foundations of sociology

foundations

of sociology

DAVID C. KING
Center for War / Peace Studies

MARVIN R. KOLLER
Kent State University

RINEHART PRESS / HOLT, RINEHART AND WINSTON
SAN FRANCISCO

Cover: Amish barn raising (Wide World Photos)

Foundations of Sociology by David C. King and Marvin R. Koller

A revision of *Modern Sociology* by Marvin R. Koller, David C. King, and Harold C. Couse

Library of Congress Cataloging in Publication Data

King, David C.
  Foundations of sociology.

  Includes index.
  1. Sociology. I. Koller, Marvin R., joint author.
II. Title.
HM51.K492 1975   301   74-23219
ISBN 0-03-007756-7

preface

While major portions of this text are devoted to explaining basic sociological concepts, we have strayed considerably from the format of traditional texts. For one thing, we have tried to indicate the diversity of sociological thought and approaches. This has occasionally involved presenting some of the major areas of disagreement and conflict within the field. Strict scholars might find such an approach disquieting. However, the authors felt it was essential to show sociology as a healthy, often argumentative, search for knowledge, rather than a body of theories and data stamped Ultimate Truth.

The book also represents an attempt to relate sociological knowledge to the concerns of life in the last quarter of the 20th century. Modern society is in a state of ferment; conflict and often disruptive change will be major characteristics of our lives for the indefinite future. Sociology can make important contributions in helping us to cope with our age of uncertainty. It is not a "science of society" in the sense of offering a blueprint for remedying social ills or establishing a more equitable and fulfilling life. But sociology does provide important ways of looking at this and other societies, offering an element of understanding that is a beginning for rational social action.

A concerted effort has been made in the writing of this text to enhance its readability and usefulness for the beginning student. Jargon and technical language has been reduced to a minimum for ease of reading. Highlighted summaries and end-of-chapter glossaries are provided to increase comprehension.

Finally, interesting and informative features such as issue-oriented "perspectives" and focused essays on the work of particular men and women in the field are included to bring home to the student the breadth and excitement of a fascinating discipline.

The authors wish to express their gratitude to Kenneth Magoon, Kay Ann Turbak, Sharon Flitterman and Cathryn Long for their work in preparing materials. Our thanks, too, to Cliff Snyder of Holt, Rinehart & Winston and to Emmett Dingley of Rinehart Press for making the book possible.

David C. King

Marvin R. Koller

contents

Penology
&
Connections

Planning
&
Professional Sociology

photo credits

foundations of sociology

STUDYING SOCIAL LIFE

THE SCIENCE
OF SOCIETY

The young science of sociology is devoted to the examination of human groups. Born scarcely a century ago, it has emerged as a full-fledged academic discipline, using specialized techniques for applying the scientific method to the study of man's social environment. This chapter examines some of the techniques used by sociologists, and highlights some of the general aims of sociological study.

WHAT IS SOCIOLOGY?

As one of the newest of the social sciences, sociology takes its place beside history, geography, anthropology, political science, and psychology. Each of these social sciences has produced (and continues to produce) important insights into human affairs, although each takes a different approach to the subject and focuses upon a different set of problems. History, for example, records the activities of people in the past and shows the relationship between these activities and the passage of time. Anthropology deals with the development of the biological characteristics of human beings and with the various customs people throughout the world have adopted. The workings of the human mind, as expressed through the phenomenon of consciousness, provide the raw data for the field of psychology.

Taken together, it might appear that the other social sciences have exhausted the various ways to study people by accumulating knowledge about human beings in time, in space, as remarkable creatures with unique ways, in terms of power, in making a living, and in individualistic behavior. Sociology, however, has also made its contribution through the study of *human groups*. This young science adds to our understanding by focusing its attention on the ways in which human groups come together, on what keeps them together, and on what effects these groups have on each other and on their participants. A group becomes a unit of sociological study whether the interactions involve two persons or the population of the earth.

Technically, therefore, sociology may be defined as *the scientific study of human groups*. Any human group—be it a family, a tribe, a labor union, a band of revolutionaries, or whatever—is of interest to the sociologist. In studying these groups, sociologists concentrate on one of the most important aspects of human existence, the social aspect. Humans have long been described as "social animals," which is another way of saying that they live most of their lives and perform most of their activities as members of various groups. In fact, as we shall see, group living (or social living) is essential to the full development of the human personality. And the whole web of social living—the entire system of relationships existing among humans—is called *society*. Thus, sociology is also often described as *the science of society*.

Foundations of Sociology

For thousands of years people have been intrigued by human behavior. Both Plato and Aristotle, for example, speculated upon the relationship between individuals and their societies. In the course of their speculations, these two remarkable Greek thinkers constructed social theories that have remained topics of academic discussion ever since. However, Plato and Aristotle approached social phenomena as philosophers, not as scientists. And this type of philosophical approach characterized social thought for generations thereafter. It was not until the early 19th century that the groundwork for a truly scientific study of society was laid.

Comte. While no single individual "invented" sociology, the man who set the stage for the appearance of modern sociology was a French mathematician and philosopher named Auguste Comte (1798–1857). Like many other scholars of the early 19th century, Comte was deeply impressed by the accomplishments of physicists, chemists, biologists, astronomers, and other natural scientists whose discoveries were giving human beings greater and greater control over their environment. Comte became convinced that the methods used by these scientists in dealing with physical phenomena could be used effectively in studying social phenomena. It was this idea that induced him to suggest a new academic discipline, which he called sociology.

In his *Positive Sociology,* Comte viewed his new discipline primarily as a vehicle for social reform. It was to be a scientific tool with which people could study the structure and operation of their societies. Comte believed that social organization was governed by laws which individuals could discover readily if they made use of the proper scientific methods. Once these laws were understood, Comte *believed,* a person would have sufficient knowledge to reorganize society along lines which would eliminate most social problems. In the new social order which Comte envisioned, sociologists would play a major role, acting as the directors of human progress.

Time has proved both the merit and the defects of Comte's ideas about the new science of sociology. His belief that the discipline would enable humanity to achieve social harmony easily and quickly was far too optimistic. This idealism, plus some of his suggestions for social reorganization, laid his ideas open to considerable criticism. It would be a mistake, though, to pass over his contributions lightly. Comte was one of the earliest and staunchest advocates of the idea that human society is a fit subject for scientific study, and it is this idea that has motivated sociologists ever since. And, although they did not become the social engineers that Comte envisaged, sociologists have helped provide the storehouse of knowledge needed to deal adequately with modern social problems.

Spencer. Among the many Europeans who became interested in a science of society was the English philosopher, Herbert Spencer (1820-1903). A contemporary of Charles Darwin, Spencer viewed society as a product of evolution not unlike that of living organisms—complex social systems evolved out of simpler, primitive structures. Thus one could learn a great deal about modern industrial societies by studying contemporary primitive societies.

One of Spencer's most important contributions was his popularization of the *comparative method.* Relying heavily on the reports of travelers, missionaries, and explorers, he compared ways of life all over the world with modern societies. Both Spencer's method and the assumption upon which it rests are still used by modern cultural anthropologists in their efforts to discover the origins of social institutions.

Ward. The ideas of Comte and Spencer were enthusiastically received by a number of American scholars, such as Lester Frank Ward (1841-1913). Like Comte, Ward believed that sociology should be used as a guide for social planning. In his *Dynamic Sociology,* he said that the proper aim of sociology is to benefit humanity, and toward that end, he suggested that sociological education be devoted to creating a new, highly planned society to be called a "sociocracy." He advocated the establishment of an academy of social sciences in Washington, D.C., where sociologists would be trained to advise government officials on social planning and effective legislation.

Although he had received his formal training in law and botany, Ward's fame as a sociologist was such that in 1903 he was elected president of the International Sociological Society, headquartered in Paris. When he returned to the United States, he helped organize the American Sociological Society and became its first president in 1906. Known today as the American Sociological Association, this body is the chief professional organization for American sociologists. The association publishes the *American Sociological Review* and the *American Sociologist,* two of the many journals now published on the research and theory of sociology as well as the professional problems within the field.

Sumner. William Graham Sumner (1840–1910) was another important figure in the development of American sociology. Differing sharply with the social planning visions of Ward and Comte, Sumner felt that sociology could not bring about positive changes in society. He believed there were tremendous social forces or laws at work which would not be affected by puny human efforts. What intelligent people could do, according to Sumner, would be to understand the true nature of society and to learn to accept inevitable changes and processes that were beyond human capacities to alter. In modern terms, Sumner would probably be regarded as a "conservative" in contrast to a "liberal," or an "activist," who urges a reforming role for sociology. Advocates of both schools of thought are represented among modern sociologists and are noticeable by the different ways in which they approach current issues.

The work which brought Sumner fame was *Folkways,* in which he made good use of Spencer's comparative method. It is a fascinating collection and analysis of customs among societies throughout the known world and left a legacy which modern sociologists still follow in studying different ways of life both within and outside American society.

Even this brief survey should suggest that much of the work of those who guided sociology through its infancy was less than scientific. Some, like Comte and Ward, were intrigued by grandiose but impractical schemes for social reorganization. Nearly all were far better at concocting theories than at proving them. While they were anxious to study human groups in a scientific manner, they frequently did not know how to go about it. It was one thing to apply the scientific method to physical phenomena, but quite another to apply it to human behavior. Only when a number of

specialized research techniques had been developed would this latter task be possible. And it was not the earliest sociologists, but rather their immediate successors, who were to devise the necessary techniques.

The process of making sociology a reasonable scientific discipline began late in the 19th century. The process is still going on and undoubtedly will continue for some time to come. Today, as in the past, sociologists are continually developing new ways of applying the scientific method to the study of human society.

THE SCIENTIFIC METHOD

The phrase "scientific method" refers collectively to a regular series of steps which begins with observation. The scientist rejects as unproven any conclusions not supported by observed facts. Thus, when the ancient Greeks reasoned that the universe must be spherical because the sphere is the most perfect of all shapes, they were not adding to humanity's store of scientific knowledge. Only by measuring it could they have established *scientifically* that the universe is spherical.

A close approximation of how sociologists scientifically study human groups is outlined in the following steps or stages. The process is designed to check upon old or new knowledge, to relate a variety of factors, to seek to understand why events occur as they do, and to formulate some overall framework into which findings can be placed.

1. Defining a Topic

The initial step is to know precisely *what* one seeks to study. This requires as thorough a knowledge of what is already known as is possible; and of course, as the amount of information available has grown, so has the need to specialize. Sociologists "search the literature" or examine published information in related areas to discover prior knowledge, to locate gaps in knowledge, and to isolate contradictory evidence. This preliminary work helps to narrow the research to a specific topic, a topic of manageable size that can be studied and yield worthwhile results.

2. Forming a Working Hypothesis

An hypothesis is an "educated guess" that certain items under study are somehow related. A "working" hypothesis is carefully worded to guide the researcher to a designated target. It serves to keep scientists from straying off into attractive, but irrelevant, sidetracks; it focuses attention upon the testing of prior ideas to determine whether or not they can still be held in the light of new knowledge. An hypothesis should not be considered a preconceived conclusion—instead, it is a tentative statement that will be tested against the available evidence. Once the study is completed, the original hypothesis will be accepted, rejected, or modified in some way for further study.

Suppose, for example, a sociologist wanted to deal with the question of how widespread juvenile delinquency is among different social classes. The institutional records and common sense would indicate that youths from low-income families commit a far greater number of serious crimes than children from middle- and upper-class families. Studies of the judicial process might lead us to theorize that perhaps minority youths from low-income families are more likely to be arrested, adjudicated, and institutionalized than their middle-class counterparts for the same offenses. To narrow the topic to manageable portions we might ask: Do criminal court records give an accurate picture of the extent of juvenile delinquency among the different social classes? On the basis of previous studies, the sociologist might create a working hypothesis which states: Official statistics from juvenile courts and institutions tend to underrepresent the extent of juvenile delinquency among middle- and upper-class youths and therefore do not give a true picture of all types of crimes and the number of youths involved in them.

3. Securing Data

As with any scientific research, sociology makes use of a number of techniques to test the validity of hypotheses. In any particular study, some combination of these techniques rather than a single one is likely to be used. The sociologist also makes use of *controls*. These controls help to isolate only those factors which relate to the particular problem. When these factors are isolated, they can be studied to see if they have the relationship to one another assumed in the hypothesis. Some of the most common techniques for collecting evidence are:

Examining available sources. A basic first step is to make use of all available sources of data, such as government records and statistics. In our sample hypothesis on delinquency, for instance, the sociologist could make use of court records, school records, the records of detention homes, Federal Bureau of Investigation statistics, and so on. He could also make use of records that have to be created, in the form of tables, data cards, files, or photographs. Too, he would want information on the types of crimes committed and also on the socio-economic background of the youths. This often consists of the incomes and occupations of the heads of the households, plus their years of education, property owned, religion and ethnic backgrounds. The categories so developed would provide a basis of social class comparisons.

Interviews and questionnaires. Both interviewing and questionnaires (either administered in person or through the mails) are common ways of gathering data. The researcher must use caution with each method, being careful that the wording of questions will bring valid responses, while at the same time trying not to lose the cooperation of the subject. In our hypothetical study, the sociologist might want to interview youths who are not in prison to determine the extent of their "self-reported delinquency." This data would be compared with official records and interviews with youths in prisons to obtain a more accurate picture of the extent of delinquency. It is important to note that when obtaining self-reported information on criminal or deviant behavior one has to assure the respondent complete anonymity to obtain honest responses.

Participant observation. Anthropologists have long been aware that they can learn only so much about a primitive people by studying them from the "outside"—that is, by simply recording such information as the people are willing to give on request. Consequently, early in this century, anthropologists began the practice of becoming participants in the societies they wished to study. They usually spend two or three years living with the people, speaking their language, eating the same food, and sharing the same work while closely following tribal rites and ceremonies. In this way, barriers are gradually broken down and the researcher often becomes an accepted part of the community.

In much the same manner, sociologists have often become "participant observers" in groups within more complex societies. Sociol-

ogists have lived in prisons, worked with street gangs, lived in ghettoes, even joined country clubs. They have investigated whole communities in the same way. As a result they have been able to get a view of these groups "from the inside," and have managed to obtain information that is normally withheld from strangers.

An example of participant observation techniques can be found in the classic study by William F. Whyte, *Street Corner Society.* This was a study of a group of young males called the Norton Street Gang, who lived in a working-class slum in Boston in the 1930's. Whyte, then a Harvard graduate student, spent three years periodically living with members of the community and hanging around with the gang. He posed as a novelist and had the gang's leader, Doc, as a confidant.

Whyte's experiences in the field and his solutions to problems of observation methods have created useful information for the following generations of sociologists. His principal contribution was to show that through participant observation the sociologist is able to see the world through the perspective of people he is studying. More importantly, a sociologist using field research methods can test his working hypotheses over and over again, based on new information and feedback from his subjects. In Whyte's case this proved invaluable because he found that what he had hypothesized to be a high degree of social disorganization and community breakdown in lower-class neighborhoods turned out to be a different form of social and community organization than found in middle-class neighborhoods. Deviance, violence, and political corruption were accepted as facts of life associated with poverty. Groups such as the Norton Street Gang provide young males, who have difficulty achieving material success through accepted middle-class means, an opportunity to gain prestige and a feeling of self-worth through their peers.

The fact that Whyte was accepted as a member of the community allowed him to gain these insights that would remain unknown to outsiders. In addition, as a trusted participant Whyte was able to gain firsthand information about crime and deviance. This presented him with several ethical problems regarding his role as a citizen and scientist versus his friendship with members of the community. These experiences and dilemmas provide the sociologist with conceptually rich data not available through other methods.

Case study. As a research tool, the case study is useful for amassing information about individuals who share a common grouping. A good illustration of this approach is a study by W. I. Thomas and Florian Znaniecki, in which they wished to learn as much as possible about the waves of immigrants who were pouring steadily into the United States during the early 1900's. Thomas and Znaniecki selected the Polish immigrants as their study group and carefully examined all records pertaining to the Poland-to-America migration. The researchers tried to find out how the Poles had lived in Europe, why they decided to leave their homeland, what happened during the migration, and what adjustments they had to make living in a new country. The two researchers paid special attention to diaries, letters, and newspaper reports; they obtained the life histories of numerous immigrants, along with accounts of important personal experiences. The information collected by Thomas and Znaniecki was edited and analyzed, then incorporated in a monumental work called *The Polish Peasant in Europe and America*, published in 1918.

Laboratory technique. A laboratory is not necessarily limited to those rooms filled with test tubes, Bunsen burners, and complicated machinery. A psychologist's laboratory, for example, might contain a maze used to test the intelligence or reaction patterns of white mice. Such a device would enable the psychologist to study the animal's behavior under controlled conditions. A botanist's laboratory might consist of a greenhouse filled with different species of flora. In such a setting the researcher would be able to control such factors as heat, light, and soil conditions to determine how they affect the plants. Thus a laboratory is any place where scientists conduct experiments under controlled conditions.

Because sociologists deal with human beings, it might be expected that they would be unable to use the laboratory technique. In many cases this is true. Human behavior cannot be controlled in quite the same manner as psychologists control mice or botanists control plants. It would be impossible, for example, to study most aspects of crime in an experimental setting.

However, there are situations in which sociologists can make use of the laboratory technique. One way of doing this is by *matching* two different study groups. For example, two different classes studying a given college subject might be matched according to numbers of students, intellectual capacities, past grades, age levels, and proportions of men to women. Then one class might be exposed to a nontraditional method of teaching, such as closed-circuit television or programmed learning, while the other class would cover the same material in the traditional manner. This second class would be serving as a control for the experiment. The sociologist thus would have controlled all the variables except one: teaching method. If there is a measurable difference in the performance or interest level of one class over the other, this would suggest that one teaching technique was more effective.

PERSPECTIVE

SOCIOLOGICAL SCHOOLS OF THOUGHT

In your brief encounter with sociologists in this course and in your later discoveries as well, you will find that some sociologists appear to be more "scientific" than others. That is, the studies of some will adhere more strictly to the methods described in Chapter 1, by carefully marshalling their evidence, explaining their procedures, drawing listed conclusions. Others will paint their picture of society with broad, almost careless, brushstrokes, filling their pages with sweeping generalizations supported more by personal insight than by empirical evidence. And the work of still others can be placed in between these two extremes.

The reason for this lack of consistency is that sociologists do not agree on any single method of analyzing social behavior. The same is true of the other social and behavioral sciences, and disagreements crop up in the natural sciences as well. Each person must follow the dictates of his own conscience and decide what path to follow in pursuit of the common goal of understanding human behavior. Alex Inkeles describes the alternative approaches in sociology this way: "Sociologists divide on the issue of whether sociology is or ever can be a science, whether its methods should be that of sympathetic understanding or the controlled experiment, whether it is nobler to build theory or to get one's hands dirty digging into the facts, whether sociology should be politically engaged or value-free. The decisions which sociologists make with regard to these issues have a profound effect on the kind of sociological investigations they conduct."

On the basis of the description, we can divide sociologists into a number of "schools of thought."

The Empiricists. Most sociologists have attempted to deal with their subject as a "pure" science, emphasizing the pursuit of knowledge in a "value-free" scientific manner. The advocates of this position are those who identify themselves with a structural-functional or social systems perspective in the tradition of Emile Durkheim, Max Weber, and Talcott Parsons. Other contemporary figures in this approach include Kingsley Davis, Robert K. Merton, and Paul Lazarsfeld. They have in common an emphasis on viewing society as an organized system of behaviors and institutions. The task of sociology is to use those methods which uncover what Durkheim called "social-facts" in the form of statistics, public records, and social surveys.

Critics of this approach, such as C. Wright Mills (*The Sociological Imagination*), point out that some sociologists become so committed to being scientific that they lose sight of the practical value that their studies might have. Very often, according to Mills, the empiricists become more interested in manipulating their research methods than being critical social scientists.

Humanistic Perspective. In contrast to the traditional "positivist" or scientific perspective of sociology, we find a growing interest in the application of humanist values to the sociological enterprise. Humanistic sociology is a philosophical orientation and sense of responsibility for the welfare of mankind, as well as an academic school of thought. The proponents of this perspective tend to emphasize an existential view of society. That is, society and its institutions should be analyzed in terms of the shared realities and actions of individuals as they understand them. John R. Stande, in his book *Humanistic Society, Today's Challenge to Sociology*, has attempted to indicate the various orientations that make up the humanistic approach. These include: ethnomethodology (Harold Garfinkel), neo-symbolic interactionism (Erving Goffman), the sociology of the absurd (Scott and Lyman), the sociology of everyday life (Marcello Truzzi), the sociology of knowledge (Berger and Luckman), and existential sociology (Tiryakian). Space does not allow us to discuss each of these orientations at length. They have in common an attitude that sociology should study "man in society" or that it should place the interaction between individuals in the center of social life. All of these approaches have a common background in the ideas of Max Weber and Alfred Schutz. Weber emphasized that sociology should base its explanations of society in the intuitive understanding of people's actions and motivations. Alfred Schutz combined Weber's inductive methods with the phenomenology of Edmond Husser which emphasizes that man creates the meaning of his experiences through an endless process of reflection and interpretation. The responsibility of sociology, according to Schutz, is to first understand the meaning that individuals give to their experiences and then construct more abstract explanations of those experiences and their meaning in a societal context. Alfred Schutz's *Phenomenology of the Social World*, Berger and Luckman's *The Social Construction of Reality*, and Peter Berger's *Invitation to Sociology* will give the student a fuller understanding of the various approaches included in this version of humanism.

Radicalism in Sociology. There is a small group of sociologists, whose numbers seem to be increasing, who believe that they have a responsibility to work towards a new form of socialism. Intellectually, they are neo-Marxists and prefer to call themselves "conflict theorists." They are the most vocal critics of traditional functional sociology.

One of the important books of the 70's, *The Coming Crisis of Western Sociology*, by Alvin Gouldner, is a radically oriented critique of traditional "academic sociology." But he also criticizes the microscopic methods of the humanists and the utopianism of Marxists. In fact, Gouldner, along with Irving Horowitz and other sociologists following the critical tradition of C. Wright Mills, is attempting to establish a new direction for sociology.

The orientation of this radical sociology is partially understandable as an outgrowth of the New Left of the mid-60's. Many of its practitioners were graduate students and professors of such limited tenure that they could criticize America's major institutions, its foreign policies, and the universities as the principle causes of imperialism, racism, and other social problems. They have a value-commitment, though, to provide the intellectual groundwork for a restructuring of the field of sociology to make it more equalitarian and responsible to democratic principles. Ideally, sociologists would then be able to fulfill a long-range goal of providing knowledge and theories that will help the American society and the world to achieve these same goals.

Critics of the radical perspective point out that such zealous commitments to social change can be taken over by extremists. This point is well taken, but as long as sociology remains essentially an academic discipline, its use will be that of an empirical and administrative instrument of the existing social order.

4. Classifying, Interpreting, Reporting Results

Once the data are gathered, they can be classified in either a nonstatistical or a statistical manner. The former would consist of word descriptions of the different classifications, how they are related, and in what order they appear. The statistical technique plots the data on charts and tables. Suppose, for example, a sociologist is investigating the high rate of juvenile delinquency in a particular neighborhood. Since it would be impossible to study all of the juveniles in the neighborhood, the researcher would begin by choosing a representative sample, that is, by selecting a certain number of youthful lawbreakers whose offenses are fairly typical. Then, using one or more of the methods outlined above, the next steps would be to discover as much about the youths as possible, arrange the findings systematically under appropriate headings, and tabulate the data mathematically. For instance, the heading "offenses" might reveal 40 car thefts, 20 burglaries, 30 instances of street fighting, and 10 attacks on police officers. Similar breakdowns might be made under such headings as "Failed to complete high school," "Relationship with parents," "Age," "Had a relative convicted of a crime," and so on.

After these and many more factors had been recorded, a comparable study would be conducted for nondelinquents from the same neighborhood. The nondelinquents would comprise a control group which could then be compared with the delinquent group. This would help the sociologist isolate the phenomenon of delinquency with a view toward relating it to other factors in the young peoples' backgrounds.

Table 1-1 provides a simplified version of how partial results might look when arranged for statistical analysis. With data like these the sociologist tries to determine if there is a *significant* mathematical relationship between any of the factors and juvenile delinquency. In this hypothetical case, there is no such relationship for two of the factors: "Had a relative convicted of a crime" and "Failed to complete high school." Only a small percentage of either the delinquent or nondelinquent groups had family members who were convicted of crimes. Moreover, the percentage of nondelinquents in this category is higher than the percentage of delinquents. Consequently, there is no indication of a significant positive relationship. Similarly, while 50 percent of the delinquents left school before age eighteen, so did 50 percent of the nondelinquents. There is no mathematical evidence of a strong positive relationship here either. However, for the category "Felt rejected by parents" a significant relationship is indicated by the statistics: 90 percent of the delinquents felt definitely rejected, but only 30 percent of the nondelinquents felt the same way.

If a real sociological study were to produce

TABLE 1-1   NEIGHBORHOOD X

	Total number	Felt rejected by parents	Failed to complete high school	Had a relative convicted of a crime
Delinquents	100	90	50	3
Nondelinquents	100	30	50	5

such findings, this would not necessarily establish a *causal* relationship between delinquency and parental rejection. However, it would suggest the strong probability of such a relationship in the particular neighborhood under study. And it would certainly suggest that this factor should be studied further. Follow-up studies, for instance, could be carried out in other neighborhoods and other communities to test the findings more thoroughly.

Whether statistical or nonstatistical methods of categorizing are used, the sociologist must analyze the findings in the light of a working hypothesis. The hypothesis either can be held to be substantiated by the evidence, or it can be rejected or qualified because evidence is contrary to what was originally thought to be true. For example, a team of sociologists who did attempt to measure the extent of juvenile delinquency in one community concluded that for certain crimes criminal court records did accurately reflect delinquent behavior. Some of their other hypotheses, particularly those concerning the extent of unreported crimes, were not proved. In fact, the study suggested that there was far more unreported delinquency in the area than the researchers had expected to find. In this case, even the rejected hypotheses provided valuable information on which to base further studies. In short, the findings have meaning or significance and these meanings are ferreted out by the sociologist for all to consider.

Once a study is completed, sociologists are obligated to report publicly on its background, purpose, design, procedures, findings, and interpretations. The study would be of little use if it were not shared. Reports usually appear as articles in professional journals, papers offered at professional meetings, or books made available to the general public. Every step of the procedure is made known and criticism is invited; if there is some flaw in the work, it can be exposed and corrected. If the work is useful it can be repeated (*replicated*) to determine if the same results occur under different conditions. It is through this process that the discipline has steadily added to our storehouse of knowledge about society.

Application of Results

One major concern of sociologists from the time of Comte on has to do with the purpose and usefulness that their work serves. Many feel that the justification for the existence of sociology as a science is that it can be an *applied science*. Applied science is a term that refers to research carried on in an effort to make practical application of scientific knowledge. Others, perhaps a majority, feel that basically sociology should strive to be a *pure science*—using research to extend the frontiers of knowledge whether or not there is any immediate utility.

Thus the sociologist engaged in "pure" research need not be concerned with the question of whether or not the work will have immediate practical application. This does not mean, however, that sociologists are unconcerned with the implications of their work in the area of social problems. Like other people, they are vitally interested in improving the societies in which they live. But sociologists do not have to be social workers, although such workers invariably are schooled in sociological theory and practice.

Despite the primary emphasis on pure science, sociologists are increasingly sought by government and business leaders. Sociological services have been used by large corporations, city planning commissions, and even the U.S. Supreme Court. Painstaking research, constant effort to refine statistical measurements, objective analyses of complex social problems, and proven ability to uncover previously neglected but meaningful information have won sociologists places on more and more scientific teams striving to improve life in our society. And these scholars have added a "social dimension" to such diverse groupings as industrial plants, hospitals, military units, prisons, newspapers, schools, universities, churches, and cities.

Sociology and Social Policy

Recently, Paul Lazarsfeld published a book titled, *The Uses of Sociology,* in which he discussed applications of sociology over the years. He pointed out that sociological theory and research have been used in law, medicine, education, social welfare, law enforcement and corrections, the military, and industry. These data were directed towards administrating these institutions more efficiently or creating public policies. These public and private agencies need information about their organization and what they can do to become more effective in fulfilling their social responsibilities. They also have funds and grants available to pay for extensive research projects. They are the principal sources of income from those sociologists working outside of academia. Often governmental research projects are sidelines of professors at prestigious universities. In the past this supplemental work has been criticized as drawing them away from their teaching responsibilities. It has been said that some professors teach no more than one course all year.

Many sociologists are critical of this activity not because they are jealous or even that they believe their colleagues should be in the classroom. Whether these sociologists are being objective and scientific is not the issue either. Instead, they are questioning the role that the sociologist is playing through his research in maintaining society and its institutions.

This criticism represents the opinions of activists and humanists in the discipline. They say that if sociologists work for social institutions that oppress minorities or the poor, then they must share responsibilities for the problems and inequities caused for these groups. A case in point is our penal system which is considered by many to be archaic at best. Most of the research on inmates, prisons, and "rehabilitation" has been done by sociologists with the goal of improving them. Today, many people are of the opinion that our system of corrections is not successfully rehabilitating prisoners. Instead it is more likely further criminalizing and alienating them. The critics of our prisons, and the sociologists who do research in them, take the position that we need much more than technical reforms to improve the situation. Instead, they say that a complete restructuring of our system of justice, laws, and philosophy of punishment is necessary. The problem with these changes is that they are considered by some authorities to be too radical and the federal and state departments of corrections are unlikely to provide research grants to aid those sociologists and reformers who would so drastically change the system.

The position of the scientific sociologists who are being criticized by their colleagues is that the radicals are failing to be value-free. That is, the ideological biases of the radicals are the source of their objections and thus their objections are unscientific. The long-standing tradition to achieve scientific respectability has kept most sociologists from identifying their professional work with social causes. They do acknowledge that their personal values and beliefs can involve them in improving society, but this would be in the voluntary capacity of a citizen.

The Ethics of Social Research

This is an issue often encountered in the study of deviant behavior by sociologists who identify themselves with the humanistic perspective and utilize field methods and participant observation research techniques. Advocates of this type of research, such as Howard Becker, say that knowledge about behavior such as homosexuality, drug use, mental illness, and crime can be best understood from the perspective of those people who are involved in them. The sociologist can contribute to the general public's knowledge about and tolerance of deviance by representing the "outsider's" or "underdog's" viewpoints. He believes that this knowledge will lead to more humanistic treatment of individuals labeled as deviant.

The radical sociologist, Alvin Gouldner, has taken exception to this position and has argued against Becker's ideas. His main criticism is that the people who are most likely to use information about deviant behavior are those who want to catch and punish the people involved. Thus, the sociologist is participating in the process of social control and possible oppression of deviant minority groups. Two cases in point include marijuana users and homosexuals. In recent years people involved in these practices have openly supported new laws which protect these groups. The established middle-class view is that marijuana use and homosexuality should be considered crimes, and it is this majority perspective on which our system of social control is based. Any research which directly describes the actions and lifestyles of people involved in these behaviors could be used to arrest them, according to Gouldner.

A recent study of homosexuality by Laud Humphreys called, *Tearoom Trade: Impersonal Sex in Public Places,* demonstrates the moral and ethical questions involved here. This study of homosexual behavior in public restrooms was conducted with Humphreys assuming a role of "watchqueen," someone who serves as a lookout for those engaging in sexual acts. Humphreys' behavior raises the issue of the moral responsibility of citizens, and presumably sociologists, to report crimes.

Perhaps a more significant issue in relation to Humphreys' study has to do with a follow-up interviewing project he conducted. In order to gain more data on participants in this activity he obtained their home addresses from the Department of Vehicles by taking down their license numbers. Posing as a researcher for a social health survey he went to the homes of the men he had observed and found out as much as possible about their lifestyles. Many of them were married with good jobs and respectable positions in the community. The lives and careers of these individuals might have been ruined had Humphreys not gone to great lengths to assure that their identities remained anonymous. All sociologists attempt to ensure the anonymity of their subjects. Yet it is possible that somehow their identities might become known.

This problem represents a potentially serious breach of the trust that subjects expect of sociologists in control of their information. Without this trust the sociologist would find it difficult to do much of his or her research. An alternative is to try to conduct research without the knowledge of the subjects. Journalist Nicholas Von Hoffman has referred to this activity as "sociological snooping." He equates the research of Humphreys with the work of undercover police or FBI surveillance. He questions whether the privacy and civil rights of individuals can be protected under these circumstances.

In defense of their colleague and the research methods he used, Irving Horowitz and

THE VARIOUS PATHS TO SOCIOLOGICAL KNOWLEDGE
EMILE DURKHEIM

Perhaps no single individual has had a stronger influence on the development of sociology than Emile Durkheim (1858–1917). Earlier sociologists had been more successful in developing theories about social life than in establishing evidence to prove those theories. In fact, in the 19th century, it was often difficult to separate the writings of sociologists from those of philosophers.

Durkheim became the pioneer in insisting that sociologists use the scientific method to test and to modify their hypotheses. This was the objective of one of his major works, *The Rules of Sociological Method,* published in 1895. He was convinced that sociologists should not deal with *all* social reality in sweeping generalizations, but rather should search out "the parts, elements, and different aspects which could serve as subject matters for specific problems." In other words, he urged social scientists to limit the focus of inquiry so that it could be dealt with in a scientific way. At the same time, he warned that such topics should not be studied as isolated phenomena—the researcher must always be aware of the relationship among "social forces."

Durkheim believed that a key element in the understanding of society lay in his concept of "social facts." These facts were social forces which existed outside the individual but had profound influence on the actions, beliefs and attitudes of the individual. Society, then, was more than a collection of individuals—it existed apart from the individual and exerted its force upon him. This concept clearly differentiated the two fields of sociology and psychology.

The study of *Suicide,* published in 1897, was a major effort to put these ideas into practice. The act of suicide appears to be a totally private matter, the concern of no one but the individual involved. But, Durkheim reasoned, if he could prove that this personal act was in part a product of social forces, then he had proved his point: social forces exist outside the individual and have much to do with determining his behavior.

Durkheim then made use of a wide array of statistical evidence to support his theories about the causes of suicide. This work remains a model of using empirical evidence to examine social behavior. Some modern critics feel he went too far in separating individual psychology from social forces. Granted that Durkheim's social facts influence suicide, they argue, but the specific act by particular individuals is still a reflection of that person's psychological experiences. Generally, though, most modern social scientists feel that Durkheim's work stressed the interplay between sociological and psychological phenomena, rather than separating them. The concept of anomie, for example, has been an increasingly important subject of research for both sociologists and psychologists.

Above all else, Durkheim was successful in establishing the scientific credibility of sociology. As one recent review stated: "Durkheim was perhaps the first to draw the full implication of the conception of sociology as a generalizing social science and to translate it into systematic empirical research on recurrent social phenomena in support of theoretical principles."

Lee Rainwater have referred to Von Hoffman's criticism of Humphreys as "journalistic moralizing." They point out that research into the everyday lives of people leads sociologists to new definitions of reality which may represent a threat to the more traditional interpretations of reality espoused by clergymen, politicians, and journalists such as Von Hoffman.

A more important point raised by Horowitz and Rainwater is that of establishing a priority between two desirable goals: the right to privacy and the right to know. They say that the issue is between the responsibilities of social scientists to seek and obtain greater knowledge and the responsibilities of the legal system to seek and obtain maximum security for the private rights of private citizens. Humphreys has met the professional criteria of assuring anonymity. His research has gone beyond the existing literature on sexual behavior and has proven once again that ethnographic research is a powerful tool for social understanding and policymaking. It is on

these grounds that sociologists feel that their work should be judged.

SUMMARY

Sociology was developed in the 19th century as a response to social conflicts and problems accompanying rapid industrialization and urbanization of Europe and America. Since its inception sociology has attempted to achieve somewhat contradictory goals of scientific analysis and social reforms. This approach has led to the development of conflicts within the discipline over the responsibilities and roles of the sociologist.

One area of conflict is over what is the best research method to use in the scientific study of social behavior. The crux of the issue centers around the question: in what form should the data that represents human behavior be? Most people in the field chose methods that result in quantitative data which can be interpreted through statistics or mathematical models. Research that involves official records, surveys, and case studies reflects this approach. These studies have a scientific advantage of being replicated by using the same or similar data.

Other sociologists prefer methods such as field research and participant observation which utilize the interaction between people and their subjective states as data. The practitioners of this approach emphasize that society exists in the on-going interrelationships of individuals. Direct observation of everyday behavior provides a richness of understanding unavailable through statistics and surveys. Critics of this approach feel that it suffers from the lack of scientific controls over the collection and interpretation of data.

The issue is whether or not sociologists should be activists in reforming society and solving social problems. The central concern here is maintaining an unbiased objective attitude towards research. The advocates for a "value-free" position state that the sociologist should not be involved in radical movements because of the obvious sources of bias. The radicals counter with the claim that to try to avoid the possible implications of research for social change is to fail to meet a responsibility to create a more equitable society.

Despite these varying positions it is reasonable to say that modern sociologists are attempting to direct their energies towards humanistic goals. These would include the maximization of human potential and self-determination. The disagreement seems to be over the means to attain them. Perhaps this disagreement is a sign of the vitality of this discipline. The diversity of perspectives in sociology can certainly provide its students with a lively education and professional careers.

GLOSSARY

comparative method   the study of different groups or societies in the effort to determine what factors lead to particular similarities or differences among them. Sometimes used to mean only the historical method, i.e., comparing primitive groups with more advanced groups to study social growth, as advocated by Herbert Spencer.

controls   arrangements which allow for isolation of the desired object of study in an experiment. In a sociological study, the experimental group will be balanced by a similar "control" group that does not undergo the experiment, in order to ensure that the experimental results are not simply due to some irrelevant element.

empirical   based on observation, experience, or experiment. The scientific method requires empirical evidence to support generalizations.

humanistic perspective   the various approaches in sociology that attempt to understand society from the viewpoint of people living in it; an emphasis is placed on enhancing social tolerance through understanding all varieties of the human condition.

hypothesis   a step in the scientific method. Consists of a tentative theoretical conclusion which is then tested empirically and verified or disproven.

laboratory technique   a research tool wherein an artificial situation is established to create the controlled conditions necessary for an experiment or study.

objectivity   the ability to see things as they are, not distorted by our social or psychological biases.   Scientific method strives to maximize objectivity.

participant observation   the research method which puts the sociologist out in the everyday "real world" attempting to gather descriptive data through personal experience.

radical perspective   the activist orientation which emphasizes the responsibility that sociologists have to uncover the causes of social inequality and then participate in social change to restructure society and remove barriers to equality.

replication   repetition of a study to check its accuracy.   Reports of sociological experiments are useful when they allow for replication so that results can be verified.

science   the scientific, objective study of empirical phenomena and the knowledge thus gained.   *Applied science* is research carried out in an effort to make practical applications of scientific knowledge.   *Pure science* is the scientific pursuit of knowledge for its own sake, with no immediate concern for practical applications.

statistical technique   a research tool involving the use of mathematical laws and logic, such as probability or systematic sampling, to collect and analyze information.

structural-functionalism   the traditional sociological approach that studies society as an abstract system of institutions, organizations, and values with an emphasis on how social order is maintained.

survey research   used in attitude studies, voting research, and opinion polling.   This method involves interviewing a randomly selected sample of people.

value-free sociology   the attitude of sociologists that they must develop their theories and research in an unbiased manner and that they must avoid promoting ideological causes in their professional work.

variable   a characteristic common to some individuals, groups, or objects but present in different degrees.   Controlled experiments isolate certain variables for study by standardizing the other variables for all the subjects under study.

SUGGESTED READINGS

Berelson, Bernard.   (ed.).   *The Behavioral Sciences Today.*   New York: Basic Books, 1963.   This general survey of the behavioral sciences illustrates the relationship between sociology and other behavioral disciplines.   It is a useful handbook of the current state of the various fields.

Berger, Peter.   *Invitation to Sociology.*   Garden City, New York: Doubleday (Anchor), 1967.   In a conversational and frequently witty style, Berger makes the field of sociology appear far less awesome than many other writers.

Bowen, Elenore Smith.   *Return to Laughter.*   New York: Harper & Row, 1954.   Although this novel deals with the experiences of an anthropologist rather than a sociologist, it is a vivid picture of the pleasures and problems of participant observation.

Cuzzort, R.P. *Humanity & Modern Sociological Thought.* New York: Holt, Rinehart and Winston, 1969. An extremely well written survey. Presents the major ideas and contributions of such "humanist" sociologists as C. Wright Mills, David Riesman, Peter L. Berger, and Erving Goffman.

Douglas, Jack R. (ed.). *The Relevance of Sociology.* New York: Appleton-Century-Crofts, 1970. In a series of essays leading sociologists deal with the problems of being objective in the study of society.

Gouldner, Alvin. *The Coming Crisis of Western Sociology.* New York: Basic Books, 1970. A far-ranging critique of traditional and modern sociology with a suggestion for the development of a radical "reflexive" sociology.

Humphreys, Laud. *Tearoom Trade: Impersonal Sex in Public Places.* Chicago: Aldine Publishing Company, 1970. The very controversial observational study of homosexuality in public restrooms. The January, 1970, issue of Transaction Magazine contains the justifications and critiques of this work.

General Sociology

Deutsch, Stephen E. and Howard, John. (eds.). *Where It's At: Radical Perspectives in Sociology.* New York: Harper & Row, 1970.

Faris, Robert L. *Handbook of Modern Sociology.* Chicago: Rand McNally, 1964.

Lazarsfeld, Paul F., Sewell, William, and Wilensky, Harold. *The Uses of Sociology.* New York: Basic Books, 1967.

Lazarsfeld, Paul F., and Rosenberg, Morris. (eds.). *The Language of Social Research.* New York: The Free Press, 1971.

Merton, R. K., Broom, L., and Cortell, Jr., L. S. *Sociology Today.* New York: Basic Books, 1959.

International Encyclopedia of the Social Sciences. New York: MacMillan and Free Press, 1968.

STUDYING
HUMAN GROUPS

Like the other social sciences, modern sociology has collected vast amounts of data, with sophisticated systems of information retrieval and analysis. Less than a century ago, however, the early sociologists were searching for the techniques and approaches that would enable them to study human groups more scientifically. Some of the early efforts are summarized in this chapter, not so much as a history of the discipline, but to give you an idea of how modern patterns and problems of investigation have developed. Chapter 2 also defines some of the key terms sociologists use to distinguish readily among the many social entities man has developed.

DEFINING GROUP RELATIONSHIPS

As every science builds up a body of knowledge, it develops its own jargon, or shorthand method of expression. Thus the geneticist speaks of DNA and RNA, the linguist refers to phonemes, allophones, or glottochronology, and the statistician uses expressions like "chi square," "fiducial limits," or "correlation coefficients."

To someone unfamilar with their meanings, these specialized terms have little value and may even be obstacles to communication. In the hands of a scientist, however, they are time-saving tools, enabling him to convey his ideas to others in his field without having to stop for elaborate explanations.

What is true of other sciences is equally true of sociology; specialized terms with precise meanings have been developed as part of the shorthand of the discipline.

The need for a special language of sociology becomes evident merely by considering the basic entity studied by sociologists—human groups. We live our lives in an almost endless variety of group relationships, the closest and most obvious being the family. Some groups, like a rioting mob or a crowd at a football game, exist for only a short period of time and are centered around a particular moment or event. Other groups are more long-lasting and have a more formal structure, such as a school, church, army, political party, and so on. Still others, formed for a specific purpose, are somewhere in between, for example, a team, a club, a professional organization. And still others may lack formal structure but will last for varying periods of time, such as a group of friends. To distinguish among this variety and to suggest the interrelationship between the individual and the group, sociologists have found it useful to agree on certain definitions.

Groups, Categories, and Social Classes

The basic concepts of sociology center around the dependency of humans on one another. The fact that we are members of groups does not require scientific interpretation. But sociologists seek to understand the direct and indirect relationships between individuals, groups, social classes, and social institutions. The traditional approach to sociology is to view these as being the interrelated elements of any society.

Groups. The sociological definition of a group is two or more people taking one another's behavior into account. The relationships between group members can be very personal and direct, as in primary group relationships, or impersonal as in secondary group relationships. These concepts will be developed more fully in the next section.

In a more general sense, people interact when they affect one another's behavior through their verbal and nonverbal communications or their presence in a social setting. Thus two people holding a conversation constitute a group because they are interacting, in this case through the medium of verbal communication. The members of a family constitute a group because they are constantly interacting in a variety of ways too numerous to mention. To cite another and rather extreme example, two perfect strangers passing one another on opposite sides of an otherwise deserted street could constitute a group under certain circumstances. Let us suppose that one of the strangers is idly kicking a can while the other is humming a tune. Suddenly, as these two draw together, each looks up and notices the other approaching. Both become embarrassed, stop what they are doing, and quicken their pace to continue on their way. They still do not know each other; they still have not spoken a word. But each has reacted to the presence of another human being, and this has affected his behavior. For a fleeting moment, therefore, they have comprised a group.

This form of social interaction has been studied extensively by sociologist Erving Goffman, in his book, *Behavior in Public Places*. His observations point out the rather complex patterns of behavior that recur in certain social settings within our culture. These involve nonverbal communication, concerns over privacy, maintenance of personal space, and creating territories in public areas.

Categories. Sociologists create social categories based on similarities that two or more people have in common. This is a process of classification according to characteristics such as age, sex, race, residence, or more complex socio-economic variables. The value in using categories is not to oversimplify human differences, but to find a common basis for comparing behavior and experiences of people. Social categories are particularly useful in establishing matching control groups and experimental groups in research projects.

Social Classes. The concept of social class has a much greater diversity of meanings than groups, or categories. Social classes have emotional connotations for most people, hence the difficulty in using this concept for theories and research. Typically, sociologists refer to social class as representing the similar values and status of people who are in the same economic situation. Income, occupation, and number of years of education and training are considered to be objective indicators of social class position. But there are other indicators, such as the reputation or prestige that an individual enjoys in the community. There is also the subjective judgments about one's own position in relation to others that may be used to distinguish between social classes. For example, we may consider any multimillionaires to be members of the upper class, yet among the most wealthy people important distinctions exist between "old" wealth that indicates high family social position and the *nouveau riche* or recently upwardly mobile people who are seen as too brash and conspicuous in their materialism or status seeking.

Groups, categories, and social classes are important concepts because they allow sociologists to find common patterns of behavior that may exist where no actual interaction takes place between individuals being compared. For example, numerous studies of community organization have compared family behavior of different social classes in the area. Also, the study of all forms of behavior through statistical rates and correlations depends heavily on the use of categorical distinctions between the types of people represented by the rather impersonal data and records. We will see the rather diverse use of these concepts in future chapters.

THE NATURE OF GROUP RELATIONSHIPS

As we have indicated, humans are members of a great variety of groups. Because not all groups have the same effect upon the individual, nor does he participate in them to the same degree, sociologists have divided group relationships into two general types. These are *primary group* relations and *secondary group* relations.

Primary Groups Shape Personality

Primary groups are distinguished by the quality of the relationships that exist among their members. These relationships are of an intimate, personal nature, involving the total personalities of the participants. Familiar primary groups include families and children's play groups. Close friendship groups are also primary.

Generally, primary relationships arouse strong emotional responses in people. The members of a primary group provide each other with love and affection. But at the same time, they are capable of hurting one another deeply when they act in a thoughtless manner. Because of their intimate character, primary groups tend to be small in size. Generally, no more than a handful of people can maintain very close ties with one another over a long period of time.

Primary groups exert a profound influence upon the development of the human personality. They are largely responsible for determining the type of person an individual ultimately becomes. Within the family and play groups the individual learns most of the habits, attitudes, and beliefs that are carried through life.

Moreover, primary groups help to transform the human infant, so utterly dependent at birth, into a capable, functioning member of society. Through early group contacts the child is gradually introduced to the demands of social living, learning what the group expects in the way of behavior, which forms are acceptable and which are not. The child also begins to assimilate the standards and accumulated knowledge of the society. Thus, an individual who reaches maturity should be capable of coping with the adult world.

Later on in life the individual continues to depend upon primary groups. The family and the friendship group provide the warmth and affection which every human being needs. They serve as havens of security into which a person can withdraw to escape the pressures and demands of modern existence.

Secondary Groups Test the Individual

As individuals begin to widen the range of their experiences, they encounter secondary groups, which are characterized by impersonal, nonemotional relationships, the ties within them tending to be much looser than those within primary groups. Labor unions, political parties, business firms, military units, and professional organizations are all secondary groups.

Unlike primary relationships, secondary relationships do not demand the total involvement of the human personality. Rather, the parties to such relationships exhibit only part of their personalities to one another. For example, between an employer and an employee there is no need for total involvement. The employee ordinarily learns comparatively little about the religious beliefs, philosophical convictions, family life, or leisure-time activities of the employer. Similarly, the employer sees only one aspect of the employee. During the day, both bring parts of their personalities to bear upon the task of running a business. At day's end, however, both go home to resume their primary relationships.

There is virtually no limit to the size of a secondary group. Its membership can number as few as two people (as with the group formed by a customer and a clerk) or soar into the millions (as with political parties). This is possible because intimate ties do not have to be established among all the members in common. However, such ties may be established among certain of the members without affecting the secondary nature of the group as a whole. For example, within a given business firm a small number of employees may form themselves into a friendship group. Indeed, any number of such friendship groups might exist within the firm. But the firm as such would still be a secondary group.

As a rule, secondary groups do not exert anywhere near the same influence upon the human personality as do primary groups. Certain secondary groups, especially those which incorporate facilities for formal training, may help in the process of personality formation. But research has indicated that the family and the play group leave a much deeper imprint upon the individual than do even such organizations as schools and churches.

However, while secondary contacts rarely alter the basic structure of an individual's personality, they often do help to modify certain personality traits. They do so by testing the individual, by subjecting ingrained habits, attitudes, and beliefs to the light of objective examination. They force the individual to take personal stock and, if need be, to adjust at least outward behavior. Business associates and the other people with whom a person forms secondary relationships during the course of a lifetime rarely make the same allowances that family and friends will make. Rather, they tend to judge the individual on the basis of performance. Thus, in a sense, secondary groups are society's "proving grounds."

Secondary groups serve as the media through which human beings perform a number of activities that they could never perform by working solely through primary groups. People organize themselves into secondary groups when close, personal ties would be a drawback to effective group functioning, or when it is necessary that a group encompass a large number of individuals. Secondary groups permit a much higher degree of organizational complexity than do primary groups. Consequently, they are extremely important to society.

SOME SPECIAL SECONDARY GROUPS

Communities provide many local services. Among the more complex social structures that human beings have created are those known as communities. To the sociologist a community is *a group of people living near one another in order to satisfy most of their daily needs.* Thus a small village containing only a few families is a community and so is a large city in which millions of people dwell. Even the camp of a band of wandering nomads can be a community, despite the fact that the camp may move from place to place during the course of a year.

Regardless of their size and location, all communities perform certain necessary social functions. For example, they all provide a marketplace where their inhabitants can engage in trade either with one another or with people from other communities. Through this marketplace the community disposes of its own surplus goods and services and obtains goods and services which are not available locally. But communities are much more than economic centers. They also serve as centers for political, recreational, religious, and other activities. Thus in virtually all American communities one finds churches, schools, recreational facilities, and some sort of governmental establishment.

Because they help people to meet so many daily needs, communities have come in for a good deal of sociological study. Sociologists note carefully any changes that occur in the nature of a people's community life. For example, American sociologists have watched carefully the growth of American cities and the accompanying decline of our small, rural villages. This movement, originating in a population shift from one type of community to another, has created a whole new way of life and brought with it many new problems. These problems will be discussed in Chapter 15.

Associations may be adapted to fit a wide variety of situations. Another type of secondary group that has been found to be extremely useful is the *association.* Associations are *groups of people who have come together to achieve some specific goal or goals.* Most associations, such as business organizations, fraternal lodges, service clubs, YMCA's, and scouting units, are voluntary in the sense that their members are free to join them or withdraw from them as they wish. But there are others, such as the Armed Forces and public schools, in which membership for certain individuals is compulsory.

Because they are organized to fulfill a specific purpose, associations tend to be structured along rather formal lines. Ordinarily, each member of an association has a fairly well-defined role to play in fulfilling an obligation to the entire group. Thus, in an association such as a fraternal lodge, some members will be lodge officers, some committee heads, and so forth. In a business firm some members will be vice presidents, others lesser executives, and others rank-and-file employees. Most organizations have sets of established procedures which every member is expected to follow. Frequently, for instance, there are procedures for conducting meetings, procedures for contacting members, and procedures for filling vacancies among the association's membership. All of this formal organization is intended to coordinate individual activity, thereby helping the association to achieve its stated purpose.

Associations abound in all modern societies, but they are especially prominent in American society. Americans have been described as "a nation of joiners." Associations for one purpose or another can be found listed in great numbers in any American telephone book, community directory, or school annual. Apparently, whenever there is a job that needs doing, a cause that needs championing, or a bit of excess energy that needs an outlet, the characteristic American response is one of forming an association.

However, associations are by no means limited to highly complex, modern societies; on the contrary, they also can be found in primitive villages. Among the Indians who once inhabited the southwestern United States, for example, associations existed in the form of secret societies which only men were permitted to join. These societies gathered to perform important religious rituals in circular, underground chambers known as "kivas." Any number of these kivas have been unearthed by archeologists digging in the ruins of ancient pueblos. Today the descendants of the pueblo-dwellers continue the kiva tradition by erecting large, circular structures which are forbidden to all save special initiates.

In similar fashion, Eskimos have been known to erect "men's houses" into which the adult males of a tribe can withdraw to escape the company of their wives, mothers, sweethearts, and daughters. The men of certain Australian tribes used to accomplish much the same thing by forming themselves into "bullroaring" associations. When these associations were in session, their members frightened away all women and children by whirling flat, oval pieces of wood or stone in the air. It would seem, therefore, that the need to associate with like-minded people is universal among human beings.

Ephemeral groups have affected history. Certain social groups, in contrast to those that we have discussed thus far, tend to develop in response to a momentary stimulus rather than an abiding human need. These are the short-lived, informal gatherings known as *ephemeral groups.* Such groups as mobs, crowds, and audiences are basically ephemeral. Among the stimuli that can call these groups into existence are sporting events, plays, political rallies, even window displays; in short, virtually anything upon which people are willing to focus their attention. Ephemeral groups tend to be spontaneous, and on the surface they frequently appear to lack direction. However, organizers who anticipate such gatherings and plan to take advantage of them can often be found behind the scenes. Many celebrities and politicians have built their careers upon their ability to influence ephemeral groups.

Although ephemeral groups can be sustained only for a short period of time, some of them have had a decided influence on the course of history. Consider, for example, the Parisian mob that stormed the Bastille in 1789; or the crowd of Hungarian students who poured through the streets of Budapest in 1956—only to have their desperate attempt for freedom crushed beneath the treads of Soviet tanks. Each of these groups was basically ephemeral in nature; yet each carved a place for itself in the pages of history. Nor can history lightly regard the Elizabethan audiences, also ephemeral, who sat in open-air theaters to witness the earliest performances of the plays of William Shakespeare. Almost unquestionably, the knowledge that he could enthrall these audiences with his artistic talent must have served as an inspiration to Shakespeare, inducing him to fashion works which have been revered as masterpieces of the English language.

Societies provide frameworks for group living. Sociologists use the word "society" in two different ways. As we saw in Chapter 1, the term may indicate the *total system* of relationships existing among human beings, as in the phrase "human society." However, it may also refer to a *particular* human group which we call *a* society. In this second, more restrictive sense, a society may be defined as *the largest group of people who share a unique way of life, occupy a definite territory, and think of themselves as a social unit.*

Specific societies are invariably distinguished by means of an identifying adjective. Thus we speak of the American society, the German society, the Mexican society, the Burmese society, and so forth. Societies are the most inclusive of human groups in the sense that they serve as the framework within which all other groups tend to operate. Primary groups, communities, associations, and ephemeral groups are usually only parts of total human societies.

In today's world the territorial boundaries of a given society usually coincide with the boundaries of a given country. Thus the French society is found within the borders of France, the Iranian society within the borders of Iran, and the American society within the United States. However, this pattern is not universally duplicated. National lines can be drawn arbitrarily, dividing a society in two. Such is the case, for example, with the African tribal society of the Bakongo, which is split by the territorial boundary separating Zaire (formerly Belgian Congo) from the Congo Republic (formerly French Congo). Moreover, there are certain countries, such as Australia, in which two or more societies manage to exist side by side. Centered principally in several large metropolitan areas along Australia's southern coast is a highly complex, modern society which was fashioned for the most part by immigrants from the British Isles. The continent's interior, on the other hand, supports a number of primitive, tribal societies peopled by native Australian aborigines.

The Changing Characteristics of Group Relationships

In his classic text, *Human Society,* Kingsley Davis created a typology of social characteristics that reflect a process of change which societies undergo as they become urban/industrial states. He refers to these characteristics as "folk society" and "urban society," a distinction which sociologists have traditionally considered to be very important.

In the 19th century, sociologist Ferdinand Tonnies described the two contrasting forms of social relationships with the concepts Gemeinschaft and Gesellschaft. Gemeinschaft is the equivalent of the folk society or "community," which involves a closely knit form of social relationships that are personal and informal and a high sense of identification with and commitment to the group. Gesellschaft refers to modern urban industrial society and to social relationships based on contractual arrangements, a specialized division of labor and rational economic thought rather than emotional ties. Davis' folk/urban typology expands Tonnies' distinctions to include the various identifying characteristics of these types of social relationships.

An observer of modern society would probably point out that these characteristics are not mutually exclusive. Even in megalopolis America, primary group relationships still predominate along with informal systems of social control. Sacred beliefs influence the values and morality of millions of people. The idea of the heterogeneous ethnic melting pot of urban America is being modified by the increasing concern of racial and ethnic minorities to maintain their cultural heritage and identity. Many "ethnic enclaves" exist in urban areas which preserve a uniform social and cultural lifestyle.

Based on these observations we might form the opinion that attempts to develop typologies of social relationships and groups result in oversimplification of social processes and change. The sociologists acknowledge that to take many of their concepts as direct representations of human behavior would be to commit the logical "fallacy of misplaced concreteness." That is, to regard abstract concepts such as primary groups, community, or urban society as being directly observable social reality is to miss the point that society exists in the form of interaction between individuals and within group settings. Even groups are only individuals acting in terms of a certain degree of involvement with one another. If we keep in mind that the goal of sociology is to develop theoretical explanations of the social aspects of human existence, then we can maintain the proper perspective with respect to the high degree of generalization inherent in this discipline.

VARIETIES OF RESEARCH TECHNIQUES FOR STUDYING GROUPS

One approach to the study of human groups is the social survey—a comprehensive study of a selected aspect of social living. The survey is broad in scope, attempting to collect a vast array of data out of which a number of hypotheses can be formed. In modern terms, surveys are exploratory, pilot studies that can help suggest directions toward a predesignated target. By providing a broader perspective, this form of study can suggest areas in which more specific types of research might be rewarding.

PERSPECTIVE

THE AGE OF "GROUP"

In the late 60's and 70's we have witnessed the development of a social phenomenon which represents a new form of group relationship. This group relationship is a combination of primary and secondary characteristics in which strangers come together and engage in intimate and intensely personal face-to-face interaction. Going under various designations such as T-group, encounter, sensitivity training, or consciousness raising, these groups are of considerable interest to sociologists because they represent an adaptation to the depersonalizing influences of urban/industrial society.

The proponents of various forms of "group" explain its popularity in terms of a present need of individuals to be recognized and treated as a person with feelings and problems rather than just another student, bureaucrat, worker, or social security number. "Groups" provide a social setting which is established on a first name, very personalized basis. Under the guidance of a leader or "facilitator," participants are encouraged to remove their masks as social role players and other barriers to intimacy and communication. An encounter or T-group may last for varying periods ranging from one weekend-long marathon session to regular weekly meetings for 6 months to a year. Perhaps the longer the group lasts the more it takes on primary group characteristics. Yet despite the degree of intimacy or the length of time the group is together, it seems that participants do not develop permanent emotional ties to one another. Very often members feel that they have reached a point of maximum personal growth within the group and either individually drift away or formally agree to disband. This characteristic of intense, yet transitory, group involvement is an interesting contrast to other forms of group relationships such as the family, work groups, or peer groups.

Sociologists and social psychologists have numerous interests in the encounter group phenomena. The main concern of sociologists centers around the fact that these groups drastically alter the norms and social roles that people are involved in. To communicate one's inner emotions and "gut-reaction"; to be honest and straight-forward; to discuss one's feelings openly rather than intellectualizing; and to be physically intimate with relative strangers, let alone one's colleagues, friends and even family represent a reversal of the trends of modern society towards predominately secondary types of social relationships. It is also significant that these behaviors occur because a leader guides groups through various activities and exercises until a sense of *trust* develops that allows people to become spontaneous in their responses to one another. Sociologists interested in the study of formal organizations, bureaucracy, and community life question whether this honesty, trust, and spontaneity can be extended to group relationships in everyday life situations. It is not that they are complete cynics, but rather, they recognize that encounter groups create an illusionary sense of reality that offers an escape from an increasingly depersonalized world. Whether this more personalized reality can be part of school, work, or community life depends on the socialization process and values.

In another sense this phenomenon represents a form of collective behavior which has been called the Human Potential Movement, a loosely organized outgrowth of the interest in mysticism, "natural living," mind expansion, meditation, and "self-actualization" during the late 60's and 70's. Needless to say, this movement draws its members primarily from the young college-educated middle classes. This category of people is characterized by a willingness to be involved in novel experiences enhancing personal awareness. Sociologically, we want to consider whether this movement will result in a permanent adaptation of group relationships and the quality of urban life or simply a short-lived fad in response to an era of rapid cultural and social change.

Social Surveys

A generation before Comte, an English humanitarian named John Howard published a remarkable survey of British prisons. Convinced that only an impressive array of facts would convince officials of the need for reform, Howard undertook a detailed documentation of conditions in the prisons of the late 18th century.

With painstaking care, Howard listed such items as the names, salaries, duties, and length of service of the jailers in all of the prisons. He recorded the length of prison sentences and noted the numbers of prisoners who were eventually found innocent of any crime. He interviewed prisoners personally and described their exposure to rats, filth, inadequate food, and ill treatment. When Howard appeared before a committee of the House of Commons, his impressive collection and command of the facts produced some action. Steps were taken for more frequent inspections of prisons along with measures to protect the lives and health of those accused or convicted of crimes.

Howard not only anticipated Comte, but he also used the comparative method nearly a century before Spencer gave it scholastic expression. To find out how other countries managed their prisons, Howard journeyed throughout Europe comparing other systems with the British; in fact, he died from a fever contracted while inspecting prisons in Russia.

Another early experimenter in social surveys was a Frenchman named Frederick Le Play, who published a six-volume work in 1885 on the subject of *European Workers*. Le Play's work was notable not only for its thoroughness but also for some of the techniques he developed. He theorized, for example, that he could tell a great deal about the nature of the lives of French working-class people by examining their family budgets.

Through the use of such now-standard methods as direct observation, uniform schedules, and standardized questionnaires, Le Play managed to create a more scientific and accurate picture of the French workingman, replacing guesswork, assumption, and distortion with factual evidence.

One final social survey that should be mentioned is B. S. Rowntree's study of York, England in 1899 and 1936. One refinement Rowntree developed was the effort to establish some kind of baseline for minimum subsistence—what we commonly refer to today as "the poverty level." Rowntree also made use of another category he called "secondary poverty," in which incomes were sufficient to sustain life, but the quality of that life remained woefully poor.

Rowntree also proved the usefulness of studying a sample rather than an entire population. First, he secured data on the total number of households in York, over 16,000 of them. Then he selected an evenly distributed sample of 10 percent of the households; if 1600 households revealed information as valid as surveying all 16,000, the savings in time and energy would be amazing. This turned out to be the case. He narrowed his sample even further, repeating it with one household in 20, then one in 30, and so on. It is now an accepted practice to make use of carefully selected samples to provide data on total populations, a practice followed not only by sociologists but census bureaus, public opinion polls, consumer survey organizations, and various other types of research.

Observing Groups

To avoid the common misconception that sociologists use only social surveys and statistical research techniques to gather indirect information about group behavior, we will discuss the various types of observational studies conducted by modern sociologists. These research methods take several forms. They provide the sociologist with direct information about group dynamics and on-going human relationships. Surveys and statistics cannot provide this data.

Laboratory Observation

The principal criticism of directly observing group behavior is that the researcher must depend heavily on sensory impressions in gathering data. It is difficult to test the accuracy of data and to repeat the study to test the conclusions when such subjective methods are used.

Sociologist Robert F. Bales, working at the Laboratory of Social Relations at Harvard, developed a method for the recording and analysis of social interaction. He concentrated on what could be called decision-making or problem-solving activities of groups. The principal area of interest involved was the patterns of communication of task-oriented small groups.

Bales conducted his observations in a laboratory setting where, in groups of five, subjects met in a small room and were observed through one-way mirrors. The observers used a system of categorizing all the communication in terms of questions and answers related to reaching decisions and also positive or negative reactions to social-emotional aspects of group involvement. Perhaps this rather complex study is more important for its use of systematic observation techniques than its findings, yet it contributed several insights to our understanding of group dynamics under varying conditions. Bales noted that the direction and quality of group communication patterns were affected by the size of the group and type of leadership. For example, the larger the group the more communication became "centralized" around individuals who

filled leadership roles. Moreover, leadership status tended to be bestowed on individuals according to their amount of participation. This applied to leaders in the task area, as well as to those who were considered most popular. Leaders came to initiate and receive the majority of communication acts. Bales attempted to generalize these findings by concluding that the "expectation of 'equality' which is so often present in groups of our culture, is based on an expectation of an over-all balance of action and reaction rather than of an equality of amounts of output of all members, which in practice is never found."

Field Observations

The research described above is most often conducted under controlled laboratory conditions with groups "created" for the purposes of study. Many sociologists feel that while such studies provide information about some aspects of group dynamics, they fall short of the understanding achieved through observing social interaction in "natural settings." In the first chapter we discussed examples of participant observation research which is the form that field studies take. The sociologists using this method employ numerous techniques to gather data which include observation, interviewing group members, and direct personal involvement in the group or behavior being studied.

An example of observation and interviewing in the field is found in a recent work by Jacqueline P. Wiseman, titled *Stations of the Lost: The Treatment of Skid Row Alcoholics.* Professor Wiseman followed the "moral careers" of people with various degrees of drinking problems. That is, she studied how the interaction between alcoholics and people in the agencies designed to control problem drinkers, such as the police, the courts, the jails, outpatient clinics, Alcoholics Anonymous, religious "dry-out" missions, hospitals, and mental institutions, contributed to the definition and treatment of the alcoholic's "problem." Her discussion of the social interaction in "drunk court," where people arrested for drunkenness are sentenced, is of particular relevance to our analysis of group behavior.

The "drunk court" is much more informal than other municipal court settings. The judges utilized "extra-legal" methods to expedite the sentencing process which would not be allowed in other criminal hearings. Platoon sentencing is one technique used whereby 5 to 50 defendants would appear before the judge simultaneously to receive sentencing. Each case was judged in an average of 30 seconds. Wiseman observed that this was possible because the judge used social characteristics to signify drinking status. These criteria typically included: the physical appearance of the men; past arrest records; and the man's social position in the community. In addition, "drunk-court" judges depended on the advice of assistants as to the appropriate sentence for each case. Dr. Wiseman referred to this sentencing process as an "assembly-line outrage" and points out that no matter how many times a chronic drunkenness offender is arrested he never becomes accustomed to how he is treated in "drunk court."

This situation represents a nightmarish extension of the impersonal nature of modern society. Individuals treated and judged in assembly-line fashion while subjected to degrading rituals are unlikely to have respect for the judicial system or accept any attempts to rehabilitate them. In fact, many sociologists and psychologists feel that dehumanizing experiences and the lack of meaningful group relationships cause many people to retreat into alcoholism, drug abuse, or mental illness. We can hope that further studies of the type which concentrate directly upon group interaction in social situations which decide the fate of individuals will provide information on how to create more humanistic processes of social control.

SOCIAL RESEARCH AND THEORY OF GROUPS

Comte, Spencer, and many other early sociologists were social theorists on a grand scale. Theory provides a framework in which to place information so that it can be understood. The ability of those like Comte and Spencer to envision societies as having origins, development, and purposes did encourage others to build the new science of sociology. But what we might consider the second generation of sociologists discovered that theories were likely to be more useful if they were less sweeping—if they dealt with a part of society rather than the whole. A good example is provided by the work of Emile Durkheim, a French sociologist who was particularly interested in understanding those forces that hold a society together (integration) and those which led to disintegration. One way he chose to explore this subject was in his famous study of suicides.

Durkheim's study of suicides, 1897. Durkheim realized that there were many reasons why individuals committed suicide. But what puzzled him was that the rate of suicide was different for different groups in French society. Suicide rates for Protestants, for example, were higher than they were for Catholics; they were higher for single persons than for those who were married; higher for soldiers than for civilians; higher for noncommissioned officers than for enlisted men. He also found that suicide rates were lower during time of war and revolution than during periods of peace, and they were lower during periods of economic stability than when there was unusual prosperity or depression.

On the basis of these findings, Durkheim developed the hypothesis that there were group-related reasons to explain these differences. Something in the way different groups were organized made suicide either more or less likely. His organizing theory included three different types of suicides: *altruistic, egotistic, and anomic.*

Altruistic suicides were those that occurred when people sacrificed their lives for the sake of the group. The Japanese *Kamikaze* pilots of World War II would be an example—men who willingly crashed their planes into American warships. The Buddhist monks who protested the war in Vietnam by burning themselves alive would be another example.

In sharp contrast to the altruistic suicides were those Durkheim called egotistic. These people, according to Durkheim, resorted to suicide because they had *weak* attachments to their respective groups. Thus, single people were less attached to family life than those who were married and were therefore more likely to commit suicide. Egotistic suicides would be reduced during time of war or civil disturbance because at such times people stand together to meet a common crisis.

Finally, anomic suicides were described as those who could find no clearcut group rules to follow, they became unsure of what was right or wrong, and they missed the security of group controls. Out of frustration, depression, or the feeling that everything was meaningless, these people destroyed themselves.

In his study of suicide, Durkheim set a pattern that sociologists continue to follow: collecting data on group behavior, classifying the findings, and then interpreting those findings according to some organizing theory. This theory can then be tested with other groups

and in other time periods. Durkheim's particular theory of strong and weak attachment to a group has been sustained by subsequent research. His idea of anomie ("lack of rules") has been particularly important in modern sociological studies which deal with the disorientation or alienation experienced by many people in contemporary society.

Focused research. As sociology became recognized as a separate discipline in this country, there was a heavy emphasis on focused research: concentrating study on particular groups or group-related activities. Thomas and Znaniecki's *The Polish Peasant in Europe and America,* a model emulated by many sociologists during the 1920's and 1930's, built a rich body of data through specific case studies. Such titles as *The American Soldier* by Samuel Stouffer, *The Negro Family in Chicago* by Franklin Frazier, and *Mental Disorders in Urban Areas* by Robert Faris and Warren Dunham indicate some of the many uses to which focused research and theory were applied. These case studies applied to specific groups; the researchers did not pretend that they were applicable to all other groups. Data on the black family in Chicago, for example, might not apply to black families in other urban areas. However, focused research does provide a basis for comparisons among different groups that have been similarly examined.

Consolidation of research and theory. Beginning in the 1940's and continuing into the present, a great many American sociologists have been concerned with bringing together the numerous research studies and their supporting theories. Case studies or specialized interests continued to be reported, but broader interests—those that concerned the entire American society or the entire field of sociological development—were also presented in sociological publications.

THE VARIOUS PATHS TO SOCIOLOGICAL KNOWLEDGE
EDWARD A. SHILS AND MORRIS JANOWITZ

The use of attitude surveys is a common sociological tool; it enables the researcher to measure the responses of a sampling of people on a particular topic. Many sociologists have criticized this survey method, however, on the grounds that the researcher is obtaining only the intellectual response of the moment. Such expressions might not provide a clear indication of a person's actual behavior.

Despite these possible drawbacks, the attitude survey was used extensively in a widely acclaimed study dealing with the influence of primary group relations on individual behavior. The study not only provided important insights about primary groups but helped to legitimatize the use of attitude surveys. This work was a collaboration between Edward Shils and Morris Janowitz, arising out of their experiences with German prisoners of war during World War II.

Their study, *Cohesion and Disintegration in the Wehrmacht in World War II,* 1948, centered around the Allied uses of propaganda to demoralize the German Army (the Wehrmacht). At the height of Nazi power in 1942, Hitler's forces had controlled much of the European continent, and had penetrated deep into the Soviet Union as well as North Africa. Slowly, the Allied counter-offensive began to liberate these occupied territories. By 1944, Hitler's Third Reich was rapidly shrinking. The Wehrmacht was in retreat on all fronts.

Yet, the German soldiers continued to fight. Many people assumed that the reason for this was that they deeply believed in the ideology of the Nazi dictatorship. As a result, Allied propaganda efforts were aimed at attacking the symbols, leaders, and ideas of Hitler's movement. In an attempt to demoralize the German fighting man and convince him to surrender, these attacks on Nazism took many forms: leaflets, radio broadcasts, and even loudspeakers close to enemy lines kept up a continuous barrage on the futility of the German cause. Still the German army units fought on.

Professors Shils and Janowitz approached the problem differently. On the basis of initial evidence, they formed the hypothesis that Nazi ideology was not a major factor in the will to fight. Instead, they theorized, the German soldier would keep on fighting as long as he felt a deep sense of belonging to the group—not to the whole German army—but to the platoon or squadron to which he belonged.

To test their hypothesis on the importance of primary group membership, Shils and Janowitz used a number of different methods and materials. One method was front-line interrogation of just-captured prisoners of war. The second was more intensive psychological interviews that were conducted in rear areas. The third was the use of monthly opinion polls of random samples of POW's. In addition, the sociologists made use of captured enemy documents, including letters written by or to German soldiers, statements of Allied soldiers who were freed or escaped from German prisoner-of-war camps, and the reports of combat observers.

From this data, Shils and Janowitz found that belief in Nazism or adulation of Hitler were not the key factors that kept the enlisted men fighting. Instead, what was important to the German soldier was that he belonged to a group. Cut off from the civilian groups that are important to all, particularly the primary groups, the soldier gave his loyalty to the men in his squadron and received support from them. For many of the men, in fact, the army was often described as "one big family," which suggests the importance of the fighting group in satisfying the psychosocial needs of the individual. Most of the men interviewed stressed the importance of the sense of community and the spirit that they felt it gave them.

In other words, the platoon or squadron acted as a primary group. It provided the soldier with a sense of belonging. It also gave him food, shelter, leadership, comradeship, and security. Although a small percentage of the soldiers maintained a strong loyalty to the Nazi cause, Shils and Janowitz concluded that the factor of group membership was more important.

If the closely knit military group began to disintegrate, then its fighting effectiveness would quickly be lessened or destroyed. Loss of leadership, isolation of individual soldiers, lack of food, shelter or weapons, were all likely to lead to group disintegration and then surrender. In isolation, the fighting man would find all his security knocked from under him. Without this group solidarity, he lost his will to fight or resist.

From these findings, Shils and Janowitz concluded that the type of face-to-face contact found in primary group situations is more important to the individual soldier than remote factors such as loyalty to one's nation.

David Reisman and his associates, for example, examined the changing character of Americans in a class study titled *The Lonely Crowd*. The work highlighted three different modes of behavior the researchers felt dominated the way Americans conducted their affairs. The first and earliest type were those who were "tradition-directed." These persons followed closely the heritage of their families, many of them being transplanted Europeans striving for success in a new environment. Expanding America, however, called for those persons who could rely upon their own "inner resources," their own ideas based on the unique conditions in which they found themselves. These rugged individualists were called "inner-directed." Finally, Reisman and his colleagues portrayed a new type of American who tended to abandon his traditions but at the same time distrusted his own inclinations. These were the "other-directed" Americans, those who would take their cues for thinking and acting from the people around them.

Just as there has been some controversy in the field over whether the goal of sociology is to be a pure or an applied science, works such as *The Lonely Crowd* have created disagreement between those who favor sweeping, society-wide analyses and those who believe limited, empirical studies provide the only valid conclusions. More and more sociologists have come to the conclusion that there is room for both approaches within the discipline. The effort to consolidate and draw together the strands of research and theory continues in the 1970's. Such works as *Human Behavior: An Inventory of Scientific Findings*, by Bernard Berelson and Gary A. Steiner, and the *Handbook of Modern Sociology*, edited by Robert Faris, summarize numerous studies and theories and thus enable sociologists to take stock of what they have accomplished as well as new directions that should be pursued.

SUMMARY

According to the early sociologist Georg Simmel, the particular contribution of sociology to our understanding of society is the study of the social forms that human behavior takes. His ideas have been influential for the work of Erving Goffman's studies of a great variety of forms of group settings, ranging from intimate primary groups to the impersonal secondary relations of public places.

Following the ideas of Simmel, Durkheim, and Weber, modern sociology has developed the study of groups in all forms. Their interest in abstract manifestations of group living such as social categories reflects the influence of Durkheim's notion that social and economic characteristics such as religious affiliation, marital status, and occupation represent "social facts," which influence behavior patterns. Behavior patterns that Durkheim and other empiricist sociologists were interested in are observable in the form of statistical rates and categories, such as suicide, crime, or unemployment. The methods used to study society in this form include social surveys and statistical descriptions of official records of bureaucratic agencies.

Other sociologists following in the tradition of Simmel and Max Weber concentrate on interaction between individuals and between groups. For these men and women the various techniques of observation, whether in the laboratory or in "natural settings," provide direct information about the quality of group life.

A final note of caution regarding the use of sociological concepts is to recognize that the goals of this discipline are to develop theories that explain or describe social behavior. Sociologists do not expect any given social situation to exactly represent any particular concept.

GLOSSARY

aggregate   a plurel made up of persons physically close to one another, without regard for social organization or lasting relationships.   An essentially quantitative term used to refer to the people in a given place, such as a building or city.

association   a formal group of people who have come together for some specific purpose.

category   a plurel consisting of people who are classified together because they share, or are thought to share, a common characteristic.

ephemeral group   a social group that develops in response to a momentary stimulus and is short-lived.   Examples are crowds and audiences.

group   a plurel consisting of persons who are involved in mutual interaction and share some feeling of unity.

inner-directed person   as defined by David Reisman and his colleagues, a person who relies upon his own internalized goals in getting through life.

other-directed person   as defined by David Reisman and his colleagues, a person who tends to conform his behavior to the expectations and preferences of others.

primary group   an enduring group characterized by intimate, highly personal relationships among its members.   The family and the small, old-fashioned neighborhood are examples.

secondary group   an impersonal group that involves only a part of the members' lives and personalities.   Labor unions, political parties, business firms, and professional organizations are examples.

society   broadly, the entire system of relationships existing among humans.   Specifically, the largest group of people who share a distinct way of life, occupy a definite territory, and regard themselves as a social unit.

SUGGESTED READINGS

Goffman, Erving. *Asylums.* Garden City, New York: Doubleday, 1961. An observational study of social interaction and group life in mental institutions, which shows the remarkably rational behavior of people judged insane by society.

Hammond, Phillip. (ed.). *Sociologists at Work.* Garden City, New York: Doubleday, 1967. A very candid collection of "behind the scenes" accounts by prominent sociologists of their experiences while conducting research projects.

Liebow, Elliot. *Tally's Corner: A Study of Negro Street-corner Men.* Boston: Little Brown, 1967. A more recent participant observer study after the fashion of Whyte's pioneering research.

Moreno, Jacob L. *Who Shall Survive?* Boston: Beacon, 1953. Moreno developed a method of studying small groups which consisted of asking key questions, such as which members were most desirable for certain activities, which least desirable, and so on. Moreno, and others who use the procedure, are convinced that this enables them to trace the network of relations within each group.

Spiro, Melford E.   *Children of the Kibbutz.*   New York: Schocken Books, 1965.   A detailed study by an anthropologist of a particular group—the Kibbutz of Israel.

Tiger, Lionel.   *Men in Groups.*   New York: Random House, 1969.   Tiger's study of human groups raised considerable controversy because of his heavy emphasis on the biological bases of behavior.

Whyte, William F.   *Street Corner Society.*   Chicago: University of Chicago Press, 1955.   Whyte used a variety of techniques to study behavior including participant observation, interviewing, and sociometry.   The interpersonal difficulties encountered by Long John & Doc, two members of street corner groups, reads more like a novel than sociological research.   The appendix describes the field study techniques Whyte used.

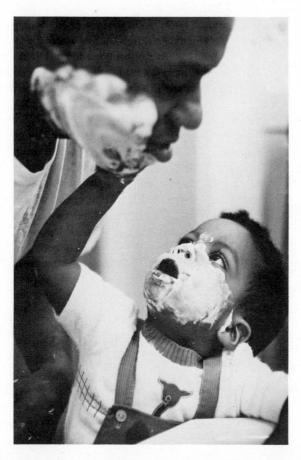

THE CONCEPT
OF CULTURE

Since humans first began the clumsy fashioning of stone tools, they have devised a variety of ways of coping with the environment, of satisfying their biological, social, and psychological needs. As new means were discovered and invented, they were often transferred from one human group to another, and the total pattern was passed on from one generation to the next. Because human societies have been scattered throughout the globe, with varying degrees of contact among them, an almost endless variety of ways of living have developed. The whole range of this human achievement is encompassed by the concept of culture.

WHAT IS CULTURE?

The word *culture* has had (and retains) a number of meanings. Originally, it referred to the arts and humanities; the "cultured" man was one who was well versed in drama, philosophy, the arts.

During the 19th century, the word came to be used almost interchangeably with *civilization*. Remember that some early sociologists (and others) were intrigued by the idea of society evolving from lower to higher stages. Thus, civilization or culture was something achieved as society evolved. People who were cultured or civilized were considered distinct from, and superior to, the primitive peoples of the world. *Civilization* is still commonly used in this sense, but the word *culture* has come to mean *the total way of life of a people*, whether that way be primitive or highly "civilized."

Culture, therefore, varies with every group or society, depending on what its historical experience has been; it represents the "distinctive way of life of a group of people, their complete design for living." The concept refers to behavior that arises from the entire range of human activity.

In broad terms, we can define culture as the *changing patterns of shared, learned behavior that humans have developed as a result of their group experiences*. A particular culture—one developed by a particular society—would consist of the patterns of learned behavior shared by the members of that society. This would include attitudes, ideas, values, knowledge, skills, and material objects. Specific cultures are usually referred to in the same manner as the societies that produce them. Thus, we can identify a Mexican culture, a Tahitian culture, a Norwegian culture, and so on. In short, we can identify as many cultures as there are societies.

Perhaps the key words in our definition of culture are *shared, learned behavior*. A behavioral trait is shared when it is practiced by nearly all members of a society, or by the members of a specific category within a society. Thus, driving an automobile is a part of American culture because automobile driving is widespread among adult Americans. Laying bricks with a trowel and mortar is also part of American culture because a specific category, American bricklayers, commonly work in this manner. If a bricklayer starts using a shovel and mud to lay bricks, this practice would not be part of American culture because it would not be shared.

But that is only half the story; shared behavioral traits are not automatically cultural traits, unless they are learned. Learned behavior stands in sharp contrast to unlearned behavior—that which is instinctive, inborn, innate, and genetic. No child is taught such behavior as breathing, circulation of the blood, digestion of food, or maintenance of body temperature. These behaviors are essential to life and are present at birth. Learned behavior is *acquired* behavior, gained after one is born through experiences with others in group situations. A normally healthy person doesn't have to learn how to jerk his knee when it is tapped; he does have to learn how to drive an automobile or to lay bricks. There are no genes that carry culture; but there are capacities in individuals that enable them to learn the ways of life of their fellow human beings.

The key to the learning of behavior patterns is language. People are unique in their ability to symbolize. They have *abstracted* from reality, developed symbols that stand in the place of reality, and these symbols become meaningful and important. Other animals live in groups, share ways of behaving, are capable of learning, and communicate messages to each other. Natural scientists have recorded intricate communicative devices among such varied creatures as porpoises, whales, gorillas,

Nature vs. Nurture

and insects. But these findings do not indicate anything of the magnitude, command, and diversity of human language.

In sharing and transmitting knowledge within their species, then, other creatures perform at a rudimentary level. Each generation attains about the same levels of learning as that of the parents. A person, on the other hand, can learn from experience and can pass this knowledge on to succeeding generations. The ideas, information, techniques of living become cumulative, enabling each generation to build on the experience of previous generations. If each generation of humans had found it necessary to relearn how to make tools, fire, shelter, etc., culture would have remained quite static. Instead, the ability to transmit ideas within and between generations has made culture a phenomenon of constant change and growth.

The Role of Culture in Determining Human Behavior

Over the years, the behavioral sciences have made a considerable contribution to our knowledge of man as a social animal. Numerous cross-cultural studies on the development of identity and personality traits, sexual behavior, and intelligence have presented considerable evidence to indicate the influence of social and cultural conditioning on human behavior.

Most sociologists agree that only to the extent that infants are reared in human society, will they develop the attributes we generally regard as the special mark of being human. In other words, what we call human behavior is learned; it is not biologically inherited. This position is sometimes called *cultural determinism.*

An extreme view of cultural determinism would suggest that human behavior is *entirely* the product of social learning. Inherited biological or physical traits would not have any influence on behavior. However, most sociologists do not go this far. Instead, the influence of genetic traits is recognized, but the social environment is regarded as a much more significant determinant of behavior.

While widely accepted, this position is not universal among behavioral scientists. In the 19th century, for example, biogenetic theories were developed to explain the causes of criminal behavior. Cesare Lombroso and his associates studied prison inmates in search of a correlation between behavior and physical characteristics. They concluded that there existed a definite criminal "type"—individuals who were genetically inferior to noncriminals. Criminals revealed *atavistic* physical traits, that is, the features of beings who were throwbacks to an earlier stage of human evolution, with low foreheads, jutting jaws, and close-set eyes. Because of their biological inferiority, these individuals were incapable of making moral distinctions or conforming to social codes. Variations on this theory have continued through the 1940's in the form of attempts to demonstrate a relationship between body size, temperament, and juvenile delinquency.

Today there are several versions of biogenetic theories used to explain different forms of deviant behavior. One theory says that some homosexuality may be caused by an imbalance of male/female hormones. The sociological response to this idea is that such theories are based on stereotypes of the effeminate male homosexual and fail to take into account the extensive learning process involved in the development of a sexual identity. Furthermore, some very feminine appearing men are strictly heterosexual, while some extremely masculine types are gay.

Another controversial genetic theory centers around the "supermale" or XYY chromosome found among violent men. This double male gene might trigger an aggressive violent impulse in those men possessing it. What we don't know, of course, is whether all men possessing this genetic trait have violent characteristics. The problem here is a lack of an adequate sample of the population. One must admit that the possibility of such a causal relationship is simultaneously intriguing and frightening. We could test infants for this trait and begin to "condition" them to control any violent impulses. On the other hand, in our effort to "protect" society we might deny them certain freedoms and label them as deviant or dangerous, which would very likely create violent impulses anyway.

Race, Intelligence, and Culture

The most important current controversy is whether intelligence is inherited or the product of cultural learning. The issue is over the 15 point average difference between the intelligence scores of whites and blacks. Most sociologists argue that this can only be explained by the fact that intelligence tests have always been culturally bound. That is, they are created by and for white middle-class oriented social backgrounds and lifestyles. When social class and education of the parents are the same, black and white I.Q. differences disappear, as do differences between Mexican-American and white children.

Two well-known proponents of the other view are Arthur Jensen, at U.C. Berkeley's College of Education and William Shockley, a physicist at Stanford University. Their argument is basically that the difference in I.Q. scores has been too consistent over the years and through a variety of tests to be entirely accounted for by cultural biases. Furthermore, according to Jensen, compensatory education has failed to eliminate the differences. Shockley requested a test of the hypothesis that intelligence differences in racial groups is biologically caused. His request was denied, and he has been rebuked for his interest in this subject. Jensen has been similarly attacked for his views by intellectuals and the public.

Most social scientists simply dismiss the theories of Jensen and Shockley. They argue that a number of tests have already indicated no innate intelligence differences exist among different racial or ethnic groups. There also may be a reluctance to dignify such theories with further research. The very establishment of such tests might aggravate racial tensions at a time when Americans finally seem to be in the process of working out racial differences.

Unfortunately, unsupported statements like those of Jensen and Shockley provide fuel for racial supremists. In a 1974 television interview, for instance, an influential newspaper publisher stated that he had always had trouble dealing with blacks. "That's understandable," he said flatly, "because they are centuries behind us in terms of evolution. That has already been proved by scientists like Shockley." Such bigoted views are not likely to succumb to further testing of the I.Q. controversy.

How Culture Is Organized

For purposes of analysis, a culture may be broken down into its component parts. The smallest element of any culture is known as a *culture trait.* These are the basic building blocks or units out of which a culture is constructed. Traits can be either material or nonmaterial. A guitar, for example, or any other musical instrument, is a material trait. From such basic elements as these, entire cultures are fashioned.

A number of combined traits form a *culture complex.* A rock group, for example, is made up of a number of different material traits: instruments, amplifying equipment, sheet music. A number of nonmaterial traits are also in evidence: the skills of the members, the rules governing harmony, the symbols on the sheet music, even the applause of the audience.

When culture complexes themselves are combined, they form a *culture pattern.* Consider a simple culture trait, the wheel. Two wheels mounted on an axle originally formed a culture complex for a cart or chariot. Wheel complexes are combined with steering complexes, electrical complexes, engine complexes, and so on to form an automobile pattern. This pattern, in turn, fits in with still other patterns, such as governmental patterns, educational patterns, and recreational patterns.

Culture Areas and Subcultures

While cultures may be broken down into component parts for purposes of analysis, it is important to recognize that a culture is not a hodgepodge collection of bits and pieces. Rather, it is an extremely broad and closely woven fabric. Each society, as we noted earlier, has its own culture, one that is at least a bit different from ways of life developed by any other society.

Despite this cultural diversity, historians and anthropologists have discerned a number of distinct *culture areas:* geographical regions in which people share many of the same basic sets of traits, complexes, and patterns. The nations of Europe formed one such area, the influence of which was gradually extended to other regions of the world, including North America. North America itself, prior to European expansion, was divided up into such culture areas as the Eastern Woodlands, Circum-Caribbean, Meso-American, Eastern, Central, and Western Arctic areas. Similarly, in the South Pacific, four different culture areas have been identified: Micronesia, Melanesia, Polynesia, and Indonesia.

Every broad culture area includes several cultures or *subcultures.* Thus, within the Polynesian area scholars have identified such subcultures as the Samoan, the Marquesan, the Hawaiian, and the Tongan.

American society can be divided into subcultures in a variety of ways. Perhaps the most obvious distinctions are those among different geographical areas: North, South, East, and West. Certain aspects of speech, dress, eating, and other forms of behavior vary from one section to another. These geographical subcultures can be broken down even further: The New Englander differs from the New Yorker and the Southwesterner from the Californian—at least in certain ways.

Subcultures can be identified in ways other than according to geographic regions. For instance, there exists an urban subculture as well as a rural one. In other words, the patterns of living of city dwellers are uniformly different in some respects from the patterns of country dwellers. Many sociologists would also differentiate a separate suburban subculture, with behavior patterns distinct in some ways from either city or rural dwellers.

It has become increasingly common to refer to almost any group with distinctive behavior patterns as a separate subculture. Thus, the "counterculture" movement associated with living in rural or urban communes is referred to as a subculture. Such terms as "teen culture," "drug culture," and "criminal subculture" are based on identifiable behavior patterns associated with those groups. There is also a subcultural difference based on sex, with males and females in this society being trained for adulthood in quite different ways, traditionally resulting in the man being the principal wage earner and the woman assigned to homemaking duties. These distinctions are not as sharp, of course, as they once were; women, for example, have become more and more "career" oriented in recent decades. The thrust of the Women's Liberation movement is to erase as many of the subcultural differences based on sex as possible.

THE DYNAMICS OF CULTURE

In our discussion of cultural influences on behavior, emphasis was placed on how cultural patterns replace instinctual traits. This learning process extends across the full spectrum of human activities. One sociological insight into the role of culture is that we take our values, beliefs, and customs for granted. Through information about the culture of other societies or our own subcultures we gain greater understanding of the world we live in.

Sexual Dimension of Culture

Human sexual behavior provides a good illustration of the importance of cultural conditioning and what can be learned by cross-cultural comparisons. Cultural learning is so deeply ingrained, and so taken for granted, that we regard as "normal" that sexual behavior which conforms to our cultural standards. At the same time, behavior which deviates from those standards is considered unnatural or "sick."

These ideas of "normal" and "sick," however, are not determined by natural instincts. Instead, they represent a complex system of cultural rules, or norms, established to control and regulate sexual behavior. These normative controls vary widely from culture to culture, as do the sanctions or penalties imposed for their violation.

Folkways are norms that have mild sanctions such as gossip and ridicule. In tradition-

al American society, premarital sexual experimentation among women was discouraged through neighborhood gossip that attempted to discredit the girl's moral character, and to suggest that her marital chances would be harmed. This was often sufficient to control premarital sexual experimentation.

Other forms of sexual behavior are considered serious enough to have legal sanctions established against them in the form of misdemeanors and felonies. The behaviors range from public nudity or "streaking," which are not likely to result in imposition of penalties, to homosexuality and prostitution, which have severe penalties attached to convictions. But these aren't always enforced either. Finally, there are mores which are norms designed to prevent very serious affronts to the social order, such as rape and incest. Increasingly, we are becoming aware of the difficulty of obtaining convictions for these crimes.

Crimes w/o victims

Cultural Diversity and Similarity

Not all societies have the same sexual beliefs, norms, and customs. The island society of Mangia is typical of the carefree south sea cultures analyzed by anthropologists like Margaret Mead in her study of Samoa. The Mangians seem highly promiscuous by our standards. They encourage teenagers to engage in as much premarital sex as they desire, often in the same room as the parents. Both boys and girls are expected to have many sexual partners before finally settling down. Females have their sexual preferences and place great emphasis on the ability of the boys to bring them to orgasm. Sex education is, of course, an important part of their cultural learning.

In contrast, there is the other extreme of the small island off Ireland called Inis Beag. Here sexual behavior in general is played down. Neither men nor women receive any sex education and are discouraged from marriage until their late 20's or 30's. Girls are kept ignorant about menstruation. For them sex is something that one should engage in as a marital duty and is never acknowledged as something pleasurable.

These extreme patterns of sexual behavior can be understood in terms of the concept *cultural relativism.* This means that behavior of others should be understood and judged within the context of their beliefs and values, rather than our own. This idea can help us to overcome *ethnocentricism,* which is the belief that one's own culture and behavior is superior to that of other societies or groups.

The goal of cross-cultural comparisons is to remove these biases in order to discover how diverse patterns of behavior might actually represent *cultural universals.* For example, through a comparison of Mangia and Inis Beag we gain information about how sexual orgasm and pleasure among women may be learned or suppressed through cultural conditioning. Another universal characteristic of social life represented in both societies is the need to control deviant behavior. Homosexuality is practically nonexistent in these island societies. Also, quite remarkably, both have a high incidence of sexual impotence among males over 30. Perhaps the Irish don't get enough sex, while the Mangians apparently get too much. Perhaps in both incidences we see the problems of male sexuality caused by cultural emphasis on aggressiveness and potency. Hopefully, there is much to be learned from these and other studies about causes of sexual dysfunction, such as frigidity and impotence, in our society.

Cultural Lag and Social Change

Sociologist William G. Ogburn used the term *cultural lag in* his analysis of the process of social change. He noted that *material cul-ture,* or technology, develops much more rapidly than *nonmaterial culture,* which includes values, beliefs, customs, and norms. This means that when innovations in communications or transportation occur, new variations in behavior become possible without traditional cultural constraints. This insight might provide understanding about communication gaps between generations over sexual behavior.

The controversy surrounding the so-called "sexual revolution" is a case in point. Several technological inventions in this century might be associated with increased sexual activity among youth. These include the motion picture, the automobile, and the birth control pill. The film industry has emphasized sexual attraction and pleasure with increasing explicitness in recent years. The automobile has allowed young lovers to find privacy and mobility necessary for intimacy. The pill has perhaps had the most liberating impact on sexual freedom by allowing women to avoid unwanted pregnancies. It allows couples a greater degree of sexual spontaneity than other forms of contraception.

Related developments in our knowledge of human sexual response through research by psychologists and sociologists have also influenced sex behavior and attitudes. The famous works of psychologists Masters and Johnson involved the measurement of physiological and psychological responses of men and women during sexual intercourse. Studies of this sort provide information on how people may maximize their sexual pleasure. Sociological studies of sexual behavior in "deviant" groups and subcultures have provided information about the "normal" or routine aspects of their lifestyles. For example, our knowledge of homosexuality has been greatly increased in recent years.

In addition to these technological developments, there are changes in the institutions of education and the family that influence sexual patterns. A more candid approach to sex education in schools tends to remove some of the anxiety about sex that young people experience. It is probably true that this knowledge has led to greater sex experimentation among adolescents. We still find the effects of a lack of openness about sexual matters, though, in the high rates of venereal disease and pregnancies among teenagers. This fact might be explained by the cultural lag theory in that the traditional values and beliefs which suppress sexuality are so influential as to negate the use of knowledge about contraception and venereal disease.

Culture Conflict and Change

Some examples of the reactions to changing knowledge and attitudes about sexual behavior will illustrate another important factor in change called *cultural conflict*. This principle is based on the notion that changes in cultural beliefs, values, and norms proceed at different rates for various segments of the population. This process creates conflicts between generations and subcultures.

In communities throughout America there have been controversies over sex education in schools. Parents and certain religious groups object to the fact that children will likely be developing sexually permissive attitudes and values while learning more about sex. Similarly, many people feel that teenagers should not learn about nor be allowed to have contraceptives.

Sexual explicitness in the arts, entertainment, and mass media has become another source of conflict within communities and nationally. In 1972, California voters defeated an antiobscenity initiative that would have severely restricted "sexually oriented" language, behavior, and content in films, literature, stage performances, and other art forms. The

"antiobscenity" forces, such as Citizens for Decent Literature, fundamentalist religious groups, and the John Birch Society, have had some success in influencing how sex is to be presented publicly.

The U.S. Supreme Court under Chief Justice Berger has ruled on related issues, one of which is that the definition of what is obscene material will be left up to the dominant standards and morals of each community. This raises the question of whether subcultural values will be considered as part of those of the "community." Depending on the zealousness of the group, extremist values and beliefs may be either eliminated from or possibly dominate the community's definition of obscenity. The possible erosion of the freedoms of press and personal expression due to censorship has already developed. Publications such as Playboy Magazine were banned from sale in some towns. Novels by Kurt Vonnegut and J. D. Salinger's *Catcher in the Rye* have been considered unfit for use in some high schools because they contain "dirty words." Perhaps we should not expect a resolution of these conflicts over appropriate sexual expression. Keeping in mind that our society consists of numerous subcultures, sociologists try to maintain a certain degree of distance from such issues as how communities shall define sexual norms. The principal contribution that sociology and other behavioral sciences might make towards the resolution of this conflict would be to indicate the wide diversity of cultural beliefs and norms surrounding human sexuality.

Cultural Pluralism

We can use the sexual dimension of behavior to illustrate another cultural concept which reflects the dynamics of modern society. This is the idea of cultural *pluralism,* a term used to describe the conditions that cause cultural conflict.

With all of our cultural diversity in the form of varying lifestyles found among different racial, ethnic, regional, and economic subcultures, we should be concerned for our liberty, if one subculture's values and beliefs about sex, for instance, ever completely dominate the others. The fact that conflicting values and beliefs influence our laws, education, and family with some disorganizing consequences reflects this pluralism. Sociologists are becoming convinced that cultural diversity and conflicts are enduring and functional aspects of social life. This develops a humanistic capacity for tolerance of the full range of human behavior and experiences.

CULTURAL DEVELOPMENT

The origins of culture are shrouded in mystery. What information we have is based on "finds" of material objects which are all that remain of once-active cultures. Relics of this kind have been found at sites scattered throughout the world. Physical evidence of human occupation of a place in ancient or prehistoric times include old fireplaces, bits of cloth or basketry, pottery, tools, and, at times, human skeletons or fragments. Refuse heaps composed of discarded animal bones, broken weapons, scattered seeds, and unfinished carvings also yield clues.

From such material items, archaeologists attempt to reconstruct the society's nonmaterial culture patterns—how they worked, governed themselves, worshiped, and so on. Like the pieces of a gigantic jigsaw puzzle, the fragments of evidence must be carefully sifted and interpreted to arrive at valid generalizations.

AMERICA'S CULTURAL HERITAGE

American society, like most others, is heir to a rich storehouse of cultural achievement. Americans have borrowed heavily from people of other ages and distant parts of the world. In fact, a good portion of American culture is an amalgam of bits and pieces brought to the United States by foreign immigrants.

Most of us are aware that we have inherited a great deal from the cultures of Western Europe. Our basic forms of government, art, science, industry, technology, education, philosophy, and religion were forged in Europe and passed on to us intact. Yet we often tend to overlook the contributions of non-Western peoples. These are both numerous and impressive, ranging from Arabic numerals to Chinese paper and gunpowder, and foods introduced to Westerners by American Indians.

In a satirical article titled "One Hundred Percent American," sociologist Ralph Linton illustrates something of the cultural transmission, diffusion, and contact that have shaped the lives of Americans. He describes a "typical" morning of a "typical" American, where, at breakfast:

... His food and drink are placed before him in pottery vessels, the popular name of which—China—is sufficient evidence of their origin. His fork is a medieval Italian invention and his spoon a copy of a Roman original. He will usually begin his meal with coffee, an Abyssinian plant first discovered by the Arabs. The American is quite likely to need it to dispel the morning-after effects of overindulgence in fermented drinks, invented in the Near East; or distilled ones, invented by the alchemists of medieval Europe. Whereas the Arabs took their coffee straight, he will probably sweeten it with sugar, discovered in India; and dilute it with cream, both the domestication of cattle and the technique of milking having originated in Asia Minor.

If our patriot is old-fashioned enough to adhere to the so-called American breakfast, his coffee will be accompanied by an orange, domesticated in the Mediterranean region, a cantaloupe domesticated in Persia, or grapes, domesticated in Asia Minor. He will follow this with a bowl of cereal made from grain domesticated in the Near East and prepared by methods also invented there. From this he will go to waffles, a Scandinavian invention, with plenty of butter, originally a Near Eastern cosmetic. As a side dish he may have the egg of a bird domesticated in Southeastern Asia or strips of the flesh of an animal domesticated in the same region, which have been salted and smoked by a process invented in Northern Europe.

Breakfast over, he places upon his head a molded piece of felt, invented by the nomads of Eastern Asia, and, if it looks like rain, puts on outer shoes of rubber, discovered by the ancient Mexicans, and takes an umbrella, invented in India. He then sprints for his train—the train, not the sprinting, being an English invention. At the station he pauses for a moment to buy a newspaper, paying for it with coins invented in ancient Lydia. Once on board he settles back to inhale the fumes of a cigarette invented in Mexico, or a cigar invented in Brazil. Meanwhile, he reads the news of the day, imprinted in characters invented by the ancient Semites by a process invented in Germany upon a material invented in China. As he scans the latest editorial pointing out the dire results to our institutions of accepting foreign ideas, he will not fail to thank a Hebrew God in an Indo-European language that he is a one hundred percent (decimal system invented by the Greeks) American (from Americus Vespucci, Italian geographer).[1]

PROCESSES INVOLVED IN CULTURAL GROWTH

Now that we have sketched in the general outlines of cultural growth, we can examine

[1] Ralph Linton, "One Hundred Percent American," *The American Mercury,* Vol. 40 (April, 1937) pp. 427-429.

the processes through which such growth takes place. These are *invention, diffusion,* and *transmission.*

Cultural Invention

Invention is the discovery of new material and nonmaterial objects or ideas which serve as a stimulus to cultural growth. In many instances, new materials or findings were discovered by accident. Such was the discovery of fire, soft metals, or, in more recent times, the vulcanization of rubber, an "invention" which occurred when Charles Goodyear inadvertently spilled sulfur on a batch of hot rubber.

On the other hand, invention can be deliberate. Thomas Edison was fond of insisting that invention is "one percent inspiration and ninety-nine percent perspiration." His development of a workable incandescent bulb was a case in point. He carefully tested a wide variety of materials for use as the filament in such a lamp before he settled upon slivers of charred bamboo. Other examples of deliberate invention would be the development of the laser beam or the harnessing of nuclear energy.

Inventions may be classified as either *primary* or *secondary.* Primary inventions are those which make possible significant advances in humanity's struggle to shape the environment. They are, in effect, the basic building blocks upon which many other cultural developments rest. Such discoveries as fire, the wheel, the phonic alphabet, ore smelting, and atomic energy may all be considered primary.

Secondary inventions, by contrast, are those which represent improvements upon existing designs rather than unique breakthroughs. For instance, when the rudder replaced the steering oar at the rear of sailing vessels, it

PERSPECTIVE

CULTURAL LAG IN AMERICA'S INSTITUTIONS

We live in a world marked by tremendously rapid change, especially in science and technology. Our ways of making a living have changed dramatically, but other aspects of our way of life have altered much more slowly. As a noted anthropologist has stated: "Our economic political and social institutions have not caught up with our technology. . . . Part of us lives in the 'modern' age—another part in medieval or even Greek times."

Can our basic institutions—economics, government, family, religion, education—change fast enough to meet the needs of space-age society? Or are these institutions in the process of becoming cultural dinosaurs, no longer capable of adjusting to changes in the environment?

These are questions that Americans are desperately wrestling with, and so far no one has come up with any universally accepted answers. From the point of view of some members of the radical left, our institutions are "death traps" and must be torn down, by revolution if necessary, although no one has suggested what would replace them. In underground-press style, here is how a student leftist views American political institutions: "The 1854 donkey elephant political institution is a death form. After 113 years of success, the people in the country are where they're at. Straight people, we don't like to break your stiff security, but let's dig the cliche 'it's time to change' and let's blow our brains and do more than just change candidates—let's change from a political system to a free form. . . . The only alternatives open for these free people are either to ignore the city's political institution or to violently attack it."

On the other hand, people of an extreme right-wing persuasion feel that we must preserve our institutions as they are; any attempt at change raises fears of a Communist conspiracy. A publication of the John Birch Society proclaims that "right before our eyes" those who attempt to change our institutions "are gradually changing our whole economic framework into a socialist system . . . our whole political system from a republic, to a democracy, to a mobocracy, to a dictatorship. . . . There is an even more forceful and more immediate drive to destroy the family as a fundamental structural unit in our civilization."

In between these two extremes, responsible citizens and public leaders express the concern that our institutions must be changed to meet the needs of modern society. Senator George McGovern warned that ". . . it is important that the leaders of our major parties—and of other established institutions in our society—understand that the question is not who will control these organizations but, rather, whether these organizations will continue to exist at all. We can be sure that unless there is a new responsiveness in the old institutions, the young people of this country—and others shut out by the atrophy of our democratic processes—will ignore them or seek to bring them down by their own improvised means."

And President Nixon, in a speech on a college campus, urged that a constructive attitude is needed if we are to achieve the needed changes without violence: "Our institutions are undergoing what may be their severest challenge yet," he said. "I speak not of the physical challenge: the force and threats of force that have wracked our cities, and now our colleges. Force can be contained. . . . The challenge I speak of is deeper: the challenge to our values, and to the moral base of the authority that sustains those values. . . . Avenues of peaceful change do exist. Those who can make a persuasive case for changes they want can achieve them through orderly process."

In other words, if social institutions are slow to change in response to our changing needs, it is up to society to struggle to modify those institutions. And the struggle does not have to involve revolution or violence. The challenge for this generation, as publisher Otis Chandler has said, is that "we must determine how to adjust our institutions and modify our living styles to meet the conditions of the latter part of the twentieth century."

represented a secondary invention; likewise, the self-starter in an automobile. Needless to say, secondary inventions outnumber primary ones by a huge margin.

It has been said that "necessity is the mother of invention," a statement which obviously contains a grain of truth. Individuals rarely invent things which don't help to meet some human need. However, the mere existence of a need does not automatically bring about an invention. For countless centuries people have experienced a need to rid themselves of disease; yet the cure for many diseases eludes even the most exhaustive research.

The overwhelming majority of human inventions are really the end products of long chains of events, often stretching back in time far beyond the lifetimes of any individual. Dr. Jonas Salk will always be remembered as the discoverer of polio vaccine, but he was able to make the discovery only because he could draw upon a store of medical knowledge which had been accumulating for centuries. Similarly, the automobile was invented near the end of the 19th century by a number of men in different places. What these men did, in effect, was to combine elements of accumulated mechanical knowledge into a new, useful form.

This storehouse of knowledge, in all fields, is what sociologists call a society's *culture base*. Every culture has a base, but no two cultures have precisely the same base. That is, no two cultures are made up of exactly the same combinations of traits, complexes, and patterns.

Cultural Diffusion

The second process involved in cultural growth is diffusion. Diffusion takes place when societies borrow traits, complexes, or patterns from one another. Hence it is popularly known as cultural borrowing.

On a very broad scale, the influence of diffusion can be seen in the spread of the Industrial Revolution. From the early beginnings in mid-18th century England, the factory system of production spread first to Western Europe, then to North America. In the succeeding years, the influence of industrialization became felt in just about every corner of the planet. One of the primary goals of modern Third World nations is to "borrow" culture traits, complexes, and patterns needed to create higher levels of industrialization.

Any number of specific instances of diffusion can be culled from the Industrial Revolution. In 1789, for example, a man named Samuel Slater emigrated to the United States, carrying in his head the detailed plans of an English spinning machine. Slater's knowledge enabled him to supervise construction of a cotton mill in Rhode Island, and it was this mill that is commonly considered the starting point of American industrialization.

The experience of Japan is also illustrative. After centuries of avoiding contact with the West, the Japanese in 1853 suddenly faced the persuasive influence of the warships of American Matthew C. Perry and agreed to "open their doors" to Western trade. Aware of the technological (and military) advantages the West had achieved through industrialization, the Japanese very deliberately set about trying to "catch up." European and American experts were brought into the country to school the Japanese in Western innovations in industry, education, government, and military science. Within 50 years, Japan had become a modern industrial nation; in fact, it now ranks as the third largest industrial power in the world.

Diffusion may be either *direct* or *indirect*. The direct spread of culture takes place when the members of different societies come into face-to-face contact with one another. Migration, trade, war, and missionary activities are primary instruments of direct diffusion. Indirect diffusion, on the other hand, does not involve personal contact; it depends instead upon communications media, such as the printed page, radio, television, and films.

Various factors affect both the rate and direction of cultural diffusion. For example, the spread of cultural elements is usually from the more advanced cultures to the less advanced, although movement in the opposite direction is by no means unknown. As a rule, material traits diffuse much faster than nonmaterial traits. Societies are far more likely to accept technological innovations than changes in their basic social structures. Most primitive groups, for instance, will adapt the tools or science of more advanced groups long before they will change family patterns, governmental organization, or religious ceremonies.

The attitudes of a receiving society also help to determine whether the society will accept new ways of doing things. Often, there is a strong resistance to innovations, sometimes involving taboos against changing certain aspects of a culture. At other times there is a strong feeling of superiority which makes the people look down on anything foreign. The Chinese for many centuries refused to accept most foreign innovations because they considered their own culture far superior to any other. This voluntary isolation was one of the factors responsible for the contrast between China's struggle to industrialize and the success of the Japanese in this area.

The prestige of the "lending" culture may also be a contributing factor. After World War II, American culture enjoyed a high level of prestige, which undoubtedly helps explain why our culture was diffused throughout so much of the globe in so short a space of time. Similarly, President Nixon's 1972 trip to China initiated in this country something of a fad for Chinese ideas, art, and manufactured goods.

Finally, the culture base of a society helps to determine whether that society will borrow and what it will borrow. To cite an extreme example, it would be impossible for a preliterate society to adopt a new printing technique. And it would be just as unlikely that a modern nation would be interested in a modification of the bow and arrow to serve as a weapon of war. There are exceptions to this pattern. Many Americans, for instance, have begun to show a new appreciation for the traditional values of American Indians, particularly in regard to their attempt to live in harmony with nature.

As the examples above indicate, cultural diffusion depends upon intercultural contacts, which result in an exchange of ideas. Societies which fail to establish contacts with neighboring groups cannot benefit from diffusion. The isolated society is forced to rely solely upon its own resources; it cannot profit from the advances made by other people. It is tied to its own culture base and bound by whatever limitations that base imposes.

Normally, cultural isolation is the result of geographical accident, although it can be deliberate, as in the case of the Chinese attempt to isolate themselves from Western influence. The Indians of North and South America, for example, were cut off from European developments and the individual societies were quite isolated from each other. Although some of these societies developed high levels of civilization (the Aztec, Mayan, and Inca Empires), most remained at a fairly primitive level of cultural development. And none of these cultures was prepared for the penetration of Europeans, with their advanced weaponry and technology.

Even in modern times, some cultures have remained isolated in remote geographical corners. The densely jungled island of New Guinea, for example, was the site of fierce battles during World War II. Yet, some of the interior tribes had never seen a white man until a group of Australian explorers made their way across the island in the 1960's. Isolated for centuries, the New Guinea tribes continued to live in a Stone Age culture, with only the most rudimentary forms of clothing, shelter, and governmental organization. Perhaps the last such totally isolated cultures is represented by the Tasaday of the Philippine Islands, who were not "discovered" until 1970. The Tasaday remained Stone Age hunters and gatherers while the rest of the world was charging into the Space Age.

Cultural Transmission and the Sociology of Knowledge

Transmission is the process by which the accumulated knowledge of one generation is passed on to other generations. Within societies that possess a written language, traits, complexes, and patterns can be transmitted in written form. Within nonliterate societies they are transmitted by word of mouth.

There is always the danger that transmission will take place imperfectly, with certain aspects of a culture being lost. Such culture loss is especially apt to occur during the transmission of knowledge and skills which are the exclusive property of small groups or categories rather than entire societies. During the Middle Ages craftsmen who specialized in the making of stained glass windows developed techniques for achieving exquisite shades of coloring. However, many of these techniques were known only to individual families or guilds. The secrets were apparently transmitted for a time and then allowed to die out. Consequently, the medieval knack of staining glass has been lost to the world. Today's craftsmen, despite the benefits of modern technology, have been unable to duplicate the work of their predecessors.

Occasionally, even widely shared cultural patterns manage to become lost through imperfect transmission. Such was the case with the written language of ancient Egypt. For centuries no one knew how to interpret the Egyptian hieroglyphics; even trained scholars were unequal to the task. It was not until the famous Rosetta stone was discovered by the soldiers of Napoleon Bonaparte that the key to this mystery was supplied.

Most instances of culture loss may be attributed to changes in social conditions rather than faulty transmission. When a society adopts a new way of doing something, it often discards the old way. Thus, the adoption of different vernacular tongues by Europeans caused Latin to all but vanish as a spoken language. And the invention of the automobile had a devastating effect on the craft of blacksmithing.

The *sociology of knowledge* deals with the process by which knowledge arises in a particular culture. It also analyzes how cultural knowledge is transmitted and controlled, and the effects that this has on behavior within the culture. The importance of this perspective for our discussion of how culture is transmitted lies in the idea that if knowledge is socially constructed, rather than being innate in the human mind, then our perceptions of reality are greatly effected by our social position and cultural background.

The Radical View

It should be noted that there are disagreements among sociologists as to the process of how knowledge is developed and distributed within society. The Activists believe that knowledge is developed and controlled to serve the interests of the power elite or ruling class. According to this view cultural knowledge transmitted through major socializing institutions of the family, education, religion, work, and the mass media represents cultural programming or conditoning designed to perpetuate the dominant ideology.

The "Scientific" View

Traditional sociologists reject the radical views as being too deterministic. This group, following the early ideas of Durkheim and the leading proponent of functionalism, Robert K. Merton, take the position that knowledge as a social product is part of a dynamic system that is a reality independent of the schemes and ideologies of members of society. As such, cultural knowledge is still socially developed and distributed, but is not controlled or conditioned as the radicals believe. Ideas thus are a reality which effects behavior and culture depending on social conditions.

For example, in the 1970's we find a resurgence of knowledge and beliefs surrounding the occult, supernaturalism, astrology, and parapsychological phenomena. These ideas, while not replacing scientific and religious interpretations of reality, are of considerable interest to members of the mass media, clergy, social scientists, and the "respectable" middle classes. Furthermore, the fact that this is occurring during a critical period of political and economic uncertainty lends support to the functional perspective. That is to say, the current interest in mystical or supernatural belief systems reflects the anxiety and uncertainty about social conditions and a failure of the dominant cultural knowledge system to provide answers to problems of the times. Thus, some people are seeking a form of escapism through an alternative reality beyond the realm of political scandals, high prices, and gasoline shortages.

The radicals would probably also see the interest in alternative definitions of reality as an attempt to escape from the mundane problems of living. Yet they would add the judgment that this preoccupation shifts attention away from those in positions of political and economic power and responsibility.

The Humanistic Perspective

There is still another viewpoint on the relationship between knowledge and culture, associated with the humanistic perspective in sociology. This approach has been developed by Peter Berger and Thomas Luckmann in their book, *The Social Construction of Reality: A Treatise in the Sociology of Knowledge.* Their approach is to point out that knowledge and social institutions exist on multiple levels of social reality. Ideas and knowledge are created as a social product stemming from shared experiences. As time and generations pass, the shared experiences and knowledge become institutions and part of external reality. As even more time passes the experiences may no longer exist, yet the knowledge and institutions remain a part of cultural heritage. New members of society, the young for example, and minority groups are expected to internalize the knowledge as part of their own subjective reality (or values and beliefs).

The potential for conflict between generations and groups is probably evident to the reader at this point in the discussion. It might also be suggested that this disparity between objective and subjective social realities is one of the causal factors in the "generation gap" and perhaps the basis for the development of the "youth culture." A number of "pop" sociologists, such as Charles Reich (*The Greening of America*) and Theodore Rozak (*The Making of a Counter Culture*), have attempted to analyze the values and ideologies of the "youth culture." While they may not have followed the dialectic approach as indicated by the sociology of knowledge, their studies provide information about the involvement of the youth in mysticism, spiritualism, and radicalism.

Both Rozak and Reich point out that the turbulent era of the 60's, with its numerous racial, political, and antiwar confrontations; drug and venereal epidemics; and various radical attacks on the family, work, and higher education, was basically an illustration of culture conflict. What was unique about this situation was that the conflict developed within the dominant middle-class culture. While being socialized for positions of responsibility and leadership, the offspring of the affluent middle classes internalized values of equality, justice, and individualism as part of their subjective realities. The external or objective reality presented knowledge that racial inequality, corporate irresponsibility, and environmental neglect lay deep in American social structure and institutions. Moreover, science and technology, while providing affluence, also threatened to deteriorate the environmental quality. Television, with its emphasis on advertising and violence, developed into a communication wasteland that numbed its viewers, hence the label "boob tube." Finally, materialistic and competitive values were perceived as separating people from natural and spiritual consciousness.

According to the sociology of knowledge the various elements of the so-called youth culture or counter-culture are responses to a sense of reality not experienced by previous generations. The search for new values and lifestyles in the form of different social arrangements, such as communalism, and the back to nature movement along with the quest for altered consciousness through drugs and spiritualism does not actually represent the creation of new knowledge. Almost all of the information needed for this culture is available

from the past. The important sociological fact is that these changes away from technological values and urban lifestyles are occurring at this point in history. Probably the children of the counter-culture types will long for the more "far-out" experiences of going to drive-in movies and drive-in-restaurants for hamburgers and cokes.

CULTURAL VALUES AND SOCIAL CONTROL

Social control is defined as the techniques and strategies for regulating human behavior in any society. It has long been recognized by politicians, theologians, psychologists, and sociologists that actual or threatened physical force is not a long-term deterrent from social deviation. Thus, the state with its laws, sanctions and prisons is not the main source of conformity and social order.

Social Control in Folk Societies

Historically, in what has been called "folk society," the institutions of the family and church were combined with the local rural community in maintaining a high degree of conformity. Means of social control in folk society are informal. Gossip, ridicule, and threatened ostracism and banishment from the community are sanctions imposed on those who would deviate from community norms. Face-to-face interaction is an effective means of control in such communities. Traditional values and religious beliefs dominate without threats from conflicting ideologies because the population is homogeneous and not very mobile. Strangers are kept at a friendly distance and tolerance of eccentric behavior is low.

Emile Durkheim referred to this type of social control as "mechanical solidarity." He meant that in folk societies normative controls were so internalized in the individual and his every day contacts with members of the community that conformity was almost automatic. In other words, social control was a very informal, but effective, process in such communities.

Social Control in Urban Societies

In contrast, Durkheim used the concept of "organic solidarity" to describe the formal system of social control found in urban societies. He theorized that the fulfillment of diverse social and economic roles is more crucial to the organization of society than uniform acceptance of beliefs and values. People would be tied together by the fact that they were indirectly dependent on one another to perform specialized tasks and thereby contribute to the maintenance of the social and cultural order.

The problem with this system of control is its openness. The individual is expected to develop a high degree of self-control without the reinforcement of consistent community pressure and values. There is greater possibility for deviant behavior and *social disorganization*. Durkheim called this form of disorganization *anomie*, or a state of normlessness in which social control of individual behavior becomes ineffective. Anomie occurs when social and cultural changes occur too rapidly and there is a breakdown of traditional norms and values. In urban societies with a high degree of social mobility and conflicting subcultural values and lifestyles, anomie and deviant behavior become a more or less permanent condition. Increased tolerance of deviance, or behavior that violates social and cultural norms, can be viewed as an *adaptation* to cultural diversity and social change.

Crimes Without Victims

Sociologists have used the term "victimless crimes" to refer to the forms of deviancy that represent this rather gray area of conflicting values and norms. In his classic book, *Crimes Without Victims*, Edwin M. Schur defines homosexuality, abortion, and drug use as falling into this category. It is interesting to note that in the 1970's we have seen various attempts to legalize all sexual behavior between consenting adults, abortions, and the use of marijuana. The fact that most of these bills and initiatives failed to pass in legislatures and by the voters indicates the cultural resistance to changes of traditional morality and beliefs.

Norms, Values, and Cultural Adaptation

What are the possible consequences of continuing cultural conflicts? Recently, two sociologists, Rubington and Weinberg, in their text *5 Perspectives on Social Problems*, suggested three possible responses to the condition of social disorganization. The first is that widespread violation of social norms would be allowed to continue without enforcement of the laws.

A case in point is marijuana use which is still a felony in most parts of the country. It was estimated that by 1973, 20 million Americans had used marijuana at least once. The regular and occasional users must also be in the millions. The actual number will never be known. This situation is undesirable because knowledge of massive violation of the law

THE VARIOUS PATHS TO SOCIOLOGICAL KNOWLEDGE
ROBERT S. LYND AND HELEN MERRELL LYND

In studying American culture, a number of sociologists have concentrated on analyzing life in a single community, an approach that is sometimes referred to as community studies. Rather than breaking down community life into separate segments (such as class structure or government), an attempt is made to present an overall view of the community and its cultural values.

Robert and Helen Lynd were among the first to employ this form of research. Using Muncie, Indiana, as their field laboratory, they produced a profile of the community in 1929, using the title *Middletown.* Then, in a further attempt to determine the extent to which cultural values were influenced by social change, a follow-up study called *Middletown in Transition* was published in 1937.

In the first study, the Lynds tried to determine how cultural values were affected by the widespread mechanization of industry. In *Middletown in Transition*, the major social change to be dealt with was the Great Depression, which caused such great economic and social dislocation throughout the country in the 1930's.

The findings of both studies suggested that cultural values tend to persist even during periods of marked change. People continue to express the traditional values, respect them, and try to live up to them, even though such values may appear to have little relevance to current realities. The ideal of rugged individualism is one example. The culture of Middletown was centered around the ideas of competition, every person for himself, and the just reward for hard work.

But mechanized industry was making it increasingly difficult for many to achieve the goals connected with such ideals. The use of machinery blurred the lines between skilled and unskilled workers. The worker found himself part of a citywide labor pool, in competition with unseen others, and getting a job no longer requiring expert skills. The idea of working hard to get ahead no longer seemed to work out; massive economic forces were just as likely to lower wages as hard work was to raise them.

The value of upward mobility was also made difficult for those who had hopes of going into business for themselves. By the 1920's, large sums of capital were needed to start many kinds of businesses, and the production of goods was becoming increasingly complex. Despite these new obstacles, the people of Middletown continued to believe in the traditional values; in fact, they seemed to see no contradiction between the value system and the changing economic conditions.

Similarly, cultural values remained intact during the Depression upheavals. Part of the individualistic value system had been the stress on self-help—one did not look for handouts or government assistance. The economic realities of Depression times, however, made large-scale government programs essential. Again, the Middletowners continued to insist that their values had not changed. There was unlimited faith in progress and the American way. The trauma of the Depression had upset their lives, but not their values.

The advantage of such community studies is that they reduce the examination of American culture to manageable proportions. Following the lead of sociologists like the Lynds, a number of more recent researchers have analyzed class structure and power systems within particular communities, such as the Yankee City series of W. Lloyd Warner or Floyd Hunter's *Community Power Structure* (1953). An even larger number of studies have focused on ethnic or racial relations within individual communities, one of the earliest being John Dollard's *Caste and Class in a Southern Town* (1937).

threatens the credibility of the whole system of formalized social control.

Another response to the violation of norms would be to strictly enforce the laws and impose maximum penalties. Whether this action adequately deters others from engaging in the behavior is debatable. In the case of marijuana use, strict law enforcement would have the consequence of "criminalizing" many people who are otherwise law abiding. We might then lose the talents of many potential and presently employed industrial workers, businessmen, civil servants, and professionals. Convicted felons are unable to find good employment and are denied positions of social responsibility.

A third response involves the process of changing the laws. The resistance to legalization of marijuana use has already been discussed. What has happened is that many states have decriminalized their laws by making marijuana use a misdemeanor rather than a felony, or allowing the courts the discretion to reduce the charge to a misdemeanor, as in California. Thus, formal normative social control is maintained. But the existence of diverse values and lifestyles is at least tacitly acknowledged and tolerated.

Through the above discussion we have attempted to indicate that the relationship of cultural values and norms to social control is dynamic. The existence of subcultures in complex urban societies increases the likelihood of social conflict. The position of most contemporary sociologists with respect to social and cultural conflict is that it represents a process of adaption to change and is an indicator of a viable democratic society. In contrast, totalitarian societies are less tolerant of deviant lifestyles and conflicting values and beliefs. Social control may be more uniform, but perhaps the quality of life is lessened.

POSTINDUSTRIAL SOCIETY AND THE CULTURAL REVOLUTION

American society is entering a postindustrial era. This means that the majority of employment opportunities are in areas other than the production of goods and merchandise. Today more people work in sales and distribution of merchandise, or providing business services, civil services, and the most recently developed occupational area called human services. Job opportunities for unskilled and semiskilled workers are declining. Those people who do find employment in factories will be more like computer operators than assembly line workers.

The postindustrial era, which some people say is already upon us, has several distinguishing characteristics. These include: phenomenal growth of technological development, in transportation, communication, and medicine; alternative forms of traditional institutions of the family, work, and education; greater efforts at "social engineering" and increasing human awareness.

The impact of these changes on our total way of life will be significant. With the exception of the technological innovations, all of our future developments will be tremendously influenced by cultural conditions. Whether or not the future brings with it greater fulfillment of the human potential, and equality of life experiences for all people, will depend on the flexibility of values, beliefs, and social norms.

The concept of cultural revolution has been coined to describe an accelerated process of cultural change. This does not mean that we should cast aside our traditional or sacred values and beliefs. Rather, the challenge is to take the best humanist values from the past and integrate them with knowledge from the behavioral and social sciences. Neither the traditions of the past nor the technology of the future should be allowed to dominate the human spirit.

SUMMARY

The study of cultures involves analyzing those aspects of social life that we take most for granted. All of our shared and learned behaviors including language, knowledge, beliefs, values, and norms are elements of nonmaterial culture. Inventions and technology represent material culture. The theory of cultural lag has been developed to explain that nonmaterial culture changes more slowly than technology. This presents problems in that different segments of society, especially youth, may adapt their behavior to the latest technology. When this behavior is in an area of strong cultural constraints, such as sexuality, a high degree of cultural conflict is likely to occur. From a scientific perspective, the sociologist is interested in analyzing the processes through which culture conflict is resolved, regardless of the outcome. As a humanist and activist, the sociologist is concerned that the outcome of such conflicts does not result in the oppression of members of deviant subcultures.

Both anthropology and sociology are interested in the similarities and diversity of cultures. Studies of cultural patterns tend to emphasize universal functions that they tend to fulfill in the maintenance of the society or group. Sexual socialization patterns and the definition of deviant behavior establish the boundaries for conformity and maintain social bonds within the family and community. Whether traditional cultural values are to prevail and be the basis for these forms of social control will depend on the institutional and political experiences of successive generations. New definitions of social reality and rapidly increasing knowledge from the behavioral sciences will bring continuing pressures on the existing norms and customs. Rather than returning to the "simpler times," based on traditional morality, we are likely to see an ever more complex and conflicting cultural revolution.

GLOSSARY

biological determinism the belief that inherited characteristics cause behavior, to the exclusion of social and cultural factors.

cultural determinism the belief that only learned variables can be considered as a cause or explanation of human behavior.

cultural lag William Ogburn's concept which explains how related segments of society change at different rates, usually applied to the slower change in values than technology.

cultural pluralism the simultaneous existence in society of diverse values, beliefs, and norms associated with varying lifestyles.

cultural relativism the view that behavior cannot be morally evaluated by universal or absolute standards.

cultural transmission the process of passing beliefs, values, and behavior patterns onto successive generations.

culture conflict the existence of competing value and belief systems.

determinism the belief that one variable, such as biology, culture, psychology, or economics, causes human behavior and social change.

ethnocentrism the tendency to evaluate the norms and values of other cultures as being inferior because they differ from one's own cultural standards.

folkways patterns of behavior common in and typical to a group.

mechanical solidarity Emile Durkheim's concept that describes the almost automatic conformity that exists in small-scale societies.

mores norms from which a group or society tolerates very little deviance, such as murder, rape, or incest.

organic solidarity Durkheim's concept to describe the form of conformity existing in complex urban-industrial societies.

social control   the techniques and strategies for regulating human behavior, ranging from gossip and ridicule to law enforcement and imprisonment.

social disorganization   the breakdown of groups and institutions usually attributed to internal conflicts over values.

sociology of knowledge   the school of sociology concerned with how knowledge is culturally created and socially distributed.

subculture   the different values and folkways developed among various groups within society.

values   ideas about desirable goals or social conditions that have an "ought to be" quality to them.

SUGGESTED READINGS

Ardrey, Robert. *African Genesis.* New York: Dell, 1961.
————. *The Territorial Imperative.* New York: Atheneum, 1966.
————. *The Social Contract.* New York: Atheneum, 1970.
Ardrey is a popularizer of the field of ethnology. In these three works he suggests that man's use of weapons, his desire for property, and his relationships to fellow men are related to innate genetic codes.

Benedict, Ruth. *Patterns of Culture.* Boston: Houghton Mifflin, 1961. This is a widely read, and well-written, study of three primitive societies. Although written in the 1930's, it remains one of the best introductions to the study of culture.

Berger, Peter L. and Luckmann, Thomas. *The Social Construction of Reality: A Treatise in the Sociology of Knowledge.* Garden City, New York: Doubleday, 1966.

Davis, Kingsley. "Extreme Social Isolation of a Child." *American Journal of Sociology,* 45 (January 1940), pp. 554–565; "Final Note on a Case of Extreme Isolation." American Journal of Sociology 52 (March 1947), pp. 432–437.

Eysenck, Hans Turgen. *The IQ Argument: Race, Intelligence and Education.* New York: Library Press, 1971.

Jensen, Arthur R., *et al.* *Environment, Heredity, and Intelligence.* Harvard Reprint Series, No. 2. Cambridge: Harvard University Press, 1969.

Kluckhohn, Clyde. *Culture and Behavior.* New York: The Free Press of Glencoe, 1964—or *Mirror for Man,* Greenwich, Connecticut: Fawcett, 1964 (originally published in 1944). Kluckhohn is a leading anthropologist and an outstanding writer. In addition to describing the influence of culture on behavior, he presents a strong case for what the layman as well as the social scientist can gain from a study of culture.

Mannheim, K. *Ideology and Utopia.* New York: Harcourt, 1936. One of the leading writers in the sociology of knowledge, Mannheim established much of its direction in this work.

Skinner, B. F. *Walden Two.* New York: Macmillan Co., 1969. The famous behaviorist offers a view of possible future cultures.

Williams, Jr., Robin M. *American Society: A Sociological Interpretation.* New York: Knopf, 1966. Williams attempts to sort out what he perceives as the basic cultural values of American society. He admits that his classification is largely hypothetical—it is also provocative.

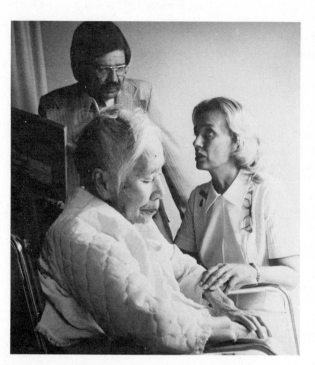

SOCIAL
INSTITUTIONS

Every human society must design ways to perform certain basic functions: new members must be born and socialized; the basic necessities of life must be produced and distributed; order must be maintained; and people must feel that life has meaning and purpose. The basic structures designed to fill these needs are social institutions. Institutions have been referred to as the "building blocks of society"; without them, the social structure would collapse. Each major social institution provides the focus for a special branch of sociology.

DEFINITIONS AND FUNCTIONS

In the broadest use of the term, a group is not an institution, but "an organized way of doing something" is. An institution is normally established over a long period of time and is usually recognized by the society. A college classroom, or even a particular college, is not an institution; the educational institution is made up of all schools, at all levels, and all the patterns of laws, mores, roles, and so on that are associated with the basic function of education. An institution, then, can be defined as a *system of norms which have grown up around a major social function.*

Institutions are structures that have evolved to meet the basic needs of the individual: food, shelter, beliefs, order, the transmitting of culture. At the same time, these "systems of norms" are important ways of regulating behavior, providing the society with necessary stability and continuity. Sociologist Peter Berger explains this point by stating that "institutions provide procedures through which human conduct is patterned, compelled to go, in grooves deemed desirable by society. And this trick is performed by making these grooves appear to the individual as the only possible ones." To illustrate, Berger offers the example of a young person in love. That person potentially has a wide number of options—a harem, a communal family, arranging for someone else to raise children, and so on. But society leads him, through its institutions, to think in terms of only one or two alternatives, such as monogamous marriage.

Primary Functions

Each of the five major institutions (family, the economic, religious, political, and educational institutions) has an area of paramount responsibility which is known as its *primary function.* The primary functions can be summarized as follows:

The family, which is regarded as the most basic social institution, is found in every society and serves three primary functions: (1) it provides for the expression of affection and concern among males and females; (2) it offers the structure for reproducing the population; and (3) it manages the early care and socialization of new generations.

Mere maintenance of the population is not enough to ensure the survival of a society. There also must be some means of transmitting the cultural heritage from one generation to the next. The socialization of the young and teaching them the patterns of behavior they need to know to fit into their social environment are the primary functions of the educational institution.

Humans in every age and every society have encountered forces they could neither explain nor control. The very nature of life and death raise disturbing questions which seem to defy human understanding. These uncertainties have led people in all societies to acknowledge a power greater than themselves, thus providing the basis for religious beliefs. For the individual, religion has served the function of supplying an orderly system to explain the chaos or mystery of events and also helps people feel that life has purpose and direction. The religious institution also serves society by supporting and influencing the values of that society.

The economic institution provides a pattern of norms that makes possible cooperation in meeting basic needs, such as providing food, clothing, and shelter. A division of labor is required in which different tasks are assigned to different people, and some way of distributing goods must also be worked out. The basic function of the economic institution, then, centers around the production and distribution of goods and services.

Finally, all societies require some means of maintaining order among the people and groups comprising the society. This maintenance of order is the primary function of the political institution, or government.

Secondary Functions

No social institution stands entirely independent of all other institutions within its society. Social institutions share many functions with each other and these are referred to as their *secondary functions.* Families, for example, socialize the young, but they are not the sole agencies for the process. Important aspects of socialization occur in job situations, through religious associations, and through participation in government. The political institution does not merely govern, but also provides for the welfare of families, regulates commerce and transportation, and supports schools among a host of secondary functions. And religion does not merely provide answers for the mysteries of life, but also provides a moral foundation for marriage and family, actively participates in welfare work, and supplies an ethic which influences both the economic and political institutions.

Other Social Institutions

Family, education, religion, economy, and government are *fundamental* institutions and are to be found in all societies. In addition, many sociologists distinguish a number of other social institutions that have developed to serve important functions in complex, industrialized societies. Recreation, health, social welfare, and science are representative examples. Recreation, for example, would include a wide array of social structures that deal with vacations, show business, sports, music and art,

parks, and so on. Similarly, health care has become such a huge and complex concern as to be considered a separate institution. This would include the many varieties of hospitals and health care centers, the training of personnel, nutrition, sanitation, accident prevention, and research. Social welfare is an institution which covers a wide range of functions such as charity, family planning, social security, community centers, and unemployment compensation. And science, in the sense of research and development, is frequently regarded as a distinct institution. The National Aeronautics and Space Administration (NASA), for example, does not properly fit into any of the major institutions and yet covers a wide network of activities, norms, and roles concerned with research and development in the exploration of space.

Transfer of Functions

The emergence of the subsidiary institutions above suggest a basic fact about the world we live in: modern society is so complex and social change is so rapid that the basic institutions cannot always fulfill their primary or secondary functions. Public health and social welfare have achieved the status of institutions through the *transfer of functions* from other institutions. For much the same reasons, there is often a transfer of functions between major institutions. In a simple society, for example, the socializing function is carried out primarily by the family. But in a modern industrialized society the need for specialized skills and knowledge has led the educational institution to assume more and more of the socializing function.

In the United States one of the most dramatic examples of transfer of function occurred during the Great Depression of the 1930's. At that time, the nation found itself in serious economic trouble. The stock market had crashed, many banks were either insolvent or close to it, and millions of people were out of work. Those who controlled capital had little confidence in the country's financial future. The entire economic institution seemed on the brink of collapse and was not able to meet its primary function of producing and distributing goods and services.

To meet the economic crisis, the federal government began taking over some economic tasks. Some agencies, such as the Works Progress Administration (WPA) and the Tennessee Valley Authority (TVA) literally "went into business," providing work for thousands and giving an important boost to the economy. Other agencies, such as the Federal Deposit Insurance Corporation (FDIC) and the Securities and Exchange Commission (SEC) represented government attempts to control the economy in order to avoid future collapse.

This transfer of functions created a good deal of controversy and the conflict has continued into the 1970's. Those who are generally labeled "conservatives" argue that the political institution should not interfere in the economy. Those of a "liberal" persuasion usually feel that the government should be doing more, not less, in the economic field. Today, most Americans recognize the necessity of at least some governmental activity in business, but disagreement continues over the extent of this activity. It is significant that when Americans discovered in 1973 that the nation faced an energy crisis, nearly everyone assumed that the federal government would play a key role in the search for solutions.

Institutional Domination

Some societies tend to emphasize one institution over all others. The society is then said to be dominated by the favored institution.

Thus, it is possible to describe certain societies as essentially familistic, essentially religious, or essentially political. Ancient China provides an example of an essentially familistic society. The family pervaded every aspect of Chinese life. The dominant position of the family in the religious sphere was reflected in the practice of ancestor worship. In the area of economics the family's importance was equally evident. The basic means of livelihood was farming, and each family owned and worked its own plot of land.

Politics in ancient China was dominated by those families which had useful connections with the emperor or regional rulers. The family was instrumental in keeping order because it assigned a specific role to each of its members. Older members wielded authority over younger members, and women were subordinate to their male relatives. Finally, the home served as the chief educational unit because children received most of their instruction directly from their parents.

In contrast to China, life in medieval Europe was dominated by the religious institution. The Church influenced medieval society in much the same way the family influenced Chinese society. The Church was the largest landholder, dispensed charity, and provided the moral force behind "just" wages, prices, or business transactions. Most scholars were clergymen, and schools and universities were run by the clergy. In the area of government, the Church's influence can be seen in the practice followed by the Holy Roman Emperors of having themselves crowned by the Pope. The emperors, like most other European rulers of the time, knew that Church recognition of their right to rule was necessary to maintain popular support.

The family also reflected the strong influence of religion. Marriage was contracted solely under Church auspices; and the marital bond, because it was confirmed by a sacrament, was considered inviolable. Individual families were expected to maintain homes where piety, devotion to the faith, and a high standard of morality were taught and practiced.

Few societies are dominated by a single institution to the same extent as were those of ancient China and medieval Europe. Nevertheless, there is no society in which all the institutions are perfectly equal. Invariably, one or more of these social structures tends to assume a leading position.

In the United States, there is considerable debate over which institution most influences our way of life. Most scholars agree that the family, the school, and the religious institutions are important, but tend to play a somewhat lesser role than government and economics. The question, then, is whether the political or the economic institution is more influential, and perhaps the most accurate answer is to describe the United States as a politico-economic society.

THE SOCIOLOGY OF INSTITUTIONS

Each of the social institutions provides the focus for a specialization within the sociology of institutions. Some sociologists concentrate their attention on the family, others on religion, education, economics, or the government. There is a massive and growing literature on the sociology of health, recreation, social welfare, science, and militarism. The limits of a single chapter on social institutions cannot do justice to such material. What can be done is to briefly examine some of the basic features of each institution and to survey the stresses encountered by these institutions in rapidly changing modern societies. With the exception of the family, which is reserved

for the next chapter, the remainder of this chapter deals with these selected institutional issues.

Education and Social Change

Education is universal. In every society some provision is made for socializing new members. But this does not mean that every society has a formal educational structure, such as a system of schools. Where the cultural heritage is fairly simple, it can be passed on from generation to generation through informal procedures. Thus, among preliterate people (those who do not possess a written language) the function of education is centered largely in the family and the tribe. Within these groups children learn vocational skills, tribal history, religious beliefs, and all the other mores and folkways of their society. They learn largely by observing their elders.

It is only within literate societies that we find formal educational structures. And it is only within modern, industrialized societies, like our own, that we find elaborate school systems staffed by specialists. However, these school systems have not eliminated informal education as an important element in life. Today, as always, children are socialized within their families and play groups.

Moreover, informal socialization does not stop with childhood but continues throughout life. Therefore, congeniality groups, work groups, recreational groups, and a host of others combine to influence an individual's total education. In a sense, all experiences in life are educational, and the bulk of them occur when people are consciously attending to some activity other than formal learning.

The beginnings of formal education in the Western World can be traced back to the ancient civilizations of the Nile and Tigris-Euphrates valleys. The early Egyptians and

Babylonians were among the first literate peoples, and therefore among the first to require formal educational structures. These civilizations did not develop schools as we know them today, but they did have scribes and priests whose duty it was to teach reading, writing, and mathematics.

The first true schools appeared in Greece, and these were copied by the Romans. After the fall of Rome, education in medieval Europe was almost exclusively in the hands of cathedral schools and monasteries. By the 13th century this system had produced the first European universities.

After the 15th century, however, the entire pattern of European life began to change, and education changed along with it. Several factors were responsible for this. First was the Renaissance, with its emphasis on the individual and his role in the secular world. The Renaissance broadened the scope of education and made a place for the lay scholar. Secondly, there was the Protestant Reformation. Protestantism urged individual study and reading of the Bible, which could only be done if the average person were taught to read. In addition, many of the Protestant leaders insisted on elementary schools, where instruction could be given in the local, vernacular tongues of the people instead of the Latin used in Catholic schools.

A third factor that influenced European life and education was economic change. The revival of trade after the Crusades laid the foundations of modern capitalism and gave rise to a growing middle class of merchants. This middle class required formal education to keep records, carry out monetary transactions, and perform numerous other business activities. The Industrial Revolution, which began in England in the 1700's, helped broaden the educational base even further. Industrialization helped to weaken the grip which the hereditary landed classes had upon education.

It led to wide-scale urbanization, bringing millions of people into the cities where the intellectual climate was far more stimulating than in isolated villages.

A final factor influencing education was the growth of representative government. Once large numbers of people were given a voice in the affairs of state, the need for an educated citizenry became widely recognized. All of these changes helped to bring about the attitude that education should be for the many, not just for the few.

In the United States, there has been a prolonged struggle to extend education to all citizens rather than to reserve it for a privileged elite. The fight for a tax-supported compulsory education system open to all Americans has been won, but remnants of an elitist educational system remain. Apart from the remaining exclusive, private schools, educational inequality is most noticeable in regard to the opportunities open to minority group members. In an age when specialization requires advanced skills, many people have found themselves shut off from such learning by financial barriers or lack of adequate preparation. Scholarships, government loans, adult education, and a more open and diversified educational system have helped to reduce elitism, but full equality still eludes us. Women, too, continue to push for broader opportunities in advanced education and specialized training.

A good deal of research in the field of educational sociology is concerned with the relationship between social change and the educational institution. A number of studies, for example, have focused on the impact of desegregation in particular school systems and communities. Another illustration of the concerns of educational sociology is provided by studies into the changing role of education in the socialization process. For instance, some researchers deal with the subject of how the sex or racial composition of a school's faculty influences learning and socialization. They explore such questions as: do male and female students respond differently to a woman teacher as an authority figure; or, are racial attitudes altered when students are instructed by a member of another racial group. These and dozens of other problem areas are providing an important body of data in sociological research.

Religion and Social Control

Religious structures reflect a society's values. All religions are based on the belief that supernatural forces beyond man help to shape his destiny. All human societies, from the most primitive to the most modern, have established religious institutions to give direction and meaning to life.

Among primitive peoples, religion generally is interwoven both with magic and with everyday life. Rarely are there any formal structures, such as organized churches, to carry out the religious function. And there are no differing creeds because everyone shares the same core of traditional beliefs. Yet primitive peoples do define roles which are at least partly of a religious nature. The shaman is a religious figure in that he invokes the spirits to assist with his spells and cures.

Religious structures and roles were carried to a high point of development by the ancient polytheistic societies. Among the Egyptians and Babylonians, as well as the Indian civilizations of the Western Hemisphere, great temples were erected to the several deities, and were staffed by a powerful priesthood. Such societies may be described as *theocracies*— societies dominated by religious leaders and ceremonies. All other social institutions were subordinated to religion.

In modern Western societies, religion has become highly formalized. Religious adherents generally form themselves into secondary groupings known as churches. (The term "church" refers here to any body of worshipers professing a common belief and organized for a religious purpose.)

Among the most important secondary functions of the religious institution is that of lending support to the society's mores. There have been times in history when religious values and social mores were practically synonymous. This was the case in the theocratic societies mentioned above. It was also true to a great extent in medieval Europe, where Christianity was the principal faith and the Church exercised considerable control over the moral climate.

In modern, pluralistic societies, like our own, there are a number of faiths and an effort is made to maintain a line of separation between church and state. Under these circumstances, the influence of religion upon social norms is not so direct. However, even in our society, religions do give powerful support to our mores. The three major faiths of the United States—Protestantism, Catholicism, and Judaism—all endorse moral codes based on the principles of reward and punishment and a sense of life's high purposes. These codes have a pronounced effect on individual conduct, whether or not the person professes to be a devout follower of one of the religions. Clearly, then, religious sanctions serve as important instruments of social control.

Religion, like all institutions, changes over time as new needs arise. In our modern, materialistic society, religions have undergone considerable change, including transitions in the secondary function of supporting society's mores. During the 1960's, for example, there was a widespread Protestant movement which declared, "God is Dead." The movement developed from the feeling of a number of Protestant leaders that traditional beliefs and

religion & mores

CONSPIRACY THEORIES OF INSTITUTIONAL CONTROL

Two decades ago, a Republican Senator from Wisconsin, Joseph McCarthy, delivered a speech which shook the nation and set off a terrifying witch hunt. Our government, McCarthy said, had been infiltrated by Communist agents who were in the process of seizing control of the machinery of political power. He waved a sheet of paper before his audience and declared: "I have here a list of the names of 108 known Communists who hold high positions in our government."

The reaction to the speech was electrifying. In those early years of the Cold War, there was enough fear of communism in this country to make people believe what the senator said. No matter that the names he claimed to have were never revealed—clearly a man in his position would not make such a statement unless there was some truth in it.

The famous witch hunt which followed created tremendous fear and dissension throughout the nation, shaking the faith of many in our basic institutions. Riding high on the wave of alarmism, McCarthy, joined by a few other senators and congressmen, held hearings throughout the country, intent on ferreting out all Communists and Communist sympathizers. McCarthy never proved that a single person he accused was a Communist agent, but the very fact that a man or woman was called before an investigating committee was often enough to "blacklist" him or her as "Fifth-Amendment Communists" in his or her community and place of employment. The senator saw the conspiracy in other institutions as well: religion, education, the military, even the entertainment industry. It was in a televised hearing on communism in the military that enough people saw the shallowness of McCarthy's charges that his power quickly collapsed.

Such conspiracy theories are not new and are certainly not a uniquely American phenomenon. Over a century ago, Karl Marx developed what might be considered a conspiracy theory of institutional control. Marx argued that the class in control of the economic "means of production" used its power to subjugate the other classes, and all other institutions were simply used as tools of the ruling class. (Religion, for example, was called "the opiate of the masses.") A few years later, France was rocked by its own conspiracy theory which culminated in the famous Dreyfus case. And, of course, Adolf Hitler rose to power partly by posing as a defender of Germany against the "conspiracy of international jewry."

Today, in the United States, conspiracy theories persist and frequently polarize larger segments of the population. Those on the left of the political spectrum see our institutions so firmly in the control of conservative or reactionary forces (i.e., the Establishment) that the great majority of citizens are totally powerless. After a flurry of resistance in the mid-1960's, many of the extreme left came to feel that further struggle was useless. An article in the *East Village Other,* for example, considered the American political process to be nothing more than "the largest spectator sport in history. . . . We will enter the sport at the last possible moment," the writer went on, "run home to watch it happen on TV as the election returns come pouring in, to see how our moment of active participation fared, and all brought to us live by the makers of who, what— Reality?"

Ironically, the ultra-conservative fringe of our society sees a danger that these radical leftists, led by Communist agents, are in the process of gaining control of our basic institutions. A pamphlet of the extreme right-wing Minutemen recently proclaimed: "Our nation is in immediate danger. It is possible that within a very few years, perhaps even within months, our nation could be conquered and enslaved by the Communists." And, when Barry Goldwater was defeated in the presidential election of 1964, the John Birch Society's newsletter, *On Target,* opened with this sentence: "The hopes of millions of Americans that the Communist tide could be stopped with ballots instead of bullets have turned to dust."

Sociologists, too, can be susceptible to the idea that a powerful elite is trying to control key institutions. In his controversial work, *The Power Elite,* C. Wright Mills presented the theory that American society is divided into two groups: the power elite, that small group which controls the means of death, production, and political power; and the great mass of the population, themselves controlled like sheep by the elite. Speaking of the elitists, Mills said: "They rule the big corporations. They run the machinery of state and control the prerogatives. They direct the military establishment. They occupy the strategic command posts of the social structure in which are now centered the effective means of the power and wealth and the celebrity which they enjoy."

Probably few sociologists would agree with the sweeping generalizations of Mills' theory. In fact, many would probably agree with the statement of one of Mills' critics who wrote: "Some men hunger for theory as for salt; and those who do not yet see the inadequacies of Marxism will find in Millism a doctrine which satisfies many of their yearnings."

Power Elite

practices no longer applied in space-age society. Instead, they emphasized a form of social action to replace the earlier emphasis on doctrine. This wave of social involvement represented one response of the institution to the changes in the society. A quite different response emerged in the 1970's in the so-called "Jesus movement," touching especially the younger generation with the appeal of a return to a simple form of faith in reaction to the materialism of society.

Sociologists who study religion are confronted with a difficult task when they seek to determine membership of a religious faith. World-wide figures are available, but they are only approximations because no adequate religious census has ever been taken. No religious census has ever been taken in this country principally because we have not wanted one. There is a strong feeling among Americans that religion is a private matter and should not be made the object of official prying. Consequently, we must depend mainly upon the various faiths themselves for information on their membership.

However, all denominations do not apply the same criteria when listing their adherents. Some groups automatically include as members all those whose parents were members. Others base membership upon participation in a particular ceremony, such as baptism. Still others will count only active participants while excluding those who attend functions rarely or not at all. Consequently, it becomes almost impossible to measure the impact of changes within particular faiths, even in terms of church membership.

Problems of Church and State

In ancient times political and religious institutions were very closely allied. Primitive peoples scarcely distinguished between the two because they had no need to. Every aspect of their existence, including religion and government, was inseparably bound up with their total culture. Religious differences could be found between cultures, but not among members of a single culture.

As civilization emerged and both government and religion became more highly developed, the two institutions tended to become mutually supporting. Such was the case in the Roman Empire, which until the 3rd century A.D. had a polytheistic state religion with the emperor as its head.

During the Middle Ages the Pope was considered the head of all Western Christendom, and the various European monarchs were considered only the temporal rulers of their states. However, there was much overlapping between the religious and political institutions, with the result that church and state were often in conflict. The Reformation altered the medieval church-state relationship by creating several Protestant denominations, none of which acknowledged the Pope's authority. Some Protestant groups affiliated themselves with political leaders, thereby becoming state churches.

Today there are several nations in which there is an established, or favored, religion. Among these are Great Britain (Anglican), Spain (Roman Catholic), Sweden (Lutheran), Israel (Judaic), and Pakistan (Islamic). Most of the countries which have established religions also grant freedom of worship to members of other faiths.

In the United States, of course, there is no established church. This is expressly forbidden by the First Amendment, which also guarantees religious freedom. The political and religious institutions are regarded as operating within separate spheres: the principle which is known as the separation of church and state. This separation, however, does not mean that all sources of tension between the two institutions have been removed. The question of government aid to church-operated schools, for example, has frequently caused controversy. On the one hand, the mounting costs of education make it increasingly difficult for such schools to survive; on the other hand, large portions of the population believe that separation of church and state must be strictly observed.

Religion and Science

The relationship between religious adherents and scientists during the past several centuries has often been marked by conflict. Generally, such disagreements arose when scientific investigation brought to light knowledge or theories that challenged long-standing beliefs. For example, during the 16th century, men like Galileo and Bruno endorsed the theory of Copernicus that the sun, not the earth, is the center of the universe. This theory seemed a direct challenge to a traditional belief and was branded as heresy. Both Galileo and Bruno were given the choice of either retracting their statements or risking the death penalty provided for heretics.

The 19th century was another period when scientific findings appeared to challenge religious doctrine. Perhaps the most important controversy arose after the publication of Charles Darwin's theory of organic evolution. The members of many religious denominations denounced Darwinian theory on the grounds that it contradicted the story of Creation as recorded in the Bible. In the United States, disputes over the evolution theory reached a climax in the famous Scopes trial of 1925, which involved the removal of a public school science teacher for presenting Darwin's theory to his class. Although the theory of evolution is now widely accepted, the controversy is still not over. Members of some churches con-

tinue to insist on a literal interpretation of the Bible; as a concession to these beliefs, a California textbook commission in 1973 ruled that science texts must include the Biblical interpretation of life's origins.

Such conflicts have sometimes been cited to support the view that religion and science are necessarily opposed. However, this view is by no means universal, either among scientists or among members of different religious faiths. Instead, most people in Western societies accept the proposition that religion and science operate in separate spheres. Science deals with matters which may be tested empirically, that is, on the basis of observed evidence. Religion, on the other hand, deals with matters of faith which often cannot be proved or disproved. On this basis, then, religion and science need not come into direct conflict.

Although direct confrontation between religion and science may be a thing of the past, many people feel that it has been replaced by a more subtle form of conflict. Modern societies tend to become technologically oriented, with a faith in science which in itself may be considered religious in nature. What place does religion have in such a society? What functions does religion serve both for the individual and for the society? In what ways do religious ideas influence, and how are they influenced by, changes within the society? Such questions as these are asked by members of churches themselves as the various faiths continue a process of self-examination. These questions are also asked by sociologists of religion in seeking to assess the role of religion in contemporary society.

Government and Social Order

We have noted earlier that a basic need of every society is to maintain order among its members; that is, all societies devise some means of securing conformity to their norms. This need for social control has led to the development of the political institution.

In simple, tribal societies, there is usually a chief or council of elders responsible for making decisions affecting the community's general welfare. There is no additional political structure because there is no need for one. Mores and folkways in a simple society tend to be universally shared and largely internalized, with the result that informal negative sanctions, such as gossip, are effective means of keeping order. Social control, therefore, can be handled quite readily by the large kinship groups, or clans, which are the basic units of society. If an individual violates a taboo, his clan generally will punish him. If a clan member is injured by an outsider, the task of punishing the offender usually falls to other clan members. Justice frequently takes the form of vengeance and is privately administered, resulting in little distinction being made between public and private justice.

In modern complex societies, on the other hand, there is a definite need for formal political structures. Such societies are not organized on a kinship basis. Their populations include millions of people, all of whom are viewed as members of a political entity known as the state. Informal social control continues to be important; many folkways and mores continue to be defined and enforced by the family and other nongovernmental groups. But it is also necessary to have specialized agencies to handle the three basic functions which every modern government must find a way to perform: the making of laws, the administering of those laws, and the settling of disputes.

Each society develops its own structures for carrying out these functions. The result is a wide spectrum of government forms, ranging from democracy to totalitarianism, with most of the world's governments leaning toward some form of dictatorship. In the United States, of course, the three basic functions are the primary responsibility of three separate branches of government: legislative, executive, and judicial. This separation of powers is not common. In most other systems, such as the British, the chief executive officer is also a member of the legislative body.

In addition to the formal structures of government, there may also be informal arrangements or associations in the political sphere. In the United States, for example, no Constitutional provision was made for political parties; the party system developed informally in response to the society's needs. Lobbies and pressure groups developed in much the same way. Such arrangements form part of the political institution, but are not part of the formal structure of the government.

The growth of both informal and formal political structures has become a matter of growing concern both for sociologists and for the average citizen. The needs of modern society have led to ever-increasing government activity, and this, in turn, has meant the mushrooming growth of governmental bureaucracy. As early as the turn of the century, sociologist Max Weber felt that bureaucratization was both the most important source of institutional change as well as the greatest danger to the forces which held society together. He expressed the concern that a society dominated by bureaucracy would be a society "filled with nothing but those little cogs, little men clinging to little jobs and striving towards bigger ones." Weber believed that a vital question facing democratic societies was "what can we oppose to this machinery in order to keep a portion of mankind free from this parcelling out of the soul, from this supreme mastery of the bureaucratic way of life."

Many political sociologists do not share Weber's pessimism. While recognizing the weaknesses of bureaucratization, they argue that the process is important for maintaining social order. Bureaucrats, for example, are well known for their resistance to change. In our stereotyped view, the bureaucrat shuffles along at his own pace, carefully adhering to regulations and ignoring the grandiose plans of those elected to office. This pattern, frustrating though it may be to the general public, may offer an important element of cohesion to the society. If massive shifts in policy occurred every time a new politician was elected, the process of government might be weakened by political strife. It is argued that newly formed nations which lack a stable bureaucracy are subject to greater instability and unrest than those new nations which preserved the bureaucratic structures inherited from a colonial power.

Economic Systems

In primitive societies, almost by definition, there is very little economic diversity. One or two forms of activity such as hunting, fishing, and perhaps marginal agriculture constitutes the only means of livelihood. Consequently, there is little or no need for formal economic structures to handle the functions of production, distribution, and consumption. All of these functions are taken care of by the family, which provides for its members' food, clothing, and shelter. Moreover, primitive peoples do not need economic specialists. Instead, the division of labor is based primarily on the categories of age and sex. In other words, if the society defines hunting as a task for adult men, virtually all adult males will be hunters. If basket weaving is considered the task of adult women, all women will weave baskets.

In modern complex societies, by contrast, economic productivity is extremely diversified, with the existence of a great many formal structures. There are secondary groupings, such as business firms, to handle nearly every phase of production and distribution. To a great extent, the division of labor is still based on age and sex, although important changes are occurring. The traditional roles of the man as wage earner and the woman as "homemaker" are gradually changing and women now make up nearly 40 percent of the labor force. The professions and top-level management positions continue to remain a bastion of "male dominance."

As with political institutions, the modern world reveals a wide variety of economic systems. In general terms, the major types can be distinguished according to who owns and controls the producers' goods and services. (Producers' goods and services are those that can create more goods and services, such as factories, banks, supermarkets, as opposed to consumer's goods and services which are used by the individual—his clothes, home, food, etc.)

In a capitalist economic system, there would be complete private or individual ownership of producers' goods and services. Capitalism operates according to the law of supply and demand, with no interference from the political institution. Pure capitalism has never really existed in the United States, because from the very beginning of the nation, there was at least a degree of government involvement through taxes and tariff barriers. Instead of the ideal of capitalism, the American system is usually characterized as one of regulated capitalism. While most business remains in private hands, the government has increasingly regulated economic activity.

Fascism can be considered an extreme form of regulated capitalism. Ownership of producers' goods and services remains in private hands, but the state exercises tight control over key elements of the economy. Varying degrees of fascism can be found in nations

THE VARIOUS PATHS TO SOCIOLOGICAL KNOWLEDGE
PETER L. BERGER

Peter Berger exemplifies the general approach to sociology referred to as the humanist school. While he believes that sociology can and should make use of scientific procedures, he also sees the discipline as having a great deal in common with humanistic endeavors such as philosophy and history. In this regard, Berger feels that sociology can make an important contribution in helping us to gain an understanding of ourselves and the world around us, and how we can make use of that understanding. "Unlike puppets," he writes, "we have the possibility of stopping in our movements, looking up and perceiving the machinery by which we have been moved. In this act lies the first step towards freedom."

Part of the "machinery" we must deal with consists of our social institutions. Berger has applied his humanistic perspective to the study of institutions. Although some of his studies have focused on religion (*The Sacred Canopy*, 1967, and *The Precarious Vision*, 1961), more general works have dealt with the institutional structure of contemporary society (*Invitation to Sociology*, 1963, and *The Social Construction of Reality*, 1966).

Berger expresses in his works a concern that humans can become imprisoned by their societies, surrendering their freedoms to "standardized" ways of behaving within institutional structures. Our institutions, he states, present us with "imperatives," leading us to behave in certain ways which we do not question. When carried to extremes, this can make society and its institutions seem "more like a gigantic Alcatraz than anything else."

We allow ourselves to be imprisoned, he argues, when we act in "bad faith"— when we say we act simply because that act is expected of us:

The terrorist who kills and excuses himself by saying that he had no choice because the party ordered him to kill is in 'bad faith,' because he pretends that his existence is necessarily linked with the party, while in fact this linkage is the consequence of his own choice. It can easily be seen that 'bad faith' covers society like a film of lies.

The very possibility of bad faith, however, shows us the reality of freedom. Man can be in 'bad faith' only because he is free and does not wish to face his freedom.

Sociologists, too, are capable of such "bad faith." Berger suggests that a sociologist might work in the field of racial discrimination out of a conviction that social and political action are needed. But then, as he proceeds with his work, he becomes the "expert," the scientist, and his work becomes the objective writing of the "coolly scientific commentator." Such a person is acting in "bad faith" because he has lost the sense of personal involvement.

In other words, Berger is saying that knowledge of how society functions is essential, but only if it shows us how we can free ourselves from its constraints, how we can best take advantage of the choices open to us. Instead of surrendering blindly to social forces, we must make our institutions the means of expressing our own free wills.

ruled by dictators. While the state leaders insist they exercise control over the economy for the benefit of all the people, the rationale is usually a thin disguise for maintaining a rich and powerful elite.

If major elements of the economy are controlled and owned by the government, the system is socialistic. In the mixed economy of the United States, highways, the post office, many educational facilities and railroads are owned and controlled by the government or by government corporations. Many people regard this political activity in the economic sphere to be a form of "creeping socialism," and controversy continues over how far the United States ought to go in the direction of public ownership. The nations of Western Europe are also characterized by mixed economies. Most of these countries have gone further in the direction of socialism than has the United States, with key industries as well as transportation and communications being state-owned and-operated.

Communism represents the ultimate socialistic economic system in which *all* producers' goods and services are owned and controlled by the government, or more correctly by the political institution. Communism, of course, is generally associated with the systems found in the Soviet Union, Eastern Europe, and China. But even in these nations, the system does not exist in its pure form. All Communist countries reveal some examples of what amounts to regulated capitalism.

Many observers feel that there is now occurring a blurring of lines between economic systems. In other words, the Communist countries tend to become more capitalistic, particularly in the area of consumer goods. The capitalist nations, on the other hand, increasingly lean toward public ownership of large-scale industry. In the United States, for example, concern over environmental problems and the supply of scarce resources such as oil have led to increased government control over some segments of the economy, and these steps are seen by many as evidence of the nation moving closer to socialism.

SUMMARY

Institutions are systems of norms created to carry on essential social functions. The five major institutions—family, education, religion, economic, and government—are universal social structures.

The *primary function* of the family is to allow for expression of affection among males and females and provide for the birth and upbringing of children. The prime objective of the educational system is to transmit the cultural heritage from generation to generation. Religion helps men discover a sense of purpose in life and lends support to cultural values. The production, distribution, and consumption of goods are the primary functions of the economic system. The chief concern of the political institution is the maintenance of order.

In addition to their primary functions, each of the major institutions provides varying degrees of support to the other institutions. *Secondary functions* of the political institution, for example, include providing for the welfare of families, regulating commerce and transportation, and supporting schools.

In complex industrialized societies some further institutions have appeared, such as recreation, health, social welfare, and science.

The primary functions of each institution are so essential that they may be transferred to other institutions when they appear to be inadequately handled. An example of this was seen in the depression of the 1930's when the government intervened into economics.

In some societies one of the major institutions may become dominant. Ancient Chinese society centered around the family. Life in medieval Europe was strongly dominated by the Church. In the United States, the most influential institutions appear to be government and economics.

A special branch of sociology is centered on each major social institution. Much research in the field of educational sociology concentrates on the relationship between social change and the educational institution. Sociologists of religion seek to assess the role of religion in society, dealing with such issues as the relation of church to state and of modern "faith in science" to traditional belief. Other sociologists study the forms of government and such related social problems as bureaucratization. Sociologists of economics examine such issues as the blurring of lines among the traditional types of national economies.

GLOSSARY

bureaucracy   a formal organization characterized by specialization, departmentalization, and a hierarchy of authority based on status and rank. Bureaucracies thrive in urban societies.

capitalism   an economic system characterized by private ownership of means of production, economic motivation through profit and competition, and determination of wages largely through supply and demand.

Communism   a socialistic economic system in which all producers' goods and services are owned by the political institution.

fascism   a political-economic system characterized by rigid state control over all aspects of life. Means of production remain in private hands but the state tightly regulates the economy.

pluralism   the peaceful coexistence within a society of differing groups, each of which maintains certain identifying characteristics.

polytheism   belief in many gods and/or goddesses.

socialism   an economic and political system characterized by state ownership and control of major elements of the economy.

theocracy   a society dominated by religious leaders and ceremonies.

SUGGESTED READINGS

Blau, Peter M. *The Dynamics of Bureaucracy.* Chicago: University of Chicago Press, 1963. This is a scholarly work, well written and well documented.

Mills, C. Wright. *The Power Elite.* New York: Oxford, 1956. In this classic, Mills shows the interrelated nature of the military, economic, and political institutions and the people who lead them.

Peter, L. F. and Hull, R. *The Peter Principle.* New York: Bantam Books, 1970. This work is a satirical treatment of bureaucratic organization and inefficiency.

Townsend, Robert. *Up the Organization.* New York: Knopf, 1970.

Rozak, Theodore. *The Making of a Counter Culture: Reflections on the Technocratic Society and Its Youthful Opposition.* Garden City, New York: Anchor Books, 1969. A popular analysis of the rebellion of many youth against the dehumanizing consequences of bureaucracy and technology.

Ruitenbeck, Hendrik M. *The Dilemma of Organizational Society.* New York: E. P. Dutton & Co., 1963. This collection of essays raises disturbing, and often penetrating, questions about the individual's ability to maintain his identity within a bureaucratic, technological society. Essays include Max Lerner's "Big Technology & Neutral Technicians," "The College Student in an Age of Organization," by David Reisman, and Richard H. Rovere's "The Invasion of Privacy."

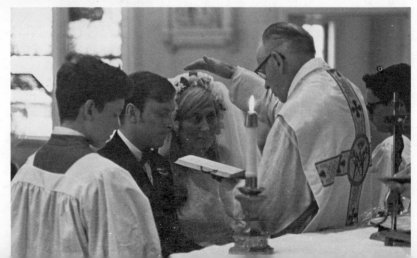

5

THE FAMILY

The basic social web in which all humans live is the family. It is the family which provides vital biological and psychological support for the infant as the child goes through the long process of maturation. The family is the initial and essential transmitter of culture, and it forms an important social and economic unit. In all societies, the family fulfills many of the same functions. But the very concept of family, as well as its functions and dynamics, varies widely from culture to culture. In industrial and post-industrial society, the family institution is undergoing rapid change, raising often disturbing questions about what is happening to the family and what its future will be.

THE FAMILY AS A SOCIAL INSTITUTION

The family is a universal social institution. All societies have established some form of family structure to provide for the birth and rearing of children. In addition, all societies recognize that blood ties create a special bond among people—a bond that helps mold them into a tightly knit group. However, there is no universal mode of deciding just who should be considered a blood relative of whom, or which relationships should be viewed as closest. Different societies have different norms governing these matters. The result is that family size, family residence, kinship boundaries, and the means of determining descent vary widely from culture to culture. In this section, we will discuss the family as it exists in various societies.

The Nuclear Family

The basic family unit, called the *nuclear* family, consists of three related roles: mother, father, and child. These roles of course are biologically determined and cannot be filled indiscriminately. While the nuclear family is found in all societies, it is subject to a number of variations. For example, among the Trobriand Islanders of northeast New Guinea, the role of father is shared by the child's biological father and his maternal uncle. The biological father helps with the child's upbringing for several years, but then the uncle assumes more and more control. Eventually, the child looks solely to the uncle as his male parent.

The Extended Family

In the United States, the typical family unit is the nuclear family. Americans tend to live in nuclear groupings consisting of only two generations—parents and their children. There are, however, many societies in which the typical family unit is what anthropologists call an *extended* family. An extended family is created when young people live with their parents even after they have their own families; in other words, several nuclear families are combined to form one large unit. For many centuries the traditional Chinese family consisted of at least three generations: a grandfather and grandmother; married sons and their wives (plus unmarried sons and daughters); and the children of the married sons. While this traditional pattern is breaking up in modern China, extended families are still common in parts of India, Japan, Iran, Turkey, and some African nations.

The Variety of Family Forms

Nuclear and extended families can be classified further according to the number of marriage partners, residence, lines of descent, and power. In terms of residence, for example, extended families can be classified according to whether each newly married couple resides with the bride's or the groom's relatives. If custom decrees that they join the groom's family, the society is called *patrilocal*. Chinese, Moslem, and Hindu families tend to be patrilocal. However, if the new couple is expected to live with the wife's family, the society is *matrilocal*. Among the American Indians, the Hopi, Navajo, and Iroquois were matrilocal societies. This can be an important matter in societies where the land is worked by families and it also operates among some nomadic peoples. The dynamics of family life are influenced by the fact that one spouse is living among comparative strangers. The spouse who remains "at home" often gains certain powers and privileges. In the United States, as in most industrial societies, neither of these patterns applies. Most American families are *neolocal,* with each husband and wife establishing an independent home.

The way families trace their lineage can affect the generational transfer of property and privileges as well as the daily conduct of family affairs. In *patrilineal* societies, descent is traced through the father, with children assuming the father's name, inheriting from him, and generally considering themselves closely related to his family. When descent is traced through the mother, it is called *matrilineal,* and if neither maternal nor paternal side takes precedence, then it is a *bilateral* line of descent.

Usually, the tracing of descent through one side of a family accompanies a similar residential pattern. Thus, the patrilocal Chinese were also patrilineal, while the matrilocal Iroquois were also matrilineal. However, there are exceptions in which lineage and descent patterns are dissimilar. The Trobriand Islanders, for instance, have patrilocal families but trace descent through the mother's line.

In families, as in most groups, there is a discernible power structure. The authority for making final decisions has to rest with some individual or combination of individuals. In most societies, the father is the dominant figure and the family is called *patriarchal.* *Matriarchal* societies, in which final authority is vested in the wife, are less common. Several American Indian tribes, including the Zuni, Hopi and Navajo, are classified as matriarchal. However, in most matriarchal societies it is the mother's family—rather than she herself—that actually exercises authority.

There is considerable variation in the power structures of American families. Some are largely patriarchal and some lean toward matriarchy, with perhaps the majority being considered *democratic-cooperative,* in which decision-making is shared among all the family's members.

Societies also differ according to the *forms of marriage* which refers to the number of mates an individual may have. In the United States, of course, *monogamy* is strictly observed—a man or woman may have only one spouse at a time. By contrast, many societies of the world permit *polygamy,* in which a man is allowed to have several wives at once. Sociologist William Goode states that polygamy exists in 193 of 234 known societies; it is most widespread in Africa, where an estimated 88 percent of the sub-Saharan tribes allow polygamy. However, Goode stresses the point that this form of marriage exists as an ideal, attainable only to the few who can afford it or who can attract more than one marriage partner. The roughly equal proportion of men to women in most parts of the world, as well as the expense, mitigates against widespread practice of polygamy.

A third form of marriage, *polyandry,* exists when one woman has several husbands at the same time. Polyandry is quite rare, although it has been reported among several peoples, including the Tibetans, some Eskimo tribes, the Bahimas of east Africa and the Nayars of southwest India. Sometimes polyandry seems to be associated with the practice of female infanticide (the killing of females during infancy). This practice could account for the higher proportion of males to females that is characteristic of polyandrous societies.

Most societies place certain restrictions on the process of mate selection. For example, young people may be required to marry someone from outside their own group. This practice, known as *exogamy,* is prevalent among peoples who reckon descent on a strictly matrilineal or patrilineal basis. Extended kinship ties among such people tend to be very strong. Often an entire society is divided into several large clans, with all the members of a given clan regarded as blood relatives. Hence, marriage among members of such a clan is strictly prohibited.

Exogamous regulations were prevalent among Indian tribes in North and South America as well as societies in parts of Asia, Oceania, and Africa. An extreme form of residential exogamy is found among the Masai of East Africa, where the society dictates that no two people living within one hundred miles of each other should marry.

The counterpart of exogamy is *endogamy*, the practice of marrying within a particular group. Endogamous restrictions were particularly important in ancient India, where marriage between members of different castes was prohibited. Many religions have endorsed a form of endogamy by urging their members to marry within their own faith. Sometimes cultural norms not only restrict people in their choice of a spouse, but actually take that choice completely out of their hands. In many societies marriages between individuals are arranged by their respective families. In general, this custom reflects a belief that the social and economic aspects of marriage are the most important, and that families are better judges of a match than are the people immediately involved.

Until the past century, arranged marriages were common in many European countries, and the practice has not completely disappeared. In the United States the selection of a marital partner is regarded as a personal matter; parents are often asked to approve of a choice, but their approval is not considered essential. However, this represents something of a break with the past. At one time, American norms gave parents considerable influence over their children with regard to the choice of a marriage partner.

THE CONTEMPORARY FAMILY

Many complex problems are associated with contemporary family life in our society. While the family still fulfills its function of creating, maintaining and socializing its members, it is no longer the center of activities it once was. And recent social changes and pressures have complicated the relationships between family members. Sociologists have noted that the traditional family structure is weakening, and a new family pattern is emerging. What is the pattern of contemporary family life? What are some of the sources of strain faced by the modern family?

The Changing Family Role

In trying to determine how American family life has changed, it is important to know what the family was like in the past, and that is not always easy to measure. For example, our stereotyped view of the traditional American family suggests that, among other things, the father was a figure of absolute authority, children tended to stay near their parents even after marriage, and parents played an important role in their children's choice of marriage partners. While there is some truth to this view, there were also many exceptions. As early as the 1830's, for example, a French visitor was struck by how little Americans conformed to traditional patterns. The visitor wrote that:

A very remarkable custom in the United States gives girls the freedom to choose a husband according to their fancy. . . . As soon as they have their growth, the Yankees whose spirit now predominates in the Union quit their parents, never to return, as naturally and with as little emotion as young birds desert forever their native nests as soon as they are fledged.

In other words, there is a danger of idealizing family patterns of the past, which William Goode refers to as "the classical family of Western nostalgia." With these limitations in mind, it is still possible to identify some of the major changes in the family.

A century ago, American family life was relatively stable. The patriarchal tradition, family centeredness, and the differentiation of status based on age and sex were seldom challenged. The traditional family was usually a large one, and often included more than one generation within the household. There was little confusion regarding family roles because these were relatively fixed. For the most part, the family was at the center of economic, religious, and educational activities.

Contemporary family life is quite different from the stabilized patterns of the past. The modern family no longer functions as the center of life. Where family members once worked together on farms or in household industry, they now work outside the home. In the past, it was an important function of the family to uphold religious faith and practices. Although there are exceptions, today, religious activities are predominantly the function of the church. Education also is handled as much by teachers and schools as by parents and the home.

In other areas, too, where the family once fulfilled important responsibilities, it no longer predominates. For example, the sick and the aged were once cared for by the family. Today, this function is largely in the hands of specialized agencies. Similarly, outside agencies such as the police and the courts have generally supplanted the family's function of protecting its members.

Another major area in which the contemporary family differs from that of the past is in the lessening of the patriarchal tradition. For the most part, the husband and father is no longer regarded as the decision-maker and authority figure. One reason for this is that the father seldom works in or near the home as he once did. The greater independence of women, both economically and socially, has also tended to reduce male domination. Nevertheless, the status of a family still tends to be associated with the father's occupation. In making important family decisions, such as where to live, the father's occupation is likely to be the determining factor, even when the wife has her own career outside the home. And, for the most part, the male still has the legal and economic responsibility for taking care of the family.

Modern families also differ from traditional families in terms of size. A gradual drop in the birth rate over the past century is reflected in the smaller overall size of the modern family (see Table 5-1). The rural family of the

TABLE 5-1 FAMILIES GROW SMALLER

Year	Population per Household
1790	5.79
1850	5.55
1860	5.28
1870	5.09
1880	5.04
1890	4.93
1900	4.76
1910	4.54
1920	4.34
1930	4.11
1940	3.77
1950	3.52
1960	3.38
1970	3.23

Source: U.S. Bureau of the Census.

past tended to be larger primarily for two reasons: first, children were economic assets because their labor was needed to help run the family farm or business; second, there was a tendency toward an extended family household in the practice of older people living with their married children.

Causes of Change

A major factor in the differing pattern of modern families is the status of women. Economically, politically, and socially the woman's role has been changing for more than a century. Before industrialization, the economic value of women was within the home, with responsibility for traditional household tasks. She had little other choice than to work within the family; even women with wealth or advanced education were considered to have the basic role of homemaker.

Industrialization contributed to change by introducing labor-saving devices into the home. It also gave women the opportunity for outside employment. As industrialization progressed, more and more women sought work in factories, offices, schools and shops. The increasing role of women in economic life continues to increase their areas of independence. And the fact that women generally do not have to rely economically on the family has contributed to the concept of marriage as an equal partnership. These changes have also created confusion and conflict over the roles of men and women in the family.

Women have been agitating for many years for full equality with men. The early suffrage movement and todays Women's Liberation movement have sought to give women more power in the political, economic and social spheres. More and more, women are moving into areas that were once almost exclusively dominated by men. The increasing activities of women outside the home, and their greater awareness of opportunities have brought into question the traditional family roles.

Another factor in changing family patterns has been the urbanization process. In our society, the traditional family is thought of as the family on the farm or in the small town. But today, 3 out of 4 Americans live in urban areas, and only 6 percent of the population earn a living by farming. The lifestyle of cities and suburbs is geared to mobility and anonymity, and more emphasis is placed on activities and interests outside the home. These factors tend to reduce further the ties and loyalties of the family.

Is the family becoming a "defunctionalized" institution? Some people feel that this is the case—that the family is in danger of "going out of style." Many argue that more and more family functions are likely to be taken over by other institutions. As women achieve greater independence from the home, for instance, the movement toward day-care centers for preschool children gains strength. At a White House Conference on Children, attended by 4000 social scientists and physicians, most of the delegates supported the idea of government-financed day-care centers. They reported that day care provided "a means of rescuing children from the effects of affluence and isolation as well as poverty and neglect, rather than merely relieving mothers of the nine-to-five responsibility of child rearing." Many people, of course, feel that such a transfer of functions will further reduce family ties. Psychologists Jerome Kagan and Phillip Whitten warned that the issue "might be regarded as an evolutionary test of the durability of the family."

On the other hand, most social scientists are convinced that the nuclear family will remain our basic social institution for the indefinite future. Additional changes, such as an increase of day-care centers, will require adjustment, but such adjustments have been taking place for well over 100 years. In general, the majority of observers would probably agree with anthropologist Margaret Mead in her statement that: "Again and again, in spite of proposals for change and actual experiments, human societies have reaffirmed their dependence on the family as the basic unit of human living. . . ." Ms. Mead does not suggest that the stability of the traditional family patterns will return, but rather that the family will continue to survive continued change and stresses.

Divorce

A major area of change in the contemporary family has been the increase in the divorce rate. In the United States the number of divorces and the divorce rates have fluctuated

"I now pronounce you His and Hers."

PERSPECTIVE

THE INCEST TABOO

The taboo against incest has been known in practically all human societies throughout history. Normally we think of it as a powerful sanction against sexual relations between a brother and sister, or a parent and offspring. There are, however, a number of variations from culture to culture. Until the mid-19th century, for example, the British had laws against the "incestuous" marriage of a man to his deceased wife's sister, a practice that would be considered acceptable in most societies. People usually assume that the incest taboo is natural, a biological barrier to unions that might lead to harmful genetic effects. However, there does not seem to be a clear biological basis for the incest taboo; if incest had been practiced in the past, harmful genes would be eliminated by natural selection.

A number of sociologists theorize that the incest taboo serves a cultural, rather than a biological, function. Claude Levi-Strauss, for example, believes that the incest taboo has been a basic factor in the development of the family institution. He points out that the taboo would help to define family roles clearly. Chaos would result if free sexuality were possible among family members, but the incest taboo insures that members will be brother and sister or mother and child only.

Levi-Strauss goes further and suggests that the incest taboo is an important pillar in the establishment of society. It dictates that families will join other families, since each family requires two other families in order to be established, one to provide the husband and the other the wife. The web of families which results then constitutes a society. "What makes man really different from the animals," Levi-Strauss explains, "is that, in mankind, a family could not exist if there were no society; i.e. a plurality of families ready to acknowledge that there are other links than consanguineous ones. . . ."

If the taboo did not exist, humanity might be set off in small, closed biological families, each caught in its own ignorance and prejudice, constantly warring with one another. The fact that marriage between children of rival families has been a traditional way of making peace might lend support to this theory. One could say, then, that not only does the family depend on society, but that society itself is the creation of this particular form of family. Levi-Strauss speculates that the incest taboo is "a kind of remodeling of the biological conditions of mating and procreation . . . compelling them to become perpetuated only in an artificial framework of taboos and obligations. It is there, and only there, that we find a passage from nature to culture, from animal to human life. . . ." While one might not agree with Levi-Strauss' sweeping generalizations, his arguments do suggest that the incest taboo has served important cultural functions.

over the years. The lowest incidence of divorce occurred well before 1860, then climbed to a peak in 1946, the first peacetime year after World War II, before declining for a period of about 15 years. Beginning shortly before 1960, divorces again began to rise steadily, with more than 700,000 divorces recorded in 1973 (compared to 610,000 in 1946).

This high rate of divorce does not mean that marriage in the United States is doomed to failure. For one thing, with larger populations, with greater numbers of marriages, and with greater expectations for marriage under rapidly changing conditions, a parallel increase in divorce can be expected. For example, in 1910 there were 948,000 marriages and 83,000 divorces in the United States. This is a divorce rate of 0.9 per thousand population, or about 1 divorce for every 12 marriages. In 1973, the ratio had changed to roughly 1 divorce for every 3 marriages, or about 4.3 per thousand population.

This, of course, does not mean that divorces in a single year came from marriages made that same year. Divorces in a single year will come from marriages made in previous years as well as from that particular year. In 1950, for instance, the median duration for marriages affected by divorce was 5 years; 20 years later, in 1970, the median duration of marriages affected by divorce was 7 years. A fair summary of all studies of first marriages is that somewhere between 20 and 25 percent of American marriages terminate in divorce. High as this figure sounds, it also means some 75 to 80 percent of first marriages do not end in divorce.

Those who divorce are not necessarily discouraged about marriage. Three-fourths of divorced men in the United States remarry as do about three-fifths of divorced women. The old stigmas about divorce are not applied as strongly as they used to be. And those that remarry report that the second marriages are far more successful.

The traditional plea that divorce should not occur because of the potential harm to children may have some basis in fact. And yet, there is convincing data from such studies as that done by Ivan Nye that children from broken homes showed less delinquent behavior, less mental illness, and less antisocial behavior than a matching sample of children from unbroken, but unhappy, homes.

Despite changing attitudes toward divorce, many states still require *adversary action* in court before a divorce can be granted. This requires one party to be "innocent" and the other to be "guilty" on whatever grounds the state laws provide. But the new freedom to divorce can be seen in the increase in no-fault divorce laws, in which it is simply acknowledged that the couple have become incompatible, and the court makes no judgment of fault.

The Sexual Revolution

More open divorce laws and the increased divorce rate are related to a great extent to what is often referred to as the "sexual revolution." Within the past 20 years attitudes and mores regarding sex have undergone considerable change. Behavior that was once considered "sinful" or simply "not done" has now become widely practiced if not totally accepted. One aspect of these changing attitudes has been a new approach to marriage—increasingly Americans have come to regard personal happiness as being paramount in family and marriage. Consequently, a marriage that detracts from that happiness is considered better terminated than maintained for the sake of social custom.

More liberal attitudes toward sex and marriage have influenced the family in a variety of

THE VARIOUS PATHS TO SOCIOLOGICAL KNOWLEDGE
E. FRANKLIN FRAZIER

E. Franklin Frazier (1894–1962) was a leading black sociologist whose interests ranged over a wide area, including class structure, community organization, prejudice, race, culture, and socialization. To a great extent, he combined these interests in *The Negro Family in the United States,* published in 1939. Studies of the family have been and continue to be a major field of interest to sociologists; Frazier's chief contribution lies in establishing what might be considered a sociology of the black family.

Looking at the black experience in the United States from a broad historical perspective, Frazier was convinced that major historical traumas had profoundly influenced the development of family structure for American blacks. The major events he related to family organization were: the slavery experience, the readjustments required by Emancipation, and the immigration of blacks from the rural South to urban areas in both the North and South.

The experience of slavery placed a tremendous barrier in the way of family life for blacks. All ties with African culture and the family life that is connected with such a culture were destroyed. Under slavery, the black male was treated as a child and the prerogatives that usually go with being a husband and father were not tolerated. The constant threat of being sold hindered the formation of close relationships. What is more, in the early days of slavery there was a disproportionate number of males to females. It was not until the 1840's before parity between males and females was achieved. In these conditions, blacks tended to have casual sexual encounters that did not bind them with a permanent partner.

In addition, many slaveowners mated their slaves as they did their livestock—without any regard for the preferences of the slaves. As a result, the duration of the marriage as well as its execution depended on the will of the masters rather than the participants.

Perhaps the miracle was that any family life managed to survive at all. But where it did, strong family ties tended to result. This was especially true in those situations "where husband and wife were permitted to cultivate patches of ground as a means of supplying themselves with extra food or better clothing. . . . It seems, too, in some instances that a sort of public opinion in the slave community had some effect on the significance of the marriage bonds.''

Emancipation did not solve the problems of blacks, but rather brought about a new general crisis. New ways of thinking and acting had to be learned by the newly freed people. At the same time, the black did not have real freedom. The widespread discrimination known as Jim Crow replaced the slavery system. Therefore, the full dignity to which the black was entitled was not granted. It was an important factor that in gaining their freedom blacks were not given any land. This effectively kept many of them from gaining the economic security that was necessary for strong family life.

By and large, in those cases where there had been some kind of family ties before emancipation, those ties were strengthened after freedom was granted. In those cases where black males showed a pattern of casual mating, this was continued after emancipation. It is important to stress that where the black managed to gain some land this was an incentive to strong family ties.

Frazier takes as his assumption that the family that is male-dominated is the most stable. And therefore he gives his greatest compliments to those families that were organized in this way. In reality, the situation of the black usually favored female domination. This was due, under emancipation, to two factors. The first was that black men could easily cut themselves off from the family relationship and join the great number of men both white and black wandering about the country in search of work. In general, this option was not open to women. Second, the position of the grandmother in the black family was uniquely powerful. On the plantation, she had been ''the repository of the accumulated lore and superstition of the slaves, and was on hand at the birth of black children as well as white.'' After emancipation, it was often the grandmother who kept the generations together. She always had an important function as midwife.

In the years after emancipation, blacks gradually moved away from the areas they had lived in as slaves. By 1910 1.6 million of them had left the state of their birth. Of these, 400,000 had left the South altogether and were living in the North. Much of this migration was to the cities, because jobs there held out the promise of a better way of life. The flood of migration was dramatically increased during the 1930's, when millions were in search of jobs. In the North, blacks filled the need for labor that had formerly been filled by immigrants.

Life in the city meant a relaxation of primary group control over behavior. Sometimes the dissolution of family life had begun before the family reached the city. But even if the family retained its cohesion until it reached the city, the urban conditions of poverty and discrimination often forced blacks to seek homes in deteriorated slum areas from which practically all institutional life had disappeared. Hence, at the same time that these families were losing their ties to primary groups, they were freed from controlling forces of public opinion and communal institutions. Family desertion in cities, therefore, seems to be a factor of urban life on simple family organization. The resulting disorganization in the family life tends to produce social problems for the black.

Although Frazier's research is now more than three decades old, much of it is still highly relevant. The basic patterns he described, including the obstacles to cohesive family structure, continue although some of the statistics have changed. And, despite progress toward equal rights, many of the same pressures and tensions remain. More recent studies of black family structure have built on the evidence and analysis supplied by Frazier. An example of such research is the U.S. Government sponsored study, *The Negro Family: The Case For National Action,* published in 1965. This work, often referred to as the Moynihan Report, created new awareness of the ideas presented by Frazier a generation earlier.

ways. Premarital sex, for example, is more widely accepted than it was a generation ago and is probably practiced more widely than in the past. Living together before marriage—or with no plans for marriage—has also become more common. One result of this changing pattern has been that many couples have made important adjustments to each other prior to marriage. On the other hand, the freer approach to premarital relations, particularly living together, has often contributed to family tensions since it is difficult for most parents to approve the practice. Instead of the traditional stereotype of the timid youth asking a father for his daughter's hand in marriage, thousands of parents have faced the difficult task of adjusting to the letter or phone call reporting that their offspring has just moved in with a boyfriend or girlfriend.

Another result of the "new morality" has been an increase in alternatives to marriage. Many young couples feel free to live together indefinitely without marrying or they push marriage off into the future, usually when the decision is made to have children. More extreme alternatives to traditional marriage are tolerated, if not accepted. Some people have experimented with group marriages, particularly within commune settings, although the arrangement is rare and often of short duration. Also, marriages between homosexuals have now become possible, although opinion polls show that the great majority of Americans still regard such unions as "immoral" or wrong.

Does the new morality present a further threat to the viability of the family institution? Although some people argue that this is the case, most Americans seem to be adjusting to the changes. Certainly the bond of marriage does not seem to be going out of style; in fact, the percentage of the population that is married is considerably higher now than was the case 30 years ago.

The Older Generation

An area of growing concern for scientists is the study of the aged and the aging process, particularly since this segment of the population has become so numerous and because changes in the contemporary family have created special problems for the elderly. A relatively new discipline called *gerontology* deals with this subject. Natural scientists such as biologists and biochemists work in *biological gerontology*, while social scientists work in *social gerontology*. A third specialized field, *geriatrics*, applies available knowledge from gerontology to the practical needs of the elderly.

Recent studies have shown that the aged segment of the American population has grown remarkably over the past few decades. For purposes of convenience these studies generally use the accepted definition and designate as aged all persons 65 years of age or older. Such persons currently number over 20 million and represent nearly 10 percent of the population. Projections for the future indicate that the aged segment will continue to grow both in numbers and in proportion. It has been estimated that by the year 2050 the elderly could number between 48 and 80 million people, comprising between 15 and 20 percent of the total American population.

Although the extension of life expectancy is generally considered one of the major achievements of modern science, the existence of a large aged population has proved a mixed blessing. Older persons are forced to make difficult adjustments in order to cope with the problems that accompany advanced years. As the aged population expands, these problems affect increasing numbers of people. Since elderly persons frequently require assistance in caring for themselves, a growing older population places heavy demands on the resources of society.

In the United States, changes in family life have strongly affected the status of the elderly. As we noted earlier, the traditional American family lived in a more-or-less extended pattern. The older members stayed on with their married children and had definite roles to play in the running of the household. The modern family follows the neolocal, nuclear pattern in which children move away upon marrying, and the average modern household consists of only 2 generations. As a result of these changes, older people have been forced to surrender many of their familiar roles and usually have little to do with the training of grandchildren.

Without family support, many of the elderly face extreme economic hardship. Government programs and pension plans have assumed some of the burden that traditionally fell to the family, but these efforts have proved far from adequate. According to the poverty levels of $1850 per urban couple, $1470 per urban individual, and 30 percent less for farm aged, over one third of the elderly in this country are living in poverty. Opportunities for employment are few; the health of the aged generally declines; and their level of education tends to be below that of the younger generation. In addition, rising prices reduce their real income, and economic assets such as homes or cars are either reduced or nonexistent.

The economic plight of many of the elderly is also worsened by their need for medical assistance and adequate housing. The Medicare program, instituted by Congress in 1965, has helped to provide needed health care and has reduced much of the strain on the limited economic resources of the elderly. Medical costs to the individual can still be a great burden and there are indications that older persons are paying more for health care than they did before Medicare because of rising hospital costs and physicians' fees. Studies of housing, too, indicate that, in spite of massive government programs, the needs of this segment of the population are not being met. With 800 persons reaching the age of 65 every day in the United States, there remains a question as to whether or not the efforts of federal programs will merely keep up with conditions or will make headway in providing greater economic security for the aged.

In addition to federal, state, and county assistance programs, many local communities have accomplished a great deal in caring for the aged. A number of programs provide opportunities for the elderly to help one another and, at the same time, to become more actively involved in local affairs. The elderly themselves have developed a number of organizations to help find part-time employment for retired persons, to lobby for additional government assistance, and to plan and operate retirement communities.

SUMMARY

While the family is a universal social institution, it takes different forms in different cultures. In our own society the typical family grouping is *nuclear,* consisting of a mother, father, and their offspring. In other societies the nuclear family is submerged in a larger unit called the *extended* family of several generations living together.

Nuclear and extended families can be classified further according to the number of marriage partners, residence, lines of descent, power, and limits on mate selection.

Our own family system has undergone striking changes. The large, rural families of our colonial past have given way to the smaller, urban families of today.

Fixed roles have been redefined so that there are multiple roles available to family members. The exclusive functions of the family have come to be shared with other institutions or nonfamily agencies. Two important causes of these changes are the increasingly independent role of women and the urbanization process.

While some people fear that the family may be a dying institution, most social scientists agree that while the family may change, it will survive as the "basic unit of human living."

Three major areas of change in the family that have come in for special study by sociologists are divorce, the sexual revolution, and the state of the older generation. Although 20 to 25 percent of American first marriages end in divorce, some studies show that divorce may be a prelude to a better second marriage or a more happy situation for children. New freedom to divorce may be seen in the new "no-fault" divorce laws which have replaced *adversary action* in some states.

The "sexual revolution" has created some strains, but it has also allowed for important adjustments before marriage and resulted in a variety of alternatives to traditional marriage.

GLOSSARY

bilateral descent   tracing of descent through both the maternal and paternal sides of one's family.

endogamy   the practice of selecting a mate from within one's own group. Familiar types are religious, racial, tribal, and national endogamy.

exogamy   the practice of selecting a mate from outside one's own group. Tribal or clan exogamy are somewhat common among primitive peoples.

extended family   a family unit in which married sons and daughters and their offspring continue to live with their parents. Includes three or more generations.

gerontology   the scientific study of aging and the aged, and of the impact of a large aged population upon societies.

matriarchy   a family in which authority rests with and is exercised by the mother.

matrilineal   relating to the tracing of descent through the mother.

matrilocal residence   the custom of a newly married couple living with the bride's parents.

monogamy   the most common form of marriage, wherein the individual weds only one spouse.

neolocal residence   the practice of a newly married couple setting up its own household, rather than living either with the bride's parents or the groom's parents.

nuclear family   the basic family unit consisting of the roles of father, mother, and child.

patriarchy   a family in which authority rests with and is exercised by the father.

patrilineal   relating to the tracing of descent through the father's line.

patrilocal residence   the custom of a newly married couple living with the groom's parents.

polyandry   a form of marriage wherein a woman takes two or more husbands.

polygamy   plural marriage, or marriage in which one has two or more spouses simultaneously.

SUGGESTED READINGS

Delora, Joann S. and Delora, Jack. (eds.). *Intimate Life Styles: Marriage and Its Alternatives.* Pacific Palisades, California: Goodyear Publishing Co., 1972. An analysis of both traditional and emerging patterns of behavior involving intimacy and sexuality.

Goode, William F. *World Revolution & Family Patterns.* New York: The Free Press, 1970. Goode deals with changing family patterns in a wide range of cultures—Japan, China, India, the United States, sub-Saharan Africa and the Arab nations. In highly readable prose, he deals not only with *what* is changing, but why these changes occur and what their implications might be for the future of human societies.

Gordon, Michael. (ed.). *The Nuclear Family in Crisis: The Search for an Alternative.* New York: Harper and Row, 1972. Several articles dealing with group marriages, Kibbutz life, communes and the family in socialist nations are presented as alternatives to the nuclear family.

Koller, Marvin R. *Social Gerontology.* New York: Random House, 1968. The study of aging and the aged, as a special field of sociological research, is relatively new and is becoming increasingly important. The author draws on the increasing body of research to deal with major questions of aging in American society.

Koller, Marvin R. *Families: A Multigenerational Approach.* New York: McGraw-Hill, 1974. The author suggests a new way of examining families in the United States. He stresses the relationships of past, present, and future generations within a wide variety of socioculturally "different" families.

Komarovsky, Mirra. *Blue-Collar Marriage.* New York: Vintage Books, 1964. Ms. Komarovsky based her study on extensive interviews with 58 couples in an eastern community. The picture she creates is often a gloomy one, leading her to the conclusion that the drabness of life puts a heavy burden upon the marriage relationship.

SOCIAL STRATIFICATION

Close observance of any society reveals the existence of social inequalities—not everyone receives all the benefits the society has to offer. These inequalities seem to pervade every facet of life: the clothes one wears, food choices and type of dwelling, educational level and type of work, interests, language, companions, and so on. The people in each layer or strata may or may not know each other, but they do share common characteristics that have a marked effect on the type of life they lead.

THE MEANING OF SOCIAL CLASS

In all societies, people are assigned to different social classes according to the way they are ranked by members of that society. Generally speaking, those people who enjoy a maximum share of society's material and nonmaterial benefits are said to belong to the upper classes, while those who enjoy a lesser share are arrayed among the various levels below. This layering of society can be compared to the layers or *strata* of rock that form the earth's crust; in fact, the geological term *strata* is often used in referring to social classes. However, there are important distinctions in this analogy. For one, social strata are not visible to the naked eye; an understanding of them requires the analysis of social data. Further, social strata are not fixed or set in place, but are subject to considerable changes. Finally, the lines between social strata are often blurred or difficult to establish clearly.

The study of social classes is made even more difficult by the denial that social classes even exist. The "myth of classlessness," for example, has been promoted both in the United States and the Soviet Union. In the United States, the statement is frequently made that "everyone is as good as everyone else" or that there is "equal opportunity for all." In the Soviet Union, the same notion of classlessness is promoted by an ideology that insists "everyone is a worker . . . everyone is a laborer for the common good." Such myths are not easy to dispel, but they are challenged by the findings of sociologists. Americans, for instance, reveal an awareness of class levels in the struggle "to get ahead," or to be selected to a particular club or organization, or to live in a particular neighborhood or suburb.

Social Class Criteria

Social classes, then, are categories in which people live at different levels of society, some few at the top enjoying full benefits, others at the lowest levels receiving the least benefits, and the remainder of society distributed somewhere in between these extremes. The criteria or standards used to distinguish one social class from another include wealth, education, family ties, occupation, length of residence or seniority, and the possession of selected personality traits. Which of these is most heavily emphasized will vary from culture to culture.

Wealth. In most societies the amount of wealth an individual possesses is related to one's social class standing. But only to a limited extent is it valid to say the greater the wealth, the higher the class level. The mere possession of wealth is not always sufficient to confer high rank on its owner. One may be quite wealthy and still not be considered a member of the upper classes. An underworld figure who amasses a great fortune, for example, does not necessarily qualify as a member of the upper class, nor would a recluse who lives in squalor while hoarding great wealth. There is often great social friction between those who have just acquired wealth—the so-called *nouveaux riches*—and the older, established upper-class families. Not until the upper-class families accept them can the newcomers establish their claim to that status. By contrast, it is also possible for a person with little in the way of material possessions to be given a high social rank. This is true of many "impoverished" European nobles who have lost their family fortunes but retain their family titles and are still considered members of the upper social strata.

Family Ties. As the reference to European nobility suggests, blood relationships can be most instrumental in determining social levels, especially in societies which are stratified along caste or estate-system lines. In the United States, access to certain private schools, "name" colleges, and even certain businesses is much easier for those with the "right" family connections.

Occupation. How one earns a living has a

great deal to do with one's social class; in fact, it may be the most important criterion in industrialized societies like the United States. Occupation is related to wealth in the sense that better-paying jobs frequently are accorded higher prestige. But here again, wealth is not the sole determinant. Certain occupations are prestigious in themselves; a clergyman, for instance, may earn far less than a truck driver, but will be regarded as higher in social class position.

Length of Residence. A consideration which frequently enters into the determination of class is residential tenure—how long one has lived in a certain place. The older, more established residents of a community, the so-called "first families," tend to be respected more than the newer arrivals. People who are descended from the founders or first settlers of towns are generally accorded higher prestige than newcomers, provided other factors in class determination are more or less equal. A notable exception to this, of course, is provided by the experience of racial minorities in the United States. All American Indians, as well as many blacks and Chicanos, can claim longer residency than whites, but this residential seniority clearly has not been a determinant of their social class.

Education. Formal education often serves as a factor influencing social classification, with individuals who have received more education ranking above those who have received less. This ranking may be because the society values educational achievement for its own sake; or, in developing nations particularly, it may be because the society so desperately needs the talents of people with advanced training. In modern societies, of course, certain degrees are essential "union cards" for many professions and occupations; thus, education makes possible a career that will be important in social advancement.

Personality Traits. Finally, an individual's personality can enter into the determination of social class level. That is, a person who pos-

sesses (or is thought to possess) personality traits which are approved and respected by one level of society will be ranked higher than one who does not. Of course, the same personality features are not approved in all societies. In one culture such traits as good manners, courtesy, thoughtfulness, tact, honesty, intelligence, and taste may improve a person's social position, while in another culture, the approved traits might be strength, courage, imagination, or ruthlessness. George Bernard Shaw satirized the frequent over-emphasis on personality traits in his play *Pygmalion* (which became the musical *My Fair Lady*), in which he had a lower-class flower girl transformed into a lady accepted by the upper classes only through training in speech and manners.

Special Factors in the Study of Social Classes

A numer of points should be kept in mind in the sociological study of classes: (1) class is determined by a combination of factors; (2) the criteria can be both objective and subjective; (3) criteria are subject to change; and (4) social classes are essentially prestige ratings, but they are also associated with social power.

1. *Combinations of social class criteria.* While occupation has been mentioned as, perhaps, the best single criterion of social class, social classes are too complex to be judged by a single-factor analysis. Accordingly, sociologists rely on a number of indicators, which explains, in part, why social classes are often described as socio-economic levels rather than simply the results of location and type of housing, wealth, work, or use of leisure time.

2. *Objective and subjective criteria.* In the determination of social class, much depends on the perspective of the person making the determination. Sociologists, for example, can distinguish various socio-economic levels by using the "objective" criteria we have just out-

lined.   In much the same way, Americans rank other people according to much the same set of factors.   When the perspective becomes "subjective," however—that is, when people are asked to rank themselves or their families—the criteria changes.   Studies of how people rank themselves usually reveal that Americans prefer to be ranked in the middle class; few assign themselves to the "lower" class, but if the designation "working" class is used, many will place themselves in that group.   The study of *Deep South*, mentioned earlier in this book, suggested that people tend to stress their own importance.   Upper-class people viewed the upper-middle class as "nice, respectable people," but saw them-

"And what sector of the economy are you folks from?"

selves as "people who should be upper class." Lower-middle class participants saw themselves as "we poor folk," but they ridiculed those above them as "people who think they are somebody."

3. *Changes in social class criteria.* The dynamic nature of human systems applies equally well to social class systems. What has been valued in the past may be devalued in the future, and vice versa. When the military came to dominate Japanese society in the early years of this century, military leaders were held in high regard. After the disastrous national experience of World War II, however, militarists were not favored and the most prestigious positions are held by business, industrial, and intellectual leaders. In 19th-century America, the family physician enjoyed about the same prestige as a clergyman; both were respected, but were rarely regarded as members of the upper classes. And a doctor who wanted to perform autopsies to find the possible cause of death was likely to be tarred, feathered, and run out of town. Today, of course, the specialized branches of medicine, including research, are often regarded as possible stepping stones to upper-class prestige. Such change in criteria often reflects social changes; consequently, a society that is undergoing rapid social change, such as a new African nation in the 1970's, is likely to see social class criteria altered dramatically.

4. *Social classes as prestige and power systems.* It is difficult to determine to what extent social classes embody both prestige and power. Prestige refers to the "high," "middle," or "low" ratings applied to persons so they may be categorized in ranks. Power refers to the ability to control the lives of others. It is clear that prestige and power are not necessarily correlated, because we find people with high prestige, such as college professors with very little power, or we find people with considerable power, such as military or political leaders, who may have low prestige.

Some sociologists, however, are convinced that a small handful of families, a "power elite," actually controls American society. Most sociologists would dispute this contention, pointing to "multiple blocs" of power, such as those represented by numerous lobby and pressure groups, which exert an influence on societal policies. And such groups as the poor, the aged, youth, racial minorities, and women have organized sufficiently to make demands on government, business, and society in general—demands which cannot be ignored. These interest groups cut across social class lines and weaken the argument that social classes represent gradations of power as well as prestige.

SOCIAL MOBILITY

At birth, a child automatically becomes a member of the parents' social class. Usually, the family's position in the structural framework of the society is determined by the father's status, although in societies which trace descent through the mother's line, the mother's position becomes the determining factor. Even in our society the female parent's status may be more important than the male's, especially when the mother's position is higher than that of the father. Such a situation might occur when a woman who has achieved fame in a career or who comes from a famous family marries a less well-known husband. But regardless of which parent is more instrumental in conferring social standing, the fact remains that most of us begin life with a social heritage that includes a certain class membership.

In many societies, however, an individual can change class position through personal effort. Such movement within the class structure is known as *social mobility;* the movement may be either *vertical* or *horizontal.*

Vertical Mobility

In vertical mobility, the individual changes his social class level, either moving upward in what is called *ascending* vertical mobility, or downward in *descending* vertical mobility. Extreme examples of both types are easily recognized. The famous surgeon whose father was a laborer has experienced ascending vertical mobility. The child of wealthy, highly respected parents who "drops out" to live on a commune has experienced descending vertical mobility.

In the United States a heavy emphasis is placed on upward vertical mobility. The "rags to riches" or "log cabin to White House" theme has long been central to the American system of values. Beginning in the late 1960's, many middle-class young people reacted against what they felt to be the hollow materialism of this tradition. Great numbers refused to join the "rat race" of striving for economic and social success. Instead, they searched for "alternative lifestyles" in the pursuit of inner peace, or harmony with nature, or personal pleasure, or simply by "dropping out." In the 1970's, this "revolution" seems to have slowed considerably, but it did succeed in reducing some of the pressures felt by many students. And work in such low-paying jobs as teacher's aides, welfare work, or handicraft industries, for example, is now much more acceptable than was the case a generation ago. On a society-wide basis, however, the admiration for upward movement remains.

Horizontal Mobility

In *horizontal* mobility, the individual does not change class level but does make a change within the same class. For example, a lathe operator who moves from one plant to another for a higher salary remains a lathe operator and therefore retains roughly the same class

standing. Or a doctor who decides to specialize in a particular branch of medicine does not substantially alter social position. In horizontal mobility, then, an individual may improve a position within a given social class, but does not cross class lines.

Social Mobility in the United States

A number of sociologists have attempted to chart the general trends of social mobility within American society. These mobility studies generally use occupations as their guidelines. For example, to see how much social movement has taken place during an individual's career, researchers will compare his occupation with that of his father. Studies such as those of Seymour Lipset and Reinhard Bendix (*Social Mobility in Industrial Society,* Berkeley, University of California Press, 1958) indicate that there is a good deal of social movement in our society, although most of it is horizontal rather than vertical. That is, only a few people hold exactly the same jobs as their parents, but most hold jobs with roughly the same level of prestige. Thus the sons of blue-collar workers tend to become blue-collar workers of a different type. At the upper levels of occupational strata, there appears to be greater selectivity than at the lower levels. Top managerial positions usually are filled by people from the upper and middle strata, rarely from the lower strata. This does not mean, of course, that great upward mobility is impossible; it does mean that movement from one class to a higher class is not particularly common.

The research also confirms that our highly industrialized society offers increasing opportunities in professional and technical work and in many white-collar occupations, with a corresponding decrease in the opportunities for unskilled and semiskilled laborers. In 1900, for example, fewer than 20 percent of the employed population was engaged in nonmanual work; the proportion had risen to 32.7 percent in 1940, and today more than half are employed in nonmanual jobs. This has also meant a general increase in educational level and in real income. The percentage of adults who had completed high school, for instance, was 24.1 in 1940; 25 years later it had almost doubled to 49 percent. The percentage of those completing at least four years of college also increased from 4.6 to 9.4. Using 1964 dollars as a standard, sociologist Herman P. Miller found that in 1947, only 7 percent of American families had annual incomes above $10,000; by 1964, the figure had changed to 22 percent.

In terms of income, occupation, and education, then, there seems to have been a steady upward movement in American society, drawing more and more people into the middle and upper levels. The lower levels remain much the same in terms of income and occupation. To many, this is a clear indication that the rich are becoming richer, and the poor are falling even further behind. The contrast between the affluent and the poor, whether white or nonwhite, is clearly one of the major causes of social tensions in our contemporary society.

TYPES OF CLASS SYSTEMS

Sociologists distinguish between 3 different types of class systems, which differ according to the degree of upward mobility permitted. In a *caste* system the class lines are sharply drawn and little mobility is allowed. In an *estate* system there are a few openings through which people can rise, but the number who can ever make use of these opportunities is limited. An *open class* system offers free movement between classes. Open class sys-

tems can be better understood if we have an understanding of the other two.

Caste Systems

The word *caste* is derived from the Portuguese *casta*, meaning "family," "race," or "lineage." As applied to social class systems, the word refers to stratification along lines of descent—the individual is born into a given social category and remains there for life. Caste systems have been maintained by many societies throughout history—the ancient Egyptians, the Indians of Mexico and Peru, many African kingdoms, and the peoples of New Zealand and Tahiti. But the most familiar of all caste systems was that of ancient India.

The origins of the Indian caste system can be traced back to the Aryan invasions of India, around 1500 B.C. The Aryans, a light-skinned people, conquered the dark-skinned Dravidians and imposed an unequal form of accommodation on them. Only the invaders were allowed to become priests, warriors, or craftsmen, forcing the Dravidians into laboring jobs. It was this division along racial lines that marked the beginning of the caste system; in fact, the Hindu word for caste, *varna*, means "color." Once the Hindu religion was adopted, this reinforced the stratification according to the division of labor.

By about 600 B.C. the lines of the four major castes had been established and remained remarkably rigid until a quarter-century ago. The uppermost caste included the Brahmans, or priests and learned men, whose duty it was to teach the other castes. Next came the Kshatriyas, the warriors and rulers, who were expected to protect the society. They were followed by the Vaisyas, the merchants, craftsmen and farmers. The final caste, the Sudras, were the hired laborers. Beneath the Sudras were the outcastes, or untouchables, who

The perfect Communist society, as first envisaged by Karl Marx and Friedrich Engels, would be a society with no social class distinctions. A classless society, they theorized, would be free of the tensions and sufferings caused by an uneven distribution of wealth, power, and prestige. "From each according to his ability, to each according to his needs" became a key slogan of Communist movements—everyone would receive what he needed from the society and each would contribute to the common good whatever he was able to.

Today, more than a half-century after the Communist Revolution in Russia, the people of the Soviet Union cling to the dream that they are on the verge of achieving a society free of social class distinctions. But the realities of Soviet life clearly make the dream more of a myth than an actuality.

As in all modern industrial societies, the Soviet Union has different strata based on occupation, income, education, responsibility, and so on. The Russians recognize that distinctions do exist, but insist that they are gradually disappearing. But, in recognition of these class distinctions, the slogan quoted above has been altered to conclude ". . . to each according to his *work*," indicating that the work of some deserves higher rewards than others.

While the Institute of Russian Studies at Columbia University draws a distinction among nearly 100 different classes in the U.S.S.R., it is easier to think, as the Russians themselves do, in terms of three basic classes: the workers, the peasants, and the *intelligentsia*. This last group, making up about 20 percent of the population, includes government officials, factory managers, engineers, scientists, teachers, artists, military officers, and party officials. Basically it is a group set off from the rest of the people by education and positions of responsibility. And even within this group there are differences of income, power, and prestige.

Journalist Charlotte Curtis reports that "Soviet sociologists like to compare the existing class structure with a popular Russian dessert that has cake on the bottom, cake on the top, and a thin layer of jam or icing in the middle. The peasants and workers are the cake. The intelligentsia is the icing." In other words, the elite class tries to give the impression that they are in the middle of the social structure rather than dominating it.

Whenever possible, the government tries to blur the distinctions between classes and to build feelings of solidarity. The three major divisions are often referred to as "the three pillars of Soviet society" to create the impression that each is of equal importance. "Practical work" of any kind is glorified, and a woman who operates a street-cleaning machine is encouraged to think of her position as being as prestigious as that of a prominent scientist. Occasionally, the press notes complaints of supervisory personnel "treating workers in a rude and insulting way"—a practice very much frowned upon. Farm and factory workers who produce beyond their quotas are rewarded with special bonuses in terms of income or extra vacations and this gives them a special status within their own groups.

Despite these efforts, "class consciousness" does exist and frequently creates tensions and antagonisms. With the scarcity of consumer goods, it is obvious to all which groups manage to get the lion's share of such treasured items as automobiles, new homes, and appliances. The peasants, particularly, seem to chafe at their lot and clearly see themselves "at the bottom of the ladder." They are often annoyed by the fact that the chairman of their collective farm is usually a young political activist brought in from the outside, thus giving them less chance to rise in the farm hierarchy. And, since rural schools still lag behind those in the city, their children, unless they show some unusual talent, have little chance of acquiring a higher education.

The picture of social class structure is complicated by two distinctive features of Soviet life. First, party membership makes a great deal of difference in potential for upward mobility. Education and occupation can overcome the handicap of not being a party member, but the road up the social pyramid is much smoother for an individual active in the party. A common saying is that "party membership is not a right but a privilege granted the few"—even a peasant who is a party member will receive special privileges fellow farm workers do not have.

The second distinctive feature of Soviet social class structure has to do with ethnic and national minorities. Only about half the population of the U.S.S.R. is Russian; the rest consist of more than 80 ethnic and national groupings, such as Ukranians, Georgians, Cossacks, and Armenians. These minority groups are often distinctive in appearance and language, and they are definitely at a disadvantage in the social hierarchy. The positions of highest wealth, power, and prestige almost always are occupied by Russians, even in the non-Russian states of the Union.

The people of the Soviet Union have made some progress in bringing the various classes closer together, at least in terms of income, and they are proud of the social mobility open to women. Although seldom prominent in high party positions, Soviet women seem to feel they have achieved equality with men and experience few barriers to progress in education or careers. For example, 75 percent of the physicians in the Soviet Union are women, as are 70 percent of the teachers and, in Moscow at least, 40 percent of the lawyers.

were members of no caste and were outside the Hindu religion. These people were forced to live on the outskirts of towns and villages, and included those Dravidians who struggled to survive by such trades as scavenging and refuse-sweeping. A serious crime, called a *chandalas*, could also make one an outcaste.

Over the centuries, the system hardened until there was practically no upward mobility. With few exceptions, each person retained for life the social position of his father. Where caste rules were violated, however, downward social mobility was possible. For example, if a man married a woman of higher position than himself, their children would become outcastes.

The major castes of Brahmans, Kshatriyas, Vaisyas and Sudras represent only the barest outline of this elaborate caste system. The last formal tabulation of castes, made in 1901, listed some 800 castes and subcastes. It has been estimated that if local variations were taken into account, nearly 5000 castes and subcastes could be distinguished. The rigidity of caste lines permitted very little interaction between members of different castes. Each lived in segregated residential areas, and distinctive marks on the face or special costumes served as a sign of social rank. Money payments from a lower-caste person to a higher-caste member were first wrapped in cloth or palm leaves to avoid close contact; there was a deep belief that the lower castes could "contaminate" the upper castes by touch or coming too close.

Since achieving independence from Great Britain in 1947, the Indian government has steadily tried to break the hold of the caste system. The Indian Assembly outlawed untouchability and extended the vote to all citizens regardless of caste. The forces of urbanization and industrialization have also done much to undermine the system, making closer contact and collaboration between castes all but essential. In rural villages the impact of commerce, education, travel, and communication is less noticeable, and many of the old ways remain. Despite remnants of the rigid caste system, it is far from what it was in former times.

The Estate System

The estate system is associated with feudalism, the economic and social order which prevailed in Europe from about the 10th to the 15th centuries. The so-called first estate consisted of the nobility—the princes, lords, kings, dukes, and so on who controlled much of the land and political power. These temporal, or worldly, leaders shared authority with the second estate made up of the higher clergy, such as bishops and cardinals, who controlled about one-third of the land, and engaged in political intrigues and wars as vigorously as the nobility. In the centuries of disorder following the breakup of the Roman Empire, these two estates provided a necessary social function of giving protection to the rest of the people. A cathedral town or a castle became an oasis of security in a troubled world, each manor or town being a practically self-sufficient economic, social, and political unit.

The third estate was made up of everyone who did not belong to the first two—craftsmen, parish priests, and peasant farmers. At the bottom of this estate were the serfs, the farmers who were bound to the land of a particular noble and could never leave it, thus placing them in a category only slightly above slaves. A serf could gain his freedom only by the permission of the noble, or lord, or if he ran away and avoided being caught for a year and one day.

The estate system resembled the caste system in that people were born to one situation or another, and vertical mobility was extremely unlikely. However, the estate lines were not as rigid and could be crossed. A serf could gain his freedom, and a commoner could gain access to the upper estates, either through political or military achievement or, later in the feudal period, by being extremely successful in commerce.

The estate system had arisen out of particular needs, primarily the need for protection. As commerce developed in the late Middle Ages and powerful rulers welded their kingdoms into modern nations, the rationale for the system began to disappear. Gradually, the system was replaced by a more open class system. Sometimes this transition was relatively peaceful, but often, as in the French Revolution of 1789, the old system succumbed to violent assault. Today, the remaining traces of the feudal regime include the titles of royalty and nobility, most of which are borne more as badges of honor than of authority.

Open Class Systems

In an open class system the social position one inherits at birth is not nearly as hard to change as in an estate or caste system. On the contrary, opportunities for advancement are abundant for those who qualify. And the basis for qualification is *merit*—the individual can earn a higher rank by virtue of personal achievement. Certain pathways of upward progression are built into the structure of open class systems which a person may follow. In a modern, urbanized society, the principal pathways would include education, business, and the professions. Marriage, too, can change a person's rank when one marries a person whose class level is superior to one's own.

Strictly speaking, a "perfect" open class society does not exist, because no culture has managed to base social advancement solely on merit. Certain groups and categories in all societies are granted special privileges which they do not earn. However, many modern societies have approached the open class ideal to varying degrees, and probably American society has come closer to it than any other.

The Social Class System of the United States

The social class system of the United States is one that *mixes* elements of the caste, estate, and open class systems. Although more open than perhaps any other society, the fact remains that merit is not the only basis for the superior status of some and the inferior status of others. Some in the upper classes are there because they were born there; some in the lower social class strata are there because the channels of education, business, and profession have been closed to them.

Evidence of caste-like conditions are found in racial, religious, ethnic, or sex discriminations despite numerous laws that seek to prevent such acts. The bulk of the population in the United States has been described as WASP, an acronym that means *w*hite, *A*nglo-*S*axon and *P*rotestant. Some who are non-white, non-Anglo-Saxon, and non-Protestant have succeeded in rising in the social class system, but their upward mobility continues to be hampered because of a residue of subtle hostility that is not easily eradicated. The commitment to establish an open class system remains, of course, but few sociologists would predict achievement of the ideal in the very near future.

Within this mixed system, the factor which seems to be the best indicator of social rank in the United States is occupation. Occupation seems to reflect the other significant criteria better than any other. That is, if we know what a fellow American does for a living, we can usually tell a fair amount about his educational level, his income, the type of community in which he lives, and so on.

Moreover, there is a broad consensus among Americans regarding the placement of different occupational categories. In one survey (see Table 6-1), occupations were rated on a scale from 20 to 100 and their scores confirmed the hypothesis that occupations carry with them different degrees of prestige. No-

tice that the occupation is the prestige factor, not necessarily the income associated with it.

The ranking of people according to occupations is fairly easy, but the placement into classes is more difficult. Even on an occupational basis it is not easy for us to assign a given individual to a particular social level. This difficulty stems partly from the fact that we have no traditional class categories. Most people recognize three classes, usually desig-

TABLE 6-1   THE RATINGS OF OCCUPATIONS

Occupation	Score	Occupation	Score
U.S. Supreme Court Justice	94	Biologist	85
Physician	93	Sociologist	83
Nuclear physicist	92	Captain in the regular army	82
Scientist	92	Accountant for a large business	81
Government scientist	91	Public school teacher	81
State governor	91	Building contractor	80
Cabinet member in the federal government	90	Owner of a factory that employs about 100 people	80
College professor	90	Artist who paints pictures that are exhibited in galleries	78
U.S. Representative in Congress	90	Author of novels	78
Chemist	89	Economist	78
Diplomat in U.S. Foreign Service	89	Musician in a symphony orchestra	78
Lawyer	89	Official in an international labor union	77
Architect	88	County agricultural agent	76
County judge	88	Electrician	76
Dentist	88	Railroad engineer	76
Mayor of a large city	87	Owner-operator of a printing shop	75
Member of the board of directors of a large corporation	87	Trained machinist	75
Minister	87	Farm owner and operator	74
Psychologist	87	Undertaker	74
Airline pilot	86	Welfare worker for a city government	74
Civil engineer	86	Newspaper columnist	73
Head of a department in a state government	86	Policeman	72
Priest	86	AVERAGE	71
Banker	85		

Occupation	Score	Occupation	Score
Reporter on a daily newspaper	71	Streetcar motorman	56
Bookkeeper	70	Lumberjack	55
Radio announcer	70	Restaurant cook	55
Insurance agent	69	Singer in a nightclub	54
Tenant farmer	69	Filling station attendant	51
Local official of a labor union	67	Coal miner	50
Manager of a small store in a city	67	Dock worker	50
Mail carrier	66	Night watchman	50
Railroad conductor	66	Railroad section hand	50
Traveling salesman for a wholesale		Restaurant waiter	49
concern	66	Taxi driver	49
Plumber	65	Bartender	48
Barber	63	Farmhand	48
Machine operator in a factory	63	Janitor	48
Owner-operator of a lunch stand	63	Clothes presser in a laundry	45
Playground director	63	Soda fountain clerk	44
Corporal in the regular army	62	Sharecropper—one who owns no	
Garage mechanic	62	livestock or equipment and does	
Truck driver	59	not manage farm	42
Fisherman who owns his own boat	58	Garbage collector	39
Clerk in a store	56	Street sweeper	36
Milk route man	56	Shoe shiner	34

Source: Robert W. Hodge, Paul M. Seigel, and Peter H. Rossi, "Occupational Prestige in the United States, 1925–1963," *American Journal of Sociology* 70, (November 1964), pp. 286–302.

nated upper, lower, and middle, but often disagree over who belongs in each.   Many people, including a number of sociologists, make a further distinction by referring to such subdivisions as "upper-upper," "lower-upper," "upper-middle," "lower-middle," "upper-lower" and "lower-lower."   When it comes to fitting even a given occupation into our class structure, we are often at a loss.   For example, we might agree that an unskilled manual worker belongs somewhere in the lower class, but is the semiskilled worker upper-lower or lower-middle?   And should the owner of a small manufacturing firm be classified upper-middle or lower-upper?

Although these considerations may seem academic, how the people in each community decide such questions about an individual has much to do with how they will interact with that person.   To put the matter another way, an individual's class level is reflected in what sociologists call his "life chances."   This means that the *average* lower-class person is not likely to have the same opportunities as the *average* upper-class person.   Opportunities and the full benefits of society are not closed to a working-class individual, as they might be in an estate or caste system, but the chances of enjoying them are less than if the person has been born in the upper class.   Even something as seemingly unconnected as life expectancy can reflect class differences.   Studies have shown that the average individual from the highest strata of our society may expect to live

THE VARIOUS PATHS TO SOCIOLOGICAL KNOWLEDGE
AUGUST B. HOLLINGSHEAD

A leading sociologist has said: "Nothing is more likely to influence the individual or the social history of a nation than the system of stratification. For this reason stratification is the sociologist's favorite independent variable." Not surprisingly, then, a great deal of sociological research has dealt with the influence of social class systems within American society.

The researcher involved with social ranking can follow a number of procedures. One is to ask people to rank themselves. A second approach is to ask people to rate others—how do they see members of their own community. A major drawback of this method is that it works only in small communities where people know one another reasonably well. And a third method is to use objective criteria, such as statistics on income, occupation, educational level, and so on. An example of the successful combination of all 3 approaches is provided by the research of August B. Hollingshead. Using a small midwestern town for his work, Hollingshead produced a major study titled *Elmstown's Youth,* published in 1949.

The study "describes the relationships existing between the behavior patterns of the 750 adolescent boys and girls in the study and positions occupied by their families in the community's class structure." It covers 7 major areas— the school, job, church, recreation, cliques, dates, and sex. The members of the sample group were about equally divided between boys and girls. The data was derived from participant observation, interviews, official pamphlets, the local newspaper, and visits with the adolescents and their parents along with local people in the community. Five classes were established for the study on the basis of the following factors: the way the family lived, income and possessions, participation in community affairs, and prestige and standing in the community. The classes ranged from an upper class where wealth and lineage was passed from generation to generation, to those who were living on charity.

"Elmstowners in general are inconsistent in the way they talk and act with reference to the ideas of classes. If they are asked bluntly, 'Do you believe there are classes in the community?' they are very likely to say, 'No.' Yet they will tell you the Binghams are 'a leading family here.'"

The author found that the behavior of adolescents was significantly related to class in every major phase of social behavior. In other words, adolescents from different backgrounds or classes followed different behavior patterns from each other.

Elmstown's residency pattern affected this rather rigid class system. Since early socialization takes place within the home and play area, the fact that the classes were clustered together was important. Moreover, this early period of socialization is perhaps the most important in the individual's life. Later, these attitudes and manners learned in the home are brought to the school. Here, the behavior of the upper 3 classes was generally rewarded, and the lower classes scorned. By the time of adolescence, the attitudes of the youth toward himself and society were formed. Further impressions would tend to confirm these early experiences of class.

as much as ten years longer than the average individual from the lowest strata. This is probably due to the differences in wealth which enable the upper class person to spend more on proper diet and medical care. And, despite efforts to equalize educational and career opportunities, the life chances of the average lower-class person in these areas is clearly less than those of an upper-class individual.

The Marxist Interpretation of Social Class Systems

Although Karl Marx did not develop a theory of social classes as such, the concept of social class was central to his philosophy of socialism. Recognizing changes in the old estate system of the feudal era, he felt that the industrial revolution had led to the creation of two classes which replaced the old structure: the *bourgeoisie,* by which he meant those who controlled the means of economic production; and the *proletariat,* those who were industrial or agricultural workers.

The history of the industrial age, according to Marx, was and would continue to be a con-

stant struggle between these two classes, with the bourgeoisie (capitalists) gaining wealth by exploiting the working classes. Inevitably, the proletariat would develop a "class consciousness" which would enable them to unite and revolt against their "chains" in one industrial society after another. These socialist or communist revolutions would gradually become worldwide and would lead to the eventual creation of a "classless" society.

Without disputing the philosophical and political impact of Marx's theories, most sociologists reject his ideas of social class. For one thing, the Marxian interpretation places too great an emphasis on economic considerations. Social class is determined by more than occupation, as we have seen. By making economics central to his thinking, Marx predicted that government, once the "tool" of the bourgeoisie, would become a tool of the workers, a necessary evil that would "wither away" within time. Obviously, the complexities of a modern urbanized state have not enabled the Communist nations to come close to eliminating the institution of government.

Another criticism is that the idea of two classes, one ruling and the other being exploited, is an oversimplification. When Marx was writing in the middle 19th century, it may have looked as though industrial societies were headed in that direction. But a number of social changes have served to disperse political and economic power. The development of trade unions was one of many changes not foreseen by Marx; unions enabled workers to gain better wages and conditions, including pensions, medical care, profit-sharing, and so on. One of the great complaints of old-style Soviet Communists is that American and West European workers have become "bourgeois."

SUMMARY

Social classes are categories to which people are assigned on the basis of prestige. Class systems are found in every human society.

Wealth, family ties, occupation, length of residence, education, and certain personality traits constitute the chief criteria for determining social rank.

Four points are especially important to the study of social classes: (1) class is determined by a combination of factors; (2) the criteria can be both objective and subjective; (3) criteria may change; (4) social classes are essentially prestige systems but are also associated with social power.

Initially, an individual acquires his social rank from one of his parents, but in many societies he can change his class position through his own efforts.

Movement within a social class system may be *vertical* or *horizontal*. Vertical mobility means movement between classes; horizontal mobility means movement within a class. In American society, there has been a steady upward movement into the middle- and upper-class levels, while lower-level incomes and occupations remain much the same.

Class systems may be labeled according to the degree of upward vertical mobility they permit. If a system provides little or no opportunity for one to improve his position, it is called a *caste* or *caste-like* system. If it permits some upward mobility but only on a selective basis, then it is called an *estate* system. If relatively free interclass movement is permitted, then the system is called *open class*.

The caste system is usually associated with India, where it was most fully developed. It also existed, however, in parts of the Middle East, and in tribal Africa. The estate system, a product of medieval Europe, has now largely been discarded. American society probably has come closest to the open class ideal, although elements of caste and estate systems are mixed with it. The best indicator of social rank in the United States seems to be occupation.

GLOSSARY

bourgeoisie   originally, the urban middle class that emerged in medieval times between the peasantry and nobility. Used by Karl Marx to describe the owners of the means of economic production in a capitalist society.

caste system   a rigid social class system based on heredity that allows virtually no upward social mobility.

estate system   a social class system permitting some upward social mobility, but only for a select few. Feudal society in medieval Europe is an example.

horizontal social mobility   movement within a given social class.

open class system   a system of social stratification in which there are numerous channels permitting upward mobility.

proletariat   according to Karl Marx, a modern lower class consisting of the industrial or agricultural workers.

social class   a large category of people in a social system who are viewed as having similar socioeconomic and prestige status.

vertical social mobility   movement between classes, either upward to a higher class or downward to a lower one.

SUGGESTED READINGS

Gans, Herbert J.   *The Urban Villages.*   New York: Free Press of Glencoe, 1962.   Gans makes extensive use of interviews and personal observations to explore the influence of class on the lives of Italian-Americans.   Presents some strong criticism of urban planners who destroy viable working-class neighborhoods.

Lipset, Seymour and Bendix, Reinhard.   *Social Mobility in Industrial Society.*   Berkeley: University of California Press, 1959.   A major study of the degrees of mobility in American society—and also something of a model of comparative sociology—relating social trends in this country with others.   A collection of studies on the subject, compiled by Lipset and Bendix, is *Class, Status and Power,*   Free Press, 1966.

Mills, C. Wright.   *White Collar.*   New York: Oxford, 1951.   This is one of Mills's major works and also one of the most devastating.   He is particularly critical of the "status panic" that grips members of the American middle class.

Warner, W. Lloyd, *et al.*   *Social Class in America.*   Chicago: SRA, 1949.   This is one of the classic studies of stratification in American society.   Warner's delineation of social classes is still widely used.   Much of his data and analysis come from his "Yankee City Series," including such titles as *The Social Life of a Modern Community,* Yale University Press, 1941.

INDIVIDUAL IN SOCIETY

7

SOCIALIZATION AND PERSONALITY FORMATION

We saw earlier in our discussion of culture (Chapter 3) that the accumulated store of cultural ideas and behaviors of any peoples must be relearned by each new generation. The process by which this relearning takes place is referred to by sociologists as socialization. However, no two people are ever socialized in exactly the same way. Each of us is affected by different social-environmental forces. In other words, each of us develops a more or less unique personality. In this chapter we will examine these important processes and the contributions sociologists have made to our understanding of socialization and personality formation.

SOCIALIZATION

Socialization refers to the process through which the individual is trained to meet the demands of group living. It is primarily influenced by environment, especially cultural environment. To put the matter another way, it is through socialization that culture is transmitted from one generation to another. It is the process by which the individual comes to share in the cultural heritage of society and learns to become a participating member of that society.

This process takes place in largely unnoticed ways. Being taught to walk, to talk, and to adhere to the social rules of the family are obvious and noticeable forms of socialization; but a child is also socialized through the receiving or absence of affection, nonverbal indications of approval or disapproval, and so on. In fact, the child even serves a function in the socialization of the parents. As sociologist Gertrude Selznick points out: "Social control transforms biological mating into the social institution of the family; the helplessness of the child thus contributes to socializing the adult."

Practically everyone plays a socializing role in a primitive society where the child is involved in, or a witness to, just about everything that goes on in the village. The daily experiences of the group, plus the model of numerous adults are examples which mold the youngster's pattern of behavior.

In more complex, urban societies, the task of socialization becomes more complicated. The initial responsibility, of course, lies with the parents, who are the main agents of socialization during the early years. Communication also plays an important role. Language is vital to transmitting culture in a folk society, but this requires verbalization in a face-to-face way unless the society has attained literacy. In a literate society, the individual is exposed at an early age to books, pictures, television, and radio. However, these forms of communication are not usually as effective as face-to-face relationships, which involve the emotions and attitudes of the person on a much more intense level. Thus, the influence of the family, even in an urban society, remains the most effective agent. In fact, such groups are called primary at least in part because they are the primary means of socialization.

One indication of the importance of family is indicated by intelligence tests. At one time, it was thought that these tests measured the innate ability of the child. However, sociological studies have made it clear that the life of the family has a great influence on the scores achieved. A study by Virgil E. Herrick indicated that children from poorly educated, low-income families will tend to score lower than children from more highly educated families. As Herrick pointed out, the child must "learn to learn"; and his ability to do so is influenced by his family background.

Socialization and Education

Particularly in modern, complex societies, much of the socialization process devolves on the educational system. The student, from kindergarten at least through high school, is exposed to the patterns and standards of behavior he or she is expected to learn. In some ways, the socializing function of schools can be considered at least as important as the intellectual or academic function.

From the first day of school, the child learns that group living makes a great many demands. Rules of conduct become increasingly well-defined and the student learns to conform rather than risk a variety of possible social sanctions. Sometimes this social learning requires a necessary suppression of individualistic tendencies—like resisting the temptation to throw a punch whenever annoyed.

Socialization through education is also a conservative process to the extent that the child is taught the norms, mores, and cultural values of the existing status quo. Normally, the student is not encouraged to challenge these standards or consider radical alternatives, but rather is encouraged to learn an often idealized description of the nation's institutions. This aspect of education was particularly important when the society was absorbing millions of immigrants—the newcomers learned about the workings of American government in preparation for citizenship. An understanding of, and appreciation for, traditional values remains an important part of the educational system.

This socializing function of American education has been criticized for a number of reasons. Some social critics find the process too far removed from reality. The young person, it is argued, does not learn to question or explore, but rather is taught that comformity to a treadmill pattern is the only way to achieve success. Many students have probably found cause to agree with Edgar Friedenberg's assessment of America's adolescents as our "most oppressed minority."

A second criticism is that education actually delays socialization in the sense that the individual is held back from useful participation in the society. Gordon Pettit, in a book titled *Prisoners of Culture*, points out that youths in primitive societies become functioning group members as soon as they can prove their ability to hunt, gather foods, or perform some other useful task. In modern societies, on the other hand, education becomes a delaying process, keeping young people out of the labor force and frequently overtraining them for the jobs they eventually find. This enforced adolescence runs counter to the need to be a participant. "Contemporary Americans," according to Pettit, "seem to assume that this instinctive urge of young hominids can be postponed almost indefinitely if their attention is sufficiently occupied" with toys, sports, entertainment, and school.

Third, some sociologists are critical of the idea that the values and norms instilled are essentially those of the white middle class. The children of racial or ethnic minority groups often find pressures and expectations placed on them which are not consistent with the socialization process at home. Thus, an American Indian child is taught the values of individual achievement and competition. But, depending on tribal heritage, this child may have a background that stresses cooperation and regards competition as a sign of selfishness. Similarly, American education stresses business success and material consumption, ideals which are often beyond the reach of minority-group children. This, plus the emphasis on competition, creates what Jules Henry calls "the nightmare of failure." American children, according to Henry, are taught to hate themselves when they fail; and they learn to hate or envy the person who is successful. The child who stands in front of the class without the right answer faces a "forest of hands" raised by those who want to succeed; his failure represents a painful aspect of socialization in an American school.

Adult Socialization

As the person matures, a great variety of agencies become involved in the socialization process. Some, such as formal education or job training, will be more important than others, such as a club or the daily newspaper. A number of sociologists stress the importance of

PERSPECTIVE

ISHI: SOCIAL ISOLATION IN TWO WORLDS

The time: an early morning in late August, 1911. The scene: the corral of a slaughterhouse in the bustling California town of Oroville.

The slaughterhouse butchers looked up from their work to see a strange apparition of a man stumbling toward them—a lone Indian, scarcely clothed in a poncho made of wagon canvas, and clearly on the point of collapse.

The men were accustomed to seeing Indians in their town, but never a savage, frightened looking creature like this. Not knowing what else to do, they called the sheriff who, as gently as he could, led the shivering, speechless man to the town jail. It turned out to be a wise move because, in a matter of minutes, the whole town knew that some "wild Indian" had staggered into their midst and a huge crowd had gathered in the hope of catching a glimpse of him.

Sheriff Webber tried to make his "guest" as comfortable as he could. But the Indian, clearly shaken with fear, would not speak, eat, or sleep. Local Indians and half-breeds, and even Mexicans and Spaniards, tried talking to the "prisoner" in a variety of languages—Maider, Wintua, and Spanish. The man listened to each politely, his keen, sensitive face intent, but he showed no signs of understanding, and when he spoke it was in an incomprehensible tongue.

No one knew it at the time but this man—his name was Ishi—was the last wild North American Indian, a man from a Stone Age culture who had stumbled into the 20th century. Already past middle age, he found himself stranded between the extinct culture of his people and the industrial world of modern society.

Theodora Kroeber, in her remarkable biography of *Ishi in Two Worlds* (University of California Press, 1968), describes how Professors Kroeber and Waterman, anthropologists at the University of California, began to unravel Ishi's story. They read about his strange entrance into civilization, which had appeared in countless newspapers. On the basis of their field work they theorized that the man was a member of the Yana Indians. And so, armed with a copy of Indian vocabularies, Waterman set off for Oroville.

This is how Mrs. Kroeber described the dramatic encounter between Waterman and Ishi: "Waterman sat down beside Ishi, and with his phonetically transcribed list of North and Central Yana words before him, began to read from it, repeating each word, pronouncing it as well as he knew how. Ishi was attentive and unresponding until, discouragingly far down the list, Waterman said siwini which means yellow pine, at the same time tapping the pine framework of the cot on which they sat. Recognition lighted up in the Indian's face. Waterman said the magic work again; Ishi repeated it . . . correcting his pronunciation, and for the next few moments the two of them banged at the wood on the cot, telling each other over and over, siwini, siwini!"

It turned out that Ishi had had trouble with most of the words because he was a Yahi, the southern-most tribe of the Yana Indians—a tribe which had long been thought to be extinct. Ishi, in fact, was the sole surviving member of his tribe.

Like many California Indian tribes, the Yahi had lived in a small and intimate Stone Age society. The boundaries of their world had always been limited to a few days' walk from the village. No one dared to venture into the strange and frightening world beyond their close, secure community.

Then came the white man, pouring into California in great numbers during the gold rush shortly before the Civil War, just about the time Ishi was born. Many of the Yahi were killed off within a few years, or sold into prostitution or slavery. The rest succumbed to the white man's diseases—venereal disease, TB, chicken pox, smallpox, flu, and so on—diseases for which the Indians had no resistance or cures.

The rapid extinction of the society continued until only Ishi was left. Sick and alone, he left his ancestral home and wandered in search of someone, anyone, "his tribal heritage" giving him "a stubborn will to fight to the end." It must have seemed like the end when he reached Oroville and found himself in the hands of the white men, whom he knew only as the strange creatures who had murdered his people.

But he discovered that he was treated kindly and, with Waterman, he had found a way to communicate. They tried out more words and phrases. "After awhile," Mrs. Kroeber writes, "Ishi ventured to ask Waterman, 'I ne ma Yahi?' ('Are you an Indian?'). Waterman answered that he was. The hunted look left Ishi's eyes—here was a friend. He knew as well as did his friend that Waterman was not an Indian. The question was a tentative and subtle way of reassuring and being reassured, not an easy thing to do when the meaningful shared sounds were so few."

It was decided to take Ishi to the University of California at Berkeley. At first he was terrified of the train that would take him to San Francisco. He had seen them when he was young, and his mother had told him that the train was a demon "who followed white men wherever they went, but that Indians need have no fear of it; it never bothered them."

At the University of California, Ishi was housed at the Museum of Anthropology, which remained his home until his death a few years later. Indian guests were a natural part of the Museum life, which helped Ishi to feel more secure. He learned some words of English and communicated freely with the anthropologists who could speak to him in Yahi. "... Kroeber says that the first impression of him was one of gentleness, and of a timidity and a fear kept under severe control. Ishi started at the slightest sound. . . ."

Although he gradually became more relaxed, it was always clear that Ishi felt himself to be alone, to be isolated from all others even though they were kind to him and he seemed to enjoy their companionship. It was as though he sensed from the beginning that, cut off from the culture he knew, it would be impossible for him to become adjusted to the strange and different culture in which he found himself.

"His aloneness," according to Mrs. Kroeber, "was not that of temperament but of cultural change, and one early evidence of his sophisticated intelligence was his awareness of this. He felt himself so different, so distinct, that to regard himself or to have others regard him as 'one of them' was not to be thought of. 'I am one; you are others; this is the inevitable nature of things,'—is an English approximation of his judgment of himself."

the peer group in the socialization process. For example, David Riesman in *The Lonely Crowd* suggested that one's intimate group of friends may be more important in socializing the individual than the family. According to Riesman, the "other-directed" man of modern society gains approval and acquires standards of behavior from those he wants to be his friends, thus emphasizing sociability, similar tastes and attitudes, and getting along with others. While few sociologists would go as far as Riesman in this interpretation, there is agreement that the peer group is an important socializing agent.

Adult socialization is particularly noticeable during periods of great stress or transition. Divorce, the death of a spouse, a change of jobs are the sort of events that require considerable adjustment, and may lead to great changes in a person's self-image, and in habits and attitudes.

The Unsocialized Person: The Effects of Isolation

A clear idea of the importance of socialization to personality development can be gained by viewing the effects which extreme isolation has upon a human being. Since most people experience social interaction throughout their entire lifetimes, instances of such isolation are very rare; but there have been a few cases of children who experienced only a minimum of group contact throughout their formative years. Two such cases have been carefully studied and described by Kingsley Davis in the *American Journal of Sociology*. One involves a girl called Anna, the other a girl who had been given the pseudonym of Isabelle.

Anna was rejected by her mother and spent the first few months of her life being shifted from home to home. She finally ended up with a grandfather, who permitted her to live in an attic room of his house so long as she was never brought downstairs. For nearly 6 years, Anna received only enough attention to keep her alive. She was fed little but milk and was rarely cleaned, moved, or given any sort of instruction. She experienced practically nothing in the way of human affection.

Eventually, Anna's plight was discovered by a welfare agency. Although she was more than 5 years old by this time, she exhibited almost none of the characteristics of an average child her age. She could neither walk nor talk, and was either indifferent or antagonistic toward other people. After her discovery, she was placed first in a county home, then in a foster home, and finally in a private school for defective children. In these new surroundings, she received patient care and attention. As a result, she finally learned to speak, to dress herself, to string beads, to follow other children, and to walk, although clumsily. Anna died less than four years after she was found.

The case of Isabelle is strikingly similar. Born a month later than Anna, Isabelle also was shut off from normal human contact for several years. Her only companion was her deaf-mute mother, with whom she shared a darkened room away from the rest of the family. She was able to communicate with her mother, but only by means of gestures.

When Isabelle was discovered by welfare authorities, she was 6 years old; but, like Anna, she could not speak except for a few croaking noises. She failed to respond to sounds made by others and was extremely fearful of strangers. Isabelle was placed in the care of specialists who made every effort to get through to her. Their first step was to teach her to use her voice. Once she had mastered this, she made rapid progress. Within 2 months, she began to form sentences, and 9 months later she was able to write a bit and could count to 10. By the age of eight-and-a-half, she had reached a fairly normal level of development. Professor Davis, who saw Isabelle some 18 months after she was discovered, said that she appeared to be "a very bright, cheerful, energetic little girl."

There can be little doubt that the subnormal behavior displayed by these 2 children was directly related to their social isolation. In the case of Anna, there is reason to believe that she may have been mentally retarded, which suggests the possibility of a biologically based as well as a social impairment. In Isabelle's case, however, there is no evidence of a biological affliction. Her later history indicates that she was mentally sound. Yet, like Anna, Isabelle developed practically nothing resembling a normal human personality until she was exposed to human society. Her history points clearly to the vital role played by socialization in the process of personality formation.

SOCIALIZATION AND PERSONALITY

Physical characteristics such as height, weight, and the color of hair, skin, and eyes are elements of an individual's personality. While these are greatly influenced by heredity, 2 more significant ingredients of personality—habits and attitudes—are almost entirely the product of socialization.

Habits and Attitudes: Selected Elements of Personality

Habits are personal actions that occur consciously or unconsciously through constant repetition. Once acquired, a habit becomes nearly automatic, whether it's a simple personal quirk like doodling when you're talking on the telephone or performing a more complicated task such as writing, driving a car, or operating a machine.

Habit formation is vital for human survival. A person who did not have the capacity to acquire automatic responses would be unable to compete successfully in the struggle for existence. Unlike other animals, human beings are helpless at birth; they have few unlearned capabilities with which to face their environment. Instead, the overwhelming bulk of the behavior an individual needs to survive must be learned, and learned so thoroughly that it becomes habitual.

Many habits, especially those learned during the early stages of life, become thoroughly ingrained within the individual's personality. A child may show a tendency to be either right-handed or left-handed, for example, but it used to be quite common in American society to train all children to be right-handed. A child who persisted in using the left hand gradually learned through constant repetition to use the right instead; eventually, the behavior became automatic enough to be termed habitual, and later in life such a retrained person would have great difficulty in using the left hand. Many habits become so deeply ingrained that they are difficult to change or modify. And the importance of the formative years is suggested in the observation by psychiatrist Bruno Bettelheim that a "disturbed" 7-year-old would require at least 7 years of appropriate therapy to show signs of recovery (although, of course, more would be involved in such a case than the changing of habits).

While habits are more or less automatic responses, the term attitude refers to a disposition or readiness to respond in a certain manner toward a person, situation, or idea. Each of us possesses a great variety of attitudes, some of them lying so deep within our personalities that we may not even be aware of them.

THE VARIOUS PATHS TO
SOCIOLOGICAL KNOWLEDGE
RUTH BENEDICT

Many social scientists have speculated on the question of whether or not the socialization process in a particular culture leads to the creation of a "national character." That is, does socialization create a distinctive personality type within each society?

A qualified "yes" answer has been provided by the anthropologist Ruth Benedict. Sociologists often rely on the work of anthropologists since much of the latter's research is centered on simple, or primitive societies, enabling them to study all aspects of culture at the same time. Such overviews provide the basis for comparative analyses of such processes as socialization.

Forty years ago, Ms. Benedict published her most famous work, *Patterns of Human Culture.* She developed the hypothesis that socialization produces a consistent personality type within each culture—a national character that was quite distinct from that produced in other societies. Her study focused on 3 primitive societies—the Zuni, Dobu, and Kwakiutl. Child-rearing practices, along with other socializing forces, produced in each culture "a more or less consistent pattern of thought and action." Thus, a behavioral act that would be considered abnormal or wrong in one society might be rewarded or approved in another.

Benedict recognized that the simple patterns she encountered in her research could not be applied to modern, complex societies without qualifications. In the United States, for example, there is a greater variety of forces involved in socialization. Regional differences, as well as such factors as class, income, and education will have a determining influence on how a particular individual is socialized. This variability does not mean that consistency is lacking in the socialization process. Children of a particular socio-economic class will learn much the same set of values and behavior patterns as their contemporaries who come from similar backgrounds.

Even within a particular class, Benedict suggests that there can be a "discontinuity in cultural conditioning." In the post-World War II period, for example, white middle-class parents were becoming increasingly permissive in their child-rearing practices. But, at the same time, they continued to hold high expectations for their offsprings' performance—in social matters, in school, and in careers. Some sociologists have suggested that this discontinuity created confusion in the minds of many young people. Their socializing experiences were presenting them with conflicting messages of what behavior was expected or permissible for them. Such discontinuity is not likely within the relative stability of a primitive society. In a modern culture, it may be a contributing factor in the desire to escape the contradictions by "dropping out."

Social scientists generally subdivide human behavior into overt and covert types. The former is the behavior which is visible in an individual's actions, while covert refers to the "covered" behavior that goes on within the individual. Attitudes are located within covert behavior and may or may not be visible in a person's actions. A solicitous mother, for example, who zealously tends to every need of her infant would overtly seem to have an attitude of being eager to please the child. Covertly, however, she may resent the demands the child makes on her. In this instance, the overt behavior would not evidence her covert attitude.

Attitudes are not always consistent. A person can experience mixed or conflicting attitudes toward the same stimulus. These ambivalent attitudes are common in close personal relationships when we find that we can love and hate the same person. We may appreciate the warmth or help given by a friend, for example, but also feel deep resentment at the demands of friendship. While contradictory attitudes are essentially normal, many people develop deep feelings of guilt about them.

Like habits, attitudes are learned; they are developed as socialization takes place and the individual is exposed to different group situations. And, for the most part, primary groups exert the greatest influence on attitude formation. This is particularly true of the family, where attitudes as well as habits are first developed. The young child is so dependent on its parents and has such faith in their judgment that many of their attitudes are adopted without hesitation. Later, the child begins to derive attitudes from other sources as well—from playmates, friends, and teachers. As a rule he is likely to accept the attitudes of those whom he holds in esteem. Once again, the early years are extremely important. For instance, the studies of the political socialization of children by educational psychologist Judith Torney suggest that most individuals have adopted a political outlook and set of attitudes by the time they reach adolescence that are not likely to change over the course of their lives.

Attitudes help to determine the type of adjustment an individual makes to the social environment. If these attitudes harmonize with the mores and norms of the society, the adjustment is made easier. If they conflict with social standards, however, the individual may end up being rejected or in serious trouble. It is for this reason that the formation of attitudes considered proper by a society is supervised carefully.

The Concept of Self

How one sees oneself is perhaps the most important attitude an individual develops, whether consciously or unconsciously. Do I regard myself as a worthwhile person, or as someone inferior to others? Sociologist Charles H. Cooley, in describing how these self-attitudes are formed, used the term "the looking-glass self." By this he meant that a person creates a self-image by observing and interpreting the reactions of others, using them as a "mirror." For example, the male who is convinced that members of the opposite sex are tremendously impressed by his humor or his approach is likely to develop into an outgoing, sociable individual. On the other hand, the person who imagines that his early efforts have been rejected or scorned may develop a self-attitude that causes him to avoid social situations.

Clearly, imagination plays a vital role in the formation of the looking-glass self. Conceivably, the 2 people described above could be quite equal in their appeal or attractiveness. However, one views the reactions of others as favorable while the other views these reactions as unfavorable, and each acts accordingly. This is not to say that self-attitudes are purely figments of imagination. An individual's self-attitude may correspond quite well with reality. In fact, failure to form self-attitudes that correspond in a general way with the views of others may be a symptom of mental imbalance; distorted self-appraisals are nearly always evident in mental and emotional disorders.

Self-attitudes have a strong influence on behavior. An individual must have a certain amount of self-respect and self-confidence to perform effectively. A person who feels inferior to others and unable to cope with life may become apathetic and lose the will to improve or to develop fully.

Socialization and Personal Adjustment

As we said earlier, a personality is something more than a collection of physical characteristics, habits, and attitudes joined together in a haphazard fashion. Rather, these components are organized into a pattern that is unique for each individual. To grasp the significance of this organization, we first have to understand the interrelated concepts of adjustment and integration.

Personal adjustment may be described as the harmonizing of an individual's behavior with the demands of the physical and cultural environment. It is not an absolute concept because no one ever adjusts completely. Adjustment, therefore, has to be considered in terms of degree. To some extent probably everyone is somewhat maladjusted, although this term is usually reserved for those people whose behavior is significantly out of step with their environment.

Integration refers to the individual's internal harmony rather than to the harmony between the person and society. The verb to integrate means to make whole, so the well-integrated personality is one in which the various parts fit together smoothly to produce a unified entity. Conflicts between divergent habits, attitudes, and values may be present, but the individual can resolve these in such a manner as to preserve his essential unity.

Both integration and adjustment are directly dependent on socialization. It is through social contact that children acquire their first true sense of personal responsibility. The first simple patterns of reward or punishment help the child to realize that cooperation with others is necessary if one is to get along with a minumum amount of difficulty. In other words, the child learns to adjust. In time, the realization comes that life has a certain purpose, that one should aim for certain goals which will complement one's learned values. These goals will help to give meaning to life; they act as unifying forces and assist with personal integration. The individual who has definite purposes and who has assimilated acceptable values finds it much easier to resolve potential personality-disrupting conflicts.

In general, then, integration and adjustment go hand in hand. An individual who does not have a well-integrated personality will probably have difficulty adjusting to the demands of society. On the other hand, the maladjusted person is not likely to be well integrated. However, there are exceptions. Some criminals, for example, possess well integrated personalities in the sense that they have definite goals and know how to achieve them, but their goals and values are at variance with those of society, or at least the majority mores and values, so they are clearly not well adjusted to their social environment.

SUMMARY

The process by which an individual is trained to meet the demands of group living is called socialization. Since each individual is subjected to a slightly different social environment, this leads to the development of differing personalities.

Socialization is an on-going process throughout the individual's life-span. Primary groups, particularly the family, are the vital forces in the socialization of the child. Adult socialization may depend more on the reactions of real or potential friends.

Cases of social isolation illustrate the important effect on the formation of personality. Without social interaction, as in the cases of Anna and Isabelle, the individual develops little that can be called a normal human personality.

Two major psychological components of personality are habits and attitudes. Habits are automatic forms of response, learned through repetition, which are necessary for human survival. Attitudes are dispositions to act in a characteristic fashion. They often lie hidden well below the level of everyday conscious activity, to be brought to mind when the proper stimulus is applied. Moreover, they are sometimes ambivalent—that is, in conflict with one another. Like habits, attitudes are learned through socialization.

Every personality is integrated according to a unique pattern. When this pattern enables an individual to achieve harmony among the components of his personality, we say the person is well integrated. When it enables him to harmonize effectively with his environment, we say the person is well adjusted. Both integration and adjustment are achieved through social contacts.

GLOSSARY

adjustment   the harmonizing of an individual's behavior with the demands of his physical and cultural environment.

ambivalence   a state of contradictory emotions or impulses in reaction to the same stimulus.

ambivert   a person who exhibits both introverted and extroverted personality traits. Most people are ambiverts.

attitude   a predisposition to evaluate and respond to a given person, object, situation, or idea in a consistent, predictable way.

environment an individual's physical and cultural surroundings.

extrovert a personality type, as described by Carl Jung, whose interests and energies are directed to people and events outside himself. An outgoing person.

habit a learned personal action that one repeats almost automatically in an appropriate situation.

heredity the transmission of physiological characteristics from parents to their children. Determines the physical and mental potential with which one begins life.

integration personality integration is a state of internal harmony wherein the various aspects of the personality fit together smoothly.

introvert a personality type, as described by Carl Jung, who tends to be occupied with his own thoughts rather than with other people. Tends to withdraw from interaction with others, especially when under emotional stress.

looking-glass self Charles H. Cooley's term for a person's view of himself as determined by the way he thinks others regard him. Important in developing self-attitudes.

maturation the unfolding of a person's innate nature. Biological growth.

peer group a group consisting of people who have approximately equal status. A student's peer group, for example, consists of his fellow students.

personality the organized sum total of an individual's personal traits, including physical characteristics, habits, and attitudes.

social psychology the branch of sociology that deals with how individual behavior is affected by social factors. It is also concerned with the study of groups in terms of the behavior of their individual members.

socialization the process through which the individual learns his society's norms and becomes a functioning member of the society.

symbolic interactionism the social psychological perspective developed by George H. Mead which emphasizes the role of group membership in shaping the self-development of individuals.

SUGGESTED READINGS

Becker, Howard S., *et al. Boys in White.* Chicago: University of Chicago Press, 1961. A team of sociologists studied the "anticipatory socialization" of premed students who were learning how to act and feel like doctors while in medical school.

Cooley, C. H. *Human Nature and the Social Order.* New York: Scribner, 1902. One of the "fathers" of social psychology, Cooley sets down the theories and methods of the study of the socialization process in this work.

Erikson, Erik H. *Childhood & Society.* New York: Norton, 1964. Erikson writes of the need for a constant restructuring of identities. We are constantly reordering our identities to prepare for "anticipated futures."

Greenwald, Harold. *The Elegant Prostitute.* New York: Ballantine Books, 1970. A firsthand account of the socialization of women into the occupation of call girls.

Henry, Jules. *Culture Against Man.* New York: Vintage Books, 1963. One of the writers who sees the individual as a "prisoner of society." The author is highly critical of the role of American education in the socialization process.

Keller, Helen. *The Story of My Life.* New York: Dell. New York: Doubleday, 1954. The touching autobiography of how this famous lady "became human" only after learning to use symbolic communication.

Lynd, Helen M. *On Shame and the Search for Identity.* New York: Harcourt Brace Jovanovich, 1970. This book relies heavily on sources from literature to present a particular, and provocative, slant on the search for identity.

I'm Jamie and I want to be a teacher because my mother wants me to be one.

I'm Roger and I want to be a sailor because I can sink ships and get a medal.

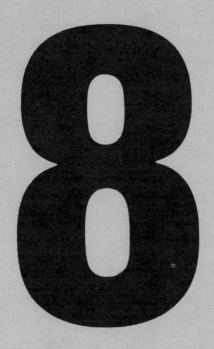

PERSONALITY INTEGRATION AND SOCIAL ROLES

If a human group is to survive, it must find the means to satisfy the basic needs of its members. These go beyond food and shelter, and include needs that can be considered both social and psychological. We need to have people respond to us; we need to achieve recognition for our efforts; we need to feel secure in our surroundings. Society provides the structure for satisfying those needs, such as through the establishment of an elaborate system of statuses and roles. In seeking to satisfy these personal needs, the individual adapts to the means offered by the society.

PSYCHOSOCIAL ADJUSTMENT

If a person is to develop a well-integrated personality—in fact, if he is to survive as a functioning member of society—his nonbiological needs must be satisfied, just as physical survival depends on satisfying biological needs. Those needs which are not strictly biological can be referred to as *psychosocial*, a word which indicates that they have both psychological and social aspects. They are psychological in that they affect one's mental, or conscious, equilibrium; they are social in that they can be satisfied only within the social environment. Much of human behavior can be related to one or more of these needs.

Identifying Psychosocial Needs

Many scholars have attempted to classify psychosocial needs. For the sake of simplicity, we can follow the lead of sociologist W. I. Thomas and group them into 4 general categories: response, recognition, security, and new experience.

Response. Each of us has a basic need, partly rooted in our biological natures, for some response to our emotions. We need contact with other humans, and when we feel such emotions as love, friendship, or sympathy for another person, it is important to have that feeling acknowledged or returned.

Recognition. We all want to have our achievements and our basic worth as individuals recognized by others. Recognition, whether praise or merely acceptance, reinforces within us the idea that our efforts are worthwhile and bolsters our self-esteem. Recognition may take an almost infinite variety of forms, depending on the individual and the situation. A child just learning to walk may need nothing more than a parental word of praise. On the other hand, a playwright who has written one Broadway hit may feel dissat-

isfied if his next play is not received as successfully.

Security. Every human being must be able to count on some certainties. There must be reasonable assurances that the familiar environment will not suddenly crumble. In addition, he must be sure of himself, must not doubt his own abilities or intrinsic worth.

Of course, few people have a totally secure life; to varying degrees, we all go through periods of insecurity. At least 3 kinds of insecurity can be distinguished—economic, social, and emotional. Perhaps the most familiar of these is economic. The person who faces financial difficulties not only feels uneasy about this aspect of his life, but may also question his worth as an individual. Social insecurity often results from the breakup of a social unit, such as a family, upon which one has learned to depend. This is a "crumbling" of the environment that can require a good deal of personal adjustment. Emotional insecurity usually arises from self-doubts, often taking the form of jealousy. The jealous person feels unsure of his emotional hold on someone he loves.

New Experience. While the individual needs a consistent element of security in his life, he also needs to have new experiences. On occasion, all of us yearn to break out of the old routines and try something new. The need might be satisfied by something simple like an evening at the movies or a day off from work, or it may require something more elaborate such as a new job or living somewhere else. Some sociologists have suggested that such diverse behavior patterns as art, dance, magic, and war are partially a reflection of the need for new experiences.

Needs as Motivating Forces

Both biological and psychosocial needs help to motivate people or dispose them to action. This is true whether or not the need is consciously recognized. The relationship between needs and motivation becomes clear when one considers the manner in which humans experience needs during various stages of life.

Needs originate in tensions caused by the absence of some required thing, such as food, rest, or recognition. In the early stages of life, the infant is aware of such tensions, but not of the need as such. A baby cannot formulate thoughts or words to express the need and does not know at first how to satisfy it. Later, through experience, the infant begins to connect satisfaction with certain objects or forms of activity. Eventually, the child realizes that certain goals will give him satisfaction and that he must take certain actions to reach those goals.

A need, therefore, may or may not be conscious. When it is consciously understood in terms of a goal, it may be called a *want* or a *desire.* In either case, whether conscious or not, the need is a powerful motivating force since it disposes one to action.

Need Frustration

Not all of a person's needs and desires can be satisfied. When something prevents a person from reaching a sought-after goal, the need or desire is said to be *frustrated.*

Many different situations can be responsible for need frustration. Sometimes the source of frustration exists within the environment. If, for example, you want to buy a new car but can't afford it (or can't secure a loan for the amount), the lack of money would constitute an environmental block.

The frustrating block is often not so much within the environment as it is within the individual. This is frequently the case with people who aspire to goals they cannot attain due to their own limited capacities. Thus, an individual may have a tremendous desire to be an

actor but simply doesn't have enough talent to make a success of it. His own limitations serve as a block and he is frustrated by his inability to reach his goal.

Frustration can also be traced to conflicting needs. For example, many people feel a real need to eat more than they need for healthy living. Food for them becomes a desired goal. But they also feel a need to remain slim enough to be socially acceptable. Similarly, people in love often retain a strong desire for independence, which is an expression of the basic need for new experience. But they also need the security that their relationship provides. In both of these instances, two different needs are in conflict, and one cannot be satisfied without frustrating the other.

The tensions accompanying prolonged or continual frustrations are called anxieties. If an individual is to develop and maintain a well-integrated personality, he must find some means of either meeting needs and desires or of avoiding the anxieties which result from those that go unsatisfied. Moreover, the solutions he works out must be acceptable in terms of his own values and standards plus the values and standards of his society. Otherwise, the solutions themselves can lead to even further difficulty. For example, the adolescent who feels the need for recognition or new experience might be tempted to join a street gang and engage in crime or vandalism. Since this is socially unacceptable behavior, he runs the risk of having society's sanctions imposed on him; at the same time, unless he has totally rejected the norms of his society, he is likely to find the behavior personally unacceptable or at least the cause of further anxiety and conflict.

Defense Mechanisms

In order to avoid the anxieties accompanying unsatisfied needs, an individual may resort to one of several largely subconscious devices known as *defense mechanisms*. Defense mechanisms enable the person to adjust to the realities of a situation while preserving the integrity of his ego or self-image.

Rationalization. When confronted with obstacles to their goals, people sometimes resort to the mechanism of *rationalization.* This means that they turn away from the goal but explain their failure to attain it in terms acceptable to themselves. A student who tries out for the college basketball team and doesn't survive the cut, may rationalize his failure with a "sour grapes" attitude by saying that he really didn't want to play because it wasn't going to be a good team this year anyhow. Or he might vary it a little and say that he failed to make the team "because the coach didn't like me."

Psychologists differentiate among a variety of forms of rationalization. *Projection* is the blaming of one's shortcomings on others. A worker who does poorly on a task may project his failure onto others by blaming his fellow workers. *Delusion* is insistence that one is capable of achieving a goal despite strong evidence to the contrary. If the basketball player who didn't make the team persists in claiming that he is really a superstar, the chances are he is engaging in delusion. *Repression* takes the form of trying to forget that something unpleasant or painful ever occurred. A person rejected in love may refuse to discuss the relationship and may try to avoid thinking about it. *Negativism* involves refusing to cooperate with people one blames for a frustration. An example would be a family situation in which a child adopts a negativistic stance toward his parents because they have thwarted some special desire. Finally, *regression* refers to returning to childhood methods to get what one wants. An adult who experiences a frustration may regress to childlike pouting or tears.

A distinction should be made between ratio-

nalization and excuse-giving. Rationalization is a subconscious act; the person is not fully aware of using a mechanism to avoid anxiety. The individual who consciously invents an alibi to escape the consequences of an action is not rationalizing but giving an excuse.

Substitution. Rationalization can be useful in helping to preserve one's self-image, but it has a shortcoming: it fails to result in the attainment of goals. Substitituion, on the other hand, involves a switching of goals; the individual converts a desire for one goal into the desire for another.

People who successfully employ substitutions often save themselves a good deal of unhappiness and anxiety. For instance, a college graduate who fails to gain acceptance to medical school, or cannot afford the extra years of schooling, might find substitutes within the same general field by aiming toward such goals as being a laboratory technician, physical therapist, nurse, or hospital administrator.

One of the subtypes of substitution is *compensation*, which consists of trying to fill the void left by failing with original goals. In compensating for lost objectives, individuals tend to overdo or overexert themselves because they are still trying to comfort themselves for their past failures. Theodore Roosevelt, for example, was weak and sickly as a child, and engaged in a variety of compensation activities later in life to make up for this feeling of shortcoming. Throughout his adult life, he placed heavy stress on physical fitness and exertion, spending some of his time as explorer, cowboy, athlete, big game hunter, and soldier.

Sublimation, another form of substitution, refers to seeking a goal "higher" than an original. Sublimation occurs in some religious orders, including the Roman Catholic Church, in which such goals as marriage and family are sublimated to the spiritual goals of the religious calling. Somewhat similar would be the case of unmarried schoolteachers (such as the hero of *Good-bye Mr. Chips*) who devote most of their time and energies to becoming "master teachers." And Gandhi, the great spiritual leader of India, could be considered a master sublimator in that he sublimated all personal desires and needs to the higher goal of gaining independence for his people.

Identification. Sometimes people who cannot achieve certain goals themselves overcome their frustrations vicariously—they gain satisfaction not through their own efforts but by sharing in the efforts of others. This is done by identifying one's self with someone who has a better chance of reaching a desired goal. This sort of vicarious satisfaction is common in the pleasure parents receive from the success of their offspring. It is particularly true if a parent has been denied a particular goal, such as a college education, but can share in the achievement of a son or daughter who achieves that educational level.

Fantasy. Frequently, the entire process of identification takes place on the level of imagination. The person with whom one identifies,

"*Alice, do you have greater ambitions for me or is treasurer of R. T. Caulkins Company, Inc., as far as I'm going?*"

WOMEN'S LIBERATION IN COMMUNIST CHINA

A variety of groups in American society have experienced numerous, often very subtle, barriers to achieved status. This has been true of racial, religious, and ethnic minorities, youth, and women. American women have been struggling for "equal rights" for many years, beginning with the suffragette movement in the last century. Today, the Women's Liberation Movement continues to try to tear down the barriers to achieved status. Do such barriers exist in other modern societies? Do women in Communist countries really have the equality of status and opportunity claimed by their country's leaders?

As the society of Communist China has become more "open" to American visitors, we are beginning to gain more knowledge about how the status of women in China has fared under communism. Here is a glimpse of the picture that is emerging.

Not long after the successful Communist takeover of mainland China, Chairman Mao declared: "China's women are a vast reserve of labor power. This reserve must be tapped in the struggle to build a great socialist country."

In the years since, women have played an increasingly active role in the economy of the nation, many as factory and farm workers, but a growing number of women are participants in the professions as well as in party and government leadership. As one woman bus driver commented, "politically and economically we are equal. In the new China there is no opposition of men to women. A person's sex doesn't matter. It is the deeds of the individual that count."

There is evidence of at least some truth in this rather extravagant claim of complete equality. In the textile industry, for instance, an estimated 60 percent of the workers are women, as are nearly half of the farm workers. Most large factories have day-care centers, and school facilities for the children so that mothers can work; in fact, some centers are open 24 hours a day to accommodate shift workers.

Teaching is becoming an increasingly important occupation for women who now make up more than half the elementary and secondary school faculties and one-quarter of Peking's college instructors. Roughly 1 out of 5 members of the Chinese Academy of Sciences are women. In a country where education of girls was considered as "useless as spilling water," all children now receive an education, and one-third of the students at the University of Peking are females.

Although government and Party affairs are still controlled by men, at the last Party Congress 20 percent of the delegates from rural areas were women, and the powerful Central Committee contained a membership with 12 percent women. In contrast, there were 11 women members of the U.S. Congress in the most recent session, representing only 2 percent of the total.

The press and radio present frequent stories of the career successes of women as an incentive for others to try harder:

—Mrs. Wang Ung-wu, who was the daughter of poor peasants and illiterate until 1950 when she learned to read in an adult education class. She has been named executive director of the Evergreen Commune, a cluster of villages with a population of over 40,000.

—Chang Yu-mei, a young party member who has gained her "wings" as a member of the air force and is now a deputy squadron leader.

—Peng Chia-kuei, a mother of 3 who is 1 of 100 women in a geological team in Kiangsi province. The women set up their own drilling machines and built a mobile laboratory for testing samples.

Despite the gains and the fact that equal rights for women are guaranteed by law, some of the old habits remain. *People's Daily*, for example, the Peking newspaper, recently criticized the fact that in some places "greater attention is paid to boys than to girls" in preparing students for entrance into the universities. And the Kansu province radio had harsh words for an official who argued that men were superior to women for many occupations.

Some women have hurt the cause of equal rights for members of their sex by openly stating that they prefer to stay at home and to raise children. Equality with men does bring new opportunities, but it also brings hard physical work and occasional hardship, especially for a woman with children. It also means that they must engage in intensive political study. Peking radio recently issued a typical criticism, this one aimed at a province in Manchuria where, the broadcast said, "many women stay at home all day gossiping and think of nothing but their families and household chores."

Although complete equality has not yet been achieved, it is clear that great strides have been made since the "Liberation" in 1949. One of the first American visitors was initially surprised that Chinese women did not seem agitated by the signs of inequality that persist. But, "as women talked," the visitor reported, "we suddenly began to understand. The gains for women in China have been so enormous, so dramatic, and all within the memory of anyone over 30, that we could see why they were not upset about the inequities that remain."

the action needed to reach a goal, and the goal itself are not real but imagined. This type of mechanism is called fantasy.

All of us engage in a bit of fantasy at one time or another. Even when we identify with an actor in a play or film, or simply indulge in daydreaming, we are involved in fantasy.

As long as one recognizes fantasy for what it is and does not confuse it with reality, it can be both pleasant and useful. Properly channeled, fantasy may result in imaginative and creative activity, or merely in a relaxing of tensions. But when it is used purely as a defense mechanism, it can be dangerous. People who constantly resort to fantasy just to escape from reality are not really adjusting to the demands of their environment; they are merely avoiding those demands.

STATUS AND ROLE

The satisfaction of psychosocial needs is directly related to the social structure of which one is a part. The goals we seek and the means we have for seeking them are influenced by the cultural environment. More specifically, they are influenced by the unique positions each of us holds within the society. This is where the statuses and roles one occupies become important.

Group Membership Confers Status and Role

The word *status* is used in two related ways. First, it refers to the position an individual holds within a group. The titles "lawyer," "doctor," "professor," "carpenter," "bus driver" all identify statuses. They do not refer to specific individuals but to positions which fit into a larger social framework.

Status is also used to refer to a rank of hierarchical position in society. Thus we think of certain people as having a higher status than others, in terms of occupation, income, or educational level; to some extent, status can also be related to birth or heritage, although this is not as frequent in the United States as it is in many Western European nations. Quite automatically, we regard a banker as having a "higher" status than a maintenance man, and a college graduate has a higher status ranking than someone who only completed grammar school.

The status of a person may be indicated by material symbols, such as a badge or uniform, or a nonmaterial symbol like a title (doctor, baron, etc.). While Americans often pride themselves on not being status conscious and having few symbols of status, as long ago as 1899, Thorstein Veblen, in his *Theory of the Leisure Class*, pointed out that signs of status were very important to our society. Higher statuses, he argued, were revealed by "conspicuous consumption"—the businessman's wife who wears an expensive diamond necklace is using this form of conspicuous consumption to indicate her status in society.

No matter how we rank a particular status, *role* is the consequence of occupying a status. A role requires certain forms of behavior and involves a variety of relationships with others. The role of doctor involves keeping up with the latest medical advances and watching over the health of patients; it also involves relationships with other doctors, with nurses, patients, medical supply salesmen, and so on. The role of carpenter involves the use of certain tools and materials; it also includes relationships with foremen, assistants, lumber yard personnel, contractors. The behavior associated with each role reflects the norms of society.

Like status, role is independent of individual personalities. Just as many different actors can perform a role in a play, so can many different types of people perform any of society's many roles. Of course, individual differences enter into the picture, so no 2 people will perform the same role in precisely the same way. Doctors, for example, may perform the same basic role of examining patients, but one might perform the task while carrying on a running conversation while another remains completely silent. Similarly, two architects will perform the same role of designing buildings, but the types of buildings they design will be quite different. In other words, while roles may be the same, *role behavior* is likely to show considerable variation.

Role Personality

An individual may fill several different statuses simultaneously. A businessman, for example, may be at the same time the head of a household, a church member, and the officer of a club. Each of these is a different status and demands a different role. Depending on which group he is in at any given time, he will use that facet of his personality which best suits the role he is playing. When he is at home, for example, he may be informal and relaxed, while at his office he may be abrupt and efficient. That part of his personality which he exhibits in connection with any given role is called his *role personality*. Each of us has as many different role personalities as we have statuses.

There has been some disagreement among sociologists concerning the degree to which the role personality is determined by the particular role. A bureaucrat or an office worker, for example, might be seen as conforming to certain behavior patterns similar to those of other office workers or bureaucrats. The natural assumption is that almost anyone, placed in the same role, will respond in much the same way, will form the same role person-

ality. Robert Merton, in a study published in 1949, suggested that the values and pressures of large-scale organizations induced people to adopt the "bureaucratic" personality. "As a result of their day to day routines," he wrote, "people develop special preferences, antipathies, discriminations and emphases." In other words, the role personality, in this case, is learned on the job.

However, more recent sociological and psychological studies have indicated that, while the job may shape the person to some extent, a more important factor is that organizations tend to select people whose personalities seem most compatible with the demands of the job. For example, a study of college students on job preferences showed that those who had high scores in a test on "faith in people" were likely to choose careers which involved a high degree of personal contact, such as sales or personnel work. Similarly, those who were described by their tests as "detached" personalites were more likely to choose careers which involved little interpersonal contact, such as art or architecture.

No matter how one chooses a particular role, his personality will influence how well he performs it and, in turn, how successfully the role satisfies his needs. Whether one has the status of mother, student, lawyer, or bowler, it is through various roles that a person tries to fulfill the needs and desires for response, recognition, security, and new experiences.

Role Conflict

Because we all have several roles to play, there are times when 2 or more of these roles will conflict, or interfere, with one another. That is, it will be impossible to play 1 role properly without denying another. Perhaps the most familiar type of role conflict is that between one's occupational role and one's role as a family member. The businessman who has to make a weekend business trip is caught in a role conflict because he must neglect his role as father and husband. Similarly, a woman who pursues a career may find herself in a role which conflicts with being a wife and mother.

In a highly complex society, a certain amount of role conflict is to be expected for almost everyone. Consequently, people have to find the means of resolving those conflicts. Women, for example, are experiencing increasing success in combining careers with marriage and family. However, when roles cannot be made to mesh properly, the resulting situation may be a source of frustration. Although different roles make demands on different aspects of the personality, it is not always easy to keep one's role personalities separate. The individual who feels that one role is detracting from another is likely to develop new anxieties. In the person who brings personal problems to the office, and whose work suffers thereby, we can recognize someone caught up in such a dilemma.

Young women in American society often experience role conflict because of differing role expectations. Sociologist Mirra Komarovsky conducted a study of college women in 1940, asking them to describe the sort of role conflicts they were encountering. For a large number of the subjects, their conflict emerged from what their parents' expectations were for them. A typical comment would be: "I talk to my parents on the telephone every weekend. My father wants to know what my grades are; my mother wants to know if I had a date last night." A replication of this study, conducted in California in 1971, revealed that in spite of the increasing career opportunities for women, exactly the same sort of conflicts were expressed by this generation of students.

Prestige and Esteem

As we suggested earlier, there is a tendency in every society to rank statuses according to a system of values. Thus in one society government workers will be held in higher regard than businessmen, while in another society the situation will be reversed. These differences in social rank reflect what sociologists refer to as differences in *prestige*. Prestige is, so to speak, "built into" a status, especially an occupational status. For example, in the United States, the job of congressman automatically carries with it greater prestige than the job of county clerk. In the Soviet Union, a concerted effort has been made to eliminate status ranking, although clearly, high government and Party positions continue to be held in highest regard. The government's efforts have generally taken the form of glorifying work of all kinds; thus a woman who operates a street-cleaning machine is made to feel that her contribution to society is as important as that of a factory manager.

A person who holds a position of high prestige will not necessarily be held in high *esteem*. Esteem depends on the way an individual carries out role behavior. A custodian in a large office building does not have the same prestige as a company president; but if he carries out his duties conscientiously, he can still win the esteem of those with whom he deals. Likewise, the company president who abuses executive authority may fail to win the esteem of employees or colleagues. In the language of sociology, it is said that status confers prestige and role behavior confers esteem.

Both prestige and esteem are vital in satisfying psychosocial needs, especially the need for recognition. Most of us are well aware of the prestige which accompanies our occupational or educational status. We gain satisfaction from holding jobs and carrying on activities viewed as important by our society. And individuals who do not occupy positions of high prestige still gain satisfaction by trying to win the esteem of others.

Psychological and sociological studies of status and role, prestige and esteem, have been important for increasing our understanding of our highly complex social system. This knowledge also has practical application: job counseling and training personnel try to match the needs and talents of the individual to a particular occupation.

Achieved and Ascribed Status

In every society certain statuses are assigned to people automatically on the basis of broad categories such as sex or age. These are called *ascribed statuses*. They are affixed to people by society, leaving no room for personal choice.

Ascribed statuses, like all others, carry with them certain roles. Males and females are expected to act in certain ways simply because they are male or female; this is demanded by social norms. To ensure conformity to these norms, society socializes each sex in a different manner. Boys are taught to display masculine behavior and girls feminine behavior. The particular roles ascribed to each sex, of course, will vary from society to society. And the roles change as cultures change; the increased occupational opportunities available to women in our society is an obvious case in point.

Roles are also ascribed on the basis of age. In most societies, the "older" members are expected to act with a certain measure of dignity and are looked upon as possessing considerable wisdom. Younger members are permitted greater behavioral leeway in the sense that minor transgressions are often over-

looked or written off to a lack of experience. But their opinions may not carry the same weight as do the opinions of elders. In the youth-oriented American society, the role ascribed to the elderly is quite ambiguous, creating problems which we will discuss in a later chapter.

Teenagers are particularly apt to resent the roles ascribed to them as a consequence of their age. They often feel ready for adulthood but find they are granted neither the freedom nor the opportunities of those a few years older. One of the chief arguments in the recent controversy over lowering the voting age to 18 ("Old enough to die for their country, but not old enough to vote") indicates the sort of tensions that can arise from this situation.

When status is not automatically assigned, but is determined by individual choice, it is called *achieved status*. In our society, occupational statuses are ordinarily achieved because people reach them by following a personally selected cultural alternative; there is no cultural requirement that certain people must enter certain fields. Similarly, educational status depends largely on what the individual decides.

Both achieved and ascribed statuses and their accompanying roles help people to satisfy personal needs. However, in every society there is some conflict between what an individual is capable of achieving and what society *permits* that individual to do. In the United States, many career women resent the fact that they are denied certain business opportunities not because they lack ability or training, but simply because they are females. Older workers resent the fact that they are kept from certain jobs simply because of their age. Such occurrences can not only be personally upsetting but detrimental to society as a whole. And even more damaging are the

THE VARIOUS PATHS TO SOCIOLOGICAL KNOWLEDGE
ERVING GOFFMAN

The field of sociology involves more than the compilation of vast amounts of data and statistical evidence to support statements about particular aspects of social structure and behavior. Some sociologists have made important contributions through the development of sweeping theories which challenge other researchers to prove or disprove them. And some have relied on careful observation, combined with research into various fields of scholarship, to provide important insights into the complexities of human behavior.

Perhaps the best modern example of the latter approach is provided by Erving Goffman. Using novels, short stories, scientific studies, and his own detached observations, Goffman has become one of the outstanding scholars in the psychosocial study of role behavior. He is a prolific and often entertaining writer, his best known works being: *The Presentation of Self in Everyday Life* (1959); *Encounters* (1961); *Asylums* (1961); *Behavior in Public Places* (1963); *Stigma: Notes on the Management of Spoiled Identity* (1963); *Interaction Rituals: Essays on Face-to-Face Behavior* (1967); *Strategic Interaction* (1969); and *Relations in Public* (1971).

A basic theme running throughout this work is the idea that in playing our various roles, we are behaving very much like actors in a play. There is nothing startling about that idea, until one begins to see how Goffman develops it and explores its implications.

In being "performers," Goffman says, we have surrounded ourselves with complex symbols, gestures, costumes, setting, and language. These we use for purposes of communication—we are trying to make others believe something, and we are occasionally trying to fool ourselves. In a word, we are all engaged in a great confidence game, each of us out to "con" the "audience"—whether that audience is a person we're trying to seduce, a business group we have to cope with, a clerk we encounter in a store. All human interaction reduces to this common denominator of trying to put on a good performance.

The skill of the performer is the major determinant in how well the audience accepts his performance. Often, we put on a good acting job simply because we have to rather than because we believe in what we are doing. The businessman might hate the person he is dealing with, but masks his dislike behind the kind of performance which determines his success as a businessman. This is what Goffman calls "cynical behavior." But what about "sincere behavior"? Clearly there are times when we are sincere about the way we act out our roles. One of the difficulties of human interaction is precisely this problem of distinguishing the sincere from the cynical. A lover can convince his "mark" provided the performance is good; the behavior is the same as that of a person sincerely in love.

We often protect ourselves from these social necessities by what Goffman labels "role distance." We go through the performance when we have to, but remain detached from it and let others know we are only acting. For example, when the boss walks in, everybody is busily at work, as though the office or shop always functions this way. Once the boss leaves, there is a backstage exchange of ironic jokes or sarcastic comments that signal other performers about one's awareness.

Does this mean that our social structure and our role behavior amounts to nothing but one big swindle? Not really. Instead, Goffman is arguing that it is wrong to idealize roles—to see people as the collection of actions they present to us. Rather, our behavior should be seen as exceedingly complex, designed to help us cope in a world which surrounds us with symbols and symbolic behavior. Many people are sincere, and many put on a good performance primarily to please others or to allow them to feel comfortable. What is necessary, then, is to learn to judge the total performance—to distinguish an "artful" performance from one which is merely "con" art.

disparities which result from ascribed statuses based upon race, religion, or ethnic background. Although job opportunities have been improving for nonwhites, it is an undeniable fact that many people are barred from achieving in proportion to their abilities simply because they belong to certain racial, religious, or ethnic groups. The chapter on minority groups will deal more fully with these problems.

SUMMARY

A great deal of human behavior is directed toward the satisfaction of psychosocial needs, especially the 4 basic needs for response, recognition, security, and new experience. Like all needs, these originate in the tensions caused by the absence of some required thing. As he matures and is socialized, the individual learns to identify some of these tensions and connect them with goals. Once recognized, the need is said to be a *want*, or *desire*.

Those of an individual's needs which go unsatisfied are said to be *frustrated*. The source of frustration can be either within the individual himself or else imposed by his environment. Often, frustrations arise from conflicting needs, some of which cannot be satisfied without frustrating others. In order to preserve the integrity of his personality, a person has to find some way of resolving unsatisfied needs.

Certain largely subconscious devices used by people to resolve frustrations are called *defense mechanisms*. One such mechanism, *rationalization*, consists in turning away from a desired goal while explaining one's failure to achieve it in personally acceptable terms. Familiar forms of rationalization include *projection, delusion, repression, negativism*, and *regression*. Another defense mechanism is *substitution*, whereby an individual pursues a new goal in place of one he cannot obtain. When the individual actually retains his attachment to the original goal and tries to make up for it by pursuing the substitute goal vigorously, the mechanism is known as *compensa-*

tion. *Identification*, another defense mechanism, consists in mentally associating one's self with another person who is able to achieve a goal. *Fantasy*, the final mechanism, is one in which imaginary identification takes place.

Need satisfaction is closely related to status and role. *Status* is the position one holds within a group, and *role* is the consequence of occupying a status. *Role behavior* refers to the way an individual performs a role, and *role personality* refers to that part of his total personality which he exhibits in connection with a role. Different roles sometimes *conflict*, or compete with one another for an individual's attention. Anyone who holds a given status automatically has a given level of prestige. However, he must earn esteem.

Ascribed statuses and roles are those automatically conferred upon people according to membership in broad categories, such as sex or age. *Achieved* statuses and roles are those an individual attains for himself. People often feel thwarted because some status ascribed to them by society prevents them from achieving in proportion to their abilities.

GLOSSARY

anxiety   a tense emotional state of apprehensiveness, lacking a clear focus on a specific object. Anxiety can result from prolonged or continual frustrations.

compensation   a defense mechanism involving emphasis on a new goal that is really a substitute for an old lost objective.

defense mechanism   behavior motivated by a person's wish to preserve the integrity of his self-image in a frustrating or potentially embarrassing situation.

delusion   a form of rationalization involving the insistence that one is capable of achieving a goal despite strong evidence to the contrary.

esteem   the evaluation of an individual's performance in his role, as determined by others.

fantasy   imagined experiences, usually pleasant and satisfying. Can be used as a defense mechanism to overcome frustration in real life.

identification   a social-psychological process in which a person mentally associates himself with someone else's values and achievements. Can be a defense mechanism.

negativism   a form of rationalization consisting of refusal to cooperate with those one blames for a frustration.

prestige   the social recognition and regard that is "built into" a status rank.

projection   a form of rationalization wherein a person attributes his own shortcomings to others.

rationalization   a defense mechanism in which a person subconsciously tries to give an acceptable argument justifying his own failure to achieve a goal.

regression   a kind of rationalization characterized by a return to a childish pattern of behavior in the attempt to get what one wants.

repression   a kind of rationalization wherein the person excludes a painful event from his memory.

role   the pattern of behavior associated with a particular status position.

role conflict   incompatability between 2 or more roles that a person is supposed to be playing.

status   a position in the social structure of a group.   May be *ascribed* (assigned automatically by virtue of a characteristic) or *achieved* (earned by the individual's own choices and efforts).

sublimation   a form of substitution in which a person puts energies that would have gone into one activity into achievement of a "higher" goal instead.

substitution   a defense mechanism that allows one to overcome frustration by converting desire for one goal into desire for another.

SUGGESTED READINGS

Banton, Michael.   *Roles: An Introduction to the Study of Social Relations.*   New York: Basic Books, 1965.

Benedict, Ruth.   *The Chrysanthemum and the Sword: Patterns of Japanese Culture.*   Cleveland: Meridian Books, 1967, originally published in 1946.   This pleasantly written analysis of family life and sexual identity development in Japanese society provides excellent comparative data with our own culture.

Berne, Eric.   *Games People Play: The Psychology of Human Relationships.*   New York: Grove, 1964.

Goffman, Erving.   *The Presentation of Self in Everyday Life.*   New York: Doubleday, 1959.   While this is probably his best known work, others, particularly *Asylums,* New York: Doubleday, 1961, and *Stigma,* Prentice-Hall, 1963, are also highly recommended.

Whyte, Jr., W. H.   *The Organization Man.*   New York: Simon & Schuster, 1956.   Whyte presents evidence and good writing to explain role behavior in terms of a person's position within various structures.   For example, he can predict which people in a housing project are most likely to be social leaders on the basis of where their house is located in relation to others.

Nobody gives A DAMN!

9

ALIENATION

In 1973, a poll conducted for a U.S. Senate committee reported that 55 percent of Americans in the sample considered themselves to be alienated. The term alienation has been the subject of much of modern fiction, poetry, drama, and art, as well as a major concern of modern social scientists. In terms of sociology, Melvin Seeman has written that "in one form or another, the concept of alienation dominates both the contemporary literature and the history of sociological thought." What is alienation? Who are the alienated? How do people cope with this phenomenon? These are questions we will be dealing with in this chapter.

WHAT IS ALIENATION?

The word *alienation* has a long history. In the law, the term was used to describe the transfer of property or ownership. For example, after the Reformation, alienation of Church property meant a transfer of ownership to the state or individuals. In addition, under the law it used to be common to sue a third party in divorce cases for alienation of affection. Still another meaning of the word connected it with insanity. Even today, in Europe, an alienist is one who treats persons suffering from mental disorders. But gradually the word came to be used to identify feelings of aloneness from others. It is in this usage that the term is meaningful today.

Recognition of Alienation

Expressions of alienation have existed throughout recorded history. Four thousand years ago, an Egyptian chronicler lamented that ". . . No more do we hear anyone laugh . . . Great men and small agree in saying: 'would that I had never been born.' . . . No public office stands open where it should, and the masses are like timid sheep without a shepherd." Most writers and social scientists, however, are concerned with alienation as an outgrowth of modern industrial society. The depersonalization of work, the crowding together of "faceless masses" in huge cities, the growth of big government, big business, big bureaucracy, the tedium of mass culture— these are the factors that contribute to the new alienation of the modern world. The extent of the phenomenon is described by psychologist Erich Fromm: "Alienation," he writes, "as we find it in modern society is almost total; it pervades the relationship of man to his work, to the things he consumes, to his fellows, and to himself."

Alienation has been a concern of social scientists since the 19th century. Karl Marx had much to do with developing an awareness of the concept. Marx saw alienation as a major outgrowth of the capitalist system; the working person is cut off from the satisfaction he once had in skillful execution of a product, and he becomes merely an extension of machinery owned by someone else. He sees himself as an object and treats others as if they, too, existed only to be manipulated.

Many writers, including sociologists, expanded on and modified the ideas of Marx. In his class study *Suicide*, 1897, Emile Durkheim sought to explain the factors that alienate persons to the point of their own self-destruction. Earlier, William Graham Sumner had stressed the importance of folkways and mores to an individual, and throughout his analysis was conscious of the penalties alienation from these norms caused. Robert E. Park and Everett V. Stonequist were early sociologists who developed the concept of the *marginal man;* an individual who is alienated from 2 or more cultures, never being able to become a full participant in either one. More recently, Robert Merton has stressed the breakdown of values as the major form of alienation, emphasizing the societal role rather than the individual one. And David Riesman and his associates, in *The Lonely Crowd*, made the concept central to their study.

From such studies, a basic definition of the term can be formulated. Alienation may be defined as a *feeling of estrangement from one's society and culture*. Thus, the values and norms that other members of the society share seem meaningless to the alienated person, and this contributes to feelings of loneliness and frustration. This definition is broad and has been used to cover a wide range of psychosocial problems. In an attempt to provide greater precision in dealing with the concept, sociologist Melvin Seeman has suggested that alienation is not 1 entity, but rather a composite of various components. Seeman has identified 6 different elements that make up what we refer to as alienation. These facets are, in Seeman's terms, *individual powerlessness, meaninglessness, normlessness, cultural estrangement, self-estrangement,* and *social isolation.* A brief summary of these can help clarify the study.

Individual powerlessness. In the face of the tremendous power and complexities of social systems, one person alone seems totally lacking in power. In a mass society in which primary groups seem to be eclipsed by secondary groups, it is difficult for the individual to feel that his efforts count. Whether one is voting, working in a factory, or shopping at a supermarket, the person is often unable to see that he or she makes a difference in any endeavor. Psychologist Ernest Schachtel suggests that this aspect of alienation is symbolized by the fact that a person's identity is fixed by the paper certificates he is forced to carry—driver's license, social security card, and so on.

Meaninglessness. Alienation, of course, goes beyond the submergence of individuality to social structures and processes. It incorporates the idea that everybody is insignificant, inconsequential, or superfluous. Life may seem dull and flat. Modern drama is particularly concerned with this outlook on modern life, perhaps most noticeably in the theater of the absurd.

German sociologist Georg Simmel argued that this feeling of meaninglessness was an outgrowth of urban living. The city person, he argued, is constantly faced by a multitude of rushing impressions which he is unable to handle emotionally. In defense, the individual becomes more and more detached and intellectual in his approach to life, emotionally insensitive to the stimuli that bombard him. Suzanne Langer, in *Philosophy in a New Key,* associates this meaninglessness with the city dweller's lack of connection with nature. Her thesis is that once we lose awareness of the motions of sun and moon, the growth of crops or the change of tides, we have lost a basic spiritual sense of the order of things and life has less meaning.

If individuals or groups reach the state where life is regarded as completely meaningless, alienation can produce severe mental disorder. Alienated from their present circumstances, they may become receptive to whatever new visions they may encounter. Sociologists who have studied alienation report that alienated persons and groups are eager to engage in what they call a search for meaning. Such persons or groups are susceptible to almost any simplistic policy proposed by a charismatic leader. In a certain program or in a leader's enthusiasm, alienated individuals can find a direction and a sense of purpose and personal worth.

Normlessness. Normlessness is a condition in which the individual feels a lack of social values to guide him in different situations. Without the guidance of norms, the consequences of any action are judged to be of equal value whatever the alternatives. Normlessness can be the result of either of 2 conditions. One is a feeling by an individual that none of society's norms have meaning. The other form of normlessness can arise when there are many norms to choose from. Since he or she cannot make a choice among the values offered, an individual may withdraw from choosing any set of norms.

This state of normlessness is also known as *anomie,* the term used by Emile Durkheim. Durkheim, however, stressed the societal factor in anomie, in contrast to the individual's response to the condition. Thus, in Durkheim's definition, anomie referred to the social and cultural structure, not to the people confronting that structure. Therefore, anomie involved the breakdown of the norms of the society, resulting in confusion for the individuals. The experience of conflicting loyalties and values is part of each individual's condition today.

Cultural estrangement. To be alienated is to be estranged from one's own culture. Historically, there have been numerous expatriates from their cultures who lived or wandered far from their original homes. They were embittered and eager to discuss the defects of their native lands with anyone who would listen. *Émigrés* are particular types of expatriates who have fled their society because they can no longer tolerate the political conditions at home. Those who left France, Russia, or Germany during political upheavals were émigrés. So too were Americans who turned from their country during the American Revolution. Among recent émigrés have been those who moved to other countries because they disagreed with American government policy in Southeast Asia.

One does not have to travel in order to become estranged from one's culture. A person can remain at home and still feel that he does not participate in his culture. Many people, for example, feel estranged from the materialism of modern society, and see little value in the money economy or the vast production of consumer goods. There is a tendency among those who are "turned off" to feel separated from their culture.

Self-estrangement. As Seeman noted, alienated persons strongly resent their feelings of powerlessness and the emptiness of their lives. Many alienated persons, however, do value their own potential. They see a great difference between what they really are and what they might become. Thus, alienated persons often describe themselves as unfulfilled or unproductive. Alienated persons are at odds with their culture and even with people close to them. But it is their internal struggle with themselves that keeps them in turmoil. Sometimes their subjective, inner distress is acted out in frequent cynicism or in hostile episodes that deepen their unhappiness.

What many are doing by such overt behavior is often asking for help. Psychological counseling and group therapy have often been able to help such individuals gain a degree of self-respect. This partially explains why we observed in the discussion of attitudes that the most important attitude is toward the self. One's self-attitude determines more than any other factor how one will handle life situations.

Social isolation. Finally, alienation carries with it the feeling of being absolutely alone, excluded from the meaningful company of others. It seems to the person involved that no one else has suffered in quite the same way. He or she feels this to be a unique and unshared deprivation. Of course physical isolation is not necessary to create this sort of feeling. The loneliness of a crowded city can be just as terrifying.

Social isolation is particularly devastating because it is the extreme opposite of what sociologists have called the essential explanation of humanity's achievements and qualities; that is, that humans are social animals. Without others, the development of human potential is impossible. He is without reference points to judge where he is, who he is, or what he would like to become.

By discovering that others have experienced similar feelings of social isolation, the first step in the direction of potential recovery has been taken. The basis for many sensitivity and encounter groups has been this desire to reach out and make contact with others. Many of the socially isolated, however, make only falteringly feeble contact with others and suffer the consequences of being lost in the "lonely crowd."

"*Put me down as 'Don't know and don't want to know.'*"

THE EXPRESSION OF ALIENATION

People may be alienated and not be aware of it. Studies of such groups as voters, factory workers, bureaucrats, and students create a picture of the alienated as quiet, accepting, and apathetic. Research suggests that the alienated do not even have to feel estranged—they may simply become automatons whose actions are controlled by outside forces. These are the alienated C. Wright Mills refers to as the "cheerful robots."

Others who are alienated, however, are acutely aware of their feelings of separateness or aloneness. Rather than accepting "lives of quiet desparation," they seek some means of expressing their alienation. Some individuals may engage in antisocial behavior; others will seek escape, including the ultimate escape of committing suicide. Many find they can join together with others who face similar problems, thus forming their own dissident groups. Sociologists have called this tendency to join a *consciousness of kind.*

Fighting the System

One means of expressing alienation is to attack those aspects of society from which the

PERSPECTIVE

LITERARY EXPRESSION OF ALIENATION

Much of modern literature is deeply concerned with the plight of the alienated. Alienation, in fact, may be considered the central theme of modern writing. Here are two brief illustrations:

1. Fyodor Dostoyevsky, in *Notes From the Underground,* attacks the growing reliance of 19th century society on science and materialism. A rational approach to life, he argues, would only increase humanity's alienation:

> The only thing one can't say (about human history) is that it's rational. The very word sticks in one's throat. And, indeed, this is the odd thing that is continually happening: there are continually turning up in life moral and rational persons, sages and lovers of humanity, who make it their object to live all their lives as morally and rationally as possible, to be, so to speak, a light to their neighbors simply in order to show them that it is possible to live morally and rationally in this world. And yet we all know that those very people sooner or later have been false to themselves, playing some queer trick, often a most unseemly one. Now I ask you: what can be expected of man since he is being endowed with such strange qualities? Shower upon him every earthly blessing, drown him in a sea of happiness, so that nothing but bubbles of bliss can be seen on the surface; give him economic prosperity, such that he should have nothing else to do but sleep, eat cakes and busy himself with the continuation of the species, and even then out of sheer ingratitude, sheer spite, man would play you some nasty trick. He would even risk his cakes and would deliberately desire the most fatal rubbish, the most uneconomical absurdity, simply to introduce into all this positive good sense his fatal fantastic element. It is just his fantastic dreams, his vulgar folly, that he will desire to retain, simply in order to prove to himself—as though that were so necessary—that men still are men and not the keys of a piano, which the laws of nature threaten to control so completely that soon one will be able to desire nothing but by the calendar. . . .

2. And, in a more modern vein, James Baldwin, in *Another Country,* describes a man for whom nothing else remains but self-destruction:

> . . . The train gasped and moaned to a halt. He had thought that he would get off here, but he watched the people move toward the doors, watched the doors open, watched them leave. It was mainly black people who left. He had thought he would get off here and go home; but he watched the girl who reminded him of his sister as she moved sullenly past white people and stood for a moment on the platform before walking toward the steps. Suddenly he knew that he was never going home anymore.
>
> The train began to move, half-empty now; and with each stop it became lighter; soon the white people who were left looked at him oddly. He felt their stares but he felt far away from them. *You took the best. So why not take the rest?* He got off at the station named for the bridge built to honor the father of his country.
>
> And walked up the steps, into the streets, which were empty. Tall apartment buildings, lightless, loomed against the dark sky and seemed to be watching him, seemed to be pressing down on him. The bridge was nearly over his head, intolerably high; but he did not yet see the water. He felt it, he smelled it. He thought how he had never before understood how an animal could smell water. But it was over there, past the highway, where he could see the speeding cars.
>
> Then he stood on the bridge, looking over, looking down. . . .

individual feels estranged. For many people in the 1960's and 1970's an important activity has been protest against the materialism, the militarism, and the rigidity of American social structures. The waves of unrest that have swept across college campuses in the United States have had their counterparts in such countries as France, Japan, Mexico, Greece, Korea, and Thailand.

Particular grievances in each case may differ, but the movements tend to follow similar patterns. Formerly passive students object to infringements of their rights as persons and demand an acceptance of policies they believe appropriate. A self-appointed leadership usually exists to press these demands and to rally uncommitted students to its cause.

Typically, there is a period of quiet organization in which grievances accumulate. Then, there is an incident that touches off discontent and demonstrations, sometimes followed by violent collective behavior. Such was the pattern in the Free Speech Movement at the University of California at Berkeley, in the taking over of buildings at Columbia, and in the display of loaded weapons at Cornell. The loss of lives at Jackson State, the University of Wisconsin, and at Kent State gave cause for even deeper alienation for some and for a determination that these overreactions never occur again. Particularly in the years between 1968 and 1970, the country seemed in danger of becoming hopelessly polarized between the "anti-Establishment forces" and those who were considered the defenders of that Establishment.

The protests of minority groups can also be seen as an expression of alienation by those who feel estranged from the majority culture. During the 1950's and early 1960's, the Civil Rights movement was normally a nonviolent form of protest. Increased frustration led to outbursts of violence in the late 1960's. In the Watts area of Los Angeles, for example, blacks

had long been alienated but had remained generally passive and indifferent. Then, in one burst of protest, large groups of community people exploded into rioting, looting, and burning.

These forms of activism serve important functions for those who are alienated. For one thing, active protest involves others and this creates new feelings of loyalty to a group. Second, normlessness is replaced by a sense of values, even though these may not be values recognized by society. And third, such movements provide a way of throwing off one's apathy and feelings of powerlessness.

Escaping the System

There are a number of ways in which individuals and groups seek to cope with alienation by escaping it. Some people manage to avoid feelings of aloneness or rootlessness by concentrating on the routines of life. In *The Organization Man*, for example, William H. Whyte describes individuals who become deeply involved in the mechanized details of work and carefully avoid questioning the ultimate value of purpose of what they are doing. Others may seek escape by devoting themselves to acquiring material things or submerging themselves in television viewing.

Another escape route, the use of drugs, has become a major social problem in the past 2 decades. Normally, drugs had been thought of in terms of the "hard stuff" like opium and heroin, and addicts were the very dregs of society. Beginning in the 1950's, health officials became alarmed at the widespread use of so-called "socially acceptable" drugs, particularly diet pills as stimulants and various forms of tranquilizers as "downers." The bored suburban housewife, it was discovered, was just as likely to seek escape from alienation through drugs as was the beatnik in Green-

THE VARIOUS PATHS TO SOCIOLOGICAL KNOWLEDGE
DAVID RIESMAN

A very few modern sociologists have made important contributions by establishing important theories—theories that seem to ring true but have not been empirically proved, disproved, or modified. Such "pseudoscientific" writers often create considerable controversy, but their ideas prove too provocative and challenging to be dismissed. Perhaps this is the best way to characterize the work of David Riesman and his associates in *The Lonely Crowd*, published in 1958.

On the surface, Riesman's theories appear relatively simple: He distinguished among 3 different social types, each reflecting a model of conformity to social control, and each representing the "national character" of particular types of society. He labeled these types as: tradition-directed; inner-directed; and other-directed.

The tradition-directed person is the product of a stable, preindustrial society, where one encounters a strong loyalty to tradition and resistance to change. The tradition-directed person accepts the standards of his society without question and finds stability and security in such acceptance. ". . . The individual in a society dependent on tradition-direction has a well-defined functional relationship to other members of the group."

Social changes, such as those occasioned by the Reformation and the Industrial Revolution, as well as demographic changes, such as population expansion, lead to the breakdown of tradition-directed societies. They are replaced by those characterized by the "inner-directed types." There is a sense of expansion and growth in such societies, which leads to exploration, invention, colonizing, and the accumulation of capital. The inner-directed individual is reaching for generalized goals, rather than being guided by tradition, and so considerable nonconformity is allowed and rewarded in the name of achieving those goals.

The mobility, expansion, and exploration of the inner-directed society leads inexorably to the next "historical type." When the economy has expanded to a certain level, when areas of open space and growth have been used up, the situation develops where there is abundance, leisure, little work, and crowding. It is at this point that people discover that "increasingly, *other people* are the problem, not the material environment."

The new, "other-directed" person has developed as the emergent American type in the years since World War II. These individuals now begin to respond to those around them for their sense of direction: "What is common to all the other-directed people is that their contemporaries are the source of direction for the individual—either those known to him or those with whom he is indirectly acquainted, through friends and through the mass media. . . . This mode of keeping in touch with others permits a close behavior conformity, not through drill in behavior itself, as in the tradition-directed character, but rather through an exceptional sensitivity to the actions and wishes of others."

The delineation of social types was not new—although Riesman's is probably more widely used than others—but what was startling about *The Lonely Crowd* was the manner in which Riesman used his typology to make incisive comments about almost all aspects of American life. Many Americans had come to feel themselves to be lost in the lonely crowd of modern mass society, and Riesman offered some explanations as well as some hope.

Riesman's discussion of sex in the different types of society offers an illustration of the wide range of his commentary. For the inner-directed person, Riesman argues, sex was important, but secondary to other considerations such as success in business. Marital sex often became a rather grim affair, the woman being expected to subordinate her sexuality to the other concerns of economic and social life. Sex outside of marriage tended to be sordid and repressive; jokes or humorous treatment of sex in literature was allowable, but serious study of the subject was frowned upon.

The other-directed person is sexually liberated, but this liberation creates problems. Since the other-directed person is gaining his sense of direction from others, sexual performance becomes competitive, and the individual develops anxieties about how he measures up with others. Part of the problem, in Riesman's analysis, was that the individual had no way to judge his or her performance in relation to others. Many readers of *The Lonely Crowd* identified their own anxieties with his discussion; the fact that such personal uncertainties remain a central topic in such settings as encounter groups suggests that the problem remains a major concern to many Americans.

Such broad social comments caused considerable criticism of Riesman by his fellow sociologists. However, this approach also won him, in the words of one sociologist, "a host of concerned readers who were wrestling with the problems of what it means to be an American today."

wich Village. Despite government efforts to regulate the distribution of such drugs, great numbers of Americans still look to them as a form of relief.

A more noticeable aspect of the drug age, of course, has been the widespread use of marijuana products and the hallucinogens. Marijuana may be a special case. Harmful effects for the drug have not been established and there are indications that "grass" may soon become as widely accepted as alcohol, although its sale or possession is still illegal.

An area of special concern for social scientists is the tendency for the use of drugs to be a basis for group formation. The "conscious altering" drugs such as LSD, which became popular during the 1960's, have often served to mark a kind of fraternity of the alienated, mostly white middle-class young people who were seemingly expressing dissatisfaction with the materialism, oppressiveness, and moral hypocrisy of society. Andrew Malcolm, a member of the Addiction Research Foundation of Ontario, Canada, compares the group use of hallucinogens and hard drugs to the initiation rites of religious groups. According to Dr. Malcolm, the drug use serves the dual purpose of sealing the initiate's commitment to the group (because the act is illegal and makes him an outlaw to the society) and producing a mental state receptive to "conversion." That is, the drug serves to break down the rational mental processes so that conversion becomes a matter of exaggerated sense perceptions and distorted emotions. Along with others concerned with drug addiction, Malcolm expresses the fear that this form of drug use tends to attract and mislead "the immature, the mentally disturbed, the socially disadvantaged, and the psychopathic."

Another method of dropping out by those who feel estranged from society has been the search for alternative lifestyles, including the commune movement. The idea of a group breaking off from the mainstream of society is certainly not new. Religious groups, such as the Amish and the Hutterites, have purposely separated themselves from society. The Amish, for example, are well known for their reluctance to use any form of modern machinery, and the Hutterites rarely intermarry with outsiders.

During the 1920's and 1930's, a colony of alienated American writers and artists expatriated themselves from American society. Most of this "lost generation" established themselves in Paris. The Beat movement of the 1950's was another attempt by alienated individuals to create some sense of community, primarily in Greenwich Village. The commune movement that developed during the 1960's has had a wider geographical distribution and a greater variety of lifestyles. Communes range from the houseful of people sharing a "family" life but going out to conventional jobs in the city to virtually self-sufficient farm communities. Accurate statistics on the number of communes are impossible to obtain because many of the communes form and dissolve so often. However, a spokesman for the National Institute of Health estimated that in 1971 there were more than 3000 communes in the United States.

Like earlier American movements toward communal living, some of the communes are built around religious, economic, or philosophical ideals. Many, though, involve no particular creed but are rather the result of people's sense of belonging together. Some social scientists, such as anthropologist Margaret Mead, see in the communes an attempt to return to the tribalism of the past in order to escape the alienation of modern society. Despite the temporary nature of many communes, along with economic or social failings, the value of the communes probably lies in providing alienated persons with an important sense of belonging. Sociologist Hugh Gardner writes, "What's happening now is mostly family farms and groups of couples dividing their collective meadows. Not really communes, but still communities . . . and in our age that's the significant event, not their ideological purity."

The Urge to Join and Belief Groups

The hippie counterculture, the commune movement, and the drug cult suggest that a major response to alienation is for the individual to seek out some group that will help him gain feelings of belonging, meaning, and a sense of purpose. In the 1960's and 1970's a number of "belief groups" have emerged which seem to serve these purposes. Many Americans, for example, have sought solace in religious groups—not in the traditional established churches, but in new religious movements that seem more responsive to their needs. Zen Buddhism was once espoused in this country primarily by a handful of the bohemian beat generation of the 1950's. Today, there is a wide variety of cults based on Eastern religions, ranging from transcendental meditation to the Spartan lifestyle of the Hari Krishnans.

Other religious groups, sometimes referred to collectively as the "Jesus movement," have splintered off from Christian churches. Appealing primarily to the young, these groups now include a great number of churches, "homes," "centers," and other formal or informal organizations. The beliefs and religious works of people in such groups take precedence over concerns about job or social status. The greater society from which they are alienated ceases to have importance for them; their faith forms the basis for personal and social integration within the group.

Other popular beliefs, less powerful perhaps than those centered on religion, are equally defiant of the rationality and materialism of the majority society. Enthusiasm for astrology, witchcraft, and the occult has grown almost to a movement in the 1970's. The back-to-nature movement, the revival of handcrafts, pride in race, sexual liberation— all have attracted people who feel alienated from the "Establishment."

The widespread popularity of various kinds of encounter groups also represents the "urge to join." The very nature of these groups suggests their relationship to alienation: the people who join often have never met before, and may have no common bond such as occupation, beliefs, interests, or neighborhood. Their major purpose in joining an encounter group is to build relationships, to release emotions, and to seek honesty in human interaction.

SUMMARY

Alienation is a feeling of estrangement from one's society and culture. The elements of alienation, in sociologist Melvin Seeman's terms, include:

Individual powerlessness in the face of social complexities, *meaninglessness* in the sense of a loss of direction or purpose, *normlessness* in the refusal to follow any group's expectations, *cultural estrangement* from one's own heritage, *self-estrangement* in the sense of feeling unfulfilled, and *social isolation* in the sense of being out of contact with all other persons.

People may be alienated and not know it. They act as "cheerful robots" controlled by outside forces, while other alienated persons engage in antisocial behavior, try to escape, or "fight the system." Some attempts to attack and change society, such as student activism and minority protests, have provided group unity, new values, and a sense of power to the estranged. Escapes from the sense of alienation include concentration on the material details of life, the use of drugs, and the formation of alternative lifestyles, such as the commune movement, outside the mainstream of society.

The commune movement, drug cult, and hippie counterculture suggest that a major response to alienation has been to seek a group that will give the individual a sense of belonging and meaning. Certain belief groups have grown up in the 1960's and 1970's that also serve this purpose, including religious groups, occult-centered groups, and encounter groups.

GLOSSARY

alienation   a feeling of estrangement from one's society and culture.

anomie   state of normlessness.

consciousness of kind   a feeling of identification with people who are similar to oneself. A group bond.

émigré   a person who leaves his native country because he cannot tolerate the political conditions there.

encounter group   a group of people who meet to interact very directly and honestly for purposes of psychological therapy.

estrangement   *cultural estrangement* is a sense of being distanced from one's own society or culture; *self-estrangement* occurs when a person senses a gap between who he is in his thoughts and the way he behaves.

marginal man   a person who is alienated from 2 or more cultures, never able to become a full participant in either one.

norm   a group-shared expectation of certain behavior.

SUGGESTED READINGS

Camus, Albert. *The Stranger.* New York: Vintage Books, 1946. This existential novel deals with the alienation of a man who does not show the degree of emotion and compassion expected of him.

Ellison, Ralph. *Invisible Man.* New York: Random House, 1947. A story of a young black's experiences in the North and in the South. It is the odyssey of one man's search for his own identity.

Fromm, Erich. *Escape from Freedom.* New York: Farrar, 1941. (Avon paperback). A leading psychiatrist explores the aspects of freedom which many find difficult to live with, creating a sense of being lost or rootless in a society which requires individual direction.

Josephson, Eric and Josephson, Mary. (eds.). *Man Alone: Alienation in Modern Society.* New York: Dell Publishing Co., 1962, 1971. Essays, magazine articles, social scientific studies, autobiographies, and excerpts from novels are combined to present varied perspectives on the subject. The long introduction by the Josephsons provides an excellent overview of alienation as well as relating the different readings in the anthology.

Keil, Charles. *Urban Blues.* Chicago: University of Chicago Press, 1966. A study of prominent black blues figures, such as B. B. King, Muddy Waters, and Howlin' Wolf as representatives of the ability of a people to transcend the alienating consequences of discrimination and poverty.

DEVIANCE AND SOCIAL CONTROL

An individual branded as a deviant is a social outcast, an unwelcome member of society. A persistent violator of the society's norms and mores, the deviant is not only regarded as an inferior human being, but is likely to face the danger of criminal sanctions. In the minds of many, this "outsider" is, if anything, worse than a criminal because the unwelcome behavior represents what is considered to be a perversion of the society's ideals. The deviants, for their part, often have little recourse but to seek the company of fellow outcasts, often creating whole communities of the stigmatized. In this chapter, we will consider the special problems—for the individual and for the society—created by such forms of deviance as alcoholism, homosexuality, prostitution, drug addiction, and mental illness.

DEVIANCE

In complex modern societies, absolute adherence to all norms and mores is neither possible nor expected. A certain amount of nonconformity, in fact, is often regarded as a virtue. However, there is likely to be consensus that certain forms of deviant behavior are not to be tolerated, and the norms and mores involved are usually supported by bodies of law. Crimes against persons or property are normally areas where there is little disagreement over the need for social controls. People generally agree that such crimes as murder, rape, arson, robbery, and so on are not to be tolerated. Other forms of deviance, such as homosexuality or drug addiction, raise important questions about what sort of sanctions should be applied—or whether sanctions should be applied at all.

Changing Concepts of Deviance

In the first decade of this century, a woman named Mary Baker Eddy proclaimed a new body of religious beliefs. To many people in the small New England community in which she lived, she was considered strange and eccentric. To some, the idea that anyone would invent a new religion was a clear sign of mental instability. A move was made to have Mary Baker Eddy committed to a mental institution. With characteristic vigor, this frail woman defended herself and managed to avoid commitment. Her new sect, the Christian Science Church, has since become firmly established.

If Mary Baker Eddy had made her pronouncement in the 1960's or 1970's, it is not likely that anyone would have been upset by her beliefs. In fact, she would have been merely one of many who were establishing or reviving churches. Behavior that was considered dangerously antisocial at the turn of the century came to be considered quite acceptable 60 years later.

As Mary Baker Eddy's case suggests, people's ideas of what constitutes deviance, including insanity, is subject to change. At any given time, the definition of deviance will depend on the consensus of the particular reference group. In a homosexual community, for example, having sex relations with members of the opposite sex might be considered a deviation from group standards. In the larger society, on the other hand, heterosexuality is the norm and homosexuality is considered a serious form of deviance. Similarly, in Skid Row society, a person who looks for a job is likely to be ostracized by the group—he has deviated from the group's expectations. In defining deviance, sociologist H. S. Becker states simply that "deviant behavior is behavior that people so label."

An illustration of a changing concept of deviance is provided by the use of marijuana. A generation ago, smoking pot was an activity associated with a few Bohemian enclaves, such as Greenwich Village, or with the more unpleasant aspects of ghetto life. The suburban, middle class party-goer was not likely to suggest that a joint be passed around. A person who did so would probably have been regarded as some kind of "dope addict," particularly since little differentiation was made between marijuana and other drugs. Today, of course, marijuana usage is far more acceptable, and as much as 10 percent of the population engages in it. However, as late as the mid-1970's the American people have shown an unwillingness to change the laws regarding marijuana possession and sale. The behavior is tolerated rather than accepted widely, and much of the stigma formerly associated with this form of drug usage has disappeared.

Changing Concepts of Controlling Deviance

Just as concepts of deviance are subject to change over time, so are ideas about how deviant behavior should be controlled. Many types of deviant behavior, for example, were traditionally thought of as criminal offenses and little differentiation was made among types of deviance. The man who stole to feed him family might be hanged along with the murderer. The homosexual or prostitute might be stoned or maimed. Criminologist Nicholas Kittrie states, "To be poor, to beg in public, or to be mentally distracted was as much an offense as to commit a violent crime. And whether poor, diseased, or delinquent, all those charged with deviant status or acts were grouped together for equal treatment in the criminal process."

Gradually, during the 19th century, changes were made in the criminal law with the general purpose of "making the punishment fit the crime." The most severe penalties were reserved for the most serious crimes; other forms of deviant behavior were likely to be punished with prison sentences. The deviant was still regarded as a criminal, but the crime was something less serious than murder.

In this century, ideas about how to control deviancy have changed still further. Increasingly, reform efforts have been directed toward the *rehabilitation* of those guilty of crimes or antisocial behavior. Instead of punishing homosexuals, for example, those who favor the "therapeutic" approach urge that these individuals be regarded as "sick." Punishment, it is argued, should be replaced by treatment.

Some social scientists feel that the trend toward therapeutic treatment of deviants and those convicted of crimes can present serious problems. Thurman Arnold, for example, ar-

gues that the criminal committed to a mental institution may suffer the injustice of being "incarcerated at the whim of the board of psychiatrists for a much longer time than would have been possible had he not been acquitted on the ground of insanity." Law professor Richard Wasserstrom raises questions about the morality of changing behavior through chemicals, operations, or therapy. "Imprisonment," he states, "may be a poor way to induce a person to behave differently in the future, but imprisonment may, nonetheless, permit him to remain the same person throughout." And Nicholas Kittrie warns that "the therapeutic state" may threaten the individual's "right to be different."

Despite these objections, most observers agree that both therapy and criminal law will be used to control deviation for some time to come. For the individual labeled as deviant these dual controls can create confusion and self-doubt—the person is stigmatized as both criminal and sick. However, throughout history those "guilty" of deviant behavior have been subject to a variety of sanctions. For instance, religious sanctions probably weighed far more heavily on the deviant in the past than they do today. Traditionally in Western societies, the deviant was regarded not only as a criminal but a sinner. The homosexual, the prostitute, the mentally ill were considered to have offended God's law. Usually, the offending individuals would be literally cast out of the church; they were cut off not only from society but from the religion they believed in.

The Functions of Deviance

As we indicated in Chapter 3, all societies develop some system of social control. Norms, mores, and laws, based on the values of the particular culture, form the standards of behavior idealized by the society. For the society to survive, sanctions must be applied to those who refuse to conform. In other words, concepts of deviance outline the limits of acceptable behavior—behavior that goes beyond those limits is controlled in the interests of order and protection of the value system.

At the same time, many sociologists suggest that the existence of deviance serves positive functions for the society. Deviance may help in the redefining of the society's values and in creating a sense of cohesion. Those who conform to norms and mores regard themselves as normal, as members of the in-group; feelings of group unity are strengthened by the presence of nonconformists, those who are not normal and are therefore members of an out-group. Lewis Coser states the matter this way: "In the process of uniting itself against deviance, the community not only revives and maintains common sentiments but creatively establishes moral rules and redefines 'normal' behavior." And George Herbert Mead argued that "the attitude of hostility toward the lawbreaker has the unique advantage of uniting all members of the community."

Some forms of deviance can be said to perform positive functions by contributing to innovation. It can be argued that there would be little social change if some individuals were not willing to deviate from the society's norms. For example, until the 19th century, a physician who tried to learn more about the human body by performing autopsies was considered a danger to society and subject to criminal sanctions. A number of doctors refused to conform, believing instead in certain values that clashed with those of the larger society. Out of this conflict gradually emerged a new system of values which holds that research through autopsies on humans performs an important service. Similarly, many artists, writers, inventors, scientists, and political radicals engaged in behavior that was considered bizarre or deviant by their contemporaries but their acts were later lauded as important pioneering efforts.

THE SOCIAL OUTCASTS

In a complex modern society probably every individual, at some time in life, finds that he or she is in the role of the outsider, a person who, in H. S. Becker's words, is "outside the circle of 'normal' members of the group." For one reason or another, the person is cut off from the opportunities, rewards, and pleasures enjoyed by others. Racial or ethnic minorities, the poor, the aged, the young, women, war veterans, draft resisters, police officers—members of all these categories might feel the pressures and disappointments of being outsiders.

Those whom society labels as deviant may find it even more difficult to cast off the status of outsider and they may also live with the constant danger of criminal sanctions. Employment, recreation, social contacts, and personal freedom may all be affected by people's reaction to them as deviants. In this section, we will survey some of the special problems faced by specific categories of deviants.

Homosexuals

Practically all people are raised in heterosexual families, and the socialization process includes training for heterosexual roles. Because of the heavy emphasis on heterosexuality in our society, there is practically no way for a family to be prepared for the announcement by a son or daughter that he or she is homosexual. Similarly, the homosexual must deal with his sexual feelings within the framework of familial and societal expectations; the individual who becomes aware of homosexual tendencies is likely to face enormous waves of guilt, whether the self-discovery is made in adolescence or later in life. And since, in addition, severe social sanctions are applied against homosexuals, it is not surprising that the majority of homosexuals try to hide their sexual identity. The secrecy, of course, can increase feelings of guilt and shame.

The person who openly proclaims his or her homosexuality is exposed to constant treatment as an inferior human being. In describing his own struggles, writer Donald Cory (*The Homosexual in America*, Chilton Co., 1960) states: "Throughout his life, from the moment he awakens for the first time to the impact of the realization not only that he is a homosexual, but as such is part of a despised group of humanity, an individual is exposed to the propaganda that he is 'not as good' as other people. He is told or hears that he (or his like, with whom he must identify himself) is 'almost a man,' is 'half a man,' and that he is a degenerate, a deviate, a pervert . . . I have (even) heard the contempt of the world repeated by many of my gay friends."

There are no precise figures on how many people are members of this outcast group in American society. Studies suggest that about 3 million males and 1 million females are completely homosexual (as opposed to bisexual or people who have had only brief homosexual relations). The research also suggests that many suffer in a manner similar to that outlined by Cory. For example, reporting on a study of male homosexuals, sociologists William Simon and John H. Gagnon found that "two fifths of these men . . . indicated some serious feelings of regret about being homosexual, giving such reasons as fear of social disapproval or rejection, inability to experience a conventional family life, feelings of guilt or shame, or fear of potential trouble with the law."

Throughout much of Western history, homosexuality has been treated both as a crime and as a violation of God's law. Thus, many state laws refer to it as one of the "unspeakable and abominable crimes against nature." The homosexual, then, is regarded by society as a deviant guilty of an unnatural or perverted act which is also a sin and a violation of the criminal code. In nearly all states, homosexual acts are regarded as a crime punishable with prison sentences ranging up to 15 years.

The laws against homosexual acts are not strictly enforced. One reason for this is a growing body of opinion in American society that there should be complete sexual freedom between consenting adults. Nevertheless, arrests do occur and convictions are upheld by the higher courts. For example, in upholding a state law against homosexual offenses, a California judge in 1970 stated, "The making of unnatural sexual relations a crime is embedded in the history of the common law, and finds its sanction in the broader base of the settled mores of western civilization." And, as sociologist Barry M. Dank argues, even when these laws are not enforced, they ". . . function to degrade the homosexual and are used to justify the legal harassment and discrimination that is directed against the homosexual."

As with other forms of deviance, the tendency in the past few decades has been to regard the homosexual as sick rather than as a criminal. A 1968 manual published by the American Psychiatric Association, for instance, defines homosexuality as a mental disorder. Many homosexuals do regret their sexual deviance and would like to live "normal" heterosexual lives. In such cases, therapy has been useful in helping people overcome homosexual tendencies.

Many homosexuals, however, insist that they are neither mentally disturbed nor criminal, and struggle to gain tolerance, if not full acceptance, by the larger society. And there are ample signs that American attitudes toward homosexuality are changing. A generation ago, for example, the subject was considered taboo in the mass media. Today, newspapers, films, television, and magazines have treated the subject, sometimes with considerable understanding and sensitivity.

In the past 20 years, homosexuals have also made progress toward social tolerance by united action. Homosexual communities, particularly in such cities as New York and San Francisco, provide an environment in which homosexuals can live with freedom. Such movements as the Gay Liberation Front provide a political focus and communication has been expanded through a variety of gay publications.

The nature of homosexuality convinces many sociologists that full acceptance of this outgroup is not likely to occur. As long as children are raised in heterosexual families, parents will want their offspring to be heterosexual. Thus, it is argued, there is always likely to be a degree of hostility toward homosexuality.

Alcoholics

The alcoholic is distinguished from other types of drinkers by the *compulsive* use of alcohol. Drinking may even be distasteful to the alcoholic—and frequently this is the case—but he or she drinks not out of desire but necessity.

The compulsive factor in alcoholism is often progressive and may develop rapidly or slowly. Tens of thousands of people are "hidden" or secret alcoholics. They must drink, but the course of the alcoholism is slow enough to enable them to hide the condition, perhaps even from themselves. For others, the heavy dependence on alcohol develops to

the point where they are rarely sober. Seldon Bacon of the Rutgers Center of Alcohol Studies described the advanced stages of alcoholism this way:

The alcoholic generally lacks interest in anything outside himself and his problems. Such outside interests as he may manifest are usually temporary and directly and immediately related to a desire to show off or achieve some quick benefit. His continual comparison of all things to himself, easy cynicism about anything not connected to himself, self-pity, intense feelings of guilt and increasingly solitary existence, all bear witness to his egocentricity.

Research into the causes and exact nature of alcoholism has not been conclusive. While there is growing evidence of a physiological basis, many researchers continue to stress psychological factors. E. M. Jellinek suggests that dependence on alcohol may be physical for some, psychological for others, and in many cases some combination of the two. Sociological factors, such as environment, group associations, and family life are also likely to be contributing factors. Because of the hidden nature of much alcoholism, figures on the number of alcoholics can only be estimates. According to the National Institute of Alcohol Abuse and Alcoholism, at least 9 million Americans can be classified as alcoholics.

The stereotyped view of the deteriorating life pattern provides a fairly realistic view of how millions of alcoholics have suffered. Loss of employment, estrangement from family and friends, declining physical and mental health—all are common experiences for those suffering from alcoholism. And the alcoholic is caught in a vicious cycle; as problems grow worse, the one escape from them appears to be greater dependence on alcohol.

The alcoholic's problems are aggravated by being treated by others as a deviant. To many Americans, the alcoholic is a drunkard and a social menace, and there are grim statistics to

PROFILE OF THE SKID ROW BUM

Just about every American city of any size has its Skid Row—a neighborhood of flop houses, rundown hotels and cheap saloons. Skid Row is the home of the drifter, the bum, the alcoholic. To most Americans, this strange tawdry world seems like the final burying place of human hopes and ambitions.

Who are the Skid Row bums? What drives them to this fate? Can they be helped? Do they want help?

These questions have intrigued many sociologists and, not surprisingly, there have been a number of studies of Skid Row life. Sometimes these studies have been conducted by participant observation—for weeks or months at a time, the researcher becomes an inhabitant of Skid Row. On the basis of these studies, there emerges a picture of the varieties who inhabit this "subculture"—and the picture is frequently quite different from the stereotyped view. Here is a brief survey of some of the findings:

Probably fewer than one third of the Skid Row men are alcoholics. More than that percentage drink, but their drinking is more like that of the uptowner or suburbanite; they drink for pleasure and for sociability. The "bottle gang" has norms of behavior quite as rigid as those of the club car on a commuter train. Few of these men are loners. Especially when drinking, they enjoy company; when a man has put together enough for a bottle, he is likely to share it. They tend to regard alcoholics as inferior partly because they drink alone and do not like to share.

Most Skid Rowers are not fugitives from justice and they are not criminals. They want peace and quiet, and try to avoid trouble with the law. As one researcher stated, "Psychologists agree that the Bowery Men need a place where an effortless going to hell is the accepted way of life."

In the special hierarchy of Skid Row, one of the classes is that of "tour director." This is the man who "puts on the tourists" and sometimes exhibits considerable skill in spinning tales of personal tragedy, in exchange for the price of a bottle. One study reports: "It is probably the tour directors who have conned journalists and authors into believing many of the legends about Skid Row—for example, the myth that Skid Row is populated by alcoholic brain surgeons, defrocked priests, dope-crazed artists, and embezzling bank presidents. . . ."

While some Skid Row men were driven there by sudden traumas that seemed to destroy their lives, others seem to simply drift to that world. Wandering day laborers, seamen, returning service men with no place to go, welfare recipients who can afford to live there better than elsewhere—these provide much of the population. The Depression and the existence of transient jobs, such as railroad construction, contributed to Skid Rows. Greater affluence and the disappearance of transient work have helped reduce the numbers on Skid Rows, as have broader welfare benefits and urban renewal programs. Most of the men on Skid Rows now are in their 50's and 60's, suggesting that this often colorful corner of American life may be fading away.

suggest the relationship between drinking and accidents as well as alcoholism and crime. Consequently alcoholics are subject to criminal sanctions; in all but 4 states and the District of Columbia, public intoxication is a punishable offense.

The treatment of the alcoholic as a criminal has been common throughout American history. However, in line with the reforms outlined earlier in the chapter, there has been an increasing tendency to consider the alcoholic as suffering from illness. According to some, alcoholism is a disease and should be treated as such; but, to a growing number of doctors and researchers, alcoholism is a mental health problem. In line with the latter view, 36 states have laws providing for the commitment of alcoholics to mental institutions under certain circumstances.

Particularly within the past decade, widespread efforts have been made to learn more about alcoholism and to provide more comprehensive treatment. The National Institute on Alcohol Abuse and Alcoholism was established by Congress in 1970. Through the Institute, a variety of programs have been coordinated and financed to provide research, treatment, personnel training, and programs for intervention and prevention. Along with such self-help organizations as Alcoholics Anonymous, the chances for the person suffering from alcoholism have improved. However, many experts feel that only a beginning has been made. For example, Richard Shore, Director of the Bureau of Alcoholism for San Francisco's Department of Public Health, argues that much more could be accomplished if: (1) the alcoholic were reached earlier in the course of his or her problem; (2) treatment programs were geared to all people, rather than the current heavy emphasis on middle-class whites; and (3) educational programs were instituted to warn of the dangers of alcohol abuse.

One of the major problems in providing broader treatment programs, or instituting such reforms as educational campaigns, is in financing. After a spate of public spending in the 1960's on a great many social welfare programs, the American taxpayers in the 1970's have proved increasingly reluctant to favor more spending programs. The stigma that is still attached to alcoholism makes efforts in this area even less popular.

Drug Addicts

Millions of Americans use potentially harmful drugs, ranging from tobacco and alcohol to barbituates and amphetamines, but they are not considered deviants. The use of such legal drugs is widespread and socially acceptable, the lines between use and abuse are often blurred, and the effects on the person's life are usually not noticeable. The term *drug addict* is reserved for those who are dependent on the illegal "hard" drugs, such as heroin, cocaine, opium, and the mind-altering chemical compounds.

The lives of drug addicts are frequently associated with crime or a shadowy world on the threshold of crime. The very possession of drugs, of course, constitutes a violation of the law. Even if the cost of the habit does not lead the addict to crime, the person's life frequently involves little more than the painful craving for junk. Author William S. Burroughs, who suffered through 15 years as an addict, describes the sort of life addiction can lead to:

I had not taken a bath in a year nor changed my clothes or removed them except to stick a needle every hour in the fibrous gray wooden flesh of terminal addiction. I never cleaned or dusted the room. Empty ampule boxes and garbage piled to the ceiling. Light and water long since turned off for non-payment. I did absolutely nothing. I could look at the end of my shoe for eight hours. I was only roused to action when the hourglass of junk ran out. . . .[1]

One basic response of society to drug addiction has been to treat it as a crime. Laws are passed to attack the manufacture and sale of illicit drugs, special law enforcement agencies specialize in drug control, and the addict is in constant danger of being sentenced to prison. In the late 1960's a drug "epidemic" swept the country, with a rapid increase in the number of addicts and a variety of experiments with drugs and chemical compounds. Suddenly, the drug addict was not the outsider of the artists' colony or the ghetto, but was just as likely to be a "normal" middle-class high school or college student. While reaction to the epidemic involved considerable hysteria, there was also a growing awareness that addicts were sick and badly in need of help.

In the past decade, a wide variety of approaches have been used to combat America's drug problem. New methods of treatment, such as methadone maintenance for heroin addicts, free clinics in local communities, self-help programs such as Synanon and the Black Muslim crusade, and a growing educational program beginning in grade schools—all have helped increase public awareness and provide aid for the addict.

Widespread use of drugs, particularly heroin, by American soldiers in Vietnam increased awareness and concern. A federally sponsored program of treatment had considerable success and helped destroy the myth that there is little or no hope for the heroin addict. Jerome Jaffe, director of the program, reported to a group of 469 addicts in a follow-up study 8 to 12 months after treatment. "Only seven percent had been addicted at any time since their return," he stated. "In other words of this group of users 93 percent did not

[1] *Evergreen Review*, vol. 4, no. 11, Jan.-Feb., 1960.

become re-addicted back in the States—at least within the first eight months." A number of factors helped to explain this success and to suggest areas for future treatment as research. For one thing, most of the returning veterans were receiving treatment in the early stages of addiction. In addition, it was found that "set and setting" had much to do with drug use—heroin was readily available, very inexpensive, normal restraints were reduced, and the men lived with a sense of danger and frustration. Once they returned to their home environment, the changed circumstances helped reduce the drug problem for many men. In much the same way, sociological studies of particular schools and communities are beginning to suggest ways in which drug epidemics occur.

Prostitutes

Prostitution is often said to constitute one of the "oldest professions." While in some societies the courtesan has been the object of respect and dignity, in most Western cultures, the "street walker" is regarded as a degraded human being. In American society, the prostitute has traditionally been considered a sinful person as well as a criminal, a deviate with whom "normal" people would not associate.

A certain hypocrisy of values is evident in regard to prostitution: the customers of prostitutes are not stigmatized, and, in fact, are likely to be respected members of the community. Availing oneself of a prostitute's services is not considered a sign of deviance, but rather is often considered "normal." The prostitute, however, is regarded as an inferior human being and is frequently in trouble with the law.

The prostitute suffers many of the same consequences as those guilty of other forms of deviance. Normal relationships with family

THE VARIOUS PATHS TO SOCIOLOGICAL KNOWLEDGE
ALBERT COHEN

Albert Cohen's major study, *Delinquent Boys: The Culture of the Gang* (1955), while concentrating on the subculture of delinquent gangs, has relevance to the larger problems of deviance and social control. Cohen's method consisted of combining his own research with a compilation of research by others in the field to create a generalized theory.

The core of Cohen's message is that the American system of values actually spawns nonconformist groups. These values are essentially those of the white middle class. A brief summary of these values would include: personal ambition; the establishing of long-range goals; the careful planning of activities and time; the development of special skills; putting off immediate pleasures in order to obtain the long-range goals; good manners and self-control; good sportsmanship rather than the free expression of aggression or violence; respect for property; the profitable use of leisure time.

But, Cohen argues, many individuals are at a disadvantage in trying to measure up to these values because they emerge from segments of society where such values have little meaning. A boy in a ghetto school, for example, is expected to behave according to such middle-class norms as sitting quietly, paying attention, showing an eagerness to learn. He quickly finds the teacher reprimanding him for squirming in his seat, talking out of turn, and so on. The problems quickly become more serious. Poor grades, for instance, serve as a signal that this individual is not competing successfully for the proper goals and rewards. This sort of rejection or disapproval will carry over into such areas as applying for jobs or dealing with government agencies.

One solution open to the youth in this predicament is to "change his frame of reference." If he can make himself believe that doing well in school is bad, he has achieved something in the way of salvaging self-respect. He finds he can associate with others who are also in the process of reversing the traditional value orientation. The gang offers a new frame of reference which runs counter to that of the middle class; conforming to the new standards provides a degree of fulfillment. Cohen expresses the function of the gang in this way:

> The delinquent subculture functions simultaneously to combat the enemy without and the enemy within, both the hated agents of the middle class and the gnawing internal sense of inadequacy and low self-esteem. It does so by erecting a counterculture, an alternative set of status criteria.

The subculture, then, provides the individual with the means of adjusting to the problems represented by society. Conformity and nonconformity, in other words, represent different ways of coping with the established value system. The very same values which Americans idealize "are among the major determinants of that which we stigmatize as 'pathological.'" And, Cohen suggests, "this interpretation of the delinquent subculture has important implications for the 'sociology of social problems.'"

A major advantage of Cohen's approach has been that he deals with the issue of nonconformity and social control from a variety of perspectives. That is, he relates such factors as family structure, social class, ethnic origin, neighborhood, and individual experience to the general question of why some people become members of countercultures. Similar studies along the same line have followed this lead, a notable example being Lewis Yablonsky's *The Violent Gang* (1962). Cohen himself has explored the theory further in *Deviance and Control* (1966).

and friends are often difficult to maintain. Feelings of guilt and shame may be present. In defense, the "typical" prostitute often develops a certain hardness toward others. In *Streetwalker* (Viking Press, 1959), the anonymous English author writes of this defense mechanism:

Apart from the extremes of fear and weakness of resolution, no softness of any kind must be shown or shared, for softness has no place in our world. It is at once shunned and despised when we come across it, because to be soft is to be constantly shamed and hurt, to lose illusions before others can be built up, to invite trickery, to open the door for the profiteer, the violent or the mad, to allow that vital and precious awareness to be dulled. . . .

The sex revolution of the 1960's and 1970's has shown some signs of altering attitudes toward this outcast group. Such businesses as massage parlors, for example, have frequently become thinly disguised fronts for prostitution. Although still subject to police action, such establishments might suggest a more open and honest acceptance of prostitution. In addition, prostitution is one form of deviant behavior that many people feel should be decriminalized. "Victimless crimes," it is argued, do not harm anyone and serve to detract police and court action from more serious crimes against persons and property. So far, however, only the state of Nevada allows prostitution in its criminal laws.

The Mentally Ill

Traditionally, people of Western societies viewed mental illness as an act of God or a punishment for sin. In some European countries, those considered "mad" or "demented" were frequently executed as witches or were placed on the "ship of fools" which carried the insane to remote places. Confinement became common in the late Middle Ages, but it was not until the 19th century that distinctions were made between criminals and the mentally ill.

The removal of the mentally ill from society is still regarded as essential to public safety and well-being. However, important questions arise in connection with the role of the state in determining the grounds for confinement. Up to 60 percent of the patients in mental institutions have been placed there on an involuntary basis, and many people wonder about the grounds for such action. In Massachusetts, for example, the law provides for involuntary hospitalization of any individual found to have a "character disorder" which inhibits his "judgment or emotional control" in such a way that his or her behavior "clearly violates the established . . . conventions of the community." On the basis of such a law, almost any failure to conform might be construed as a sign of mental illness. Those regarded as mentally deficient are also subject to involuntary commitment and many state laws still use such terminology as "feeble-minded," "idiot," and "imbecile."

Those concerned with the freedoms and legal rights of the mentally ill are critical of treatment as well as confinement practices. The use of chemicals and brain surgery have been special subjects of attack. For example, in 1974 a California woman brought suit against 2 doctors after they performed psychosurgery on her son who had been subject to fits of "uncontrollable rage." She held that her son had been "destroyed" by the operation and had become "almost a vegetable." Although the doctors and others maintain the operation was necessary, such cases led 1 psychiatrist to write in the New England Journal of Medicine that, as a result of psychotherapy, "Men may be exposed to loss of their free will and thus become slaves, perhaps, to an increasingly authoritarian state."

Those who have been committed and then released find themselves in much the same position as the ex-convict. People are reluctant to accept the person as "normal" or "safe." An illustration of this is provided by the problems encountered by board-and-care centers and halfway houses. Designed to help patients readjust to society, these establishments have been the subject of conflict in many communities. Real estate prices are reduced, it is argued, and the danger of violent crime is increased, although there is no evidence to support either view.

Stereotypes of the mentally ill and the ex-mental patient are reinforced by the mass media. As Thomas J. Scheff points out, the press routinely mentions previous mental health treatment of those arrested for crimes. "An item like the following," Scheff states, "is almost inconceivable: 'Mrs. Ralph Jones, an ex-mental patient, was elected president of the Fairview Home and Garden Society at their meeting last Thursday.'" Instead, the very fact that one has been treated for mental illness causes prejudgment. A striking case of this occurred during the 1972 presidential election when the Democratic candidate for vice-president, Senator Thomas Eagleton, was alleged to have been a mental patient on 3 different occasions. Although Eagleton and his supporters insisted the hospitalization was for nervous exhaustion, the incident was enough to destroy his candidacy and he withdrew from the campaign.

SUMMARY

Social deviance, or violation of the norms and mores of society, includes such problematic areas as alcoholism, homosexuality, prostitution, drug addiction, and mental illness. While most people agree that certain deviant behavior is criminal or insane, the definition of deviance changes with time and with each reference group. Ways of controlling deviance also change; in this century, for instance, there has been an increasing emphasis on *rehabilitation* rather than punishment of those guilty of antisocial behavior.

Deviance performs certain positive functions for the society as a whole. Those who "break the rules" of society help define the limits of acceptable behavior, and may help to change those limits by challenging them. At the same time, the presence of nonconformists in a group may give the conforming majority a greater sense of unity.

Different categories of social outcasts face their own specific problems. The homosexual has been regarded as a sick or perverted person, a sinner, and a criminal in our society. In addition to such social judgments, most homosexuals have to deal with inner feelings of guilt and shame. In recent years many homosexuals have sought social toleration and acceptance. They have made some gains, but the fact that children are raised in heterosexual families seems to argue that some hostility to homosexuality may always exist.

Compulsive drinking is accompanied by a syndrome of social and psychological problems. While the alcoholic has been treated as a criminal in the past, there has been an increasing tendency to view alcoholism as a disease or mental illness. Within the last decade efforts have been made to learn more about alcoholism and develop treatment programs, but financing for such efforts has been a stumbling block.

Our basic social response to drug addiction has been to treat it as a crime, but the drug "epidemic" of the late 1960's and use of drugs by American soldiers in Vietnam have helped increase awareness and concern for the addict as a sick person. A variety of approaches to treatment have been developed in the past 10 years.

The prostitute suffers many of the same consequences as those guilty of other forms of deviance. Many people are beginning to feel that like other "victimless crimes" prostitution should be decriminalized.

The mentally ill have historically been feared and rejected by society. While removal of the mentally ill from society is regarded as necessary for public safety, questions arise as to what rights the state has over mental patients. Involuntary hospitalization and use of chemicals and psychosurgery have come under special attack. Even outside the hospital, the former mental patient suffers from social stigmas.

GLOSSARY

bisexual   a person who has sexual relations with both sexes.
deviance   consistent or repeated violations of mores.

drug addict   a person who is dependent on the illegal "hard" drugs, such as heroin, cocaine, opium, and certain chemical compounds.

homosexual   one who has sexual relations only with persons of his or her own sex.

labeling theory   the current popular theory which views deviant behavior as a "self-fulfilling prophecy" involving the attempts to create rules and agencies to enforce them.

mores   norms regarded as vital to the welfare of a society.   Violations are severely punished.

sanction   a penalty (negative sanction) or reward (positive sanction) given to a person or group to secure conformity to norms.

victimless crime   an illegal act that does not harm anyone other than the perpetrator.

SUGGESTED READINGS

Becker, Howard, S.   (ed.).   *The Other Side.*   New York: Free Press, 1964.   This series of essays presents a view of various forms of deviant behavior from the viewpoint of labeling theory.

Clinard, Marshall B.   *The Sociology of Deviance.*   3rd ed.   New York: Holt, Rinehart and Winston, 1968.   An excellent text on the subject of deviant behavior.

Douglas, Jack D.   *American Social Order: Social Rules in a Pluralistic Society.*   New York: Free Press, 1971.   Among other topics, Douglas analyzes the limitations of statistical studies of deviance in this text.

Erikson, Kai T.   *Wayward Puritans: A Study in the Sociology of Deviance.*   New York: Wiley, 1966.   Erikson indicates through this sociohistorical analysis how the public creates deviant roles and finds individuals to fill them.   Extensive treatment of social reaction to witchcraft.

Goode, Erich.   *Drugs in American Society.*   New York: Knopf, 1972.   One of the leading researchers on drug use, Goode contributes to our understanding of the causes and controls of drug use.

Matza, David.   *Becoming Deviant.*   Englewood Cliffs, New Jersey: Prentice-Hall, 1969.   A leading sociologist in the field of deviant behavior, Dr. Matza brings forth an approach to the labeling perspective in sociology which emphasizes the naturalistic study of deviance.

Schur, Edwin.   *Crimes Without Victims: Deviant Behavior and Public Policy: Abortion, Homosexuality and Drug Addiction.*   Englewood Cliffs, New Jersey: Spectrum Books, 1965.   Although abortion is considered a mute issue as a form of deviance, this book represents a major contribution to our understanding of social deviance that involves people as willing participants in crime.

Spiegel, Keith. *Outsiders U. S. A.* (Rinehart Editions). New York: Holt, Rinehart and Winston, 1973. The editors have used a broad interpretation of the term *outsiders* (including such categories as consumers). The book contains 24 original essays on various outsider groups, including pieces by Ralph Nader and leading social scientists.

SOCIAL INTERACTION

part three

SOCIAL PROCESSES AND SOCIAL CHANGE

Human society is a product of interaction—individuals and groups influence, and are influenced by, every other individual or group with which they have contact. Thus, a first step in understanding how society is organized is to understand how people and groups interact. The forms of interaction which are common to every society are called universal social processes. *Sociologists have identified 5 such processes which we will be discussing in this chapter: competition, cooperation, conflict, accomodation, and assimilation.*

COOPERATION AND COMPETITION

Of the 5 universal processes, the 2 basic ones are *competition* and *cooperation*. In Chapter 8 we made the point that people strive to achieve goals in order to satisfy their needs and desires. Competition and cooperation represent the 2 major forms this striving can take—we either work together with others to achieve a goal, or we compete with them for it.

Why do people compete? Basically, the reason is that much of what we want or need is scarce: money, prestige, power, recognition, resources. Also, we often disagree with others over values, or how things should be done, or what our goals are as individuals, and groups compete with each other to achieve their own idea of what is right or good. Competition, then, is the struggle that goes on within a society to attain those scarce goals. It is a normal and healthy process. A half-century ago, sociologist Charles Cooley observed that this form of "social conflict" is "the life of society, and progress emerges from the struggle in which individual, class, or institution seeks to realize its own idea of good."

Cooperation occurs when there is agreement between individuals or groups in pursuing a particular goal. Each party feels it will gain something by working together with the other. Of course, cooperation can be combined with competition. The members of a basketball team, for example, are in competition with other teams; the team members cooperate to achieve the common goal of winning. However, as many coaches have learned, it is difficult to approach a condition of perfect cooperation; that is, even where cooperation is agreed upon, or even essential, individuals who are supposed to be working together still find themselves in competition with each other. Thus, the smooth, cooperative functioning that a team requires is often damaged by the individuals who are more interested in personal glory.

Personal and Impersonal Competition

Competition may be either *personal* or *impersonal*. In personal competition (often referred to as *rivalry*), the purpose is to defeat or better an opponent. We know against whom we are competing and for what objective we are struggling; and the "other side" is just as conscious of the rivalry. Personalities may be very much involved and tactics are carefully planned. Two office workers after the same promotion, applicants anxious for acceptance to a college or graduate school, political parties vying in an election, 2 nations striving to be first in the "space race"—these are typical examples of what is involved in this more direct form of competition.

Impersonal competition does not involve the same sort of awareness or direct confrontation. The groups or individuals involved may not even be conscious of the competition. Auto workers in Detroit, for instance, are competing with auto workers in Japan, but neither group is likely to think much about the other or ever meet face-to-face. Similarly, as students you are already competing for jobs you have not yet been offered, and the competition is with thousands of other students throughout the nation whom you will never encounter. And a man who runs a department store is competing with all other department stores in his area; in fact, he is competing with any concern that vies with him for the consumer's dollar. Usually, however, the store owner will not concern himself with the identities of his competitors. He merely tries to secure for himself as large a share of the market as he can.

Fortunately, competition does not always

involve a win-or-lose situation. In some instances, such as athletics or elections, the winners and losers are clearly defined. But most forms of competition allow for a number of "winners"; competitors in the same field, whether automobile salesmen or novelists, students or housewives, can gain a degree of wealth, fame, or recognition.

Two Basic Types of Cooperation

Cooperation may be either voluntary or involuntary. When people cooperate voluntarily, they do so of their own accord; they work together within a group because they value the goals toward which the group is striving. These goals act as effective positive sanctions. A team of dedicated scientists working together to solve a difficult problem is engaged in voluntary cooperation.

Competing groups or individuals may decide to cooperate as a means of achieving the same goal. Church groups, for example, may decide to cooperate in social welfare programs, creating a more efficient effort than when they work separately. What is called a *superordinate* goal may also bring 2 competing groups into voluntary cooperation. This occurs when a new objective appears more important than the goal for which they were competing. Two competing businesses may cooperate when confronted by a third competitor, or by a new tax law that threatens the profits of both. Similarly, 2 nations who usually don't get along well together, may combine their efforts against an external enemy or in solving a common problem such as an environmental emergency.

Involuntary cooperation, by contrast, is achieved through the use of negative sanctions; the people involved cooperate because they have to, not because they want to. Thus the type of cooperation shown by inmates in a prison is often involuntary. Prisoners cooperate with officials to the extent that they obey established rules; but their cooperation would be likely to end if no one were there to enforce the rules.

Obviously, a group which can elicit voluntary cooperation from its members—that is, can get people to internalize its norms—is in a stronger position than one which must resort to compulsion. People who see the value of cooperating to achieve a goal are likely to work hard at the task, and this in turn reduces the cost of enforcing regulations on a sustained basis.

THE NATURE OF SOCIAL CONFLICT

The line between competition and *conflict* is extremely thin. In fact, many social scientists consider them part of the same process. Thus, we often refer to conflict between 2 teams on a football field, and in politics or business, references are often made to a "conflict of interests." In precise scientific terms, however, there is an important shade of difference between competition and conflict. In one of the most comprehensive studies of the subject (*The Functions of Social Conflict*, Glencoe, The Free Press, 1956), sociologist Lewis Coser suggests that conflict can "provisionally be taken to mean a struggle over values and claims to scarce status, power, and resources in which *the aims of the opponents are to neutralize, injure, or eliminate their rivals.*" (Italics added) This suggests that a situation of competition has developed into something where the goal is to *overcome* an opponent in an openly antagonistic way.

One can easily be led to the conclusion that conflict is harmful; that it is something which threatens to tear groups apart. While conflict can be *dysfunctional* in this way, it is also possible that it can serve positive social functions as well. First, conflict can be *functional* in helping to create a feeling of group solidarity. When 2 nations are at war, for instance, feelings of national loyalty are likely to be strengthened (unless, of course, there is conflict within the nation over whether or not the war should be fought). Similarly, in a labor dispute, workers will tend to develop a closer feeling of group solidarity as will their opponents in the conflict, management. Second, the recognition, expression, and resolution of conflict is the way in which basic differences are settled. A family, for example, will become involved in conflict, often very bitter, over any number of issues—money, jealousy, responsibility, and so on. If the conflict is openly dealt with, there is often a clearing of the air, the issue is resolved, and the unity of the group may even be strengthened. On the other hand, if the basic conflict is avoided or ignored, it is likely to create underlying tensions that will probably surface in some other way. In a similar manner, minority groups which openly express conflict (and this does not necessarily involve violence) stand a better chance of having their needs satisfied than if conflict is avoided. One might even go so far as to say that conflict is an essential ingredient in social change. German sociologist Ralf Dahrendorf states flatly, "All social life is conflict, because it is change."

Conflict and Social Change

There is an important interrelationship between social change and conflict. During periods of rapid social change, there is a corresponding increase in the incidence and intensity of conflict. The modern revolutions in technology, transportation, and communication have created a world of constant, rapid change which has no parallel in history. This also means that we live in a world seething with conflict—conflict between management and labor, rich and poor, rulers and ruled, consumers and producers, conflict involving nations, races, minority groups, and special interests.

Merely consider one change resulting from the Industrial Revolution: the new relationship between employer and employee. The change in work and social relationships led to the long and often bitter series of conflicts between management and labor. But the conflict itself has contributed to still further social change—unions, collective bargaining, government arbitration, labor and business legislation, social security, income taxes, and so on.

If we live in a world increasingly marked by conflict and change, is this the natural order of things? Or, does society lean instead towards stability and order?

Sociologists are divided in their handling of these questions. Some believe in what is called the "equilibrium model" of society. Proponents of this view, such as Talcott Parsons, argue that when any force disrupts the stability of society, adjustments will be made to "restore the balance of its equilibrium." From this perspective, the "social organism" is comparable to a biological organism: when the body is threatened by illness or disease, automatic responses in the blood chemistry occur to correct the danger or minimize it.

Sociologists who see society in this way are also referred to as "functionalists." Their studies tend to concentrate on social structures and how these structures function to control conflict and maintain equilibrium. Thus, in analyzing the worker-capitalist class structure that emerged from the Industrial Revolution, Parsons sees such stratification as creating "to an important degree an integrating structure in the social system. The ordering of relationships in this context is necessary to stability." Conflicts occur, but they are really by-products of the structure since there will always be a certain amount of resistance to order and authority. The conflicts themselves are to be studied in terms of "the ways in which the institutional integration of the system does and does not succeed in developing adequate control mechanisms." Conflict, therefore, is a useful area of study, but it is not the dominant feature of an industrial society nor does it adequately explain the "dynamic development" of such societies.

Other sociologists believe that the Parsonian emphasis is misplaced. Those who lean toward what can be called a "conflict model" of society see conflict as being perhaps the most important force shaping the world we live in. Rather than analyzing this force, they argue, the functional sociologists see it only as a sign of "tension, strain and psychological malfunctioning." Consciously or unconsciously, this can lead to sociology becoming a science of the *status quo*.

Alex Inkeles describes the conflict model in this way: ". . . Rather than consensus, the basic condition of social life is dissension, arising through the competition for power and advantages between the different groups. The dominant social force, therefore, is not the steady effort to restore harmony or equilibrium, but the endless struggle between those without advantages, who wish to secure them, and those with privileges who wish to get more or to prevent others from taking what is available."

From this premise, it can be argued that without conflict there would be no social change. As indicated above, the conflict between labor and management contributed to a wide variety of changes. Similarly, the political process in a democracy can be seen as a way of creating social change through the open expression and resolution of conflict.

Thus, an election, a legislative vote, or a judicial decision all represent the working out of conflicting interests, and, in the process change occurs.

Conflict and Violence

Conflict is most likely to become dysfunctional when the attempt to resolve it involves physical violence, as in fights, duels, revolutions, and wars. When violence occurs, the original goal over which the conflict originated may become secondary to the desire to defeat the opponent. For example, while a war may start because two nations want the same territory, the territory is likely to be forgotten during the prosecution of the war itself. Each side concentrates on trying to defeat the other, and destruction of the enemy—not title to a piece of land—becomes the immediate goal.

Social scientists in all disciplines have channeled their energies into a search for answers to the question: why do some conflicts escalate to violence while others are resolved in a nonviolent manner? Current research suggests that a variety of factors are involved in spiraling a particular conflict into violence. Collective behavior is one such factor; in the protest demonstrations of the 1960's, for instance, collective reaction, either on the part of authorities or demonstrators, often turned a peaceful rally into a bloody confrontation. The leadership role and how it is handled is also important; Adolf Hitler being a prime example of an extremely persuasive leader. A third element in the escalation of conflict to violence is the frustration encountered in seeking goals; the American colonists, for example, came to feel that the only way they could secure their rights was to engage in a war of independence with England. Paralleling this is the question of whether or not a group sees the social structure as being flexible enough for them to achieve their goals peacefully. In the 1920's, British workers practically paralyzed England with a nationwide strike in communications, transportation, and industry. Neither side, however, resorted to violence, in part at least because both felt that nonviolent means were available for settling the conflict. In the 1960's, on the other hand, many black Americans came to feel that the structure of society was so rigid that the only way to achieve change was through violent attack on that structure.

The goal of research into violent conflict is not so much the elimination of violence, but rather, the control of same. In some instances, violence is all but inevitable, as when one fights to protect his life or the lives of others. But it is also true that if one can understand the dynamics of conflict, it becomes more possible to resolve differences short of violence. In the Cuban Missile Crisis of 1962, for example, the United States found itself on the verge of war with the Soviet Union. President Kennedy, however, was very conscious of the parallels between that situation and the events of 1914 which culminated in the outbreak of World War I. He made a conscious effort to avoid the mistakes made by national leaders in 1914 and having this knowledge helped him to make decisions that avoided war. Similarly, in disputes involving labor, minority groups, anti-war protestors, or any other conflict, an understanding of conflict and violence increases the possibility of avoiding violence.

Conflict and Accommodation

Open conflict between opposing groups usually is not continuous. Sometimes it ends only after one group annihilates another, but more often it is concluded when the parties find some method for settling their differences.

The general term for the process through which agreement is worked out is *accommodation*. Like the other social processes, accommodation may take any one of several different forms.

Truce. A truce is an agreement concluded between conflicting parties stating that they will cease hostilities for a period of time. Usually, it means a recognition by both sides that the conflict has become stalemated—that neither side appears able to achieve its objective. A truce agreement often will contain provisions for engaging in talks aimed at finding a more permanent solution. If they fail to agree, the conflict may be resumed after the truce has expired; if, on the other hand, they manage to reach a satisfactory agreement, then hostilities are ended. In other words, a truce is only a temporary expedient. It does not eliminate the conflict, but it may set the stage for such elimination. Occasionally, a truce will evolve into a more or less permanent settlement even though no further agreement is reached. In 1953, for example, the United Nations and Communist forces opposing each other in the Korean War agreed to accommodate each other. They signed a truce which brought an end to the fighting, but the conflict has remained at the stage of an armed truce for 2 decades since no further agreement has been reached toward a permanent settlement.

Accommodation through a truce is not limited to nations at war but can be applied to many other settings as well. During World War II, for instance, labor and management agreed to an unwritten truce by which both sides agreed to avoid strikes, lockouts, or other work stoppages until the war was over. By and large the agreement was observed faithfully by both sides, but only for the arranged period of the truce. When the war ended, the truce no longer applied, resulting in numerous

PERSPECTIVE

A PSYCHOLOGICAL STUDY OF SPORTS

In 1963, two psychologists, Bruce C. Ogilvie and Thomas A. Tutko, established an Institute for the Study of Athletic Motivation at San Jose State College in California. After 8 years of research and counseling, they had compiled a vast amount of data on the effects of athletic competition on both participants and their coaches. Among other goals, the researchers sought to determine whether or not sports serve positive functions; particularly, whether the common claim that sports "build character" was true and if the emphasis on winning had negative effects on the personality.

Ogilvie and Tutko found that athletes in all sports tended to show certain specific personality traits. They have a strong need for achievement and "tend to set high but unrealistic goals for themselves and others;" they are orderly and well-organized, with a strong respect for authority and a tendency to be dominant personality types themselves; they possess "great psychological endurance, self-control, low-resting levels of anxiety and slightly greater ability to express aggression." At the same time, they seem to reveal little need for the support of others and no strong desire to take care of others. The researchers questioned whether or not these traits might be temporary in nature, changing after the individual left athletic competition; but on the limited basis of their studies of male and female coaches and physical educators, they concluded that "these character trends remain highly stable."

The psychologists became convinced that these personality traits were present in the individual *before* he became involved in sports, and that sports did little to strengthen or mold the personality. "We found no empirical support," they wrote, "for the tradition that sports build character. Indeed, there is evidence that athletic competition limits growth in some areas. It seems that the personality of the ideal athlete is not the result of any molding process, but comes out of the ruthless selection process that occurs at all levels of sport. Athletic competition has no more beneficial effects than intense endeavor in any other field. Horatio Alger success—in sport or elsewhere—comes only to those who are already mentally fit, resilient, and strong."

On the other hand, their research did not suggest that sport has the harmful effects often ascribed to it by critics. "Our original hypothesis about the ill effects of high-level competition turned out to be unfounded. When we completed tests on the original teams, we discovered no negative relation between athletic achievement and emotional maturity or control. On the contrary, the higher the level of achievement, the greater the probability the athlete would have emotional maturity or control."

Over the course of their research, Ogilvie and Tutko did come to feel that definite changes were taking place in the field of athletics—that a new breed of athletes was emerging by the early 1970's, with a new set of values which did not accept the "authoritative" nature of American sport or its "supreme emphasis on winning." This newer type of athlete would often find himself in conflict with his coaches over such issues as hair length, the use of drugs, and political beliefs.

The researchers concluded with a new hypothesis—that somehow a less competitive brand of athlete will change the very nature of school and professional sport. "Many coaches won't be able to stand the strain," they predicted. "Eventually, the world of sport is going to take the emphasis off winning-at-any-cost." Observers of professional football's "bloody Sundays" can probably find plenty of evidence to counter this prediction by the two psychologists.

Quotations are from Bruce C. Ogilvie and Thomas A. Tutko, "Sport: If You Want to Build Character, Try Something Else," *Psychology Today*, (October, 1971), pp. 61-63.

strikes and other labor-management disputes during the postwar years.

Compromise. A compromise is an agreement reached through mutual concessions. Each side gives up part of what it wants in order to resolve the conflict. The settlement of a family dispute often involves this sort of accommodation. Trade agreements between nations would be another example of compromise—both parties agree to give up something in the way of tariffs or quotas as a means of solving trade disagreements or of increasing trade.

American political history has been marked by numerous important compromises. The Missouri Compromise and the Compromise of 1850 are examples: both served to reduce sectional frictions over slavery, at least for a time. The Constitution itself contains many compromises, perhaps the most important being the "great compromise" which settled the dispute between the large states and the smaller states. The small states felt themselves protected by the establishment of a Senate in which each state had 2 votes, regardless of size. The large states were adequately represented in the House of Representatives in which states are represented according to their respective populations.

Avoidance. Avoidance is a form of accommodation in which one or both of the parties involved simply withdraw from the conflict situation. They place a physical or social distance between themselves and the other side. Thus, a man who can't get along on his job avoids the situation by quitting, or a married couple may resolve their differences by dissolving the marriage. Racial, ethnic, or religious conflicts can be avoided through the practice of segregation, in which the 2 sides are physically as well as socially isolated from each other and come into contact only under carefully defined conditions. Nations can also engage in this form of accommodation. At the height of the Cold War, for example, there was practically no direct contact between the United States and most Communist countries, particularly China; each side seemed to feel that overt communication would only heighten tensions.

Toleration. Toleration is that form of accommodation whereby both sides "agree to disagree." More precisely, they agree not to let their differences interfere with their peaceful relationship. A good example of 2 groups who tolerate each other is provided by the Tungus of Siberia and the Cossacks of Western Manchuria. These neighboring people are quite different from each other culturally. The Cossacks are sedentary farmers who live in permanent villages; the Tungus are wandering herdsmen who live in mobile tents. Neither group wishes to abandon its traditional way of life and each is often quite critical of the other. Nevertheless, they have frequent economic and social contacts but still manage to avoid conflict. They do this by tolerating one another, by respecting each other's right to be different.

In quite a similar way, the United States and China attempted to heal their Cold War differences by formally agreeing to tolerate one another—to try to establish peaceful trade and political contacts but still recognizing that there were important disputes between the 2 nations. At the time of the historic presidential trip to Peking in early 1972, President Nixon and Chinese Premier Chou En-lai issued a joint communique in which they stated: "The two sides agree that countries, regardless of their social systems, could conduct their relations on the principles of respect for the sovereignty and territorial integrity of all states. . . ."

Arbitration and Mediation. When conflicting parties cannot agree of their own accord, they often resort to the forms of accommodation known as arbitration and mediation.

Both of these processes involve an appeal to a neutral party in order to settle a dispute. In arbitration, the solutions proposed by the third party must be accepted by both sides; this is agreed upon before the dispute is submitted. Thus, in a conflict over custody of a child, once the court has made its decision the "award" is binding on both parties. In mediation, the third party may only *suggest* solutions, and it is then up to the disputants to decide whether or not they will accept the suggestions.

The advantage of both arbitration and mediation lies in the fact that they bring in an objective viewpoint, and this can be particularly helpful in settling disputes in which both sides are so emotionally involved in furthering their own interests that neither can see any value in the other's position. Consequently, arbitration and mediation are used very often in attempts to settle labor disputes, especially disputes in which the normal process of collective bargaining has proved ineffective. Often in such cases the government provides an impartial third party to mediate or arbitrate the conflict.

For more than a century, there have been attempts to apply the methods of arbitration and mediation to conflicts between nations. Sometimes this has been an informal process, as when President Theodore Roosevelt agreed to serve as an "honest broker" in helping to end the war between Russia and Japan. More formalized efforts have been primarily concerned with attempting to establish an international court of justice to which nations could submit disputes. Formal machinery is provided by the World Court, which has operated under both the United Nations and previously under the League of Nations. The Court has been useful in settling many minor disputes, particularly through mediation. However, nations as a rule have not been willing to submit

the sort of conflicts that so often lead to war, and no nation has been willing to surrender its sovereignty to the point of agreeing that all international disputes should be settled by a third party.

The End Products of Accommodation

Accommodation of social conflict can have either of 2 results. Either one party will emerge with a higher social position than the other, or both parties will emerge as equals. The former situation is illustrated by the type of arrangement worked out in England after the famous Battle of Hastings in 1066. By winning this battle, the Normans under William the Conqueror became the masters of England, and they were in a position to enforce an unequal peace upon the Anglo-Saxons, whom they had defeated. By and large the Normans decided to assume a superior position and to assign the Anglo-Saxons an inferior position. The Anglo-Saxons, unable to resort to arms, had no choice but to accept the accommodation even though it was on an unequal basis.

Accommodation which results in a relationship of equality is evident in the history of American labor. Labor and management are parties with opposing interests, but they have to work together, which means they have to accommodate. During the 19th century, this accommodation was often one-sided. Management could hire and fire largely as it pleased and made most of the decisions regarding pay and working conditions; workers could do little more than agree. Gradually, however, labor gained the right to form unions, to bargain collectively, and to strike. This altered the situation and now, in most disputes, each side carries roughly the same amount of strength to the bargaining table.

ASSIMILATION

The remaining universal process, *assimilation*, is similar to accommodation but goes a good deal further and usually has more lasting effects. When groups assimilate, the cultural differences between them are not maintained, as in toleration, but are either reduced or eliminated. The groups tend to merge into one new group.

One of the best-known examples of assimilation involves the American experience with immigration. In the space of a century, ending in 1920, more than 50 million people emigrated to the United States, mostly from Europe, but with many from the Near East, Asia, and Latin America as well. At first the immigrant groups tended to cling together, forming separate ethnic enclaves within American cities. In part, this holding on to old cultural ways was a method of achieving security in a strange, new environment, and it was a defense against the prejudices of "native-born" Americans who often discriminated against "foreigners." The first major non-English wave of immigrants, for example, came from Ireland and Germany. Both groups found that jobs and dwellings were barred to them by signs reading, "No Irish (or Germans) need apply." Gradually, the process of assimilation took place; the immigrants or their children became indistinguishable from other Americans. And yet, this was not a matter of the newcomers being absorbed into the mainstream of American culture, but rather a mixing together of immigrant groups and older Americans in which both sides learned new ideas and new ways of living from the other.

Later waves of immigrants, particularly in the post-Civil War period, came from Eastern and Southern Europe. These groups had an even more difficult time in adjusting to life in the United States, but assimilation has occurred. The process of assimilation has been least successful in regard to nonwhite groups; whites and nonwhites have not yet merged into one new group, although the barriers to communication among racial groupings are slowly breaking down.

THE INFLUENCE OF CULTURE

Although the processes we have been discussing take place in all societies, they do not take place in exactly the same way. Like so many other aspects of social existence, they are influenced to a considerable extent by culture. A few examples will make this apparent.

Consider the process of cooperation. Among the Polynesians cooperation often takes the form of community fishing expeditions or of joint efforts to build seaworthy canoes. Among the Pueblo Indians people cooperate in the preparation and performance of elaborate dances, feasts, and other ceremonies. In the United States cooperation is reflected in the general obedience to traffic laws, payment of taxes, and countless activities which people must perform together in order to maintain a highly complex social organization.

The process of accommodation also provides numerous examples of cultural influence. In Medieval Europe conflicts were often settled through "trial by ordeal." An accused individual was made to place his hand in an open flame or endure some other form of torture. The extent of the injury he sustained was then supposed to indicate his guilt or innocence. This system slowly evolved and was replaced by our modern courts of law in which judges, often with juries, decide which of 2 disputants has been wronged or whether or not a person is guilty of a particular crime.

The Kalinga of the Philippines do much the same thing but in a somewhat different manner. They provide for accommodation by having influential people, called "pangats," settle quarrels. Ordinarily, a pangat will provide a solution by ordering a payment of goods to the injured party.

Many other examples could be cited to show how social processes differ from society to society. However, these examples are sufficient to make our point—namely, that the goals people pursue and the ways in which they pursue them are immersed in a cultural context of shared values and practices.

COOPERATIVE OR COMPETITIVE SOCIETIES

Attempts have been made to classify societies according to the fundamental processes of cooperation or competition. Thus the Maoris of New Zealand are termed a cooperative society because cooperation seems to occupy a central position in their value system. Their high regard for cooperative activity is seen in an incident during the wars between the Maoris and New Zealand's English settlers. A British regiment had surrounded a Maori village and placed it under siege. The villagers fought back stubbornly for days and the British troops began to slow down the rate of their fire in order to save their ammunition. When the Maoris signaled that they wanted a parley with the English commander, he readily agreed, feeling sure the villagers were about to surrender. But the Maoris had no intention of giving up. Rather, they had learned of the British plight and had come to see if they could help. Having plenty of ammunition themselves, they offered to share it with their attackers!

Outstanding among people who might be called cooperative are the Eskimos. Although Eskimos have no chiefs and no regular government, they manage to work together in almost complete harmony. Everyone in the community helps in the struggle to survive in a hostile environment. Even in a crisis, Eskimos are rarely willing to assert leadership but rather prefer to hold back and wait until common consent on a course of action emerges. An extreme illustration of this quality occurred when a boatload of Eskimo hunters was swept into dangerous rapids. Rather than shout directions and otherwise try to influence his companions, each man sat quietly, lifted his paddle, and awaited whatever the swirling currents had to offer. Only when good fortune guided the craft into calmer waters did the men resume their paddling. To have acted before then would have been presumptuous according to the Eskimo value system.

In contrast to the Eskimos and the Maoris, the Dobuans, an island people dwelling off the coast of eastern New Guinea, are regarded by most observers as fiercely competitive. They appear to be extremely jealous, displaying continual fear and suspicion toward one another. Every tribesman is regarded as a potential thief by every other tribesman. To protect their yam crops, which they value highly, the Dobuans develop secret magical incantations intended to keep away intruders. Even husbands and wives show great distrust of each other and keep separate yam crops which they insist on planting and harvesting alone. The Dobuans seem to enjoy few things more than bargaining, but they always bargain—"wabuwabu" as they call it—with an eye toward getting the upper hand. The Dobuan who can wabuwabu better than anyone else is a most envied person.

With primitive societies such as those just mentioned, classification according to cooperative or competitive tendencies can be interesting and perhaps even valuable as an

THE VARIOUS PATHS TO SOCIOLOGICAL KNOWLEDGE
LEWIS COSER

In 1950, sociologist Jessie Bernard wrote an article titled "Where is the Modern Sociology of Conflict?" Bernard was struck by the fact that the dynamics of conflict, which some regard as the "most powerful force" shaping the world we live in, were being ignored by modern researchers. One reached far back in time for the most important works on the subject—the class conflict theories of Karl Marx, written in the late 19th century, and a study of social conflict by Georg Simmel, published in 1904.

Since the time Bernard raised that question, a sociology of conflict has begun to take shape. Research now deals with such topics as community conflict, management-labor disputes, political conflict, the easing of intergroup tensions, and international conflicts, including war. And a *Journal of Conflict Resolution* has presented a major forum for dealing with the subject from a variety of perspectives.

One of the major figures in the development of this new field has been Lewis Coser. Building on the earlier works of Simmel, Coser published a study titled *The Functions of Social Conflict* in 1956, in which he placed heavy emphasis on the positive aspects of a subject we usually regard as essentially negative. Coser states: "To focus on the functional aspects of social conflict is not to deny that certain forms of conflict are indeed destructive of group unity or that they lead to disintegration of specific social structures. Such focusing serves, however, to correct a balance of analysis which has been tilted in the other direction."

In some cases conflict within a group may help to establish unity or reestablish cohesion where it has been threatened by hostile and antagonistic feelings among the members of the group. This is not always the case, and not all types of conflict are apt to fit into this scheme. It seems that whether social conflict is beneficial or harmful to a group is dependent on the type of social issues that are being contested. An additonal concern is the type of social structure within which the conflict is carried on.

Internal social conflicts which concern goals or values that do not contradict basic assumptions upon which the relationship is founded are often positively reinforcing. They may operate in a beneficial fashion for the social structure. Such conflicts can make possible needed readjustment of norms and power relations within groups. However, conflicts that are internal which involve participants in contending parties that no longer share the basic values upon which the group is based, threaten to disrupt the structure. The social structure can, however, contain safeguards against this kind of disruption. It can provide for the institutionalization and tolerance for conflict. In this manner conflicts can be resolved at an early stage before the basic consensual pattern is threatened.

Social structures differ in the manner in which they allow expression of antagonistic claims. Closely knit groups which involve the whole personality of the participant and which rely on a high frequency of interaction must strive to avoid conflict. While they provide frequent occasions for hostility, the acting out of these hostilities is sensed as a danger for the group. Often hostility is suppressed, and therefore accumulates and intensifies. When a conflict breaks out it is apt to be intense since the total personality is involved rather than a principle. Hence, the closer the group the more intense conflict will be.

In groups where members participate only segmentally, conflict tends to be less disruptive and more beneficial. Since the member's energies are mobilized in many different directions, a single conflict is unlikely to disrupt the group as a whole. Moreover, the occasions of conflict are not allowed to accumulate and are less intense. In addition the whole personality is not involved so the conflict does not seem as much a threat to the participants.

In the cases of conflict with people outside the group, the results for group cohesion are often good. In cases where groups are engaged in a long, protracted struggle with outsiders, total personality involvement is often claimed by the group. The outside threat often prevents internal conflict. However, where conflict does arise it is seen as threatening to the group. In groups where this total personality involvement is not demanded the experience of social conflict is positively reinforced.

The dynamics of conflict operate much the same in groups large and small as they do in individuals. Coser, for example, criticizes the common practice of judging the success of a marriage or family relationship according to the number of arguments reported. The family that ''never argues'' is often considered well-adjusted and happy. In reality, however, it sometimes happens that such a family is actually caught up in tensions and hostilities which no one has dared to bring to the surface.

The family that deals with its conflicts honestly and openly stands a better chance of maintaining a feeling of closeness and cohesion. It is by dealing with our conflicts that we learn where we stand in our relationships with other people. According to Coser, "Without ways to vent hostility toward each other, and to express dissent, group members might feel completely crushed and might react by withdrawal. By settling pent-up feelings of hostility, conflicts serve to *maintain* a relationship."

Conflict, then can be a disruptive and dysfunctional force; internal conflict can tear groups apart, whether a family, an organization, or a nation. It is particularly dangerous when it escalates in the direction of violence, and this, too, can happen with small groups as well as nations. But it is also important to remember that conflict is a natural part of any group life. Depending on the social structure of the group, conflict can play a vital and positive part in the internal cohesion of a group.

analytic tool. But it should always be kept in mind that these classifications are far from absolute; no society is completely cooperative or completely competitive.

With more complex societies, classification along these lines becomes even more difficult. Many people, for example, regard the United States as a highly competitive nation. Economic success rates high in the American system of values. Observers point to the frontier experience as being responsible, in large part, for a great stress on "rugged individualism." And Americans are highly competitive in regard to sports, including the vicarious enjoyment of spectator sports such as professional football.

On the other hand, there is evidence of a good deal of cooperation in American life. Some European visitors have been struck by the fact that America seems to be a "nation of joiners"—whenever there is a crisis or a problem on a project, Americans are apt to form a committee, an association, or a club to work out the problem.

Even the rugged individualism of frontier experiences seems not so individual when one looks closely at some of the practices of the open frontier such as "barn-raisings." Cooperation is also evident in such activities as charity drives, community improvement programs, and countless projects aimed at improving social and economic conditions.

SUMMARY

Those forms of interaction common to all societies are called *universal social processes*. The two most important of these are *competition* and *cooperation*. Cooperation occurs when people work together in an effort to meet their needs, and competition occurs when they pursue goals as rivals. Often, the two occur simultaneously, as when the members of athletic teams cooperate with one another but compete against opposing teams.

Both processes are subject to variations. Competition may be conducted on either a personal or an impersonal basis and may permit of either one or several winners. Cooperation may be either voluntary or involuntary. Whereas involuntary cooperation takes place under duress, voluntary cooperation is achieved because people have internalized group norms.

A third universal process is *conflict,* which emerges when competition degenerates into open struggle. Conflict is often functional, but it can be harmful and spiral into violence.

The process through which conflict is ended and the rivals work out a peaceful solution to their differences is called *accommodation.* This process also may take several forms. *Truce* consists of an agreement to suspend hostilities in an effort to work out a lasting solution. *Compromise* is an agreement reached through mutual concessions. In *toleration* the parties decide to maintain their differences but not let these interfere with their peaceful relationship. When groups cannot accommodate by themselves, they may bring in a third party to help them. Under *arbitration,* the third party has the power to dictate a settlement. Under *mediation,* the party only has the power to suggest a course of action.

The fifth universal process is *assimilation,* which consists in the social blending of different groups. As a result of assimilation, differences tend to disappear.

Although common to all societies, the universal processes are subject to cultural variations. Thus cooperation among a people like the Polynesians may take the form of a joint fishing expedition, whereas among the Pueblo Indians the people cooperate in performing certain rites. Some societies, especially those in the earlier stages of cultural development, can be classified in terms of the basic processes of cooperation and competition. Highly cooperative peoples are the Eskimos, while a highly competitive society is that of the Dobuans. American society is too complex for such classification. While Americans are a strongly competitive people, especially in economic matters, they also exhibit much evidence of cooperative activity, notably where charitable or civic projects are involved.

GLOSSARY

accommodation   a universal social process in which conflicting groups settle their differences while retaining their respective identities.

arbitration   the form of accommodation in which antagonists agree to accept the decision of a qualified neutral party in settling their dispute.

assimilation   a universal social process through which the cultural differences between groups are gradually reduced or eliminated. The social blending of peoples.

avoidance   a form of accommodation in which one or more parties in conflict withdraw from the situation.

competition   a universal social process wherein people rival one another in an effort to attain goals.

compromise   a form of accommodation in which the conflicting parties settle their differences by making mutual concessions.

conflict   a universal social process involving conscious struggle for the same goal, in which opponents strive primarily to overcome one another.

cooperation   a universal social process in which people work together to attain goals.

mediation   a form of accommodation in which a third party is brought in to settle a dispute, but the antagonists are not committed in advance to accept his advice.

toleration   a form of accommodation wherein opposing groups agree to respect each other's right to their own beliefs and practices.

truce   a form of accommodation in which conflicting parties stop hostile actions without settling the issues or resolving the conflict.

SUGGESTED READINGS

Coser, Lewis A.   *The Functions of Social Conflict.*   Chicago: The Free Press of Glencoe, 1965. In this work, Coser argues that the process of conflict is necessary for society to have stability and adaptability to change.

Maier, N. R. F.   *Principles of Human Relations Applications to Management.*   New York: Wiley, 1952.   Deals with various kinds of interaction problems in business and industrial situations, the dynamics of bargaining sessions, and the ways in which solutions are found.

Schelling, Thomas C.   *The Strategy of Conflict.*   New York: Oxford University Press, 1963. Although this is sometimes difficult reading, the book is more than worth the effort.   Schelling deals with conflict situations in terms of bargaining—how you win or lose, how threat is used—brinksmanship.

Sherif, M.,   *et al.   Intergroup Conflict and Cooperation: The Robbers Cave Experiment.*   Norman, Oklahoma: University of Oklahoma Press, 1961.   Sherif and his associates used the setting of a boys' camp to create situations of group tension and conflict.   They could then study how conflicts escalated or were resolved, and what factors were necessary to establish cooperation.

COMMUNICATION

If it were not for the ability to communicate through the medium of language, people could not have constructed even the most rudimentary form of culture. All human interactions depend on communication, the linkage that enables one person to affect another. Consequently, the study of human communication is central to sociology, and the study raises some interesting questions: How did language develop? Why are there so many different tongues? Can people overcome the barriers imposed by linguistic diversity? How do communications difficulties contribute to misunderstanding and friction? These are some of the questions we will be discussing in Chapter 12.

LANGUAGE: THE KEY TO CULTURAL GROWTH

Communication is a form of interaction. Technically, it is called symbolic interaction to distinguish it from direct physical contact among individuals. Thus, if 2 people are fighting, they are interacting but not necessarily communicating. But if the 2 people are signalling to one another by means of hand movements, they are communicating—their gestures serve as symbols which represent the ideas they are trying to convey.

Symbolic interaction is not limited to human beings. Many lower animals also communicate through sounds or body movements; they are both "senders" and "receivers" of symbolic messages. Birds, of course, have a variety of calls that warn of danger, announce the occupation of territory, or invite mates. Wolves and coyotes expose their throats as a sign of surrender when they are defeated by a stronger animal. Honey bees perform a complicated "dance-like" pattern to inform other bees of the direction and distance to nectar-bearing flowers. The high-frequency chatter of whales and porpoises is used, among other purposes, to coordinate their movements. In short, communication among nonhuman creatures is abundant and can be studied.

While each of these communicative techniques is a vital element in the survival of a particular species, animal communication is strictly limited. At best, animals can send a few standardized messages and do not seem to be capable of varying them. Instead, the content of their communication, as well as the techniques employed, remains the same generation after generation.

Communication and Culture

In contrast to other animals, communication among human beings is infinitely more varied.

Instead of being limited to a few messages, people can tell one another about almost anything they have experienced and they can exchange ideas. This ability gave humans a tremendous advantage in the struggle for survival. If an animal manages to discover some new way of doing something, it has no way of communicating this discovery. But a person who makes such a discovery can pass it on to contemporaries and also to future generations. As a result, each successive generation can build upon prior knowledge, so that knowledge itself accumulates and grows. This accumulated knowledge is what we identify as culture. In brief, then, it is the ability to communicate that enables people to construct and transmit their culture.

Communication is also important for interaction among cultures, which enables one society to learn and borrow from others. You will recall Ralph Linton's description of the "100 Percent American," quoted in Chapter 3, which illustrates how much our own culture depends on what has been learned from others. In fact, many sociologists believe that the complexity of a particular culture depends in large part on the amount of communication that society has with others. Thus, the early civilizations developed in the eastern Mediterranean where societies such as the Babylonian or Semitic served as crossroads in communication among cultures. On the other hand, societies which have remained isolated from cross-cultural contacts are less likely to attain a high level of complexity.

Communication is also associated with cultural diversity. Throughout most of history, human groups have lived in relative isolation from one another. If one group discovered a new and better way of doing something, it might take centuries for other cultures to learn of it. Thus, even though some societies such as the Maya and Inca achieved a high level of civilization in the Western Hemisphere prior to contact with Europeans, they had not developed the use of such important innovations as writing or the wheel. As communications among the different parts of the globe increased, more and more societies adopted more effective living techniques developed by others. Today, many of the world's cultures are struggling to "catch up" to the scientific and technological head start achieved by Western societies. As they attain urbanization and industrialization, these cultures become more like the cultures they are borrowing from.

The same correlation between communication and diversity is evident within cultures. In American cities at the turn of the century, for example, new immigrants tended to live in rather isolated ethnic neighborhoods—the Italians in "little Italy," the Poles in "little Poland," and so on. As long as the people in these neighborhoods had little contact with other groups, their cultural differences were noticeable. As communication within the city increased, the lines separating groups became blurred—everyone became more like everyone else. In other words, as communication between groups increases, the differences between them tend to decrease.

The Meaning of Language

Human beings have devised a great number of symbols for the purpose of communication. Even nonverbal devices have been important means of communication—such as the smoke signals used by American Indians, sign language, the Morse Code, flags, signal lights, drum beats, and so on. We also communicate through gestures and body movements in what some have referred to as "silent language": eye contact, movement of the hand, body posture, and nodding or shaking the head, for example. However, most communication among humans is performed through the medium of language.

Language may be defined as *a system of arbitrary vocal symbols used to convey information among the participants in a culture.* That statement will make more sense if we look at its component parts.

First, the term *symbols* is used in the definition to indicate that the items which make up a language—the words—stand for something other than themselves. The word "house" stands for a type of dwelling, the word "joy" represents a type of emotion, the word "verb" stands for a type of word, and the word "comfort" stands for an abstract concept. There is practically no limit to the number of such symbols that human beings can create.

Reference to a *vocal* symbol, of course, means that the sound or symbol is formed by the human vocal apparatus: vocal cords, throat, hard and soft palate, tongue, and teeth. Humans are so constructed physically that this apparatus enables them to produce an amazing variety of communicative sounds.

By saying that linguistic symbols are *arbitrary,* we mean that there is no necessary connection between words and the things they represent. Any sound may be chosen to stand for anything one wishes. The arbitrary nature of language becomes clear when one considers the variety of vocal symbols used in different language systems to convey the same idea. For example, the word for "child" in different languages may show no similarity in sound: in French, "enfant"; in Dutch, "kind"; in Swedish, "barn"; in Polish, "dziecko"; in Arabaic, "tifl"; and in Swahili, "mtoto"—all mean "child" but all sound quite different.

Finally, a language is called a *system* of vocal symbols because the words that make up a language must be used in an orderly pattern if they are to be effective. The rules governing a language—its *grammar*—specify a usual word order; in English this would be subject first, then verb, then object. To vary the order of a sentence (such as, "The dog bit the man") will often obscure the meaning ("Dog the bit man the") or destroy it completely ("The man bit the dog").

The Origins of Language

The origins of language are unknown; we have no evidence to indicate when or how it first developed. Without written records, there is no way to tell how ancient peoples communicated and, of course, written language developed thousands of years after vocal speech developed. However, the artifacts of prehistoric people that have been discovered strongly suggest that sufficient communication had developed to make possible a degree of cooperation which, in turn, would be necessary for the development of a basic culture.

Although it is unlikely that we will ever know definitely how language originated, some theories have been proposed. E. L. Thorndike suggested that language developed from the individual's ability to imitate natural sounds as a way of self-expression. He gave his theories such picturesque names as the "ding-dong theory" meaning the imitation of the sound of bells, the "bow-wow theory" such as the imitation of a dog barking, or the "pooh-pooh theory" which suggests that languages were derived from spontaneous cries emitted by people when they were surprised, frightened, amused, or hurt. Although such theories are colorful, and often quite logical, no one has yet discovered evidence to confirm any of them.

Another theory skirts the question of linguistic origins, but suggests that all languages are derived from a single ancient tongue, a protolanguage which was never recorded. In the search for such a common origin, scientists look for "root words" that various languages share. As we will see later in the chapter,

some root words have been found, suggesting that many languages share a common beginning, but so far there is no evidence that *all* languages are similarly related. The existence of a protolanguage remains a theoretical possibility, but much more research will be needed before the possibility can be substantiated.

In searching for the origins of language, scientists cannot employ the comparative method that works so well with other aspects of culture. That is, they cannot compare a "modern" language with a "primitive" language because no languages are primitive. Every language currently in existence consists of a limited number of sounds, but these sounds may be combined in an almost infinite variety of patterns. Therefore, any language may be used to express any idea known to a speaker. If a word does not exist for a particular thing, new patterns can be formed that will be recognizable to anyone familiar with the tongue. Thus, the American Indians had no word for the European invention "guns," but by combining their words for "fire" and "stick" ("firestick") they could communicate with each other about this new phenomenon.

The Importance of Writing

While it is erroneous to describe some languages as "modern" and others as "primitive," there is one respect in which language clearly reflects a difference in cultural development. Invariably, the more advanced of human societies are those which possess a method of *writing* their language—of setting their vocalized symbols down in graphic form. The reasons for this are not hard to find. Societies with no written language are limited in at least 2 ways: first, they must rely on human memory, with all its shortcomings, for the storage of information; and, second, their culture must be transmitted by word of mouth. Sociologist Robert Redfield explains more fully how the lack of writing limits cultural growth:

Through books the civilized people communicate with the minds of other people and other times, and an aspect of the isolation of folk society is the absence of books. The folk communicate only by word of mouth; therefore the communication upon which understanding is built is only that which takes place among neighbors, within the little society itself. The folk has no access to the thought and experience of the past, whether of other peoples or of their own ancestors, such as books provide. Therefore, oral tradition has no check or competitor. Knowledge of what has gone before reaches no further back than memory and speech between old and young can make it go; beyond "the time of our grandfathers" all is legendary and vague. With no form of belief established by written record, there can be no historical sense, such as civilized people have, no theology, and no basis for science in recorded experiment. . . .[1]

Clearly, then, the society that possess a written language enjoys a great advantage over the society that does not. In fact, the gulf between literate and preliterate groups is so great that scientists frequently use the phrase "preliterate" interchangeably with "primitive" in describing a society's level of cultural achievement.

Beginnings of Writing

While the origins of language are obscure, scientists can be more certain in reconstructing the beginnings of writing. The very durability of writing makes this possible; once people began to communicate in written form, they were creating records which have lasted

[1] "The Folk Society," *American Journal of Sociology*, 1947, LII.

for thousands of years and can be studied by modern scholars.

Humans took the first step toward the development of writing when they began to draw pictures. At first cave paintings and other forms of primitive art were probably intended to serve decorative or magical purposes. But by its very nature a picture is also a means of communication. A sketch showing a group of armed men surrounding an animal inevitably conveys the concept of a hunt. Once they realized the communicative potential of pictures, people began using them to record simple messages.

As the same drawings were repeated over and over, their form tended to become stylized. Unnecessary lines were omitted and the remaining strokes constituted *pictographs*, or simplified representations of different objects. By combining 2 or more pictographs, an *ideograph* was produced—the putting of ideas into graphic form. Thus, by placing a pictograph of the sun together with a pictograph of a tree, the Chinese conveyed the idea of "east"—the sun rising through the trees. The pictographs of the sun and moon together made the Chinese symbol for "light." A picture of an eye and water stood for "tears" or "crying," and the combined pictographs for child and woman stood for "good."

Pictographs and ideographs were not true writing. They conveyed messages, but they didn't necessarily depend on language. The message could be put into words in many different ways. The Egyptians and Sumerians were among the first peoples to develop what can be considered true systems of writing. Both Sumerian cuneiform writing and Egyptian hieroglyphics contained certain symbols that stood for specific words in the language, not just for ideas. Both also had other symbols which represented sounds. With these systems, then, men were putting their language into written form.

These early systems of writing were somewhat clumsy and complicated. Hieroglyphics, for example, retained many pictographs which were used in combination with more formal symbols. The Semites of Syria managed to simplify Egyptian writing by reducing the number of signs. Another important development, particularly for Western cultures, was the creation by the ancient Phoenicians of a system which made use of only 22 symbols, or letters. Phoenician traders spread this system throughout the mediterranean world, and the Greeks were among the people who adopted it. The Greeks changed the shape of the letters and, more importantly, added special signs for vowels, thereby filling a gap in Phoenician writing and producing the first complete alphabet. (The word "alphabet" is derived from the first two Greek letters—*alpha* and *beta*.)

The alphabet we use today was developed for the most part by the Romans who built on the Greek system. This system probably was carried to the Latin tribes by the Etruscans who migrated to central Italy from the eastern Mediterranean. Later, direct contact between Greece and Rome led to even further Greek influence on Roman writing. Most of the letters comprising modern English were those used by the Romans, the exceptions being the letters "j," "u," and "w," which were added at different times during the Middle Ages.

The Variety of Language

Over thousands of years, human language developed an amazing diversity. Scholars estimate that some 5000 languages were in use throughout the world at the end of the 15th century. Since that time roughly half the number have disappeared—they either fell into disuse as "dead languages" or were discarded for lack of "speakers" as tribes and bands were absorbed by larger populations.

Exactly how this great variety of languages developed is still being studied. As we mentioned earlier, the origins of language are obscure, but scholars can study the changes that have taken place in languages since the invention of writing, and they can compare various present-day languages, including those of preliterate societies. In this way they can reconstruct to some extent the process of linguistic evolution. Scholars who specialize in this field are called comparative or historical linguists.

In the development of linguistic diversity, we can be fairly certain that both migration and isolation are involved. When a group migrates, it takes its language with it; if the migrating group becomes isolated from the society it left, which is a common occurrence, its language will gradually diverge from the original. Changes will take place in the language of both the migrating group and the society from which it migrated—over a period of a few centuries, the two tongues are likely to become distinct enough to be considered separate languages. In this way, comparative and historical linguistics can provide valuable clues about human migrations throughout history.

Certain languages share a number of common characteristics. For example, the English word "brother" is similar to the Dutch "broeder," the German "bruder," Old Saxon "brothar," Lithuanian "broter," Greek "phrater," Latin "frater," and Sanskrit "bhratar." The similarities strongly suggest that all of these languages are related to one another, that they all branched from a common "stem" language. In this case the stem language is called either Indo-European or Indo-Hittite. While there is no record of the original Indo-

European tongue, scholars have been able to reconstruct it by studying its more recent descendents. It is generally agreed that the Indo-European tongue was spoken by a people who lived in eastern Europe during the New Stone Age. Over a number of centuries, groups of these people migrated in different directions, some of them moving west into Greece, Italy, and western Europe, others traveling in a southeasterly direction into Persia and India. During the course of these migrations, and the subsequent isolation of the groups from each other, the original Indo-European language was modified, creating a number of different but related languages.

Languages which branch from a common stem in this fashion are said to belong to the same linguistic "family." The Indo-European family contains the major languages of Europe, the Indo-Iranian languages, and a few scattered Asian tongues (see diagram). Other major groupings include the Finno-Ugrian, Semitic, Hamitic, Indo-Chinese, Malayo-Polynesian, Turco-Tartar, Dravidian, and Bantu families. In all, over 100 such families have been identified.

Each of these families, in turn, can be divided into various branches. The Indo-European family includes the following subdivisions: Indo-Iranian languages, such as Hindustani; Slavic languages, such as Russian; Hellenic language, or Greek; Romance languages, including French, Spanish, and Italian; Celtic, with Irish, Welsh, and Scottish being examples; and Germanic, which includes English, Dutch, Danish, and Swedish. Thus, English is one part of the Germanic branch of the Indo-European family.

How Languages Grow

A language changes and grows in the same way that other aspects of culture change and grow—through invention, diffusion, and transmission.

The process of linguistic evolution is often referred to as "word coining." Newly coined words in a language generally reflect a need to describe some innovation within the culture. The word "motel" for instance, was created out of "motor" and "hotel" in order to describe that form of travel accommodation which became increasingly popular after World War II. Similarly, the need to describe a space traveler led to the creation of the word "astronaut," formed from the Greek words "astron" (star) and "nautikos" (sailor).

Linguistic diffusion, or borrowing, is a common occurrence which may take place any time 2 cultures come into contact. Thus, the close contact between England and France, especially after the Norman conquest of Britain in 1066, has resulted in many French words being absorbed into the English language. Some of these replaced existing words: the Old English word for a group of warriors was *here,* but it was completely replaced by the French word *armee,* which became *army.* More often, though, the borrowed words (called "loan words") reflect a wider cultural exchange. That is, the English borrowed concepts or objects from the French and at the same time borrowed the words used to describe those concepts or objects. Because most word borrowing is of this latter kind, loan words strongly suggest the type of items one society borrows from another. For example, the borrowing of artistic items from Italian culture is indicated by such words as *piccolo, studio, replica, sonata, piano,* and *falsetto.* Or, if food items are borrowed from another culture, this will be reflected in the language; thus, Americans have such German additons as *sauerkraut, hamburger, frankfurter, pretzel,* and *wiener.*

The transmission of language is never perfect. As a language is passed on to a new

VIOLENCE AND MASS MEDIA

There is very little doubt that mass media in the United States serve us an entertainment diet containing more than a small serving of violence. Accusing fingers are most often directed at television since the average child, by the time he is 16 has spent as many hours watching TV as he has in the classroom. It seems safe to assume that a good deal of learning goes along with the watching. But does such learning involve a schooling in violence? How can we find out what effect violence in mass media has on the individual?

An increasing number of psychological and sociological studies have sought to find answers to these questions. One such study, conducted by social psychologist Albert Bandura and his associates at Stanford University, offers some insights, although their findings should not be taken as final proof of the influence of violence in the media. Much more study and experimentation is needed before definite conclusions can be formed.

In the Stanford experiment, nursery-school children were divided into four groups to test the extent to which young children would imitate aggressive patterns of behavior. The first group was taken, one-by-one, into a test room, where there was an adult and a variety of toys. After a few minutes of play, the adult began to attack a large plastic Bobo doll with a mallet, striking it repeatedly and shouting at it. The second group watched a film of an adult performing the same sort of aggressive behavior, and the third group watched a television showing of the adult, dressed in the cartoon costume of a cat, also attacking the doll. The fourth group acted as a control group—they played in the test room but observed no aggressive behavior.

At the end of 10 minutes the children were taken to an observation room, again one-by-one, but before they entered the room they were subjected to a mild dose of frustration: they were given the chance to play with some attractive toys, but then were told almost immediately that they would have to stop. This brief episode was based on the premise that aggressive tendencies are heightened by anger or frustration.

In the observation room, where each child was watched through a one-way mirror, the child found 2 sets of toys, some of which could obviously be used for aggressive purposes, including the Bobo doll and mallet; the other set of "nonaggressive" toys included such items as a tea set and crayons. Each child spent 20 minutes in the room and his behavior was observed and recorded.

Dr. Bandura states that "the results leave little doubt that exposure to violence heightens aggressive tendencies in children. Those who had seen the adult model attacking the Bobo doll showed approximately twice as much aggressiveness . . . as did those in the control group." The children who saw filmed or televised versions of aggression responded just as those who saw the real-life example—in fact, the group watching the cartoon figure responded with the highest score of aggressiveness.

Bandura emphasizes that there is a difference between *"learning* and *doing."* Children don't copy everything they see in real-life or on television because they are subject to other influences such as parental control and guidance. "No one should forget," he concludes, "that television is but one of several important influences on children's attitudes and social behavior, and other factors undoubtedly heighten or suppress its effects." Except in laboratory conditions, then, it may be impossible to isolate these other factors in order to measure the precise influence of the mass media.

generation, or as new words are borrowed, certain changes are likely to take place. Most of these changes are merely in the sounds of the words (*phonetic* changes), but meanings can change as well. Sometimes, the meanings will become more specific; for instance, the Old English word for "food" was *mete*, which has gradually changed to apply only to "edible flesh." The opposite process, where meanings become more general, is also common, as in the Middle English *brid*, which referred to a young birdling but has changed into the modern *bird*.

Language is intimately bound up with a society's culture and often reflects its central concerns. Americans, for example, have a few descriptive words for various types of snow, such as slush, packed snow, or icy snow. Skiers would be familiar with more specific words which are important for describing skiing conditions. And Eskimos have separate words for a great variety of snow and ice conditions indicating distinctions that are important to them in terms of their survival. Similarly, tribes in the Amazon region will have many words to describe different conditions of a jungle bird, and the language of Australoid hunters will contain numerous references to the tracks of animals.

Problems of Intercultural Communication

While language is clearly man's primary medium for communication, the variety of languages also creates serious problems. Men who share a common language can exchange thoughts with great precision, but communication among linguistically different groups is severely limited. This means, in turn, that cooperation among such groups is limited as well, since cooperation depends on effective communication.

Theoretically, there are 3 possible ways of cutting across the barriers raised by the diversity of languages: (1) have everyone learn all spoken languages, (2) have everyone adopt a single nation's language as a medium for intercultural exchange; and (3) devise a totally new language to serve solely as a vehicle for universal communication.

The first method is obviously impractical, since no individual could possibly master all the languages currently in use. Even mastery of as many as 10 languages is a prodigious achievement accomplished only by a few scholars.

The second method, that of having people adopt an established language, is within the range of human capability and has even been practiced on a limited scale. During the Middle Ages, for instance, Latin served as a common tongue for the educated classes of Europe, and it continues to serve as the official language of the Roman Catholic Church. During the 17th and 18th centuries, French was the usual language of diplomacy for much of the Western world. Once the British Empire became the leading political and economic entity in the world, English became a second language in many parts of the globe. The continuation of English as a major language for intercultural and intergovernmental communication also reflects the widespread commercial and political influence of the United States in this century.

In a few cases, there has even been some attempt to combine languages, at least informally, in order to overcome linguistic barriers. In Mediterranean ports, for example, a polyglot of languages called *lingua franca* developed in the late Middle Ages as a means of facilitating trade. It was composed of elements of Spanish, French, Italian, Greek, Arabic, and Turkish. In a similar way, explorers and traders often used "Pidgin English" as a means of communicating with tribes in Africa and the Pacific islands.

Despite these and other limited successes, there is no national language which even comes close to being a medium for world-wide intercultural exchange. People have simply not been able to agree on what language should be used to serve this purpose. Ethnocentric loyalties make such an agreement all but impossible—many groups might favor the scheme, but only if *their* language was the one that was chosen.

The third method of solving this communication problem, that of creating an artificial auxiliary language, has appealed to many people. A number of such languages have been formulated, with such names as Volapuk, Bopal, Spelin, Langue Bleue, Universal-Sprache, Mundolingue, Novial, and Basic English. While each language has had some supporters, none has come close to winning the approval needed to transform it into a working international tool.

Perhaps the most famous artificial language is *Esperanto*, developed by a Polish student of languages, L. L. Zamenhof, in the late 19th century. Esperanto has the great advantage of simplicity: it has a phonetic alphabet and there are no silent letters as there are in English and other languages. There are only 16 grammatical rules, which do not vary, and a mere 12 verb endings. English, by contrast, has over 700 verb endings and French has more than 2000. The parts of speech in Esperanto are easy to identify. All singular nouns end in "o," all adverbs in "e," and all adjectives in "a." To form any plural, one merely adds "j." Zamenhof's language won wide acclaim in the early 1900's and continues to attract supporters today, with roughly 8 million people currently able to use the language. Many countries have national Esperanto associations, and every year thousands of

Esperanto speakers from as many as 40 countries attend a Universal Esperanto Congress. But the dream of a universal language remains a distant goal.

The Problem of Semantic Variations

In addition to linguistic diversity, barriers to effective communication also emerge from *semantic* differences. Semantics can be loosely defined as that branch of linguistics that deals with the meanings of words. Communication problems arise, then, when there is lack of clarity over the meaning of words.

A common source of semantic confusion is the belief that each word has a single meaning or at most a limited number of meanings, each of which is duly recorded in a good dictionary. But, in a very real sense, any word has as many meanings as there are people who use it. That is, words are only symbols—they stand for something other than themselves. When we know a word, we know only the name of something, not the thing itself. Thus, to use a simple example, the word *chair* stands for something, but is not the thing itself; the word has meaning only if we have *experienced* a chair, and for each of us that experience is slightly different. The word conveys a particular concept to each of us, made up of common characteristics of chairs each person has seen and remembered. To put this another way, we can say that the meaning of a word for any individual will be determined by the unique experiences that individual has undergone.

Obviously, a word like *chair* is not likely to have a serious impact on human relationships. But we often get into semantic difficulties over words that are just about as simple. Consider the employer who asks a subordinate to draw up a report encompassing certain information. The subordinate performs the task, but receives anger rather than praise. "Why can't you do a simple job?" the employer is likely to say. "I told you what *I* wanted. Can't you follow directions?" What the employer probably failed to realize was that the instructions could have been interpreted in a variety of ways; a breakdown in effective communication has taken place. When this situation exists, it is also likely that a further result will be a breakdown in cooperation.

With words that refer to complex concepts, variations in meaning are more common and they can often cause disagreement. Consider, for example, the possible variations of meaning that could be applied to such words as "responsibility," "freedom," "democracy," "equality," "hope," "peace," or "progress." The difficulty in reducing semantic problems is illustrated in our governmental and legal systems. Although lawmakers generally take elaborate precautions to express their statutes in precise language, the resulting laws are still open to differing interpretations. Even a simple statement, such as the portion of the Fourteenth Amendment to the Constitution which reads ". . . nor shall any state deprive any person of life, liberty, or property without due process of law . . ." has been subject to different interpretations at different times. In the 1920's, for example, a state minimum wage law was declared unconstitutional by the Supreme Court because it was felt that such a law deprived both management and labor of their right to conclude a contract. The Court at that time was interpreting the clause in a restrictive sense. But during the 1930's, the Court reversed its former rulings, thus enabling states to pass laws governing wages and hours. Notice that the words of the "due process" clause did not change, but the *interpretation* of them did. Thus a simple semantic change had a broad impact which influenced the lives of millions of people.

MASS MEDIA

The rapid developments in communications technology achieved within the past 50 years have created a new era in human communication. The telephone and telegraph, modern innovations in printing, radio, movies, and television have brought mankind into the age of mass communication. Marshall McLuhan perhaps was not stretching the point when he said that this technological revolution had transformed the world into a "global village."

The 19th century was the great age of the newspaper as a means of mass communication. The daily and weekly papers became a source of information and entertainment for millions of people. This medium also had a powerful effect on the way people thought and acted. During the latter part of the century, for example, the large-circulation papers vied with one another for sensational stories that would capture a larger audience; this "yellow journalism" was a major factor in creating a public mood that led to the United States declaring war against Spain in 1898.

The electronic media, primarily radio and later television, broadened the impact of the mass media enormously. It suddenly became possible for government leaders, advertisers, educators, and anyone else to communicate almost instantaneously with huge, scattered audiences. There is hardly a corner of the globe that is not part of this communications network. Millions of people throughout the world, for instance, shared the grief of the American people over the assassination of President John Kennedy, by watching the aftermath of the event on television. It is significant to notice that the viewers were sharing spontaneous emotional responses as well as information.

Where television does not reach, the transistor radio does. This, too, has brought the world into closer contact, if in no other way than to make people aware of how others live. As social scientist A. Miller points out: "A generation or two ago the Colombian peasant was considerably more content with his lot in life. But the cheap transistor radio has changed that. Today the native of even the most remote Andean village is aware that a different way of life is available to some, if not yet to him. The result has been a new feeling of frustration and resentment."

The Effects of Mass Media

Radio and television, of course, touch the lives of just about everyone in American society. More than 90 percent of the homes in this country, for instance, have television sets, which is a higher percentage than that for telephones. This should not suggest that the printed word is becoming obsolete. In fact, quite the opposite is the case. More books,

*"Whom would you prefer to be Mao Tse-tung's successor—
Chou En-lai, Yeh Chien-ying, Li Teh-sheng, Chang Ch'un-
ch'iao, or Wang Hung-wen?"*

journals, and periodicals are printed today than ever before. This is true despite the fact that mass-circulation magazines such as *Life* have gone out of business, and the number of daily newspapers has declined from a peak of 2600 in 1909 to about 1700 today. Numerous special interest magazines have replaced the mass circulation periodicals of the past to a great extent, and newspaper circulation has actually increased from about 20 million readers in 1909 to well over 50 million in the 1970's. The newspaper industry has remained the 10th largest industry in the country for over 25 years.

The mass media influence how we communicate in a variety of ways. Using politics as an example, we can see that television alone has drastically changed the dynamics of the political process. Recognition of television's influence in this area became widespread following the presidential election of 1960. Many observers felt that John F. Kennedy's victory over Richard M. Nixon was largely due to his success in the televised debates between the 2 men. How much the debates influenced the voters may be open to question, but it is clear that a pattern was set for the future— every candidate for major office since then has been greatly concerned with his television "image." In fact, many people feel that no one can be elected to a major office unless he is capable of projecting the sort of TV image that people respond to. Political figures themselves seem convinced enough of this to employ Madison Avenue advertising firms in nearly all major campaigns.

Does this mean that public opinion molds the government leader and every candidate is out to please a mass audience? To some extent, this is true. Because of the mass media, government leaders are very much aware of the day-to-day fluctuations in their popularity. Both Presidents Johnson and Nixon took careful notice of opinion polls reported by newspa-

pers and television and both admitted that they did consider these polls in making many decisions.

But the media also operate in the other direction—that is, government leaders can use the mass media to mold public opinion. President Franklin D. Roosevelt was quick to notice the potential of the mass media in the 1930's. During that time, he encountered strong Congressional resistance to some of his programs, particularly to the later New Deal reforms and his desire to aid Western Europe against the aggressions of Nazi Germany. He began the practice of using the radio in what he called "fireside chats" with the American people, outlining his programs to the listening audience and seeking their support. He not only gained the support, but often succeeded in persuading Congress to become cooperative.

Television has been used in similar ways. President Richard Nixon, for example, learned that there were times *not* to use the mass media because to do so was likely to increase opposition. Instead, he would proceed with his own policies, then report to the American people to explain, and seek support for, the action he had taken. Even in less democratic countries, national leaders use the mass media to gain or maintain popularity. Fidel Castro, for instance, appears frequently on television to convince the Cuban people that his policies are designed to advance their interests and needs. In short, the mass media have made political leaders aware of a need to seek wide popular appeal; at the same time, the media provide them with a means of gaining or strengthening popular support.

Regulating the Media

Many people feel that the power of mass media to influence the public is exercised with

THE VARIOUS PATHS TO SOCIOLOGICAL KNOWLEDGE
EDWARD T. HALL

Communication between peoples of different cultures is often difficult because of language problems. Misunderstanding can also rise over nonverbal means of communication, such as "body language," facial expressions, and gestures. For example, at a time of considerable Cold War tension between the Soviet Union and the United States, Soviet Premier Nikita Khrushchev made an official visit to this country in a move toward more friendly relations. As he emerged from the airplane, Khrushchev clasped his hands above his head. To Americans, this was a defiant gesture—the prizefighter's signal of victory—and newspapers presented it that way. In Russian culture, however, the gesture was meant to convey a message of friendship.

To help ease such cross-cultural misunderstandings, a number of social scientists have tried to increase our understanding of how culture influences communication. A revealing example of this work is provided by the research of anthropologist Edward T. Hall. In *The Silent Language,* published in 1959, Hall deals with the concept of time as a form of communication. In the United States, he explains, people are very conscious of not wasting time. Time is broken down into discrete units that correspond to particular activities. Promptness is regarded as important because it shows respect for the person one is dealing with. Often, in communication with people of other cultures, Americans become disturbed when they feel there is no sense of American time. For example, American businessmen often have difficulties in their dealings with Latin Americans. Latin Americans are not as time conscious as we are. The American makes an appointment for 11 o'clock. If he is kept waiting for 5 minutes he is not greatly disturbed, but as 15 minutes go by he becomes edgy and annoyed. This is not only a conscious intellectual reaction, but also one that is rooted in his physiology. He receives bodily reactions of discomfort which increase his annoyance. By the time a half hour has passed he is disgusted, and if he has to wait for 45 minutes he feels deeply insulted. The message he has received from the Latin American businessman is one of lack of respect. Yet, this is not the message the Latin American wishes to convey. Within his culture, lateness of about 45 minutes is not meant to convey an insult. It is the beginning of the waiting period. It is equivalent to the 5-minute time scale of the American. "What bothers people in situations of this sort is that they don't realize they are being subjected to another form of communication. . . . The fact that the message conveyed is couched in no formal vocabulary makes things doubly difficult, because neither party can get very explicit about what is actually taking place."

The American views time as a material to be used. In addition, time is strictly segmented—one job at a time. Americans do not feel comfortable in doing many things simultaneously. Yet even within the borders of the United States, time has different meanings. For example, the Pueblo Indians who live in the Southwest have a completely different sense of time than other Americans. To most Americans, time is measured by a clock. For the Pueblo Indians, however, events begin when the time is ripe for them and no sooner. The Navajos have almost no sense of the future. This was a problem in the early days of range control and soil conservation. It was practically impossible to get the Navajo to cooperate in the programs necessary for soil control. The difficulty was in getting the Navajos to see that there was an advantage in giving up their sheep raising for a portion of the year—that there were future benefits in the program. The way Edward Hall dealt with this when he was put in charge is indicative of the importance of finding in another culture, a reward that is meaningful within its own context. He learned that the Navajos liked to bargain and respected success in this endeavor. Therefore, he explained that the government was giving them money to get out of debt, providing them with jobs that were near to home, and giving them water for their sheep. In return, the government demanded as its part of the bargain, 8 hours of work a day. Following this discussion, the work continued apace.

Hall's analysis also deals with ways in which concepts of space influence communication. One example is the question of how close one ought to stand to someone else for conversation purposes. "If a person gets too close," Hall states, "the reaction is instantaneous and automatic—the other person backs up. And if he gets too close again, back we go again. I have observed an American backing up the entire length of a long corridor while a foreigner whom he considers pushy tries to catch up with him." The foreigner is merely trying to establish the conversational distance that is customary in his country. Because the cultural concepts of space differ, the 2 people have difficulty communicating.

relatively few public safeguards. The debate over regulating the media became particularly sharp in the early 1970's when Vice-President Spiro Agnew attacked the press for "irresponsible" criticism of government policies and for actually contributing to an atmosphere in which civil disorders were likely.

The mass media in the United States, of course, do not operate completely free of restrictions. We have laws prohibiting deliberately false, libelous statements, and we have other laws aimed against purposely deceptive or misleading advertising. In addition, television and radio stations are licensed by the Federal Communications Commission, which means that the government has some control over these media. On the other hand, the first amendment of the Constitution guarantees that "Congress shall make no law . . . abridging the freedom . . . of the press," and this principle has been extended to apply to the other media. Americans have long considered free communications channels an essential part of a free society; Thomas Jefferson expressed the feeling of many people when he said he would prefer "newspapers without government to a government without newspapers." The belief and the tradition are so basic, that neither states nor Congress have attempted many regulatory laws; in fact, many of the laws which did exist, such as censorship of "pornographic" materials, have been declared unconstitutional.

In answer to the criticism that there is not sufficient regulation, spokesmen for the media offer several arguments. First, they point to efforts of the media to police themselves. Newspapers and broadcasters have formed various organizations for this purpose, and they have voluntarily adopted "codes of good practice." Second, they argue that our economy is geared to a continually growing market for consumer goods; therefore, vigorous advertising, which helps create a demand for products and services, is a necessary part of our economy. Finally, they note that advertising copy is by no means the only content disseminated through mass media. A great deal of information is conveyed along with the advertising, with the result that the American people today are probably better informed than at any prior time in their history.

The Quality of Mass Media

One of the major criticisms of the quality of the mass media is that the information the public receives is selected by only a few people and is often very incomplete. Sources of news, whether in newspapers or on television,

it is argued, emphasize the bizarre or sensational and are slanted according to the policies of the station or newspaper. An example from a relatively minor news event in 1968 illustrates the problem of accuracy in media reporting. On January 6th, the *Washington Post* printed the following paragraph:

French Finance Minister Michel Debré called America's proposed curbs on the dollar drain "discriminatory" Saturday and said that some of the "useless and unfair" restrictions in the program should be revised. In a meeting with Undersecretary of State Nicholas Katzenbach, Debré took a tough, uncompromising line.

The *New York Times* printed this version of the same "facts":

The French government warmly endorsed Saturday the policy announced by President Johnson last Monday for combatting the outflow of dollars from the United States . . . The French reaction emerged from a long talk between Finance Minister Michel Debré and U.S. Undersecretary of State Nicholas deB. Katzenbach.

Television presents an additional problem in that the viewer often feels that a 60-second news "coverage" of an event has provided him with full as well as valid information. Walter Cronkite expressed the concern of broadcasters themselves when he said, "I'm afraid that the public is getting brainwashed into a belief that they're getting all that they need to know from television. And this is not so. They need to know a great deal more than we can communicate to them."

Supporters of mass media feel that these criticisms are overstated. Plenty of information and varying viewpoints are available, they argue, to anyone who will take the trouble to find them. Television news is generally limited to "spot" news, because the public simply will not watch long news broadcasts. Those who want more detailed information can rely on newspapers and journals. And, if the news does seem to emphasize "three-legged calves," this, too, reflects the viewing and reading tastes of the public.

There is a similar debate, of course, over the quality of television programming. It is argued that television, like the other media, caters only to the so-called average taste level, and that quality programs are forced off the air by advertisers if they don't score a high rating. While much of this criticism is clearly justified, television is probably not as much of a "wasteland" as its harshest critics claim. Even though it seems to mean getting less for their advertising dollar, some advertisers make a conscious effort to support at least occasional programs that would appeal to what may be called sophisticated tastes. Public and educational television stations have made an even more concerted effort to provide solid educational and entertainment programming; if a public television station offers 20,000 such programs in a year, it gives the viewer a good deal to chose from. Similarly, the public can select radio stations or magazines and journals that appeal to their specialized tastes.

SUMMARY

Communication, or symbolic interaction, is not limited to human beings. However, while animal communication is abundant, it is strictly limited and does not improve from generation to generation. Man's ability to communicate is more varied and allows him to construct and transmit his culture.

Communication among cultures fosters complexity and technological progress while reducing the differences among peoples. The diversity of groups within a society is also reduced with more communication.

Language is mankind's chief medium of communication. A language may be defined as *a system of arbitrary vocal symbols used to convey information among the participants in a culture*. Every language in existence contains a limited number of sounds, but each may be adapted to express an almost unlimited variety of ideas.

When men developed *writing*, they took an enormous step forward in cultural achievement. No longer did they have to depend upon memory to store and transmit their accumulated knowledge.

Approximately 2500 different languages exist in the modern world and these are grouped into about 100 linguistic families. This multiplicity of tongues has proven a barrier to communication, and therefore cooperation, among societies.

Semantic problems also interfere with communication among human beings. These problems arise from the fact that word meanings vary from individual to individual and from society to society.

Today it is possible to communicate with huge, scattered audiences via mass media. Radio, television, newspapers, books, magazines, records, and motion pictures now disseminate information at an unprecedented rate. The enormous potential influence of mass communication has inspired continuing debate over the regulation of the media and the quality of its information or entertainment.

GLOSSARY

communication transmission of information, ideas, attitudes, and emotions from one person or group to another, primarily through symbols.

ideograph   a drawing combining several pictographs to present an idea.   Precedes true writing in the evolution of graphic communication.

mass media   the channels of communication reaching large numbers of people, including radio, periodicals, films, and television.

pictograph   stylized and simplified drawing of an object.   A precursor of true writing.

semantics   the study of the meanings of words, including usage, historical development, and the relationship of words to behavior.

word coining   the process of forming new words from parts or combinations of existing words.

SUGGESTED READINGS

Chase, Stuart and Chase, Marian T.   *Power of Words*.   New York: Harcourt Brace Jovanovich, Inc., 1954.   One of the best books in the field of language and communication.

Doob, Leonard W.   *Public Opinion and Propaganda*, 2nd ed.   Hamden, Conn.: Shoestring Press, 1966.   An analysis of public opinion and propaganda from the point of view of modern science.

Hall, Edward T.   *The Silent Language*.   New York: Fawcett World Library, 1969.   An interesting treatment of human communication, stressing cultural variations.

Hayakawa, S. I.   *Language in Thought and Action*, 3rd ed.   New York: Harcourt Brace Jovanovich, Inc., 1972.   A popular treatment of all phases of semantics.

Laird, Charlton.   *Thinking About Language*.   New York: Holt, Rinehart and Winston, Inc., 1960.   A discussion of the origins and growth of words as well as the impact of language on society.

Lee, Alfred M. and Lee, Elizabeth B.   *The Art of Propaganda*.   New York: Octagon Books, 1972.   A revealing look at the effects of propaganda.

Neal, Harry Edward.   *Communication: From Stone Age to Space Age*.   New York: Julian Messner, 1960.   Interesting treatment of the development of communications from the earliest to the most recent times.

Orwell, George.   *1984*.   New York: Signet Books, 1971.   A frightening look into the future and the possible use or misuse of mass communication.

13

COLLECTIVE BEHAVIOR AND SOCIAL MOVEMENTS

You have probably noticed that people tend to act differently when they are part of a large, excited crowd. The study of collective behavior is important to sociologists for 2 reasons: first, it can tell us a good deal about how large groups of people react to unusual or emergency situations. Second, collective behavior has been a phenomenon that has frequently altered the course of history, thus providing a dramatic indicator of major social change.

THE NATURE OF COLLECTIVE BEHAVIOR

Sociologists have long observed that people tend to exhibit strange or uncharacteristic behavior in certain group situations. Specialists in the study of collective behavior have been particularly concerned about what happens when large numbers of people find themselves in an emergency situation, a crisis in which they seem to lack guidance, structure, or norms. When usual routines are shattered by unexpected or threatening circumstances, people often panic, engaging in riots or random or bizarre behavior. Great excitement and the rapid spread of high emotional states are characteristic. Calmer, closer examination of collective behavior has revealed certain patterns that provide some basis for preparing for emergencies, for predicting what will happen, and for exercising more rational control over events.

Collective behavior is usually associated with *unstructured* circumstances—circumstances in which the usual guidelines for behavior do not exist. What we have already said about group living will make this clear.

Through long years of socialization, most people are prepared to conduct themselves adequately within the various groups they ordinarily encounter. The average individual has little difficulty in functioning effectively within the family and the community, among friends, and in business or social organizations. People have definite places within these groups, definite roles to play, and clearly defined group norms to rely on. In addition, their personality patterns are usually well adapted to deal with these familiar conditions; consequently, ingrained habits, values, and attitudes stand them in good stead.

But there are situations which people are not well prepared to meet—situations in which they have no clear roles to play, group norms are poorly defined, and the familiar patterns of personality do not seem to apply. These are the situations sociologists call unstructured circumstances.

A theater audience provides a good illustration of a potentially unstructured group situation. Audiences are ephemeral in character; they come together solely for the purpose of viewing a performance and they disperse as soon as the performance is over. Consequently, audiences have little opportunity or reason to agree on behavioral standards which would serve them in time of emergency. In such a situation, a sudden emergency, such as a shout of "Fire!" is likely to send the group into a panic, with people literally trampling one another in an hysterical effort to escape danger. Any such ephemeral gathering—a crowd at a sports event, a protest rally, passengers on a subway—is likely to produce collective behavior. The unstructured circumstances which lead to collective behavior can also occur when a normally stable group or community is faced with any sudden emergency. An earthquake, fire, flood, war, hurricanes—any crisis of this sort is likely to break down the normal behavioral patterns and produce collective behavior.

Special Characteristics of Collective Behavior

Although collective reactions can take a wide variety of forms, they are generally accompanied by a set of recognizable features. These can be described as follows:

Emotional Contagion. By this phrase, sociologists mean that emotions tend to run high during collective reactions and these feelings are speedily conveyed from person to person. In the case of a theater fire, the emotion of fear becomes dominant and is communicated throughout the audience. Moreover, the fear seems to reinforce itself, becoming stronger as it moves. For example, at a football game, if one person starts a shout or cheer or taunt and others pick it up, it quickly spreads throughout the crowd, and those who helped start it find their own emotions heightened by the wave of emotion.

Notice that in the case of the theater fire, it is the emotion—the fear itself—that is communicated, not necessarily the conviction that a fire is burning. Some people will join in the general flight even if they don't know why exactly they are fleeing. They don't have to be told verbally that they are in danger; they sense this from the reactions of those about them.

Fear is not the only emotion communicated in this fashion; almost any strong human feeling can become contagious under the proper conditions. Comedians, for example, know that laughter is contagious; consequently, many of them will send someone out ahead of their performance to warm up the audience with a few jokes. The advance man establishes the mood of the audience and the comedian makes the most of it. Political rallies are carefully staged in a similar way, often with people "planted" in the audience to spark an enthusiastic response. Or, at a presidential nominating convention, when a name is offered for nomination, the candidate's supporters will launch a long, loud demonstration, with bands, banners, slogans, and chants. This is a deliberate attempt to gain support by sweeping other delegates into a highly emotional state.

Heightened Suggestibility. A second feature of collective behavior is *heightened suggestibility*. This means that people caught up in a collective reaction often act on suggestions they might otherwise reject. Undoubtedly, such an effect is related to the highly emotional state in which the people find themselves. Their emotions seem to cloud their

reason, with the result that their ability to think critically is temporarily suspended.

Heightened suggestibility is often observed in the chains of events leading to certain forms of "mob" action, such as lynchings. Suppose, for example, the people of a town are angered and frightened over a recent crime. A crowd forms and collective feelings run high. Rumors spread. Someone mentions a name, and even with no evidence to support the accusation, the vast majority are suddenly convinced that the named person is guilty. The crowd becomes an angry mob, bent on lynching the suspected offender.

Slackening of Normal Restraints. People caught up in an emotionally charged group will often behave in a manner totally out of keeping with their normal behavior. Lacking the familiar guidelines available to them in more structured circumstances, they give vent to impulses which they would normally suppress. The most sedate individual might shout at the top of his lungs and wildly pound his neighbor after an exciting play in a football game. Or a normally law-abiding person may indulge in vandalism, looting, or attacks on others as a part of a mob.

One factor which seems related to such slackening of normal restraints is the *anonymity* inherent in crowd membership. A person "loses" himself in a crowd; an individual's actions are to a large extent concealed in the actions of others. In a large group, one becomes anonymous and can perform deeds, even socially unacceptable deeds, without fear of being recognized or punished. The impulse to throw a brick or fire a gun during a mass demonstration comes from the unusual emotional state of the moment, and is given added strength by this cloak of anonymity.

It is important to emphasize that irrational collective behavior, while potentially present in all unstructured group situations, is not a common phenomenon but rather one that is associated with unusual crisis or stress. Moreover, some people seem to be more or less immune to the contagion of collective behavior. Some people, for example, will remain very calm in an emergency, taking rational steps to avoid danger, whether it's trying to escape a theater fire or dissuade others from a lynching. And some individuals emerge as "natural" leaders in unstructured situations, in either a positive or a negative way. That is, some will take the lead in spurring a mob to fury or violent action; in contrast, during a natural disaster such as a flood or earthquake, some individuals are likely to perform extraordinary feats in trying to assist others.

The Role of Communication

So far we have referred to collective behavior in terms of large groups coming together. In the age of mass media, such face-to-face contact is not always needed to set off a collective reaction. What is needed is effective communication—radio, television, newspapers, leaflets, and the like—which may present a stimulus simultaneously to people spread throughout an entire community or even a nation. If people respond to this stimulus in a patterned emotional manner, they are exhibiting collective behavior. It is estimated, for example, that within a half-hour of the shooting of President John Kennedy, more than half the nation was in contact with the event through the media of radio and television. For some days after that moment, the vast majority of Americans and millions of others throughout the world shared in the emotion-charged atmosphere of grief and shock.

The "Martian Invasion." One of the best-documented instances of collective behavior dependent on effective communication took place in the United States on the evening of October 30, 1938. The stimulus in this case

was a radio program, a drama based on H. G. Wells' novel *The War of the Worlds.* Dealing with a "Martian invasion" of the earth, the play was presented as a scheduled offering by the Mercury Theater, written and directed by the noted actor, Orson Welles. At the outset it was announced that what was to follow was a drama, and the broadcast was interrupted on several occasions with announcements that the events depicted were not real. Otherwise, however, the performance was extremely realistic. Listeners heard from an on-the-spot "news announcer" that a meteor had fallen in New Jersey. Then they heard that the object was not a meteor at all, but a spaceship, and that strange, alien creatures were beginning to emerge. As the play progressed, various "scientists" were interviewed which heightened the effect of authenticity. "Military leaders" and "government officials" directed troop movements and ordered the evacuation of 2 New Jersey counties. In short, anyone who tuned in late or ignored the qualifying announcements was treated to a most authentic-sounding drama. The impact of the play was increased by the fact that many people did tune in late—the program's major rival, the Edgar Bergen and Charlie McCarthy show featured an unknown guest singer; when she came on, thousands of people engaged in the common practice of switching their dials and caught the Mercury Theater just as the "emergency" was announced.

Reactions to the broadcast varied. A great many people—probably the majority of the audience—soon realized that they were listening to a science-fiction story. But others were convinced that the events depicted were real; and having accepted this suggestion, they gave way to panic. Some people, believing that the end of the world was at hand, called relatives and loved ones to say last farewells. Entire families reportedly ran into the streets with moistened handkerchiefs over their faces as a precaution against poison gas. One report states that a woman tried to commit suicide rather than be caught by the "leather-faced" Martians. Telephone calls jammed the lines at police stations, bus terminals, newspaper offices, and hospitals. Ambulances were dispatched on needless errands of mercy, their sirens undoubtedly adding to the emotional contagion. Although the panic centered in and around New Jersey, similar reactions occurred at scattered points throughout the country. It has been estimated that at least 6 million people heard the broadcast and that 1 million of these became disturbed or frightened.

One factor which should be considered in connection with this incident is the world background against which it took place. By the late 1930's, radio had come into its own as a means of disseminating news to the public; people were accustomed to learning of important events from radio broadcasts. Something quite similar would be likely to occur today if a television series were interrupted by what appeared to be an authentic news flash announcing an invasion from outer space.

In addition, the daily news in 1938 reflected an extremely unsettled international situation. Nazi militarism in Europe and Japanese militarism in Asia were menacing world peace and threatening to draw the United States into armed conflict. A war scare had occurred a few weeks before the broadcast when Hitler threatened to invade Czechoslovakia. The memories of the devastation of World War I were less than 20 years old and now the airplane was recognized as a fearsome weapon, capable of inflicting heavy damage on cities and civilian populations. Consequently, people were already thinking about the possibilities of invasion, and particularly an attack by air. All of this undoubtedly helps to explain why the suggestion of a Martian invasion was accepted so readily.

The "Pitting" Epidemic. A somewhat similar incident took place in Seattle, Washington, during the spring of 1954. In the early part of that year, American nuclear testing had included the explosion of an H-bomb at Eniwetok Atoll in the Pacific, a development that caused considerable public alarm. Newspaper stories of the test discussed the dangers of nuclear fallout, including such items as a fallout "scare" tying up the Japanese fishing fleet. Then, on March 23, the papers carried reports of a strange phenomenon—mysterious damage to automobile windshields. The first reports of such damage came from a city some 80 miles north of Seattle; similar reports followed in the next few weeks.

By April 14, the windshield trouble seemed to be moving closer to Seattle. The morning paper noted that a town 65 miles away had been affected, and the afternoon papers carried similar stories from a naval air station only 45 miles to the north. By evening, the first damage was reported in Seattle itself.

During that night and the following day, the Seattle police received 242 phone calls reporting damage to over 3000 vehicles. The damage was described mainly as pit marks that grew into small bubbles, or as tiny, metal-like black specks on the glass. People began placing covers over their windshields or garaging their cars. On the next day, the mayor declared that the situation was out of police hands and called for assistance from both state and federal authorities. Then, almost as quickly as it began, the pitting epidemic died out. On April 16, only 46 calls were received; 10 calls came in the following day, and none after that. The epidemic was over.

Several explanations were offered to account for the pitting phenomenon. Blame was placed on meteoric dust, sand-flea eggs hatching in the glass, air pollution from industrial waste, cosmic rays, and vandalism. But the possibility mentioned most often had to do with radioactive fallout from the recent H-bomb tests.

Shortly after the epidemic, the governor of Washington asked the University of Washington Environmental Research Laboratory to conduct an investigation. The laboratory's report stated that virtually all of the evidence of pitting could be attributed to normal road damage. The tiny black specks were identified as cenospheres, the natural by-products of imperfect coal combustion. It was further reported that cenospheres were rather common to Seattle and that they were incapable of damaging windshields.

What then is the explanation for the remarkable behavior of the people who claimed mysterious damage to their windshields? In all probability, the whole incident was caused by some form of collective hysteria. Having heard reports of windshield damage, the residents of the city began looking at their windshields carefully. And for the first time, probably, they began to notice the effects of ordinary wear. They interpreted this road wear according to the suggestions they had received—namely that some mysterious force, such as fallout, was producing the damage.

Crazes, Fads, and Fashions

The unusual, often bizarre aspects of collective behavior are not limited to crisis situations. Emotional contagion is also evidenced in the crazes, fads, and fashions that create a collective response. In these cases, the collective behavior is not necessarily associated with a crowd or audience, but rather with a particular group within society, often limited to a particular age or category.

Crazes or manias are rapidly spreading, but usually short-lived interests that practically consume the energies and attentions of those involved. An example would be what was

called the "Tulipmania" craze which broke out in Holland in the early 1830's. Large numbers of people suddenly got the idea that the development and sale of tulip bulbs was a get-rich-quick scheme. They began to speculate in tulips, investing life savings in the process, and sending the prices of some hybrid bulbs to astronomical sums. Many people, from nobles to farm workers, made huge fortunes almost overnight. Within a few years, the bubble burst and tulip prices plummeted back to their original levels, wiping out the savings and fortunes of many.

Similar sorts of crazes occur periodically in such ventures as land speculation and gold-rushes. For a time, feverish activity seizes hundreds or thousands of people, as fortune hunters flock into a desired bit of territory. Within time, with only a handful gaining the desired riches, the harsh realities of the situation force a quick end to the boom. The same sort of motivation spurred the chainletter craze in this country during the depression years of the 1930's.

The impulse that creates a craze is not always money. Among American Indians in the Western states and territories in the last century, for example, a Ghost-Dance mania developed. The belief spread that by dancing in a particular way, the ghosts of ancestors would be encouraged to return as living Indians to help drive the white invaders from the land. For a brief time around 1890, the Ghost-Dance craze revived the hopes of many American Indians; when the promised results didn't occur, the mania died out almost as quickly as it had begun.

Fads are also short-lived, and differ from crazes only in the degree of their social significance, since they usually deal with rather trivial circumstances. Various dance steps or types of music, the hoola-hoop, computerized dating, karate parlors, dance marathons, and goldfish-swallowing are all examples of fads.

Decorative items are also frequently in the nature of fads—such as black light posters, pop art, flag-like designs, and head bands.

The line between fads and fashions is thin; usually, fashions are considered to be more enduring and represent what is considered the style of the times. The length of hair and clothing designs are obvious examples. The rapid change in clothing styles is, by and large, a deliberate effort by designers and manufacturers to take advantage of people's desires to keep up with the latest fashions. This form of collective reaction is also evidenced in such widely diverse areas as home styles, slang expressions, child-rearing practices, and the tactics of pressure groups. In child-raising, for example, the authoritative, firm control exercised by one generation of parents gave way to the permissiveness of the post-war generation, heavily influenced by Dr. Benjamin Spock's *Baby and Child Care*. Similarly, whether groups concerned with social reform use violent or nonviolent tactics can be considered largely a measure of what the style of the times happens to be.

COLLECTIVE BEHAVIOR IN HISTORY

Historically, collective behavior represents a significant phenomenon. Many important historical events have been associated with emotional group reactions. The French Revolution of 1789, for example, received much of its impetus from the angry mobs that swept through the streets of Paris demanding an end to the "Old Regime." Similarly, the Russian Revolution of 1917 showed signs of settling into a social-democratic experiment, only to have the street mobs, stirred to action by the charismatic leadership of Nicolai Lenin, provide the unrest that enabled the Bolsheviks

to seize power. More recently, the Civil Rights movement of the 1960's was in large part shaped by the huge demonstrations, both violent and nonviolent, that swept the nation from Selma, Alabama, to Washington, D.C., to the Watts district of Los Angeles.

Adolf Hitler: Manipulating Collective Behavior

We mentioned earlier that the role of a "natural" leader can be important in unstructured situations. This is particularly true of what are termed *charismatic* leaders. Charisma is one of those words that is difficult to define in precise terms, but generally it is used to refer to those people who, by the very power of their personalities, can persuade others to follow their lead under almost any circumstances. In this century, such men as Gandhi, Hitler, Martin Luther King, and John Kennedy would generally be considered outstanding charismatic leaders.

Throughout history, charismatic leaders have sought to turn the phenomenon of collective behavior to their personal advantage. Julius Caesar, for example, knew how to arouse mass support that helped him overcome the entrenched power of the Roman Senate and achieve one-man control of the Republic. Napoleon Bonaparte stirred his troops to great achievements in battle, maintaining wide popular support even in the face of crushing defeat. But perhaps the outstanding manipulator of collective behavior was Adolf Hitler.

Hitler's rise to power during the early 1930's came at a time when the German people were already subject to many emotional pressures. Germany's defeat in World War I and the harsh peace terms imposed by the Treaty of Versailles left many Germans in a bitter frame of mind. Matters were made worse a few years later when a devastating

PERSPECTIVE

INDIVIDUAL SECURITY IN A HIGH-RISK ENVIRONMENT

We live today in what Richard Falk of Princeton University has termed a "high-risk" environment—it's as though we are all sitting on a global powder keg that threatens to explode at any moment. Inside that keg are such volatile ingredients as the threat of nuclear destruction, over-population, pollution, poverty, depletion of resources, and so on. Many social scientists have become concerned with what effect these constant threats have upon individual and group behavior and upon people's feelings of security. Will the pressure of events create collective behavior such as that evidenced in many of the urban riots and antiwar demonstrations of the 1960's? Or are we capable of coping with these stresses in a calmer, more logical manner?

The primary concern of writers in all of the social science disciplines seems to be with the effect this high-risk environment has upon the young, because this is the first generation to grow up with the constant threat of world-wide catastrophe. As Stephen Spendor, author of *The Year of the Young Rebels,* has said, what are seen as "problems" by those over 30 "are built into the flesh and blood of the young." Political scientist Hanna Arendt has spelled out the problem in more precise terms:

> This is the first generation to grow up under the shadow of the atom bomb. They inherited from their parents' generation the experience of a massive intrusion of criminal violence into politics: they learned in high school and college about concentration and extermination camps, about genocide and torture, about the wholesale slaughter of civilians in war. . . .

In observing the behavior of America's young people, it is natural to look for cause and effect relationships. It is assumed that our massive global problems, especially the threat of nuclear holocaust, must have some influence on the way people behave. Consequently, whenever any major trend in youthful behavior becomes evident—whether it is apathy or rebellion or something in between—analysts try to connect this behavior to the insecurity created by the high-risk environment.

Depending on the type of behavior observed, and the vantage point of the observer, one can come to either pessimistic or optimistic conclusions. Here are some samples of pessimistic generalizations arrived at by a number of leading writers on social problems:

> • Sociologist Arnold Green: It is a world of insecurity and uncertainty, blaring headlines and sudden shocks, in which the accumulation of experience is insufficient preparation for the next, unforeseen stimulus. And meanwhile a tremendous discharge of nervous energy runs into a hundred deviant channels. Bitterness, despondency, dependency, spread like a pall, along with the belief that all is chance.

> • Hannah Arendt: The basic reason for youthful insecurity and rebellion is the simple fact that technological progress is leading straight into disaster.

• Social critic Paul Goodman: Survival is especially a youth problem because kids are deprived and powerless. As the world gets more ossified, there is no place for them. They are alienated, with little or no sense of the world.

• Supreme Court Justice William O. Douglas: . . . a black silence of fear possesses the nation and is causing us to jettison some of our libertarian traditions.

• Former Attorney General Ramsey Clark: Will we seek a little more safety by giving up a little less liberty? Can fear, affluence, or lethargy overpower our will to enlarge both liberty and security?

• Nobel-prize winning biologist George Wald, in discussing the cause of student unrest in cities around the world: I think this whole generation of students is beset with a profound uneasiness, and I don't think they have yet quite defined its source . . . I think I know what is bothering our students. I think that what we are up against is a generation that is by no means sure that it has a future.

On the other hand, it is almost as common to see signs of optimism and hope in the way youth is responding to our multiple crises. Here are some examples:

• Hannah Arendt, balancing the rather gloomy quote given above: . . . Psychologically this generation seems everywhere characterized by sheer courage, an astounding will to action, and by a no less astounding confidence in the possibility of change.

• British economist Barbara Ward sees our very problems pulling us together in a new sense of world community: [These problems, combined with instant communication] will enormously strengthen the sense of nearness and human proximity—not always for good, for who loves all his neighbors?—but always for awareness, and always for attention, for influence, for concern.

• Former President Richard Nixon: The process of freedom will be less threatened in America if we pay more heed to one of the great cries of the young today. I speak of their demand for honesty: intellectual honesty, personal honesty, public honesty. Much of what seems to be revolt is really little more than this: an attempt to strip away sham and pretense, to get down to the basic nub of truth.

• Joseph Lyford, president of the Fund for Peace: It is a remarkable and melancholy fact, which our fascination for the shortcomings of the young should not obscure, that it has been young and inexperienced people who have provided the impetus for reforms in our universities, put some life into our political parties, and led the counter-offensive against the militarization of American policy. It is because of their prodding that more and more middle-aged people are getting out of the habit of resigning themselves to sorry situations.

It should be clear that these observations are little more than educated speculations. They are not supported by what could be considered scientific proofs. Only long and intensive study can accurately reveal what effect the high-risk environment has on youth and in what ways youth is likely to respond. There are so many variables involved in one's sense of security and behavior that perhaps no scientific study of this high-risk mood will ever be possible.

inflationary period wiped out the savings of pratically the entire middle class, and this event was followed almost immediately by the world-wide depression of the 1930's, which left the country in chaos and on the verge of economic collapse. The growing strength of the Communist Party increased the fears of many, and people began searching about desperately for some solution. Their difficulties seemed caused by forces beyond the average person's control or understanding, and the government—the Weimar Republic—appeared incapable of coping with the problems. In short, for many Germans life was pretty much a matter of unstructured circumstances.

To exploit these conditions, Hitler depended heavily on mass reactions. He made every attempt to heighten the already emotional state of the German people. When he spoke in person, he held great spectacles calculated to impress the audience with his power and importance. Usually, he would arrange thousands of Nazi troops or workers in precise rows, sometimes in a massive torch-lit demonstration. His huge platforms were covered with gigantic standards displaying the swastika, that semimystical insignia he had chosen to symbolize his new order. To heighten the dramatic effect, he would walk slowly to the speakers' platform through the ranks of his troops, with muffled drums accompanying his deliberate steps. And he always followed his own advice, which he had written in *Mein Kampf:* "Always be the last to enter a group. In fact, keep them waiting for your appearance. Then, in order to be discussed by them, be sure you are the first to leave."

Hitler's speeches, whether delivered in person or over the radio, were also designed to appeal on an emotional basis. His voice often rose to a high pitch that bordered on a scream. His message was a combination of slogans, myths, and promises. He offered the German people convenient scapegoats by blaming the country's troubles on everyone from the Weimar leaders to foreign powers. He conjured up romantic pictures of former German glories and claimed that his Third Reich would restore those glories in an empire that would last "a thousand years." He spoke of German supremacy, based on the myth of an Aryan "super race," and preached hatred for "inferior" peoples, especially the Jews. The pageantry, the repetition, the emotional appeals, the power of his personality all had their effect; if we are to judge by the short but terrifying period during which Hitler held absolute power in Germany, many people threw reason and caution aside to follow him.

STUDIES OF COLLECTIVE BEHAVIOR

In recent years the phenomenon of collective behavior has been studied carefully by sociologists and other behavioral scientists. The knowledge gained has been important from a scientific point of view and has also had wide practical application. It has been useful for public officials, school administrators, business managers, and others who have to deal with large numbers of people. By knowing in advance the type of situations that are likely to set off collective reactions and by knowing how people are likely to react in times of great stress, planners can take precautionary measures. They can help to prevent an unexpected stimulus from turning a normal situation into an unstructured one.

The "War of the Worlds" Studies

Among the collective phenomena that have been studied by scientists is the *War of the Worlds* incident described earlier. The research team interviewed many of the people who heard the broadcast and discovered certain patterned reactions. For example, since many of the listeners were unsure whether or not they were hearing actual reports of a Martian invasion, they tried to check their initial reactions. Some called the radio station, while others read the program listing in the newspaper. People who checked in either of these ways quickly had their fears allayed and avoided panic.

Others who tried to check, however, remained convinced of the "newscast's" authenticity. Apparently, most people in this group had already accepted the suggestion that an invasion was underway and were only checking in an attempt to see if they were in personal danger. In their panic, they chose singularly ineffective means of testing their impressions, such as phoning neighbors and looking out their windows. Then they interpreted what they heard or saw in terms of the panic they already felt, as indicated by these samples recorded by the research team:

"I looked out of the window and everything looked the same as usual *so I thought it hadn't reached our section yet.*"

"We looked out the window and Wyoming Avenue was black with cars. *People were rushing away, I figured.*"

"No cars came down my street. *'Traffic is jammed on account of the roads being destroyed,'* I thought."[1]

Propaganda Studies

Studies on the nature and methods of propaganda have been useful in providing information about heightened suggestibility and emotional contagion. Propaganda, which may

[1] Reported in Cantril, Gaudet, and Hertzog, *The Invasion From Mars* (Princeton University Press, 1940).

be considered as any deliberate attempt to influence group opinions or attitudes, is in itself not necessarily harmful. Thus, advertising agencies, pressure groups and lobbies, even religious groups are engaged in propaganda. And actions as well as words can serve propagandistic purposes; a major motive for American foreign aid programs, for instance, has been to persuade others of this nation's friendliness.

Some studies of propaganda concentrate on how effective techniques of political or economic persuasion are. Others have been more concerned with reducing the harmful effects of propaganda and with helping societies avoid being controlled by "mob psychology." In a study called *The Fine Art of Propaganda*, sociologists Alfred McClung Lee and Elizabeth Briant Lee have isolated specific propagandistic "tricks of the trade." The chief devices—used both in personal argument as well as by "professional propagandists"—were identified as:

Name-calling—giving an idea a bad label to make people reject and condemn an idea without examining the evidence. . . .

Examples would be "loser," "whitey," "Red," "Yankee."

Glittering generality—associating something with a "virtue word" . . . to make us accept and approve . . . without examining the evidence.

Included would be reference to words like "democracy," "science," or "freedom."

Transfer—carries the authority, sanction, and prestige of something respected and revered over to something else in order to make the latter either respectable or rejected, depending on the aims.

Testimonial—consists of having some hated or respected person say that a given idea or program or product or person is good or bad.

Plain folks—the method by which the speaker attempts to convince his audience that he and his ideas are good because they are "for the people."

Card-stacking—involves the selection or use of facts or falsehoods, illustrations or distractions, and logical or illogical statements in order to give the best possible case for an idea, program, person, or product.

An example would be "don't drive God out of the public schools."

Band wagon—has as its theme "Everybody—at least all of *us*—is doing it."

Practical Applications of Collective Behavior Studies

Studies such as those mentioned here have important implications for people who have to deal with large human aggregates. They point to a need for establishing systems for dispensing reliable information and direction in times of stress. If people can be reassured during a real or imaginary emergency, the worst effects of mass hysteria can be avoided.

Studies have shown, for example, that if people are properly drilled in emergency procedures they are much more likely to behave rationally in times of crisis. This has been the rationale behind Civil Defense alerts and school fire drills. Behavioral guidelines are established that can keep even highly charged situations well structured. Similarly, the planning that went into a number of Civil Rights demonstrations, such as the march on Washington in 1963, revealed a knowledge of the reactions of large groups which helped the planners and participants maintain remarkable order.

Various "warning systems" have also been established to minimize rumor and increase effective communication in time of emer-

gency. The "Conelrad" radio warning system for example, uses 2 special radio frequencies (640 and 1240) which have been set aside exclusively for emergency use. Similar warning systems have been established to deal with potential natural disasters such as hurricanes, tornadoes, and floods. Weather Bureau warnings enable public officials and Civil Defense forces to institute calm and rational emergency procedures.

SOCIAL MOVEMENTS AS COLLECTIVE BEHAVIOR

Sociological studies of social movements were rare until the last few years. As recently as 1965, Alex Inkeles argued that social scientists had not properly explained social movements of the present or the past, nor related them to the phenomenon of collective behavior. "With a few notable exceptions," he wrote, "little has been done by sociologists and psychologists to meet this challenge." Such developments as the Civil Rights Movement, antiwar demonstrations, women's liberation, and emerging movements by Chicanos, Chinese Americans, and American Indians have spurred a new interest in this field. The growing number of studies is now providing important information about the nature of social movements.

Social Change and Social Movements

There is an important interrelationship between collective behavior and social change. During periods of great social upheaval—disasters, social unrest, war, or the end of war—normal life situations frequently take on that unstructured quality mentioned earlier. People exhibit the characteristics of collective behavior in their response to the change. The collective behavior, in turn, can trigger further social change, particularly if the collective response becomes a social movement. Here is how this apparently circular process works.

When the traditional routines of life become unsettled, there is often a period of uncertainty. People cannot decide quite how to act. Until the 1960's, for example, most Americans accepted their society as one based on ideals of industrial progress and economic expansion. A few social critics raised warning signals, but few paid any attention. Most people were far too busy getting a job or getting ahead or enjoying the increasing abundance of consumer goods and services.

Then we discovered that our "cowboy economics" had created an environmental emergency. Our resources were being squandered, our air, water, and land were in serious danger. People were not sure how to respond to this situation. The old ways did not seem to be working. And yet there was no blueprint to provide new ways.

It is in situations such as this that collective responses are likely, and these responses can develop into a social movement. A first reaction might be crowd protests or rallies, or protest through the mass media. This collective behavior evolves into a movement when: (a) the collective behavior persists; (b) it becomes organized; and (c) when it begins to take specific directions and involve a sense of action. Environmental concerns have taken on these aspects of a social movement.

A variety of groups is also likely to be involved. Each group is a collection of individuals who have pretty much the same perceptions of the situation. They can join together with other groups which have slightly different perceptions at least for the purpose of achieving action. Thus, the ecology movement has included such diverse groups as scientists, grade school children, hippies, church organizations, politicians, and businessmen.

To varying degrees, the people who join such a movement become dedicated to the cause. They are loyal to the beliefs of the movement and they might direct many of their actions toward achieving particular goals—from salvaging aluminum cans to gaining United Nations supervision of ocean pollution.

The relationship of the movement to further social change now becomes apparent. The action of the movement creates change. While the ecology movement has not been an unqualified success, it has contributed to social change. Antipollution legislation, new educational programs, increased public awareness, advances in technology, changing attitudes toward land use and industrial expansion—all are products of this social movement.

The Role of Ideology

The process of social change is also likely to contribute to new ideologies or systems of beliefs, each of which will become the organizing body of ideas for a social movement. A change that has a profound impact on society is likely to lead to a number of such ideologies. These offer explanations of why traditional methods have failed and provide action plans for future changes.

During the Great Depression of the 1930's, social upheaval contributed to ideologies of both left and right. Some people, for example, saw the economic chaos as a clear sign of the decay of the capitalist system. Some groups found that one of the varieties of socialist ideology offered a new sense of order and a plan for the future. Many Americans embraced communism during this period. Since

THE VARIOUS PATHS TO SOCIOLOGICAL KNOWLEDGE
GUSTAVE LE BON

Why does a mob behave in irrational ways? How do fads emerge and what determines which fads will become accepted customs? How does collective behavior influence dramatic events and how is it related to the process of social change?

Such questions have been of major concern to sociologists for a long time. One of the first to work in this field was Gustave Le Bon, who wrote *The Crowd* in 1895. Although methods of research had not yet been well established, Le Bon succeeded in raising important questions that influenced a number of writers and researchers. Le Bon tried to distinguish the basic aspects of collective behavior.

The most important feature of a crowd, according to Le Bon, is the intensification of emotion in its members. Concurrently, there is an inhibition of the intellect of the members of a crowd. The heightened emotion produces a rapid vacillation between conflicting emotions, such as love and hate.

In a crowd, an individual acquires, solely from numerical considerations, a feeling of invincible power which allows him to yield to sentiments that he would resist in ordinary situations. He is less disposed to exercise restraint. This is the result of the anonymity found in a crowd by its individual members.

In a crowd, every action is contagious to such a degree that an individual readily sacrifices his personal interest to the collective interest. As a result, the individual feels isolated in the midst of a crowd. Therefore, he can commit acts that would be unlikely for him in a situation affording greater responsibility.

Le Bon concludes from this that the prime characteristic of the crowd is that it acts on the unconscious level. Its motives are hidden beneath the surface. Le Bon compares the behavior of people in crowds to the behavior of primitive beings. The varying impulses of the crowd may be generous or cruel, but they will be so imperious that the interest of the individual will not dominate them.

Crowds are extremely suggestible. This is because their members are in a state of expectant attention. Yet, suggestions given to a crowd must be of a simple or extreme nature. The opinions and beliefs suggested to crowd members are accepted or rejected as a whole, and are considered as absolute truth or absolute error. Therefore, crowds are prone to authoritarianism and intolerance. Within a crowd, fundamentally opposite ideas can exist at the same time.

In crowd situations, there is an instinctive search for a leader. His will is the nucleus around which the others play their roles. As leader, he wields despotic authority, albeit for a short time. Crowd leaders may be divided into 2 clearly defined classes—temporary and permanent. Permanent leaders are much less ordinary than temporary ones. They include religious leaders and many political leaders who have reached power through the actions of a crowd.

Le Bon then applied these ideas to many different aspects of social life. He saw a danger, for example, that the psychology of the crowd could affect the stability of society and the rate of social change. Building on these ideas, a later writer, Sigmund Neumann, carried them to their logical conclusion by stating: "Mob psychology, when it seizes a whole nation, destroys the web of its complex structure . . . This process of 'massification' . . . in a way preceded the rise of modern dictators."

Other modern writers have followed Le Bon's lead into somewhat less pessimistic analyses of collective behavior. Modern studies of mass communications, urban riots, social movements, elections, and public opinion are serious attempts to deal with the questions Le Bon first raised concerning the relationship between the "crowd" and other aspects of social life.

communism at the time was nearly synonymous with the Soviet Union, this required them to close their eyes to the harsh realities of the Stalinist regime.

Quite different ideologies also grew out of those economically troubled times. Some people saw the problem as part of a conspiracy developed either by the Communists or the Jews (and sometimes the two terms were interchangeable). The Nazi ideology of Hitler's Germany and varieties of fascism, such as Mussolini's Italy, were dedicated to strengthening the capitalist system from these assaults.

The emphasis on action and the development of belief systems frequently causes splits within movements. People are searching for a new sense of order, a new consensus to replace the patterns that had previously been accepted. One ideology or one plan of action will satisfy some; others will demand more or different action or a system of beliefs that corresponds to their own perceptions of the situation. When members of the American Indian Movement seized the town of Wounded Knee in 1973, for example, they had formed a splinter movement dedicated to more revolutionary action. Other leaders of the Indian struggle insisted that the only way to achieve change was through peaceful reforms of the existing system.

The Role of Rising Expectations

Social movements generally do not grow out of desperate situations. The great movements of the past were not carried out by the starving, the wretchedly poor, or the imprisoned. Instead, this type of collective behavior is most likely to appeal to those whose lot is improving but who find that they are impatient for faster change or who feel that others are gaining relatively more. Thus, the American and French Revolutions were both largely the products of middle-class groups who felt constrained by traditional controls. The problem was not that they were deprived or suffering; rather, they saw themselves as victims of unjust treatment, and they wanted to change to correct those injustices.

Similarly, the black movement for civil rights was hardly a movement during the slavery period. Occasional outbursts, such as Nat Turner's rebellion, were spontaneous cases of crowd behavior—there was not the long-range, organized approach characteristic of movements. The Civil Rights movement gained momentum when the life of black Americans was improving at a fairly rapid rate. A study conducted in 1965 showed that the sampling of blacks was significantly more satisfied with employment, children's education, housing, and family income than had been the case only 3 years earlier. It was at this point that the rate of progress began to chafe—there were heightened expectations that now seemed attainable, but blacks could not attain

them because of the injustices of white-dominated society.

The Life Cycle of Social Movements

Social movements can become so permanent and highly organized that they are essentially new institutions. Many religious sects, for example, began as movements of protest or regeneration. Gradually, the movement's organization became permanent and the sect became an established church.

Other movements may dissolve. Occasionally, this is achieved by the repressive forces resisting the action of the movement. This was the case in a number of European countries in the years following World War I. The Bolshevik Revolution had succeeded in Russia in 1917–1918. Members of communist parties saw this as the signal for a world-wide movement by workers. The abortive uprisings were crushed by police and military forces.

Movements can disappear also by being submerged in more powerful organizations. American farmers in the late 19th century, for example, established the Grange movement to protect their rights in an economy increasingly dominated by big business. The movement lost its political cutting edge when its programs were absorbed by the major political parties. Socialism has met a similar fate in the United States. Whenever programs of the Socialist Party began to attract large numbers of voters, one of the major parties simply inserted a plank in its platform that promised the same action.

Finally, some movements depend largely on the personality of a charismatic leader. Their ability and fortune (good or bad) will have much to do with what happens to the movement. The long-time dictator of Argentina, Juan Peron, was also the leader of the Peronist movement. Although exiled for 17 years, he was able to return in 1973, win an election, and pull together diverse groups including the extreme left and extreme right.

SUMMARY

The term *collective behavior* refers to the reactions of people caught up in *unstructured* circumstances. Typically, collective reactions are characterized by the rapid spread of emotions. The participants tend to accept suggestions readily and, under the cloak of *anonymity*, to ignore the usual restraints upon their behavior.

Through an effective communications link, such as might be supplied by modern-day mass media, collective behavior can be stimulated among vast numbers of people, even if they are not physically close to one another. The collective panic following the 1938 radio broadcast about a "Martian invasion" is a classic example. Another example of collective hysteria is the "pitting epidemic" of Seattle, in which many people wrongly ascribed pits in their windshields to fallout from bomb tests which had been prominent in the news.

Collective behavior is not limited to crisis situations. *Crazes* are short-lived but rapidly spreading interests that take up most of a person's energies. Crazes are often connected with wild monetary speculations, but they may have other motivations. *Fads* resemble crazes but are less significant; goldfish-swallowing and the popularity of headbands are examples. *Fashions* represent the "style of the times" in such diverse areas as clothing and child-rearing practices.

Some collective reactions have actually helped to shape history. Emotional group reactions figured in the French and Russian revolutions, and, more recently, in the civil rights movement of the 1960's. Many men throughout the ages have managed to exploit collective behavior to their own advantage. An outstanding recent example was Adolf Hitler.

Studies have helped show how people's collective reactions are patterned. The analysis of propaganda reveals that it influences people by means of a regular set of nonrational devices.

The study of collective behavior has yielded information with highly practical applications. It is important that those who deal with large groups be familiar with the way people are apt to react in times of stress.

A growing body of sociological research deals with social movements as manifestations of collective behavior. Growing out of the unstructured circumstances accompanying social change, movements are built around a plan of action directed toward still further change; the process is actually an attempt to create a new sense of order. Movements often involve new ideologies, and these plus the desire for action lead to frequent splintering. Some will want more radical action or beliefs than others. If successful, a movement may become institutionalized.

GLOSSARY

charisma   a mystical personal quality that makes an individual seem to have special—sometimes superhuman—abilities and traits that draw others to him.

collective behavior   behavior of a number of persons in unstructured group circumstances responding to a common influence or stimulus. Characterized by emotional contagion, heightened suggestibility, and a slackening of normal restraints.

craze   a rapidly spreading but short-lived novel interest that consumes the attention or energies of large numbers of people.

emotional contagion   the rapid spread of heightened feelings found in collective reactions.

fad   a trivial, short-lived pattern of unusual behavior that spreads rapidly.

fashion   a form of socially approved behavior that is subject to periodic change.   The spread of fashions is a form of collective behavior.

propaganda   a method of presenting information in such a way as to channel the thinking or actions of a large number of people along certain lines.

SUGGESTED READINGS

Blaumer, Robert. *Ghettos, Riots and the Negro Protest.* Houston, Texas: University of Houston Press, 1966. Blaumer deals with specific episodes of the mid-1960's, particularly the Watts riot, to develop the theory that the actions were not so much cases of mob madness as unorganized attempts by blacks to gain control of their own community.

Cantril, Hadley. *The Invasion from Mars: A Study in the Psychology of Panic.* Princeton University Press, 1940. Cantril reviews the famous Orson Welles' "Invasion from Mars" radio broadcast and the various responses to it. These responses, in turn, are used as the basis for general comments on the nature of collective behavior in time of crisis.

Graham, Hugh Davis and Gun, Ted Robert, (eds.). *The History of Violence in America.* New York: Bantam Books and the New York Times, 1969. This collection of essays and research reports is particularly useful for tracing the history of collective violence in the United States. A number of studies also provide comparisons with collective violence in other societies.

Greenberg, Bradley S. and Parker, Edwin B. (eds.). *The Kennedy Assassination and the American Public.* Stanford, Calif.: Stanford University Press, 1965. This collection of essays represents attempts to assess how communication operates in time of crisis, with special focus on the role of the mass media.

Keniston, Kenneth. *Young Radicals: Notes on Committed Youth.* New York: Harcourt, 1968. Keniston analyzes the student movements of the 1960's, revealing important aspects of the collective behavioral aspects of social movements.

14

MINORITY RELATIONS

Human beings have a strong tendency to classify everything in their environment, including each other. For example, people throughout the world have recognized classifications based on race, religion, and cultural heritage. Where these classifications have been considered important, they have served as the bases for marking certain groups as "different" from their neighbors. Such "different" groups, or minorities, have experienced treatment ranging from annihilation and expulsion to acceptance and assimilation.

THE NATURE OF MINORITY GROUPS

Human societies are not always homogeneous in their population make-up. On the contrary, many societies contain groups of people who seem to stand out from their populations as a whole. Such groups are identified as minority groups, or simply minorities.

Sometimes we are inclined to think of minority groups as typically an American phenomena. And to be sure, there are many minorities in the United States. Blacks, Orientals, Puerto Ricans, and Mexicans, for example, all have been treated as minorities; so have various immigrant and religious groups, such as Jews and Roman Catholics. However, other societies also have their minority problems. In Canada, the Hutterites, Dukobors, Eskimos, and French Canadians have a minority status. The Soviet Union houses literally hundreds of minorities, including some with such exotic names as Yakuts, Tadziks, Bashkirs, Kirghiz, Chechens, Daghestans, and Chuvash. New Zealand currently is concerned about her principal minority, the native Maoris. Australians have had to make special provision for the aborigines, the original inhabitants of the Australian continent. Hungarians have been sometimes proud, sometimes fearful of their nomadic gypsies. Spain had so much trouble with her Moriscos (Moors who had embraced Christianity) that she finally expelled them in the 17th century. In the modern world, newspapers carry intermittent stories concerning the Bantus of South Africa, the Ainus of Japan, the Igorot of the Philippines, the Yemenites of Israel, the Todas of India, and the Kachins of Burma. Minorities, then, are restricted to no particular era or country. They are found throughout history and in many different parts of the world.

It often happens that minority groups not only are distinguished from the rest of the society but are also disadvantaged. That is, the minority's members are discriminated against by the society's majority, or dominant group. Such discrimination may take a variety of forms, but at the very least it usually involves a denial of opportunity for full participation in the society's life.

Discrimination against a minority is usually an outgrowth of prejudice. Literally, prejudice may be defined as prejudgment, or the formulating of opinion on the basis of insufficient or misleading evidence. As they relate to minorities, prejudices usually involve stereotypes. These are preconceived mental images which rest not on a true knowledge of a group but on half-truths, opinions, and a generally distorted viewpoint. Once someone forms a stereotyped view of a group, it is difficult for the person to think of the members of that group in an objective light.

Prejudices, of course, are learned. No one is born with built-in attitudes toward certain groups or individuals. Rather, these are acquired through social contacts. Sometimes prejudices originate in the competition among people for available jobs, wealth, or living space. Often, they develop because people mistrust groups whose norms and values are "different" or "foreign." Ignorance and fear are at the basis of much prejudice. Once learned, prejudices may be passed on from generation to generation. Sometimes they are actually woven into the very fabric of a society's culture, receiving support from the norms. Often, small groups within a society support a prejudice.

All of this is not to condemn prejudice categorically. Some prejudices are quite understandable. Most people have a favorable predisposition toward their own family, community, school, society—any of the groups to which they belong. In themselves, these feelings are not harmful; indeed, it would be hard to conceive of any society existing without them.

At times, however, group loyalties become so strong that they result in a distrust for "outsiders" and foster unjust, discriminatory treatment of others. When this happens, the inevitable results are strong tensions which can disrupt the harmonious functioning of any society. It is this aspect of minority-majority relationships more than any other that helps to make the whole subject sociologically important.

At first glance, one could easily conclude that minority groups lack power or influence in the host society—the minorities are the ones that suffer from prejudice and discrimination. This is not always the case. Throughout history, there have been situations in which a minority is in a position of greater power than the majority. In the Republic of South Africa today, for example, the Bantus are the largest single group, numbering 13 million out of a population of about 20 million. And yet, the 4 million whites of the nation hold a virtual monopoly of political and economic power. Much the same situation exists in Rhodesia, where the white minority group of 230,000 dominates a society of more than 5 million.

One other observation is in order. Prejudice and discrimination are not the exclusive properties of majorities. They are also held by minorities, sometimes directed against majorities, and sometimes directed against other minorities. No human group is immune from fostering either prejudice or discrimination against other groups.

HOW MINORITIES ARE DIFFERENTIATED

As we noted above, all minorities are somehow "different" from the dominant group within their society. Usually, they are either (1) racially different, (2) religiously different, or (3) culturally different.

Racial Categories

In Chapter 2, we noted that races are categories. People are classified within a particular race because they share or are thought to share certain common physical characteristics. At one time, it was widely believed that the task of classifying all mankind on a racial basis could be performed rather easily. When scientists attempted the task, however, it proved far more difficult than had been assumed.

One anthropologist, Alfred Kroeber, suggested that there are 3 races of men: Caucasoid, Mongoloid, and Negroid. But later he felt compelled to note a fourth race, a residual category in which he placed such people as the Australoids, the Ainu, the Veddoids, and the Polynesians. Another expert, Alexander Goldenweiser, decided that there are 5 races: Negro, Australian, Mongolian, American Indian, and White. E. P. Stibbe disagreed with both Kroeber and Goldenweiser and arrived at 6 races, namely, Mediterranean, Alpine, Nordic, Mongoloid, Negroid, and Australoid. Ralph Linton, another distinguished anthropologist, arrived at 17 races, while Malvina H. Hoffman held that she had found over 70 races. When the various attempts to set up racial categories are reviewed, one finds that the experts have listed as few as 2 to as many as 200 different races.

Such a range of classifications makes the whole search for separate races quite suspect. In their zeal to separate humanity into distinctive races, some scholars underestimated the tremendous similarities between people. All human beings, after all, belong to one common species, *Homo sapiens*. Regardless of racial "differences," they can interbreed and produce their own kind.

In modern terminology, races are *breeding populations*, persons who have pooled genetic qualities to produce an identifiable type of human being. The "differences" they reproduce vary from gross differences in body forms to microscopic differences in biochemical agents such as antibodies in blood streams.

Stanley Garn, a genetic specialist, distinguishes between 3 different kinds of breeding populations—*geographical races, local races,* and *microraces.* Geographical races are the largest categories of races and consist of a collection of breeding populations separated from other such collections by major geographical barriers such as oceans, high mountains, and huge deserts. Thus, Garn would speak of Africans, Europeans, Asiatics, and Australoids as representative of geographical races.

Local races are those that may share the same geographical area, but who remain genetically apart, not only because of great distances between them, but also because social barriers or local tabus prevent mixing with "outsiders." The Bushmen of the Kalahari Desert and Iruri-forest Pigmies are both Africans, but they are also examples of local races. The same may be said for the Eskimos of the Far North who are spread over a distance of some 6 thousand miles from the Aleutians in the west to the island of Greenland in the east. The Aleuts and Greenland Eskimos are local races who have not interbred in over 5 hundred years.

Microraces constitute even smaller segments of local races. As breeding populations, they genetically breed with persons mainly near them and so produce identifiable types. Europeans, for example, despite their fairly close proximity to each other, tend to produce microraces because they constantly select nearby neighbors as marriage partners. Italians of the North and Italians of the South are examples of microraces in Europe.

What are some of the "identifiable differences" that are used to distinguish between geographical, local, and microraces? We cannot dwell at length on the many and complex criteria that are used by scientists, but we can refer briefly to some of the better-known and widely used criteria that differentiate minorities from majorities.

Skin pigmentation. Most untrained persons like to rely upon skin pigmentation to distinguish between various races. They use color terms such as "whites," "blacks," "browns," "yellows," or "reds." But these terms are far too vague to be useful for precise distinctions.

Scientists have known for years that the key pigment is *melanin,* a brown-black or dark pigment that lies in the lower layers of the skin. Melanin is found in *all races,* from the very light-skinned Europeans in Scandinavia to the dark-skinned Africans. The only true "whites" would be *albinos,* those who lack melanin and who, consequently, need to be very careful about exposing themselves to the sun's rays. Albinos, of course, are found in every race so that one can speak of "white" blacks as a matter of fact and not fiction.

Those who are so-called "white" have varying degrees of melanin in their complexion and, thus, some can tan to a deep bronze color during the summer while others will suffer from sunburn. After a summer of intensive "sunbathing," some "whites" appear to be "brown" or "black" whites. In fact, "whites" are not really white at all. They are a light, pinkish brown and vary in reflecting light from their skins from about 40 percent in the lightest complexions to less than 20 percent in the darkest complexions.

Aside from melanin, the red coloration of hemoglobin in the blood of *Homo sapiens* accounts for additional skin hues. It is most obvious in the "pink" eyes of albinos, but it plays a part in reflecting light depending upon how close blood vessels lie to the skin's surface. *Carotene* is the rarest of the pigments and varies from yellow to a yellow-red. It is best observed in red-hair follicles of certain individuals.

Skin pigmentation, then, while widely used to distinguish between races, fails badly as a scientific means to separate individuals into distinctive races. Skin pigments are not different among people. Rather, there are degrees of coloration based upon pigments that all humans share.

Blood theory. One of the most persistent myths of modern times is the "blood theory." So-called knowledgeable persons speak of "full-blooded" or "half-blooded" individuals.

The "blood theory" is based upon the assumption that somehow, the blood carries the inherited characteristics of a person. Today, of course, we know that genes are the carriers of inherited traits and that geneticists have penetrated deeper into the structure of genes to understand their nature, to know how the various structures work, and to recognize their combined effects.

Microscopic agents or substances in the blood of *Homo sapiens* were detected through serological (blood) studies and explained why blood transfusions between healthy donors and ill, injured, or surgical recipients failed or succeeded. The best known, because they were discovered first many years ago, were the ABO agglutinates. Individual blood typing provides four categories, A, B, AB, and O. Instead of each race falling neatly into one of the blood types, the blood factors were found in each "race" in different proportions. The same was discovered for other blood factors, less well known because they were located relatively recently. These blood groupings include those known as MNS-U, Rhesus positive and Rhesus negative, Duffy factors, Diego factors, and Kidd factors. None of these blood factors is the exclusive blood grouping for a specific race. Rather, as with the ABO agglutinates, the various blood factors are distributed among all races in various proportions.

Other racial criteria. There are many more criteria that scientists have used to distinguish one race from another. They are, in these instances, visible and measurable items and would seem to lend themselves to distinguishing between the races. But, again, as with skin pigmentation and blood groupings, they occur in every so-called race and differ only in proportions from one racial category to another.

In all honesty, what usually passes as the basis for describing racial differences amounts to little more than biological trivia. The differences are simply the end products of genetic combinations and are no more biologically significant than the large ears found on some elephants and the small ears found on other elephants. They are no more significant than the fact that there are black leopards and there are spotted leopards. The angle of jaw-jut a number of persons happen to have says very little about a person except to say that such a facial structure exists. The epicanthic fold has little or nothing to do with keen or poor vision. The texture of hair, skull shape and volume, amount of body hair, nasal index, or general body stature reveal very little about individuals except to say that these are genetic adaptations that persons have biologically inherited. There are no really biologically significant differences among races; instead, the *detailed similarities* impress upon the observer the fact that all people belong to a single species.

Race and Cultural Achievement

When intelligence tests were first given to army recruits during World War I, the results indicated that Northern "whites" achieved higher scores than Southern "blacks." But subsequent and continuous studies over the past 60 or so years have not sustained the earlier conclusion that racial differences alone accounted for intelligence test differences.

What were significant factors were social class advantages such as motivation, opportunity, facilities, and training in education. When *comparable* groups of "whites" and "blacks" were tested intellectually, their scores ranged from high to low, but they were not distinctly different. In short, controlling all variables except that of race, the independent variable, did not result in one race or another being more or less intelligent than any other race.

Further, the cultural achievements of geographical races cannot be said to support the contention that one race or another is superior or inferior. It is true that European "whites" have made momentous discoveries in the sciences, technologies, humanities, and arts, but no less can be said for the genius, beauty, and accomplishments of African "blacks" or Asiatic and New World Mongoloids. Their history and accomplishments are still being revealed. In part, some of this failure to recognize the considerable achievements of every geographical race can be credited to lack of communication or to the loss of traits, complexes, and patterns over historical time. Another explanation has been that many facts have been kept out of the human record, consciously or unwittingly. This last shortcoming is being rapidly counteracted by belated scholarship that reveals the rich cultural heritage of many racial minorities. Schools and colleges throughout the country have instituted Black Studies programs in recent years and there is a growing interest in the cultural achievements of American Indians.

Religious Minorities

One need only glance at the pages of history to observe that many groups have been assigned a minority status on the basis of their religious beliefs and practices. Among the first important religious minorities in the west-

ern world were the early Christians, whose refusal to worship the pagan gods of ancient Rome earned them persecution and martyrdom. Ironically, after Christianity became the dominant religion in the Roman Empire, the situation was completely reversed and pagans became a minority against whom the overwhelming power of the state was directed. During the ensuing Dark and Middle Ages, Christianity won dominance throughout much of Europe, with the result that various non-Christian groups became minorities. Members of the Jewish faith, for example, constituted a leading non-Christian minority and frequently suffered abuse. Meanwhile, in Spain, North Africa, Egypt, and the Levant, Moslem conquests reduced the Christian population to a minority status.

After the Protestant Reformation of the 16th century, although Europe remained basically Christian, Christianity was split into a number of denominations which differed from one another in belief and practice. Some of these became minorities within one or another European society. In Protestant England, for example, Roman Catholics were persecuted as a minority during the reign of Elizabeth I, while Protestant Huguenots suffered the same fate in Catholic France. Nor was religious friction confined solely to that between Protestants and Catholics, because the various Protestant sects often disagreed among themselves.

Problems in the New World

When Europeans began colonizing the Americas, they transferred many of their religious disputes to the Western Hemisphere. Religious alignments in the New World were not always the same as they had been in Europe, but minorities definitely did appear. In the English colonies groups which suffered discriminatory treatment for their religious convictions included Quakers, Jews, and Catholics.

With the founding of the United States, the principle of religious freedom was embodied within the First Amendment in the Bill of Rights, which proclaimed complete freedom of worship for all citizens. For a time the spirit of the Constitution seemed to prevail, for America entered a period of comparatively little religious friction. But this was not to last.

The 19th century was marked by several outbursts of strong resentment against America's religious minorities. Much of this resentment was antiforeign as well as antireligious. It was tied to the fact that the ranks of the minorities were being swollen by immigrants. For example, the sizeable influx of Irish and German Catholics during the years before the Civil War helped bring about the various "nativist" movements, which were sustained, at least in part, by anti-Catholic sentiment.

Anti-Semitism in the United States

During the latter half of the century, the waves of immigrants from southern and eastern Europe brought about not only another wave of anti-Catholic feeling but also a strong resentment against Jews. The Jewish minority became the object of widely circulated propaganda. It was suggested, for example, that Jews were engaged in an international plot to gain a stranglehold upon the world's economy. This and other equally absurd rumors apparently found a fairly large and receptive audience, perhaps because of the centuries-old association in the popular mind between members of the Jewish faith and financial dealings. The association had been fostered during the Middle Ages by the church's stand prohibiting interest-taking. Unaffected by this particular

restriction, Jews became the moneylenders of the medieval world, thereby performing a necessary service but nonetheless incurring considerable resentment. Another belief that became quite popular during the late 19th and early 20th centuries was that Jews somehow constitute a racial group and that this predetermines their behavior. This belief, of course, suffers from at least 2 major defects. First, racial membership does not determine behavior. Second, Jewish people do not constitute a race at all; they merely share a common core of religious beliefs and practices. People from all 3 major racial categories may and do belong to the Jewish faith.

Anti-Semitism in the United States did not stop with propaganda; various discriminatory techniques also were employed. For example, Jews were prevented from entering certain occupational fields, excluded from certain hotels and recreational centers, and denied the privilege of living in certain communities.

Today, there are still religious minorities within the United States, at least in the purely numerical sense of the term. And there is still some evidence that tensions between minority and majority members continue to exist. However, religious tolerance has become very much of a reality in this country and discriminatory treatment seems very much reduced.

Cultural Differences

Racial and religious differences do not exhaust the bases for minority-majority group differences. Cultural differences abound in America, a land made up essentially of immigrants who came into the New World at different points in time. Aside from the American Indians, descendants of migrants who walked across the land-bridge of Beringia at the northeast corner of Asia and the northwest corner of North America, all Americans are immi-

PERSPECTIVE

BEYOND THE MELTING POT

Americans have never been entirely certain of what they mean by the concept of our nation as the "melting pot." Ideally, it suggests that our country is a great mixture of racial and ethnic groupings that have melted together into something new, something distinctly American.

This ideal was expressed in glowing terms in a play called "The Melting Pot" which had a long run on Broadway in the second decade of this century:

> America is God's crucible, the great Melting Pot where all the races of Europe are melting and reforming! . . . Germans and Frenchmen, Irishmen and Englishmen, Jews and Russians—into the Crucible with you all! God is making the American!

There is more than a grain of truth has this romantic vision. Each of the diverse groups that has made up our nation has not only absorbed American culture, but has added something to it. Frankfurters, french-fried potatoes, and spaghetti are as American as fried chicken, pork and beans or apple pie—and, of course, the mixing of cultures goes deeper that that.

Even though we have developed certain distinctly American characteristics, however, many people still cling to a certain ideal of the Anglo-Saxon Protestant. This was basically the structure of our society in the early years of our national history, and the great waves of immigrants—more than 35 million of them in the century following 1820—were expected to conform to this "WASP" ideal.

When the immigrants were slow to respond to this unspoken expectation, they found themselves ostracized by the mainstream of American society, the victims of prejudice, discrimination, and segregation. First it was the Irish and the Germans, then, in the closing decades of the 19th century, it happened to the "new wave" of immigrants from Eastern and Southern Europe who were found to be even more "different" in terms of language and customs.

Many native-born Americans were upset that these newcomers were slow to adopt "American" ways. They lived in their separate "ethnic islands," usually were poor, and maintained their national customs, languages, and newspapers. At about the same time that *The Melting Pot* appeared on Broadway, a leading American educator voiced a common sentiment when he said: "Our task is to break up their settlements, to assimilate and amalgamate these people, and to implant in them the Anglo-Saxon conception of righteousness, law, and order." When the immigrants were stubborn and confused in their response, one reaction was to close the doors to free immigration a few years after World War I.

The process of "melting" has occurred, but it has meant that the newcomers, to be fully accepted, had to learn to conform as well as they could to the Anglo-American ideal. Consequently, the result was far from being a balanced mixing of cultures, but rather, the predominance of the "traditional" American culture.

After the first generation of immigrants, the original language and most of the customs were lost. The children of immigrants usually found it easier to turn their backs on the "old ways" and to become instead "like all other Americans," with the same language, education, customs, and aspirations.

But clearly the process of assimilation has been far from complete. Our nation is still a patchwork quilt of distinct ethnic groupings and even more distinct racial minorities. The melting pot is only a partial reality; as an accurate characterization of our society it remains largely a myth. Instead, our nation consists of what sociologists refer to as "cultural pluralism," which is more like a salad bowl than a melting pot.

Nathan Glazer and Daniel Patrick Moynihan in their urban study, *Beyond The Melting Pot*, point out that New York City is nearly as much a mixture of distinct groups as it was a half-century ago. Nearly 20 percent of New Yorkers are foreign-born and almost a third more are the children of immigrants. Roughly 1 million, for example, were born in Italy or are the children of Italian immigrants; one-half million more, mostly Jews, are of Russian background. With about 15 percent of the population Negro and another 10 percent Puerto Rican, this leaves less than one-third of New York made up of "Old-stock" whites. "From almost every country in the world," the authors state, "there are enough people in the city to make up communities of thousands and tens of thousands with organizations, churches, a language, some distinctive culture."

New York, of course, is not typical of the nation because it continues to absorb the greater proportion of new immigrants. But the point that Glazer and Moynihan stress is that people who are even the grandchildren or the great-grandchildren of immigrants still tend to identify themselves for some purposes and on some occasions with the original nationality. People of Italian descent, for instance, continue to identify themselves to some extent with their Italian heritage. This is seldom common in secondary group relationships—job, school, etc. But it is often a factor in primary group ties—in the choice of neighborhoods, close friends, and marriage partners. This sense of ethnic identity does not make people any less American, but they do find a sense of belonging and common interest in considering themselves as Irish, Polish, Armenians, Russians, and so on. According to Glazer and Moynihan, even today "the ethnic group is something of an extended family or tribe."

While we have gradually come to accept the idea of cultural pluralism in regard to ethnic groupings, we have been much more confused in our attitudes toward racial minorities. We seem to be unsure whether we want total assimilation, as many tried to force on the immigrants, total separation or cultural pluralism. In terms of trying to establish sound intergroup relations and reduce the factors of discrimination and prejudice, sociologist Milton Gordon has suggested that "the United States proceeds like a race horse galloping along with blinders. He doesn't know where he's been, he doesn't know where he is, and he doesn't know where he's going. But he's making progress!"

If we accept the ideal of cultural pluralism, this means that we leave the choice up to the individual. A member of a racial minority—whether Oriental, Negro, Puerto Rican, Chicano, or American Indian—can decide whether to try to fit into the mainstream of American culture or to choose the surroundings of a racially distinct community. Again, this process applies more to primary group relationships than to secondary.

This process may prevent us from attaining the democratic values. Thus, we have room in our society for blacks who wish to assimilate culture as well as for those who believe in striving toward "black nationalism"; Indians can move to cities and seek higher education or "typical" American careers, or they can use the tribal community as the basis for rebuilding and restrengthening their proud and distinctive culture.

Black writer Ruth Turner Perst sums up this attitude which can be as easily applied to other racial minorities: "What can black power mean for America? It can mean the reaffirmation of the concept of a pluralistic American society, respect of an individual's heritage and contribution, and a respect for difference in a nation that tends too readily to become amorphous, dull, and conformist."

grants or descendants of immigrants from many lands.

Dutch colonists in New York and Swedish colonists in Delaware were cultural minorities among the dominant British colonists. Later on, Irish, German, and Scandinavians were viewed as cultural minorities by the English-speaking majority, but their common origins from northern and western Europe brought them closer together as "old" immigrants.

By the late 19th century, a drastic change in the cultural origins of immigrants to America began. This became the "new" wave of immigrants from southern and eastern Europe. Italians, Greeks, Poles, Russians, and Slavs from the old Austro-Hungarian Empire made up the bulk of these "new" immigrants. Free, arable, open land was gone or difficult to reach by the time of their arrival. They settled mainly in the cities despite the fact that they were rural people. Since America was fast becoming industrialized, the "new" immigrants had to compete with "older" residents for jobs and this, in itself, became a source of friction between them. Further, their unfamiliarity with cultural norms of their fellow Americans, particularly their limited command of English, set them apart in ethnic enclaves that aided their early adjustments to America but delayed their entry into the mainstream of American life for a time.

The "land of opportunity," however, was limited in its ability to absorb an unrestricted flow of immigrants. Gradually, the doors were closed by a series of restrictive legislation. Immigration from the Orient was closed off first and was soon followed by quota systems. The quotas were limits imposed upon immigrants from other societies, but their effect was to favor immigrants from northern and western Europe. As late as 1952, a limit of 170,000 persons was set for immigrants from the Eastern Hemisphere and 120,000 from the Western Hemisphere. Passed in 1965 and put into effect in 1968, a new system scrapped quotas in favor of a system of preferences for those who could bring desired professions or skills into the country. The present laws place the burden of proof upon a would-be immigrant who must prove able, willing, and qualified to perform work that is needed in the United States and whose entrance would not adversely affect the wages or working conditions of Americans already employed within that particular occupation.

Minorities of "Mixed Differences"

Racial, religious, and cultural "differences" are not necessarily mutually exclusive. There are a number of minorities that combine these qualities such as American Indians who have maintained their traditional ways in the Pueblos of the Southwest. These Amerinds are both racially and culturally set apart from the majority of Americans. The Amish or "Plain People" of Ohio, Pennsylvania, and Indiana are both religiously and culturally "different" from the vast majority of Americans. Those Japanese Americans who are practicing Buddhists represent the full combination of racial, religious, and cultural "differences" from the majority of Americans. If the "differences" are nonthreatening and attractive on the basis of their unique lifestyles, a minority with a number of these "differences" may be received better than a minority with only a single type of "difference" from the majority.

TREATMENT OF MINORITIES

The presence of one or more minorities within any society demands some sort of practical solution. Among the methods of "handling" minorities that have been employed by different societies are: (1) genocide, (2) expulsion, (3) segregation, (4) subordination, (5) amalgamation, and (6) assimilation.

Genocide

One way of resolving tensions between a dominant and a minority group is to annihilate the minority. As callous as this may sound, *genocide* has been pursued as an effective "solution" to certain minority problems. It was practiced, for instance, on the island of Tasmania when British colonists waged a ruthless campaign of extermination against the native population. The Tasmanians were hunted like animals by men using dogs and guns; some of them fell prey to traps baited with poisoned food. The British campaign was most successful. In less than 75 years, the Tasmanians became extinct; the last survivor, a woman named Truganina, died in 1876.

A somewhat similar drama was enacted during European colonization of the Western Hemisphere when white settlers encountered the native Indian populations. There is no evidence of an overall European plot to exterminate the Indians, but many of the colonizers' policies had the same effect. For the most part, the various Indian societies were still in the hunting and gathering stage of cultural development, or else had barely entered the stage of marginal agriculture. Hence, when the white settlers killed the game, pushed back the forests, and populated the land in large numbers, the Indian could not survive. Starvation killed many Indians, and imported diseases, to which they had no immunity, killed many more. To this, of course, must be added the number slain in battle with the more populous, technologically superior settlers. It has been estimated that, after several centuries of European encroachment, well over half the Indian population of the Americas was destroyed. The Indians did not suffer complete annihilation, but their numbers were decreased to the point where they could no longer effectively resist. Whole tribes, and even whole civilizations, were wiped out.

A more deliberate attempt to deal with a minority group through genocide took place in Europe under the direction of Adolf Hitler and his Nazi party. In this case there is no question of intent; millions of Jews were herded into special centers where they met their deaths breathing poison gas. It has been estimated that some 60 percent of the nearly 10 million Jews in Nazi-dominated Europe perished in this cruel holocaust.

Expulsion

A second means of dealing with minorities is to expel them. *Expulsion* achieves much the same effect as genocide, but at least it does not involve the direct taking of human life. Among the people to suffer expulsion were the Acadians, a French-speaking minority of British Nova Scotia, whose story has been immortalized in Longfellow's *Evangeline*. Jews have been expelled from several countries, including Spain and Egypt. An organized campaign of expulsion was used to deal with the American Indians. In 1830 Congress passed a bill authorizing the President to move several eastern tribes to new land west of the Mississippi River. This western territory was to constitute a "permanent Indian Country" where the Indians could live quietly far away from their white neighbors.

The list of tribes relocated is much too long to include here. Many northern Indians from the Ohio Valley region left with little resistance, but the southern tribes proved more troublesome. The Seminoles, for instance, fought a long, bloody campaign to retain their land. The Creeks and Cherokees (whose civilization included permanent homes, prosperous farms, large herds, well-developed trade, grist mills, schools, and representative government) resisted expulsion with everything from threats and arguments to bribes. But all of this was to no avail. By 1840 all the southern tribes had been removed. As the whites began to want the western land, the Permanent Indian Country was reduced further and further. Eventually, only Oklahoma was left; and in 1907 when this territory became a state, the last vestige of the Indian Country disappeared.

In 1941, immediately after Japan's attack on Pearl Harbor, the United States pursued a policy bordering on expulsion in dealing with the Japanese Americans who lived along our western coast. Victims of the war hysteria that swept the country in those trying times, over 100,000 persons were ordered to leave their homes and live in "relocation camps." This was done purely on the basis of Japanese ancestry; no attempt was made to discover whether or not the people involved were loyal to the United States. As it turned out, the overwhelming majority were loyal. In fact, many thousands entered the army and fought bravely in Europe and the Pacific. After the war, most of the Japanese returned to their former homes. Only a few elected to live in other parts of the country.

Segregation

If a society chooses not to annihilate or expel its minorities, it may resort to the expedient of *segregation*. Segregation consists in erecting "barriers" around a minority so as to keep its members separated from the dominant group. Usually, these barriers are social, but they may also be physical. One of the oldest segregation devices was the ghetto, a special part of a city reserved for Jews. Ghettos often were surrounded by high walls with special gateways. Jews were expected to be inside by sundown and to remain there until the next morning. They lived in a world all their own, distinctly different in cultural practices from the world outside. Eventually, many of the ghetto walls were torn down by the armies of Napoleon Bonaparte. Bonaparte's conquering soldiers found the ghettos repulsive to the ideals of the French Republic.

Because ghettos symbolize segregation, whether imposed by majorities or self-imposed by minorities, many areas in major cities have been called "ghettos." New York City's Harlem, Cleveland's Hough, and Los Angeles' Watts are contemporary examples of so-called "ghettos."

One notorious example of segregation has been the official policy of the Republic of South Africa. The Afrikaans' term for this policy is *apartheid*. To many, apartheid is interpreted as "apartness," but to those who support the dominant political party of the country, apartheid means "separate development," freedom for both blacks and whites to go their separate ways. Apartheid affects every facet of life in South Africa . . . housing, schools, recreation, employment, medical facilities, worship, and even the separate purchase of stamps in designated lines at the same desk in the post office. It is a policy that is not acceptable to many white citizens of the Republic of South Africa, but they are in the political minority thus far.

Segregation can take 2 forms, *de jure*, by law, or *de facto*, in fact or in reality. The closest America has come to de jure segregation has been "the separate, but equal" policy supported for many years by court decisions. In *Brown versus the Topeka Board of Education*, the Supreme Court of the United States ruled against this form of segregation in the public schools in 1954. Racial imbalance in both northern and southern schools has been a burning issue ever since. As many have pointed out, de facto segregation does exist in the United States and various tactics are sorely needed to change the current conditions of despair and bitterness among racial minorities. A number of studies, including those of investigative commissions of the federal government such as The National Advisory Commission on Civil Disorders, have warned that racial polarization of a "white world" and a "black world" either already exists or is rapidly approaching.

One tactic has been to bus students from de facto segregated areas to schools outside their immediate neighborhoods. It has worked effectively and quietly in some school districts. It has been violently opposed by citizens in other districts as too costly, time-consuming, and in violation of their "right" to choose the persons with whom they wish to associate. Still another recommendation has been to develop consolidated schools that provide a campus-like atmosphere in which all students in the area can enjoy the best possible educational facilities and staff.

Subordination

The essence of the segregation problem in the United States may not be segregation, itself. Rather, it may well be another form of treating minorities and that is subordination. We have discussed subordination as one of the end-products of accommodation when we discussed social processes. Subordination is what many otherwise well-intentioned people mean when they speak of "keeping people in their place"—a situation in which they can enjoy privileges while minorities must learn to cope with disadvantages. It has been popularized as a separation of the "haves" from the "have nots."

Perhaps the answer to subordination rests upon the ability to tolerate "differences." In a heterogeneous society such as in the United States, a society composed of a multiplicity of people from every portion of the globe, there is need for *pluralism*, the coexistence of a number of minorities along with the majority. But, the accommodation process needs to be a coordinate accommodation rather than a subordinate accommodation if Americans are to come closer to their ideal of democracy and human dignity.

Amalgamation

The relationship between a majority and a minority often has been affected by *amalgamation*, or the process of intermarriage between groups. A good example of this process may be drawn from the history of England. The Normans who conquered England after 1066 chose for a while to dominate the island's Anglo-Saxon inhabitants. But during the centuries that followed, barriers between the 2 groups broke down completely and intermarriage took place without restriction. As a result, England today has a fairly homogeneous society in which the differences between Norman and Saxon have long since disappeared. A country with a somewhat similar history is Italy, where innumerable peoples—Etruscans, Greeks, Latins, Goths, Lombards, and others—have amalgamated over the centuries to produce the modern Italians. In the United States, every immigrant group has intermarried with its neighbors at least to an extent. Throughout Latin America, Europeans and Indians have intermarried to produce a group known as "mestizos." Hawaii, the crossroads of the Pacific, has also been something of a crossroads for humanity. Among the groups who have contributed to the island's highly mixed population are Hawaiians, Japanese, Chinese, Filipinos, Koreans, Norwegians, Englishmen, Spaniards, and Danes.

Amalgamation between the members of different races (as distinct from people with different cultural or religious backgrounds) is called *miscegenation.* In the United States there is evidence that a considerable amount of miscegenation has taken place. It has been estimated conservatively that about 70 percent of all American blacks are mixed rather than "pure blooded." More liberal estimates place the figure as high as 90 percent. Among American Indians, at least 40 percent are gauged to be mixed.

Nonetheless, there is a strong resistance to racial intermarriage in this country—a resistance that undoubtedly is at the heart of much intergroup tension. A number of white people help maintain the social barriers separating them from nonwhite minorities out of a fear that, if the social barriers are broken down, a physical mixing of the races will follow. This fear of miscegenation has been reflected in the laws of some states. The chief target of such laws has been black-white marriages, but other nonwhites have also been specified. In 1967, the Supreme Court struck down the antimiscegenation law in one state, calling into question the constitutionality of such laws in other states.

Some of the opposition to miscegenous marriages may be traced to a concern for the offspring of such unions. The children of racially different parents often are stigmatized if they live within a society that looks down on racial mixing. Such children are forced to maintain a sort of "marginal" existence, halfway between the respective groups of their parents. Neither group is willing to accept them fully.

In the Republic of South Africa, for example, there is a special class of mixed white and nonwhite parentage who are known as "Coloreds." People within this category comprise one of the country's 4 legally recognized racial categories.

Assimilation

If minorities and majorities no longer erect social barriers against each other, the stage is set for assimilation. Assimilation is the process by which cultural differences between groups are reduced, eliminated, and eventually fused together. In contrast to amalgamation, which is a biological process, assimilation is a *social* process—one that we identified in an earlier chapter. Amalgamation can thus occur independently of assimilation or the 2 processes can occur simultaneously.

Assimilation is a far less dramatic, headline-making process than amalgamation. Yet, it is assimilation with its slow, almost imperceptible procedures that may ultimately bring minorities and majorities together.

RACE RELATIONS IN THE UNITED STATES TODAY

Well over 100 years have elapsed since the Emancipation Proclamation of Abraham Lincoln. There are those who ask for more time to bring about minority-majority group harmony, while there are those who feel that a century is more than enough time to have brought about minority-majority group accord. Within recent years, numerous minorities have become increasingly dissatisfied with conditions as they now exist. American society has been made very conscious of minority-majority tensions through race riots in many major cities, mass demonstrations of minority solidarity, and a steady effort to kindle a new spirit of in-group pride.

Sociologists have long been aware of "heightened expectations" among masses of people. These are circumstances that give rise to much hope because there are signs of achieving group goals. But they are also times of great frustration because collectivities find they are "near, and yet so far" from conditions they would like to bring about. Alternating between moods of pessimism and optimism, between violent and nonviolent tactics, between despair and dreams, America has seen the effects of the present era of "heightened expectations." The willingness to work within the present system can be seen in the election of minority group representatives to mayors' offices in major cities, in the serious efforts to train and employ minority members in formerly all-white jobs, in the growing popularity of minorities in television, or in their increasing participation in advertising. There remain, however, those who seek to work outside the system and these persons have brought on riots, shoot-outs, burnings, and lootings.

The "problem" of minorities, when all is said and done, rests with majorities. It is the majorities who have the power to make changes. It is the majorities who have created the circumstances under which minorities live and who maintain the present conditions. It will be a serious test of majorities when they experience "reverse racism" as the barriers between minorities and majorities break down. It has come as a jolt to majorities to discover that minorities have considerable group pride, and can and have treated majorities with some of the rejection that is all too familiar to minorities. When majority members experience this blind prejudice and discrimination, they are prone to react with considerable dismay. They have asked why they have been singled out for rejection when they have worked very hard to bring about improvements in minority-majority relationships. For the first time in their lives, many are getting a taste of the arbitrary nature of rejection on the basis of categorical "differences." Individual efforts and individual attitudes are overlooked in this stereotypic treatment and the experience is very difficult to accept.

There is plenty of room, however, to move beyond the present circumstances in America. Centuries of neglect and ignorance are too much time to accumulate inadequate housing, education, health, family life, and employment. It is too much time to develop personalities that have only learned to distrust others. But, it is not too late to begin to recognize that the "differences" used to keep people apart are not big enough to counter those qualities that unite them.

SUMMARY

Distinctive groups of people who seem to stand out from a given society as a whole have existed throughout history. These groups are referred to as *minority groups* and are set apart from the society in which they live because they differ in some respect from the dominant group. As a result, they are generally denied all participation in their society's life. Generally, those differences which set minority groups apart are of a racial, religious, or cultural nature.

Scientists do not all agree on a definite racial classification system, the physical differences among people being largely a matter of degree rather than sharply defined kinds. In modern terminology, a race is a *breeding population*, a group that has interbred to produce an identi-

THE VARIOUS PATHS TO SOCIOLOGICAL KNOWLEDGE
ALVA MYRDAL

The need for a far-ranging program for population planning incorporates many additional social problems. The scope of these problems is well brought forth by the Swedish sociologist Alva Mydral in her book, *Family and Nation,* 1941. She is the wife of Gunnar Myrdal who wrote the sociological classic, *An American Dilemma,* on the relations between whites and blacks in this country.

The whole concern of family planning touches on many other facets of the social existence. In the case of Sweden the problem is the reverse of that found in countries that are overpopulated. There, the population is in a state of decline after an earlier increase. Sweden is unique in that it has experienced a population decline since the end of World War I. It had maintained a relatively stable rate of growth during the early 19th century. With the coming of the Industrial Revolution and better health care, the death rate dropped sharply before the birth rate did, and there was a population increase. After this stage there was a concerted attempt to keep down population growth through birth control. This was so successful that it caused a population decline. It was to combat this decline that the Swedish government inaugurated a program to increase the birth rate.

Although the aim of the program was to increase rather than decrease the population, the policy has some significance for other countries today. This was one of the first attempts to view population growth and the quality of family life in the same program. The basic idea behind the book is that it is possible for the government to take a fundamental part in population policy. Viewing the population as a whole, it takes into account the many social variables involved. They include economic resources, employment levels, health standards, and intellectual and emotional prospects for the coming generations. Of course, Sweden has certain advantages not found in many other societies. For example, there is a homogeneous population, a tradition of planning, and the good supply of jobs.

Ms. Myrdal sees the population problem in Sweden as related to the family as an institution. So deep-rooted an institution as the family has often lacked the plasticity to adapt to modern circumstances. The inducements that government can offer can help overcome these lacks. For example, the Swedish government has effective job creation programs. Special benefits for the married have helped to offset the Swedish problems of late marriages and a high rate of illegitimacy. The programs of the Swedish government have been supportive to family life and job security.

fiable type of human beings. Still, the physical criteria used to distinguish "races" are biological trivia. The cultural achievements of the so-called races are comparable.

Religious minorities have experienced discrimination in all ages and in many societies. The classic example of religious persecution for centuries has been the restriction and persecution of the Jews. Cultural or nationalistic minorities likewise have been discriminated against in many societies, including our own. The United States has experienced wave after wave of immigration, and each group of migrants was set apart in some way. Succeeding generations, however, have been largely assimilated into the mainstream of American life.

Societies have adopted various methods of dealing with minorities within their populations. These solutions have included *annihilation, expulsion, segregation, subordination, amalgamation,* and *assimilation.* The first 4, although practiced throughout history, have invariably created more problems than they resolved. Amalgamation, which involves intermarriage and the eventual construction of a composite society, has been successful in some societies. Assimilation, in which cultural and other differences between groups are reduced or eliminated, has also been successful. One result of assimilation has been the growth of a pluralistic society in which minority and dominant groups develop a tolerance for each other's differences.

GLOSSARY

amalgamation   the biological blending of peoples through intermarriage or interbreeding.

apartheid   racial segregation in every facet of life, as practiced in South Africa.

genocide   the deliberate, systematic extermination of an entire people.

geographical race   according to Stanley Garn, a large collection of breeding populations separated from other such collections by major geographical barriers. Examples are Europeans and Australoids.

ghetto   originally a part of a city to which Jews were restricted. Now, any segregated quarter of a city in which members of a minority group live because of social, economic, or political pressures.

local race   according to Stanley Garn, a breeding population that may share an area with other populations but does not mix with them, not only because of physical separation over a distance, but because of social barriers.

microrace   a term used by Stanley Garn for a segment of a local race that breeds within itself to produce an identifiable type.

prejudice   prejudgment; that is, the formulation of opinions or attitudes on the basis of insufficient or misleading evidence.

race   a division of the human species on the basis of hereditary biological traits, such as skin color and height; or, a breeding population that produces an identifiable type of human beings. Breeding populations may be geographical races, local races, or microraces.

segregation   the process of erecting social or physical boundaries around a minority to keep its members separate from the dominant group.   Segregation may be *de jure* (by law) or *de facto* (in reality).

stereotype   a standardized mental image of a group, individual, or category which is often based on half truths, opinions, and distortions of fact.

SUGGESTED READINGS

Allport, Gordon.   *The Nature of Prejudice.*   New York: Doubleday & Co., 1958.   Allport is a leading psychologist who explores the causes and consequences of prejudice.   He deals with historical and sociological factors as well as those of individual psychology.   This is probably the standard work on the subject of prejudice.

Bettelheim, Bruno and Janowitz, Morris.   *Social Change and Prejudice.*   New York: Free Press, 1964.

Boston Women's Health Collective.   *Our Bodies, Ourselves . . .* A radical statement that provides information to women about their health and sexuality.

Engle, Madeline H.   *Inequality in America: A Sociological Perspective.*   New York: Thos. Y. Crowell, 1971.   This is a simply written book describing the sociological approach to different kinds of inequality (racial, ethnic, class, religious, age-grade).   A selection of readings includes such authors as James Baldwin, Eldridge Cleaver, and Michael Harrington.

Greer, Germaine.   *The Female Eunuch.*   New York: McGraw-Hill/Bantam, 1971.   Greer's main thesis is that the social roles that women fulfill do not supply them with self-esteem and positive sexual identity.

Mayerson, Charlotte. (ed.).   *Two Blocks Apart.*   New York: Holt, Rinehart and Winston, 1965.   Ms. Mayerson uses detailed case studies of a Puerto Rican and Irish-American growing up in New York.   The irony of the title, and the study, is that the two live in entirely different worlds although only "two blocks apart."

Myrdal, Gunnar.   *An American Dilemma: The Negro Problem and Modern Democracy.*   New York: Harper & Row, 1962.   Although written in the 1940's, this study by a Swedish sociologist remains one of the outstanding analyses of racial tensions in America.

SOURCES OF CONFLICT AND CHANGE

part four

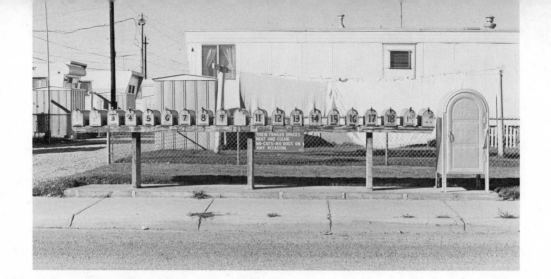

15

POPULATION

Most of us are aware that we are living in the midst of what is commonly referred to as the "population explosion." Most of us aren't sure, though, of its dimensions and we only vaguely understand its causes. There seem to be many conflicting views about how serious it is. If one is caught in a New York subway during rush hour, or trapped in a traffic jam, it's easy to become convinced that this frightening phenomenon involves the United States as well as the under-developed nations with their teeming millions. But after a flight over America's great stretches of open space, one can become just as convinced that there's no danger of overcrowding here.

How serious is this population explosion? What caused it and where is it likely to lead? In what ways does it involve us? What, if anything, can be done about it? These are some of the questions we will be dealing with in this chapter.

FACTORS AFFECTING WORLD POPULATION GROWTH

The rate of growth. Throughout the greater portion of the time human beings have existed on earth, the world's population grew very slowly. *Demographers*—sociologists who specialize in the study of population trends, distribution, and relation to resources—estimate that it took 16 centuries for the world's population to double from one-quarter billion people to one-half billion, a figure that was reached about 1650. Within just 200 years it doubled again, and we were in the beginning stages of the modern population explosion. The next doubling, to 2 billion, required only 80 years, and now, some 40 years later, we are closing in on the 4 billion mark.

This sudden upsurge is not due to any sudden increase in the birth rate. And even the rate of growth looks deceptively small—a world average of about 2 percent a year. But now that we are dealing with such large numbers, that 2 percent growth rate means that 180,000 people are added to the world's population *every day* (remember that figure doesn't refer to the number of births but to the net increase).

At this rate of growth, global population is currently doubling every 37 years. In other words, dealing with population growth is something like the complexity of working with compound interest on a sum of money. The rate may stay the same, but as the sum gets larger, that rate creates a larger net increase. If your money is growing at the rate of 1 percent each year, the sum will double in 70 years; if the interest rate is 2 percent, it will double in just 35 years.

Death Control

Rather than an increase in the birth rate, the major factor behind the tremendous population increase has been a lowering of the death rate. Throughout most of history, the rate of births barely kept ahead of the rate of deaths.

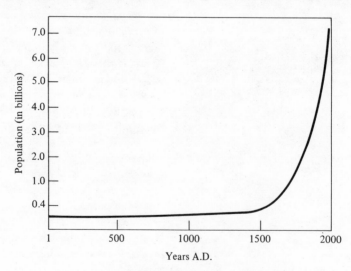

FIGURE 15-1 Estimated World Population Growth
1 A.D. to 2000 A.D.

Note: If the lefthand side of the chart were extended back
through the Stone Age, it would cover 35 to 40 feet.
Source: U.N. Demographic Yearbook, 1970-

But the miracles of modern science have cut the death rate dramatically by eliminating many diseases, especially the epidemics that in the past would frequently decimate the population of a city or region.

It is by subtracting the death rate from the birth rate that demographers arrive at the rate of population increase—or what they term *natural increase*—to distinguish it from growth by such means as immigration or territorial acquistion. These rates are usually expressed in terms of number of births or deaths per thousand people in a given population. Thus, if the death rate drops from 20 per thousand each year to 10 per thousand, and the birth rate remains the same (say, at 30), then the rate of natural increase will be double what it had been before. These numbers can become a little confusing; Harold Dorn, of the U.S. Public Health Service, expressed their significance in simpler terms by explaining that the rapid growth of population has resulted from "the combination of a medieval birth rate with a 20th century death rate."

Population Growth in the Developing Countries

For a variety of reasons that we'll discuss later in the chapter, the rate of population growth has slowed down considerably in the industralized nations of the world. The rate of increase is much greater in the poorer, underdeveloped countries. This becomes dramatically clear when you look at the rates at which the populations of various countries are currently doubling (see Table 15-1).

The reason for this faster rate of growth in the "Third World" countries is explained primarily in terms of the lowering death rate. "Death control" occurred first in the industrialized nations and was achieved over a long period of time. Modern medical and health practices were not "exported" to the developing countries until well into this century; but when they were, it created a sudden, sharp drop in the death rate. On the island of Ceylon, for example, largely through the elimination of malaria, the death rate was cut in half in a little more than a decade.

The suddenness of the population growth of these countries is illustrated by the fact that roughly 40 percent of their collective populations is under age 15. This suggests that growth in the next generation will be even more dramatic. Looking into the future, one demographer has predicted that "the underdeveloped areas alone stand to experience a population increase in the second half of this century considerably greater than that achieved by all mankind in all of the millenia of his existence up to the current year."

TABLE 15-1   DOUBLING POPULATION

Industrialized Nations	Doubling Time	Developing Nations	Doubling Time
United States	63 years	Indonesia	31 years
Great Britain	140 years	Kenya	24 years
Soviet Union	88 years	Philippines	20 years
Italy	117 years	El Salvador	19 years

Source: Population Reference Bureau.

Demographic Trends in the U.S.

Although the growth rate of the United States is not as high as that of the developing countries, it is also true that we have not experienced the same leveling as that achieved in Europe and Japan. During the Depression years of the 1930's, our birth rate—and consequently our growth rate—reached the lowest levels in our country's history. Many people became concerned that the country would not only stop growing, but would begin to show a population decline.

These fears were short-lived. The "baby boom" of the late 1940's and early 1950's has helped to swell the population from about 140 million in 1940 to over 200 million today. Demographers have pointed out that the combination of the baby boom and increased life expectancy is making us both younger and older as a nation. Almost half the population is under age 25; at the same time, the percentage over age 65 is larger than it has ever been. This has presented us with a double problem: providing educational facilities and job opportunities for the young and, at the same time, providing for the security and well-being of the growing number of elderly.

In the past 20 years the alarm has been sounded that America is growing too fast. Some demographers and population-control organizations warn that we are headed for a serious population problem despite the apparent availability of land and certainly an overabundance of food. The natural rate of growth in the United States since World War II has been about 1.6 percent per year; if this rate persists, our population will grow to 1 billion within a century. Demographer Donald Bogue points out that "this would be roughly equivalent to moving all the population of Europe, Latin America, and Africa into the territory of the 50 states."

HOW SERIOUS IS THE POPULATION PROBLEM?

Concern over crowding and the availability of an adequate food supply is not new. As early as the 3rd century A.D., Tertullian, a Carthaginian, noted the steady growth of population and concluded: "What most frequently meets our view is our teeming population; our numbers are burdensome to the world, which can hardly supply us from its natural elements. Our wants grow more and more keen, and our complaints more bitter in all mouths, while nature fails in affording us her usual sustenance."

Such early warnings, however, were rare and were made in reference to a particular region rather than the world as a whole. When the population of an area grew too large for the available food supply, famine or epidemics usually supplied a "natural" check on further growth; emigration or the invasion of neighboring territories also provided a safety valve for overpopulation.

The Predictions of Thomas Malthus

Perhaps the most famous warning about overpopulation was that written by an English economist, Thomas Malthus, in his *Essay on the Principle of Population*, published in 1798. His basic thesis was that population tends to increase in a geometric ratio (1,2,4,8,16,32), while the means of supporting that population—principally food—could only increase in an arithmetic ratio (1,2,3,4,5,6). Thus, within a century, according to Malthus, a given population would expand to 8 times its original number, while the food supply would be increased to only 4 times its original volume.

Malthus believed that this situation contributed to the existence of the human miseries of war, famine, poverty, vice, and disease. He called these miseries "positive checks," and claimed that they were necessary to hold down population growth by increasing the death rate. The only possible alternative would be for people to exercise certain "moral restraints"—marrying late or refusing to have children (although not through birth control)—to keep the birth rate down. He held out little hope that these moral restraints would be practiced and came to the gloomy conclusion that the positive checks, with all their evils, would continue indefinitely as the only means of creating a balance between population and food supply.

Malthus' predictions came during an age when the people of Western societies had come to believe that science and reason could create an era of endless prosperity and plenty. The "Malthusian dilemma" seemed to offer an impossible obstacle to those dreams. Critics attacked his doctrine, claiming it presented a distorted view of humanity, while others insisted that he had paved the way for a whole new approach to social problems.

There were many errors in Malthus' reasoning—he was really making guesses based on flimsy evidence. In addition, he did not foresee the revolutionary developments of the 19th century, such as urbanization, the industrial revolution, and the advances in agricultural technology. But he was roughly correct in seeing that there was a difference between the rate of population growth and the rate at which food supply could be increased. In recent decades, we've gained a new awareness of his dire predictions as rapid population growth threatens to outstrip the means for supporting that growth.

Modern Demographic Projections

Data on the availability of food and resources and on population trends are much more reliable now than they were in Malthus' time. Since 1800, reasonably accurate census reports have been made by more and more countries. Even today, though, less than 80 percent of the world's population is subject to accurate count. This means that, to some extent, the projections of demographers still must be based on educated guesses.

Based on past and current trends, demographers have made various projections about the future growth of world population. Most agree that, barring unforeseen circumstances, there will be a doubling of the population between 1965 and the end of the century, creating a total of well over 6 billion people. Pushing the current growth rate still further into the future, in 7 or 8 centuries there will be one person for every square foot of land surface on the globe. One is easily led to agree with the conclusion of demographer Philip Hauser that "the present rate of world population growth cannot possibly persist for very long into the future."

It should be noted that the projections of demographers are not the same as predictions. The projections will result *if* present trends continue. However, any number of factors could intervene to change these patterns. The very fact that such projections have been made may make people more aware of population problems and create a motivation for modifying the trends. It should be mentioned, too, that in spite of the growing concern developed in recent years, very little has yet been accomplished in the nature of defusing the "population bomb." The growth rate continues unabated and raises serious questions about what sort of life will be possible for the net increase in people we have to expect in the closing decades of this century.

Feeding the Growing Population

Sounding a warning similar to that of Malthus, many economists and population experts have stated that the world is losing the race

PERSPECTIVE

POPULATION AND POLLUTION—THE PARADOX OF THE AGGREGATE

A number of years ago, the famous British economist John Maynard Keynes coined the phrase "the paradox of the aggregate." He was speaking in economic terms and he used the term to explain the idea that what is in the self-interest of the individual is often not in the best interest of the community. The phrase is useful here as an aid in understanding how the various crises in our environment have come about and why we seem incapable of finding the right corrective measures.

A brief summary of our major environmental problems will show how the paradox of the aggregate reveals the relationship between population and pollution:

1. *Air Pollution.* Perhaps our most noticeable environmental problem, and certainly one of the most threatening, is air pollution. The ugly pall of smog that hangs over every American city is, of course, more than just a nuisance; it is a definite health hazard whose exact proportions cannot yet be measured. It will be years before we can determine precisely what air pollution does to our bodies—for the moment, it is frightening enough to be aware of the ruling that on smog-alert days in Los Angeles, children are told not to run, skip, or jump, indoors or outdoors, because of possible danger to the respiratory system.

In our search for the cause of this growing menace, it is easy to point an accusing finger at industry. The factory with its billowing smokestacks is an obvious target and much remains to be done to curb the pollution from this source.

But the fact remains that 60 percent of the pollutants in our air (or about 100 million tons every year) comes from the internal combustion engine—principally the automobile. Each of us who drives a car contributes to the total problem. And here is where the paradox of the aggregate enters in. When you go out on a date in your car (or the family car), or head for the nearest shopping plaza, you are merely making use of a standard convenience. The amount of pollutants emitted is insignificant and really doesn't harm anyone. But consider the aggregate: there are now more than 100 million cars in America, and it is the combined total of those innocent little trips that creates the deadly poisons.

We compound the problem by insisting on our right to drive cars wherever and whenever we please. We're not interested in mass transit systems when it's so much more convenient (for each individual) to drive to work, to school, or the store. So we spend billions of dollars each year on highway construction and only a fraction of that sum on rapid transit systems which could reduce highway congestion as well as air pollution.

2. *Land Pollution.* The 5.3 pounds of solid waste each of us is responsible for

every day is an insignificant amount. Why bother to try to reduce it by a few ounces? To do so would work against our individual self-interest—it would mean cutting down on convenient packaging, prepared foods, nonreturnable bottles and cans, and so on. From the point of view of the individual, it just isn't worth it. But, again, for the community as a whole, the matter is quite different. In New York City, for instance, that 5.3 pounds a day adds up to 24,000 tons every day! Not only does this create enormous problems of garbage removal and disposal, but it means that we are throwing away millions of tons of valuable resources, such as aluminum, tin, glass, paper, and plastics.

Much the same process applies to the use of pesticides such as DDT. The individual farmer wants a good, healthy crop—his livelihood depends on it. The amount of chemicals that runs off the soil of any single farm is a small matter—but taken together, the collective runoff is having a devastating effect on wildlife and perhaps eventually on human life as well.

3. *Water Pollution.* The rapid destruction of our lakes, rivers and streams is now clearly reaching disaster proportions. Once again, the basic cause is the difference between the interests of the individual and those of the community. The owner of a factory in the vicinity of Lake Erie—or any other body of water— is struggling for survival in a highly competitive economy. There may be other ways to dispose of waste besides dumping it into the nearest stream, but such means would undoubtedly be costly, especially since no other factory owner seems willing to take on similar additional expenses. So, in the spirit of what has been called our "cowboy economics," everyone does the easiest thing, secure in the knowledge that the waste products from a single factory can't make much difference. The collective result? The "death" of Lake Erie, along with such ludicrous but tragic side effects as the Cuyahoga and Buffalo Rivers being declared fire hazards because of their high content of flammable pollutants.

With our economy growing at the rate of about 4 percent a year, the effects of the paradox of the aggregate will become even more pronounced in the years ahead. Within a decade, we will be producing and consuming and wasting half again as much as we are now. New advances in technology can help us to ease the situation, but clearly we can't sit back and wait for science to bail us out. We need more positive programs in every community and tighter controls created by all levels of government. These actions may help us (or force us) to find ways to create a closer identity between the interests of the individual and those of the community. But even these actions are difficult to achieve. They cost money, and the individual taxpayer or legislator does not usually see it as being in his interest to vote for higher taxes. The dynamics of Keynes's theory promise to be with us for some time to come.

between increasing food supply and population growth. They point out that the tremendous efforts made by the developing countries to produce more food—even with the assistance of the industrialized nations—have barely succeeded in keeping up with the growth of population. If a country's population doubles every 25 years, it must double its food supply merely to keep the same level of consumption. Many developing countries are now exerting monumental efforts to stave off mass starvation. Eugene Black, a United Nations expert on economic development, reviewed the progress made since the end of World War II, and concluded: "I must be blunt. Population growth threatens to nullify all our efforts to raise living standards in many of the poorer countries. We are coming to a situation in which the optimist will be the man who thinks present living standards can be maintained. The pessimist will not even look for that."

The projected growth rates for the remaining years of the century have convinced many people that food supply cannot possibly keep pace. Paul Ehrlich, a biologist who wrote the controversial best-seller, *The Population Bomb*, spells out the pessimistic view suggested by Black. "The rich are going to get richer," Ehrlich wrote, "but the more numerous poor are going to get poorer. Of these poor, a minimum of three and one-half million will starve to death this year (1968), mostly children. But this is a mere handful compared to the numbers that will be starving in a decade or so. And it is now too late to take action to save many of these people."

Other experts are more optimistic. They point to the progress that has been made in developing new farming techniques and new, more prolific strains of seeds. A new strain of rice, for instance, was developed by a research team funded by the Rockefeller Foundation. This faster growing seed is now being used in many areas of the world and has doubled rice productions in some regions; in a matter of

only a few years, it enabled the Philippines to become an exporter of rice. Such increases in productivity have been hailed by some as a "green revolution," which will soon enable food production to increase much faster than population growth. Experiments in "farming" the seabeds also seem to offer some promise of increasing food supplies, especially proteins.

The Demographic Transition

Brazilian Joseu De Castro, formerly chairman of the executive council of the United Nations' Food and Agricultural Organization, has pointed out a reversal of the Malthusian logic: the areas of the world where starvation is most common are also the areas which show the most rapid growth of population. Conversely, in nations where there is an abundance of food, the rate of population growth is considerably lower.

While there is much disagreement over Dr. De Castro's theories and the proof he used to support them, there is evidence to suggest a correlation between industrialization and a lowering of the growth rate. As already mentioned, the growth rates of the industrialized nations, after going through a period of rapid increase, have tapered off considerably in recent decades. This pattern of slow increase through much of history, followed by a "population explosion" during the early stages of industrialization, and then a leveling of the growth rate is often referred to as the "demographic transition."

The experience of modern Japan is a most striking example of the dramatic changes associated with the completion of this transition. After passing through a number of decades of rapid growth, which placed great strains on the resources of the islands, the Japanese suddenly began to limit the size of their families. The births per thousand dropped from 34 to 17 in the space of just 12 years, virtually bringing to an end that country's population explosion. No other modern nation has managed to achieve such a sudden change in so short a period of time.

Does this mean that as nations achieve industrialization the rate of population growth will automatically decline? A few experts express such a hope, but most disagree. It is pointed out, for example, that the United States in the 1950's, during a period of considerable economic expansion, actually achieved a natural growth rate higher than that of India. In other words, there is little agreement over when and why the demographic transition will be completed in any given country, just as there is disagreement over how serious the gap between population and food will be in the decades ahead.

POPULATION AND THE QUALITY OF LIFE

Perhaps the real question concerning population growth is not how many people can be kept alive, but rather how many people the world can adequately support with a decent standard of living. A world half-starved and half-affluent is not a happy place in which to live. And many people have come to feel that the rapid population growth not only raises grave questions about the future, but creates the most serious obstacle to creating a decent life for those who inhabit the planet today.

Population and Economic Development

Most experts agree that the only chance the developing nations have of providing decent living standards for their people is through the process known as *modernization*—that is, the creation of modern industrial economies, not unlike those already achieved by the nations of Europe, North America, and Japan. But mod-

ernization is a complicated task. At the very least, it requires a surplus of farm production, a skilled labor force, mass education, and sufficient capital to invest in the creation of large-scale manufacturing.

Each one of these prerequisites presents imposing difficulties for the developing nations. As long as practically everything produced is needed for current consumption, very little can be set aside for future development, and this dilemma becomes more acute as populations grow. It is estimated, for instance, that India will require a minimum investment of $25 billion in the next 3 decades simply to provide some sort of housing for its growing urban population. This huge outlay does not include such other essentials as streets, sanitation facilities, water supply, medical care, or education. Nor does it involve shelter for the growing rural population or in any way solve the current urban housing problems (in Calcutta alone, an estimated 250,000 people live in the streets). In other words, India requires tremendous expenditures of labor and finances merely to keep living standards from sinking below their current level.

The picture for other developing nations is nearly as dark. One of the most ambitious development projects ever undertaken has been Egypt's construction of the Aswan High Dam, partially financed by the Soviet Union and designed to open up millions of acres of new farm land. By the time this new agricultural area is in operation, it will produce just about enough food to supply the needs of the population that has been added since the project began. Similarly, efforts to introduce mechanized farming techniques have often failed because the terrain, land distribution patterns, or the crops involved don't lend themselves to large-scale farming practices. Thus, the amount of food produced by one farmer in Asia, Africa, or Latin America is virtually the same as it was 25 years ago. The developing countries have not been able to provide the food surplus needed to form a base for rapid industrialization.

Apart from the suffering engendered by this situation, the problems of modernization involve other dangers as well. There is a tendency to look toward extreme solutions. Communism or dictatorships often seem to offer speedier paths to progress than do the methods of private initiative and democratic government although the modernization of mainland China shows that these claims are sometimes true. The promises of full stomachs and rapid industrialization are appeals that are hard to resist.

The Revolution of Rising Expectations

In the past, people who had little food and a substandard of living often seemed to accept their situation in a fatalistic manner. Occasionally desperation would drive these people to open rebellion but this was not the general pattern. In fact, some historians have suggested that revolutions occur when people's lives are improving and they become impatient with obstacles that stand in the way of further improvement. In *Anatomy of Revolution,* Crane Brinton points out that in the 18th century, the people of the American colonies and France enjoyed much higher living standards than did the populations of many other nations. The revolutions that rocked both countries were not created by starving masses, but by people who wanted to remove the shackles of the old order that were preventing greater progress.

Many authorities suggest that a similar mood is emerging in the developing nations as the people of these countries experience what is called the "revolution of rising expectations." In the age of modern communications, the "have-not" peoples of the world are painfully aware of the affluence enjoyed by the wealthy in their own societies as well as by the "rich

nations" of Europe, North America, and Japan. They are familiar with the conveniences offered by modern technology; many have access to television, whose programs parade before the viewer a taunting picture of a different and better life. In the meanest hut of Latin America or Southeast Asia, one is likely to find a transistor radio, and this too provides constant news about "how the other half lives." The people who live in the hillside slums surrounding many Latin American cities look down every day on an untouchable world of color, lights, shops, theatres, and material prosperity.

In contrast to what they know others have, the lives of the world's poor become even more burdensome. The progress so often promised never seems to materialize. In fact, according to many people, the gap between the "rich nations" and the "poor nations" is growing steadily wider. The average income for each person in Latin America is estimated to be between 3 and 4 hundred dollars per year; in Asia, it is between 50 and 100 dollars; in the Middle East it is probably even lower.

Food consumption also remains strikingly low in contrast to industrialized nations. In terms of calories alone, the per capita food intake for people in the "Third World" is about half that of Western Europe and North America. Considering the fact that most of us consume far more calories than we really need, this disparity doesn't seem too drastic. But according to a United Nations report, the lack of proteins and vitamins in their diets makes this figure a good deal more bleak; the diet of a person in the Far East is only about one-sixth as valuable as that of a person in North America.

Because of the revolution of rising expectations, this creeping pace of progress becomes increasingly frustrating. Many people are willing to accept privation today as long as there is hope for a better tomorrow. The hope has been offered but has not been fulfilled. It is this rising frustration, rather than outright starvation, that threatens to result in large-scale violence, revolution, and perhaps war. The weight of increasing numbers of people is likely to make this frustration even worse.

IS POPULATION CONTROL THE ANSWER?

Writing shortly before the Communist take-over in China, Gerald Winfield, who had spent many years as a medical missionary in that country, declared: "I suggest that public health measures which can save millions of lives should not be practiced in China on a nation-wide scale until the stage is set for a concurrent reduction of the birthrate.... The future welfare of the Chinese people is more dependent on the prevention of births than on the prevention of deaths." Obviously, Winfield's rather hard-sounding conclusion expressed his belief that the quality of life was most important. In the quarter-century since that statement, a growing number of people—scientists, social scientists, government leaders, and concerned citizens—have become convinced that birth control has become even more necessary than death control.

The Obstacles to Population Control

Perhaps the most frequently mentioned arguments against population control is that it is wrong on religious or moral grounds. It is difficult to measure just how much influence religion has in creating reluctance to plan families. Although leaders of many religions are opposed to artificial controls, the Roman Catholic Church is the only major religion that makes official doctrine of such a stand. Because of this, advocates of population control frequently point accusing fingers at the Catholic Church as presenting a major obstacle to progress in this area.

The critics lose sight of the fact that the Catholic Church is not opposed to planned families, but takes a stand against some of the measures employed, such as artificial birth control and abortion. It should be pointed out, too, that some countries with a high percentage of Catholics in their populations—such as Belgium, France, Italy, Spain, and Portugal—actually have lower birth rates than do other industrialized nations such as the United States, which seems to indicate that family planning works in spite of the church's stand on contraception. On the other hand, the highest fertility rate for any area of the world is to be found in the "Catholic" countries of Latin America. Thus, other factors besides religion are involved in determining the birth-rate of a particular culture.

In agricultural societies, it has long been traditional to regard large families as necessities. This was true in Europe and North America before the age of urbanization and industrialization. In such cultures, large numbers of children can be raised at very little additional cost, and each quickly becomes an important member of the family's food-raising team. In addition, large numbers of children usually offer the rural couple their only means of old age security—when they are too old to provide for themselves, a large number of children can produce enough surplus to meet their needs.

Conversely, in a modernized society, large numbers of children can present an economic liability. The cost of raising children is much higher than in an agricultural society; they must be cared for for longer periods of life, and are normally still in school long after rural children have become productive members of society. The cost of a college education can become a tremendous burden for a family with a large number of children. In other words, a modernized economy actually provides incentives for limiting the number of offspring. Such economic and social motivation

THE VARIOUS PATHS TO SOCIOLOGICAL AWARENESS
KINGSLEY DAVIS

The work of Kingsley Davis provides an outstanding example of the practical applications of research in the behavioral sciences.   He has produced outstanding research projects, most notably a 2-volume study of *World Urbanization,* published in 1972.   At the same time he has presented strong arguments about why population "planners" as well as demographic experts have much to gain from applying sociological concepts to their work.

A brief sampling of these arguments will help make his message clear:

From 1870 to 1932, the populations of industrialized nations tended to decline. Since this decline occurred, as Davis points out, "in the teeth of governmental, religious, and medical opposition to birth control," it clearly was not the result of nationwide population plans.   Why did the decline take place?   Demographers and economists, joined by a variety of psuedoexperts, tried to analyze the reasons and make future projections.   Many predicted a marked lowering of industrial populations over the next 25 or 50 years.

Of course, events revealed that the projections of population were far off the mark.   Quite the opposite trend occurred, creating the current worry about the "population explosion."   Are current projections any better than those made 40 years ago?   Davis suggests that we probably have not achieved more accuracy in demographic projection simply because we have tended to ignore the sociological factors responsible for changing fertility rates.   Thus, just when many slide rules were predicting an overburdened population for the United States, the 1973 Census revealed a sharp decline in the birth rate. The American population was still increasing, but at a much slower rate than anyone suspected.

The thrust of Davis' work is that we cannot adequately deal with population data—much less plan population growth—until we learn to analyze the social, economic, and cultural factors which influence fertility and family size.   Demographic trends, Davis insists, are not determined by government programs, but rather by individual families making decisions influenced by psychological and social forces.   In South Korea, he points out, the government instituted a population control program based on the premise that if "unwanted" babies could be eliminated by a birth control program, the fertility rate would decline. The program had little success in its early stages. Four years after the program started, a survey revealed that practically all the women interviewed still hoped for "two or three sons, with one or two daughters." In other words, the problem was not the unwanted children but the wanted.

Davis is saying then, that population planning through birth control clinics is not likely to have much success. "Clearly, if the conditions are such that few children are wanted," he writes, "people are not so stupid as to be unable to find the means. If, on the other hand, conditions are such that they want many, no contraceptive, no matter how perfect, will stop them from having them. . . . It follows that a national policy that confines itself to furnishing contraceptives cannot provide population control."

Davis is not suggesting that population control is doomed to failure. Instead, he says basically that success depends on learning more about the factors influencing families to have more or less children. As we learn more, programs can be aimed at influencing those sociological variables. Even with the present state of our knowledge he believes that we can do more to influence family decision-making. He suggests, for example, that governments could:

"Cease taxing single persons more than married ones; stop giving parents special tax exemptions; abandon the income-tax policy that discriminates against couples when the wife works; reduce paid maternity leaves; reduce family allowances; stop granting fellowships and other educational aids (including special allowances for wives and children) to married students; cease outlawing abortions and sterilizations; and relax rules that allow use of harmless contraceptives only with medical permission." If some of these proposals sound familiar, one reason is likely to be that Davis has been espousing them for quite some time.

is lacking in most developing nations, and, too, the presence of certain cultural norms often hinders efforts to encourage population control.

Still another obstacle to population control is that it must be carried out intensively if it is to have an affect on the birthrate. Massive education programs must be combined with adequate clinics and trained personnel. For most developing countries, the cost of such an effort has proved too high.

Population Control in the United States

Despite the growing body of literature stressing the need for reducing the natural growth rate in this country, the nation-wide response has been slow. Such organizations as Planned Parenthood and the more politically active Zero Population Growth have recently begun to reach large numbers of people, but their activities are still unwelcome in many American communities. In addition to moral and religious objections, many Americans simply feel that population control is not needed in this country. With our surplus of food, our abundance of resources and material wealth, and our vast open spaces, we seem to be in little danger of overcrowding.

In fact, the ideas of growth and bigness have long been positive values in American culture. We are proud of our growing population as a nation, just as people in California were delighted when their state surpassed New York as the nation's most populous. Even small communities equate growth with progress. Growth seems to denote strength, vigor, and improvement; business is expanding and prosperity is the status quo. Few community leaders would be pleased if census reports showed that their region was declining in population. However, states such as Oregon seem to feel differently about the benefits of continuous growth. Their official slogan is: "You're welcome to visit, but please don't settle here." These attitudes about growth are often reinforced by mass advertising, such as this sample which appeared in subway and bus posters: "Your future is great in a growing America. Every day 11,000 babies are born in America. This means new business, new jobs, new opportunities." Considering the prevalence of such norms, it is likely that efforts at population control will continue to meet some opposition in this country. The swelling ranks of the Women's Rights movement will most likely be influential in curtailing the birthrate in this country. This American obsession with

growth perhaps explains, in part, why the United States has not completed the demographic transition already experienced by Western Europe and Japan.

Government Programs to Control Population

In the past decade or two, the governments of more and more developing countries have become convinced that population control is essential to achieving a higher standard of living and eventual modernization. The governments involved have sought to gain their ends by persuading the people that family planning is necessary and by providing information and facilities.

So far, these government efforts have not been in operation long enough to determine whether they will be able to reduce the natural growth rate. Too, the programs are hampered by lack of funds, facilities, and personnel, as well as by prevailing social, religious, and economic customs. Some experimental projects, however, do seem to offer considerable promise. With the help of Swedish financing and technical assistance, 2 community-wide experiments in India and Sri Lanka succeeded in reducing the birthrate by as much as one-third in the space of just 4 years.

Despite the hope offered by such programs and by the achievements of the green revolution, the struggle to close the gap between population and food supply will continue to be one of the world's major problems for years to come. Even if a lowering of the natural growth rate is achieved, the world still faces the collossal challenge of providing a quality of life that will offer dignity, opportunity, and hope for the millions of people who so far have gained little but rising expectations.

SUMMARY

The rapid growth of the world's population over the past 3 centuries has been largely the result of an increased life expectancy achieved by the application of modern medical and health practices. While most industrialized nations have completed the demographic transition to a slower natural growth rate, the underdeveloped countries are generally growing faster than the world average. If this rate continues, the world's population will double between 1965 and 2000 to a total of over 6 billion people. The United States, which is becoming both younger and older as a nation, is growing faster than most industrialized countries.

Since the time of Thomas Malthus, there has been considerable disagreement over whether or not the world can support its growing population. Pessimists argue that increases in food production have barely kept pace with population growth. Because of this, the developing countries face insurmountable obstacles in the struggle to achieve modernization. Others are more optimistic and suggest that the green revolution and other advances promise to close the gap between food supply and population. These advances will help create the base needed for industrialization.

In recent years, a growing number of people have become convinced that population control must accompany industrialization if the quality of life is to be improved. Although birth control programs have encountered numerous social, economic, and religious obstacles in developed as well as developing countries, many governments have recently launched such programs.

GLOSSARY

death rate   a figure indicating the number of deaths within a population as compared to that population as a whole. Rates are usually expressed in terms of per thousand people.

demographic transition   the slackening of growth rates in industrialized nations after a period of rapid growth.

demography   the study of population size, makeup, distribution, and change.

green revolution   recent scientific development of means to greatly increase food productivity.

Malthusian dilemma   the problem posed by Thomas Malthus' theory that population tends to increase much more rapidly than the food supply needed to support it.

modernization   the creation of a modern industrial economy, needed to take care of a large population.

SUGGESTED READINGS

Blaustein, Arthur and Woock, Roger. (eds.). *Man Against Poverty: World War III*. New York: Vintage Books, 1968. Essays which concentrate on the gap between food supply and population, including a section on poverty in America.

Ehrlich, Paul. *The Population Bomb.* New York: Ballantine Books, 1968. One of the most widely read and pessimistic accounts of the population explosion.

Nair, Kusim. *Blossoms in the Dust.* New York: Praeger Publishing Co., 1967. Offers a collection of moving human portraits describing the problems and impact of modernization on rural life in India.

Ward, Barbara. *The Lopsided World.* New York: W. W. Norton and Co., Inc., 1968. A leading British economist describes the growing gap between the developed and developing countries, and presents a strong argument for greater economic aid by the rich nations.

Young, Louise B. (ed.). *Population in Perspective.* New York: Oxford University Press, 1968. Presents a wide variety of viewpoints, including those of demographers, religious leaders, and novelists.

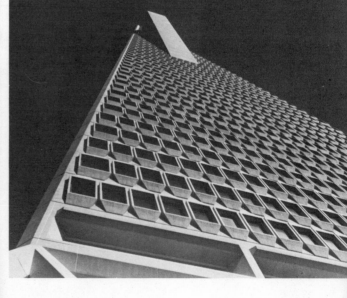

16

URBANIZATION

Government agencies and planning boards are turning more and more to urbanologists and other social scientists to help untangle the webs of the urban crisis. In this task, the sociologist's job is to scrutinize the forces that created the urban revolution, to discover what features cities have in common, how urban living differs from rural life, and what effect these differences have on the individual, the group, and the society as a whole.

As we acquire more knowledge about the urbanization process, and as we begin to understand why cities grow and change and decay, there is the hope that we can launch the sort of social planning efforts that are needed to build a decent future for our urban society.

SICK CITIES

Until a few years ago, most Americans were inclined to take their cities for granted. We knew there were problems, but these were more in the nature of nuisances than crises. Traffic was sometimes slow; there was noise, congestion, dirt; life in the slums was known to be unpleasant, but no one seemed to make much of a fuss about it—including the people who lived there. By and large, our cities were living, vital organisms, pulsating with drama, excitement, and opportunity.

Then, over the past decade or two, something happened. We discovered that our cities were sick; the once dynamic urban organism appeared to be dying. The circulatory system was failing: rapid transit systems were stricken with paralysis; highways and streets were choked with traffic. The respiratory system was suddenly unable to supply clean air, and the layers of smog grew thicker every day. Cancerous growths appeared everywhere— blighted slums, seething racial tensions, a crime rate growing at nightmarish speed, drug abuse even among children in their preteens, vast increases in welfare rolls—all seemed to be suffocating the life of the city. On a national level we discovered that our streams and lakes had become polluted; food and land were contaminated with pesticides; waste materials and sewage couldn't be carried off fast enough.

What was happening? What had gone wrong? How could we save our cities and the surrounding countryside?

Armed with only partial answers to these questions, we have spent the past 2 decades trying to restore our urban areas to some semblance of health. Millions of manhours and billions of dollars have been poured into the effort. But the problems remain. Some have even grown worse. Modern America, despite its scientific and technological miracles, continues to wrestle with the urban dilemma. The question remains whether we are capable of coping with these gigantic problems. Can we reverse the trends and make our cities habitable?

URBAN GROWTH AND URBAN SOCIETIES

Cities are thousands of years old, but the trend toward *urban society*—that is, a society in which more than half the people live in urban areas—is a phenomenon that is new and revolutionary. When the United States became a nation, less than 5 percent of the population lived in cities. Philadelphia was the largest, boasting a total of some 44,000 inhabitants.

Early Cities

Small cities have been the pattern since the first true cities appeared some 5000 years ago. Seldom did a city reach a population of more than 25,000. One of the few giants of the ancient world, Thebes, the capital of Egypt, had a population estimated at 225,000; but even that is small compared to today's cities. Through most of man's history, no society could support urban areas that contained more than 2 or 3 percent of its total population. Crowded and unsanitary conditions made it easy for epidemics to ravage entire urban populations. Secondly, the size of cities was affected by the lack of employment opportunities; with no large-scale manufacturing systems, city people made their living by trading or engaging in small handcraft businesses. But perhaps the greatest single limitation on urban growth was the lack of agricultural surplus. Farmers produced enough for themselves and their families, with very little left over. It has been estimated that it took between 50 and 70 farmers to produce enough surplus to support a single city dweller.

Modern Urbanization

Even as we turned the corner into this century, the vast majority of Americans lived on farms or in small rural villages. But cities were growing at a fantastic rate. By the 1920's, we reached that stage where the urban population outnumbered the nonurban. We had become, in a little over a century, an urban society. Today, roughly three-quarters of the population is classified as urban. So the development of the United States as an urban nation has been the product of only a few decades, and the most rapid growth has been within the past 25 years.

Not only is the "urban revolution" new, but it is becoming world-wide in scope. A number of countries in Europe are more highly urbanized than the United States, and the developing countries have not been immune to the process. The fastest growing city in the world is Sao Paolo, Brazil, with a population above the 5 million mark, more than double the figure of a decade ago. Of the 20 largest cities in the world today, half are in Asia, Africa, or Latin America.

Simply because a nation contains a number of large cities does not necessarily mean that it has become an urban society, however. India, for example, has 2 of the largest cities in the world, but India remains a predominantly rural society. Despite the global spread of urbanization, more than three-quarters of mankind still live in rural areas or small villages.

Factors Responsible for Urban Growth

Four principal developments have been responsible for the fantastic rate of urbanization over the past 150 years: (1) industrialization, (2) increased agricultural output, (3) improved transportation facilities, and (4) improved health facilities.

Industrialization. It is no exaggeration to say that the Industrial Revolution created the urban revolution. Beginning in the late 18th century in England, and then spreading to Western Europe and the United States, the harnassing of energy to replace hand labor and the introduction of the factory system led to the rapid growth of cities. Each new invention seemed to spawn a new industry, and frequently an array of supporting industries—raw materials, fuels, transportation, wholesaling, and retailing.

Around the year 1800, in the beginning stages of the industrialization process, a German observer noted that "specialized division of labor forces workers to live in large cities." Rather than nearly self-sufficient farms and villages, people now devoted their energies to the manufacture of a single product, or even only part of the final product. Other goods and services had to be provided by other people and industries. Only the concentration of large populations in small areas could make such specialization possible.

The factory system developed an insatiable appetite for workers. For the rural dweller, this need created both pressures and lures. On the one hand, industry meant jobs; the pay sounded good and the color and excitement of the mushrooming cities offered a promising change from the drudgery of farm work. On the other hand, the introduction of machinery in agriculture meant that fewer farmers and farm workers were needed. As a result, millions who took part in the vast migration to cities did so out of economic necessity; for millions more it was a matter of choice.

Increased agricultural output. An essential prerequisite for urban growth is the development of an agricultural surplus. Industrialization made the necessary surplus possible—a single reaper, for instance, could do the work of 25 men. In addition to machinery, the application of new scientific methods of farming and stock-breeding increased agricultural output. One hundred years ago, a single farm worker could produce enough food for himself and 3 other people. By 1940, he could feed himself and 9 others. Today, his output has grown to the point where he can sustain 30 people other than himself. The United States thus produces agricultural surplus far beyond its own needs, with only about 6 percent of the population engaged in farming.

Improved transportation facilities. Since the city concentrates on commercial and manufacturing interests, it depends on both short- and long-distance transportation to supply it with food, fuel, raw materials, and goods not produced in that particular city. The cities of the United States have come to depend more and more on resources and trade from distant parts of the globe, thus helping to create a worldwide network of high-speed transportation. Within the urban area itself, efficient transportation systems enable the city to spread out in all directions.

Improved health facilities. Historically, cities were not healthy places to live. Disease rates were higher and life expectancy was shorter for the city dweller. As recently as 1910, for example, the death rate in the cities of England was one-third higher than in British rural areas. All this has been changed during this century with the development of adequate water-supply systems, sewage treatment and disposal facilities, and the steady advances of medical science. Since 1950, the life expectancy of urban and rural populations in industrialized nations has been roughly equal.

THE DEVELOPMENT OF URBAN SOCIETY IN AMERICA

The transition from rural to urban society is not a gentle process. It creates tremendous upheavals in the lives of the new urban dwellers; and the rapid influx of people into the cities places great strains on living facilities and services. In the United States, the process was compounded by the great waves of immigrants who joined rural-born Americans in the movement to cities. Beginning shortly before the Civil War and ending with the immigration restriction laws of the 1920's, more than 24 million immigrants, mostly from Europe, poured into American cities. Between 1890 and 1912, immigrants were arriving at the rate of nearly 1 million per year, and roughly half the population of all cities consisted of people who had been born in foreign countries.

Because of this two-pronged invasion, the growth of American cities amounted to an urban explosion. Cities already in existence grew at almost unbelievable rates. New York, a bustling port of less than 40,000 in the age of Jefferson, had swelled to 312,000 by 1840; less than 50 years later it had passed the 3 million mark. New cities sprang up almost overnight at convenient transportation crossroads or around factory or mining sites. Chicago in the 1830's consisted of a small fort and a dozen houses. By the turn of the century, it had become one of the largest cities in the world with a population well over 1 million.

Lack of planning. Before the Industrial Revolution, it had been a common practice to draw plans for cities to insure a logical pattern of living and growth. William Penn laid out the much-copied grid pattern for Philadelphia; Pierre L'Enfant planned Washington, D.C. as a series of connected circles; years later, Brigham Young's plan for Salt Lake City created a pattern of broad avenues and open spaces.

But no one was prepared for the tremendous growth that accompanied industrialization. There were no zoning laws dictating where or how factories should be built. There were no regulations restricting the number of people who could be crammed into an antiquated, unsafe tenement building. Traffic patterns, water supply, and sanitary facilities were more a matter of accident than design. We are still living with the legacy of that unplanned growth.

Adjustment to city life. The majority of the new city dwellers were as unprepared for city life as the city was to accommodate them. Generally lacking in skills and frequently unable to speak English, they found little available but unskilled jobs at the lowest wages. Poverty and lack of housing usually forced the newcomers to pack into teeming tenement districts, often at the mercy of unscrupulous "slumlords." Nationality groups tended to cluster together for protection and security, creating ethnic islands within each city—Chinatown, Little Italy, Little Israel, and so on—many of which remain today.

Over the period of a generation or two, most of the new city residents made a satisfactory adjustment to the demands of city life. Some acquired industrial skills; their children went to school, giving the younger generation, at least, a chance to climb out of the ghetto. Gradually rural Americans and immigrant groups were assimilated into the mainstream of American urban culture. They were able to find better jobs and to move to more desirable neighborhoods or even to the suburbs.

Invasion-succession patterns. But as one group escaped the squalor of the tenement, a new minority group arrived to take its place. In this century, racial minorities—blacks, Puerto Ricans, and Chicanos—have moved into the areas deserted by immigrant groups. This process is referred to by sociologists as an "invasion-succession" pattern. A neighborhood is "invaded" when minority group people (people who are somehow "different" from the older inhabitants) move in. The original residents resent or fear this encroachment. A wave of "panic" selling (or renting) sets in, accelerating the movement to other areas and to the suburbs. As the older inhabitants flee, more and more minority members move in to take their place. When the newcomers predominate in the area, comprising 70 percent of the population, then the "invasion" is completed and it becomes a "succession." The general result has been the perpetuation, and even the spread, of "blighted areas" in the central city.

Is Urbanization Completed?

Sociologist Kingsley Davis suggests that the process of urbanization has been completed in most industrialized nations, including the United States—that is, the significant migration from country to city has stopped. Urban areas will continue to grow, but at nearly the same rate as rural population. In other words, the continued growth of metropolitan regions will be a product of natural population growth.

The 1970 census, however, suggests that a significant migration of black Americans from the rural South to cities of the Northeast, Midwest, and West Coast continues. Washington, D.C., now has more blacks than whites living within its borders; other cities also show a steady influx of blacks from the southern states. The black population of cities such as Cleveland and Chicago is now well over one-third the total population of these cities. Some sociologists suggest that the black migration will continue, and that over the next 15 or 20 years black Americans will be in the majority in a number of Northern cities.

However, part of this shift in white-black proportions is misleading. The population of many cities has grown very little and in some cases it has declined. The white population is moving to the suburbs so that only a small influx of black Americans is needed to affect the black-white ratio. In any case, the last stages of the rural-urban migration do seem to consist primarily of the various racial minorities. And even natural population growth will add another 100 million people to our urban society by the end of the century.

SUBURBAN SPRAWL AND MEGALOPOLIS

Quite early in America's urbanization process, people found the idea of suburban living an appealing one. They wanted to be close enough to the city to take advantage of its services, its culture, and its employment opportunities, but they also wanted to avoid the congestion, the noise, and the inconveniences of the central city. The result was an outward migration to less crowded areas, surrounding each city with steadily expanding residential rings. Early suburbs were linked to the city by railroads and streetcar lines; the commuter on the railroad platform, brief case and umbrella in hand, was a fairly common sight even before the turn of the century.

In the years following World War I, the mass production of automobiles made suburban living accessible to anyone who could afford one of Henry Ford's Model T's. America surrendered to what urbanologist Lewis Mumford has called the "religion of the motorcar."

Suburbs began to mushroom with unprecedented speed. Following a brief lull during World War II, the flight to the suburbs gained momentum in the 1950's and 1960's. Even industries have now dispersed to the outlying regions, and the shopping plaza attempts to offer some of the advantages of the central city.

The growth of metropolitan regions. Because of the steady spread of this pattern, it has become increasingly difficult to tell where the city leaves off and the suburb begins. As a result, the growth of metropolitan regions has become more important than the growth of cities themselves. Some cities, particularly newer ones such as Houston, have continued to grow at tremendous rates. Elsewhere, however, the population of the city proper has grown only slowly in the past 20 years and a number of cities have shown a steady decline. Pittsburgh, for example, saw its poulation decline from 676,000 in 1950 to 604,000 10 years later. But the metropolitan region which includes Pittsburgh continues to grow rapidly.

SMSA. In studying America's urban society, then, the entire metropolitan region, not just the city itself, must be considered. As a reflection of this, the Census Bureau in its last three nationwide reports has collected its population figures in terms of "Standard Metropolitan Statistical Areas," or SMSA's. An SMSA consists of a county or counties with adjoining borders containing 1 or 3 cities of at least 50,000 people, with most of the people making their living in nonfarm occupations. Two-thirds of the country's population lives in the more than 200 SMSA's identified in the 1970 census, and more than 80 percent of all the population growth in the United States since 1940 has occurred in these areas. New York, of course, is the largest SMSA. The city itself has a population that has nearly stabilized at about 8 million; but if you include the suburban areas of Long Island, Westchester and Rockland counties, Northern New Jersey and Southern Connecticut—all of which are tied to the city—the population of the whole metropolitan region is well over 14 million.

Green ghettoes. The outward spread of population has not solved the problems of urban living; it has merely distributed them over a wider area and added a few new elements. Many social critics, in fact, feel that suburban living typifies the sterility of modern life in metropolitan America. The suburbs have turned into "strip" cities, narrow bands straddling major highways, and dominated by jungles of neon signs and crowded, costly housing tracts. The very things the suburbanites sought to escape—noise, pollution, crowding, high taxes, lack of open spaces, and mediocre schools—have now become the hallmarks of suburbia. Derisive terms such as "green ghettoes" or "slurbs" have become common ways of referring to this new pattern of American life.

Megalopolis. As metropolitan areas extend outward in the endless search for new space to accommodate continued growth, a new phenomenon has occurred. In some areas of the country, the metropolitan areas have begun to run together. In the mid-1960's, Jean Gottman coined the term *megalopolis* to describe what he said was one continuous urban and suburban corridor extending along the Atlantic Coast from Southern New Hampshire to Northern Virginia. One can travel from one end of the region to the other, passing through such cities as Boston, New Haven, New York, Philadelphia, Baltimore, and Washington, D.C., a distance of more than 400 miles, and encounter nothing but one city or suburb after another. Nearly 20 percent of the country's population lives in this single megalopolis, which is often referred to as Bosnywash.

Some demographers gloomily predict that Bosnywash merely gives us a glimpse of tomorrow, and that our future growth will continue

to be concentrated in a few such megalopoli. By studying the population trends of the SMSA's, it has been pointed out that a second megalopolis is already fully developed. This second continuous city is called Chipitts, extending from Pittsburgh north and west along the Great Lakes past Chicago. Chipitts may eventually develop an arc shape, stretching south to include the St. Louis metropolitan area. A third megalopolis, located on the West Coast, is in an earlier stage of development. Referred to as Sanlosdiego, it extends from the San Francisco Bay south through Fresno and Bakersfield to Los Angeles and San Diego. There are still open spaces along this strip, at least in the San Joaquin Valley, but they appear to be closing up rapidly.

URBANISM AS A WAY OF LIFE

The urbanization of America means more than a redistribution of population—it has resulted in a radical transformation of our patterns of living. Cities throughout history have been centers of social change and ferment. The urban atmosphere, much more than the rural setting, has been charged with variety, innovation, opportunity, challenge, and heightened activity. Traditionally there was a sharp and obvious difference between the living patterns of the urban dweller and those in rural areas. In urbanized society, these differences are gradually becoming blurred. Through education, the mass media, and interaction between country and city, the values and norms of the urbanite have come to characterize the overall culture.

Many of the basic characteristics of urban living represent a sharp break with the traditional patterns found in rural societies. Four of the most important of these hallmarks of urbanized society are: (1) interdependence, (2)

PERSPECTIVE

URBANIZATION IN THE THIRD WORLD

We tend to think of the industrialized nations as the centers of urban growth, but actually it is in the developing or "Third World" nations that cities are growing at the fastest rate. There was some hint of this growth prior to World War II, but it is in the past 25 years that the "poor" nations have really been struck by the urban explosion.

And there is no sign that this unprecented growth will slow down. Eighty percent of the growth of the world's population between now and the year 2000 will occur in the Third World countries, and much of that will be in the already overcrowded cities. As one demographer has pointed out, this means that in Latin America alone "a doubling of the urban population as a whole every 15 years is the minimum outlook." There are over 2 million people in Bogota, Colombia, for example, and one-third of them have arrived within the past 5 years.

In the developed nations of the world, the growth of cities was associated with economic change and expansion. Surplus rural populations moved to the cities and were able to find jobs and shelter.

The pattern has been different in what are often called the "premature cities" of the Third World. They are not built on the base of large agricultural surpluses, rapidly expanding industry, or improved transportation and health facilities. Instead, they are the products of population growth in the cities themselves, compounded by the pressures from overpopulated rural areas. Victor L. Urguidi, President of El Colegio de Mexico, relates that these cities are:

> . . . associated with conditions where rural productivity is usually low, manufacturing is only partially developed, the levels of education, skills, health, and welfare are still grossly inadequate, and income and property are highly concentrated. Latin America's cities—even the larger ones of European vintage—are poor; poor and partially rundown, or poor and backward, or poor on the average with splashes of wealth interspersed in shockingly grim slums and ugly surroundings, held together by increasingly inadequate transportation and other services.

Unlike other cities in the United States and other developed nations, there is no room for the constant flood of immigrants within the central city. Instead, shantytowns spring up on the outskirts of the cities—the *bidonvilles* of Africa, the *favelas* of Brazil, the *bustees* of India. Robert Shaw and Sarah Jackson, researchers for the Overseas Development Council, describe the growth of these marginal communities:

> They move in with relatives, tribesmen, and fellow villagers into crowded housing in the older sections, or they set up shacks of corrugated iron, tar paper, and wood in vacant lots. With this overnight construction, they defy city ordinances and the lack of planned streets, water or sewage systems, and adequate building materials. In Rio de Janiero less than half of the registered residences had water connections and even fewer had sewer connections, and these figures do not cover the more recent unregistered homes.

The result is a picture of the central city, often a thriving center of modern buildings and bustling commercial activity surrounded by the most deplorable slum communities, the inhabitants of which seem forever condemned to gaze helplessly at the prosperity beyond their reach. These unfortunate slum dwellers and squatters make up between one-quarter and one-half of the populations of cities in India, Turkey, Venezuela, Senegal, and many other countries; their global total runs to the hundreds of millions.

Most of these people live a marginal existence, with scarcely enough food to keep them alive. Hundreds of thousands are unemployed with little prospect of ever finding full-time jobs. And still they keep coming, because life in rural areas is not much better. The city offers the promise of excitement and glamour; more than that, there is always the hope of finding work.

Experts agree that employment is the vital first step in solving the tremendous problems of Third World cities. But despite spectacular progress in some areas, few urban economies are growing fast enough to absorb the ever-increasing population. Robert McNamara, President of the World Bank, states that "in Latin America, the situation is particularly serious. There, the urban population has grown twice as fast as the number of jobs."

Some recent innovations and proposals offer at least a glimmer of hope. In some countries, for example, industries which have tried to duplicate the automated manufacturing processes of developed nations are being encouraged to use human labor instead. If this substitution of men for machines increases the cost of production, however, the scheme is unworkable, because the industry would price itself out of the highly competitive world market. But in such fields as food processing and construction, the use of more workers has not made important differences in costs.

Another promising step which has been tried successfully around the town of Dasca in the Pakistani Punjab is to spread small industrial centers into rural areas. There, 105 separate small factories are engaged in the manufacture of diesel engines. Planned regional towns, such as those developed in Israel, can also be helpful—they bring some of the advantages of city life into the country, which in turn could help to slow down the migration to cities.

The "Green Revolution," created by the development of new, higher-yielding grains, may create some of the needed agricultural surplus. This has already occurred in the Philippines and elsewhere, enabling the developing nation to import needed industrial materials and additional food items.

In spite of these gains, the progress is painfully slow; it seems unlikely that the developing countries, unaided, can provide the increase in job opportunities. And even if they can, it is only the beginning, because there are the additional challenges of providing adequate housing, schools, sanitation, water, transportation, and other services. Although aid from developed nations has lessened, some assistance is available from the United Nations and other organizations.

An example of the possibilities offered by international cooperative effort is the Mekong River Project in Indochina. Work has already started, although it will take years to complete. This major development program, which some consider even more ambitious than the Marshall Plan (a major factor in the reconstruction of Europe after World War II), involves the cooperation of Laos, Cambodia, Thailand, and South Vietnam. A variety of private companies and international organizations are involved, including a number of UN agencies. David Lilienthal, former director of the Tennessee Valley Authority, has said of the project: "The Mekong, disgorging six times the water of the Nile, could produce more cheap power—vastly more—than TVA, Grand Coulee and Hoover dams generate together. This power would spark new industries, aluminum smelting and mining, and eventually light places as far distant as Malaysia and Singapore." Such a project also holds the promise of thousands of jobs for urban dwellers in the countries involved.

heterogeneity, (3) bureaucratic organization, and (4) impersonal relationships.

Interdependence

In the past, the "typical" farm family was largely a self-contained economic and social unit. They grew their own food and made most of what they needed; a trade with a neighbor or the occasional sale of some livestock or farm surplus brought them the few items they couldn't provide for themselves.

Today, by contrast, the "average" American lives in an urban setting, works for someone else, and personally makes very little of what is needed to live on. Most people are dependent on others for their food, clothing, and shelter; for health care and transportation; and for the purchase of the products they help to make in the services they help to provide.

If one segment of the urban system doesn't function properly (for example, if there is a transportation strike or a water shortage), the urbanite will feel the effects even though he is far removed from the sources and probably has no control over it. He is mutually dependent on thousands of people whom he seldom sees and is even less likely to know personally. This web of interdependence extends far beyond the limits of the city itself and the metropolitan region that surrounds it. The urbanite depends on a miner in Appalachia for his fuel; a strike vote in a union meeting halfway across the country may have an immediate impact on his job; a political crisis or a natural disaster in some remote corner of the globe may affect the price or availability of certain foods or of raw materials vital to the wheels of industry.

Heterogeneity

Earlier in our country's history, rural Americans were generally homogeneous in terms of ancestry, occupations, outlook, and social con-

tacts. Urban Americans, on the other hand, are heterogeneous. The flood of immigrants from Europe and Asia, combined with the movement of rural peoples, including racial minorities, has made urban society a rich mixture of national, ethnic, and racial groupings. Diversity has also been fostered by heightened mobility; the stress on following in the footsteps of one's parents has been replaced by the chance to follow any of a large number of cultural alternatives, each leading to a different career. Urban Americans move frequently; they are reluctant to accept the ideas and beliefs handed down by the preceding generation; and they are accustomed to associating with people from many different social, occupational, religious, and ethnic backgrounds. This pattern of living is shaping a wide variety of people and ideas.

Bureaucratic Organization

A third feature of urban life is the prevalence of what sociologists refer to as *bureaucratic organization*. The term is commonly associated with the structure of government agencies, but it has come to mean more than that. Today, bureaucratic organization is found throughout society in the form of business firms, labor unions, religious organizations, military units, educational establishments, and the many fraternal, civic, and recreational associations that have become such an important part of American life.

Essentially, a bureaucracy refers to a large organization run by a hierarchy of officials, each of whom occupies a ranked status, usually in some pyramid form of authority. Those at the top are the decision-makers, and the lower echelons carry out the decisions. The overall task of the bureaucratic organization is usually broken down into specialized departments and subdepartments. Only the person at the top has the slightest chance of viewing the operation as a whole, and even that executive frequently cannot grasp its total significance.

Anyone who has ever stood in line to straighten out some minute tangle of redtape, or has filled out endless numbers of forms "in triplicate," has encountered some of the weaknesses of the bureaucratic system. Critics argue that bureaucracies are wasteful and inefficient, and that they reveal a dangerous concentration of economic and political power in the hands of the very few at the top. Some

"Always remember, my son, when buses come, they come not singly but in clusters."

sociologists, such as C. Wright Mills (*White Collar: The American Middle Classes*) and William H. Whyte (*The Organization Man*), have expressed concern over what effect working in a bureaucratic environment will have on the individual. They see the organization sapping the employee's individuality, turning the person into a robot-like functionary whose only goal is to complete methodical chores with enough diligence to climb up one more rung on the bureaucratic ladder.

On the other hand, no one has devised a better system of organization than the bureaucratic structure. Despite the criticisms, it is quite possible that "big" business, "big" government, and "mass" media are necessary to enable a complex society to exist. The defenders of the system argue that the concentration of power is misleading, since even the top-level members of the hierarchy are subject to the rules of the system. The corporation executive, for instance, has to answer to the board of directors and the stockholders. Regarding the impersonality of the system, it is argued that this element is overemphasized and that individuals are capable of adjusting to working for huge organizations just as they have learned to cope with other social changes. Regardless of how one views the phenomenon, bureaucratic organization is destined to remain an integral part of our society for some time to come.

Impersonal Relationships

We often look back nostalgically on the simple days of rural society when a person lived in a small, stable community and could get to know the neighbors on a rather personal basis. When we encounter this in the areas where such patterns remain, we come away with a feeling of warmth, security, friendliness. This is not always the case of course, but the image of a serene rural life is strong for many Americans.

Urban society represents a sharp contrast. The individual seems lost in what sociologist David Reisman referred to as "the lonely crowd." The urbanite deals with people as faceless functionaries rather than total personalities. The clerk, the ticket-taker, the policeman, the customer, the bureaucrat—all are encountered but never known. People can live in a high-rise apartment building—or even a suburban housing tract—without ever knowing the names of their neighbors. The newcomer to a city seems to be especially vulnerable to a depressing and dehumanizing anonymity.

Some recent sociological studies have suggested that this impersonal picture of urban life has been overdrawn. There is evidence to indicate that nearly all metropolitan residents maintain close ties with their immediate families and a small circle of friends. And within their neighborhood, many people know the local grocer, druggist, or dry cleaner as well as a few neighbors. Outside these circles, however, it remains true that the urbanite may spend many hours of his day virtually anonymous in the midst of millions, for instance, when riding on public transportation.

THE SEARCH FOR SOLUTIONS TO CITY PROBLEMS

The United States is a vast, sprawling area containing millions of acres of wilderness. And yet, more than half the population is squeezed into large metropolitan areas that take up less than 1 percent of the total land surface.

Crowding

In the search for more living, working, and playing space, some cities have expanded vertically through the creation of skyscraping apartment and office buildings. New York City, of course, is the prime example of this, partly because horizontal expansion is hampered by natural geographic barriers. As a result, the island of Manhattan has a population density of 77,000 per square mile, while the total New York metropolitan area has roughly 2000 people per square mile. The Hancock Tower in Chicago, which rivals the Empire State Building in height, offers the futuristic phenomenon of apartment dwellers on the upper floors "commuting" to offices and stores on the lower floors by high-speed elevators.

Other cities, particularly those that have "grown up" in the age of the automobile, have expanded horizontally. Los Angeles, the nation's second largest city, has a population only about half that of New York, but it is spread over a considerably larger area (approximately 455 square miles to New York's 315). In addition, over 50 "satellite" cities are clustered around Los Angeles, giving the aerial viewer the impression of one endless city stretching from horizon to horizon.

Some of the effects of the congestion are difficult to analyze. Behavioral and social scientists are just beginning to analyze the effect crowded conditions—plus accompaniments such as noise—have on human mental and physical health. The early findings of this work suggest that our spatial patterns may be more harmful than we suspect.

A more visible result of crowding is the difficulty of moving goods and people. Our transportation facilities are obviously inadequate for our ever-increasing congestion. During the 1950's and 1960's, we thought the solution was the development of multilane freeways connecting cities and providing access "belts" for commuters within each metropolitan area. This program, which is still in the process of completion, has already cost well over $50 billion in federal funds alone. The results have been disappointing. The automobile population has grown faster than our ability to provide pavement to accommodate it. In Los Angeles, for example, 60 percent of the land surface is already devoted to the automobile in the form of freeways, streets, parking lots, and service stations. And in other major metropolitan areas, traffic congestion seems worse than ever and smaller cities are already beginning to feel similar strains.

An alternative that is gaining some popularity is the development of more and better rapid transit systems—commuter railroads, subways, and buses, plus some innovative methods such as monorails and hydrofoils. The cities of the San Francisco Bay area have nearly completed an ambitious and costly rapid transit system called BART (Bay Area Rapid Transit). The potential of such efforts is still open to question. Taxpayers in most areas have turned down similar proposals and the relief offered by such systems may be only temporary. Perhaps a more serious obstacle to rapid transit is the "religion of the motorcar." Despite congestion, the difficulties of finding parking space, the expense, the noise, tensions, and pollution, most urban Americans would still rather drive their own cars than ride on public transportation. In the 1970's, crowding and traffic congestion remain 2 of the unsolved problems that make up our urban crisis.

The Environment

The decay of our urban environment was a danger that went relatively unnoticed until

THE VARIOUS PATHS TO SOCIOLOGICAL KNOWLEDGE
MAX WEBER

Max Weber (1864–1920) was perhaps the most eminent figure in the entire field of sociology. His mind was encyclopedic. His interests ranged from the study of religion, to bureaucracy, to the nature of power, to the city. There is virtually no area of modern sociology to which Max Weber has not made an important contribution. Given the concerns of the 19th-century sociologists with the Industrial Revolution and the growth of urbanization, it is not surprising that Max Weber addressed himself to these problems. The result of his studies was a long essay known as *The City.* In it, Weber stated his explanation of urbanization and the structure and function of the city.

Weber's definition of a city was that it was an urban community that incorporated the following characteristics: a fortification; a market where trading and commercial relations predominated over agriculture as the major economic activity; a court of its own with at least a partially autonomous law; and at least partial autonomy of government. Within this definition, Weber illustrates his point through the use of numerous examples drawn from different areas and time periods. Weber is more interested in the cities of the West than those of the East.

Of great importance was Weber's insistence that the city was more than just a great agglomeration of people. It could not be measured only in quantitative terms. Cities were not measured by size alone. In some cases, relatively small aggregations of people made a city; in other cases, a greater number might not qualify.

To Weber the urban community was not unstructured. It was a distinct and limited pattern of human life. It represented a total system of life forces brought into some sort of equillibrium. It was self-maintaining, restoring its order in the face of disturbances. In addition, one could distinguish cities of different kinds. There were typical producer cities which were different from consumer cities. There were also differences between commercial and industrial cities, and main and satellite cities. Moreover, cities developed and changed. For example, some of the functions of the city listed above were found to be less important at certain times. The concept of city as fortress was much more important in the Middle Ages than it is in the world today where weaponry has made it obsolete. The typical medieval city was enclosed by a wall for protection. Today, a wall would be inadequate. The modern city is no longer used for defense. Some of the citizenry are no longer expected to take up arms to defend the city. Other functions of the city in times past today have been taken over by the nation-state, which is the primary administrative unit.

To a considerable degree, Weber used his analysis of urbanization as a means of refuting the materialistic interpretations of Karl Marx. Weber insisted that material economic conditions were not the major social force in our lives. Thus, in one of his major works (*The Protestant Ethic and the Spirit of Capitalism* (1893) he argued that religion, far from being a capitalistic tool for control of the masses as Marx claimed, was instead the major force which had made capitalism possible. And, in his study of the city, he stated that the sense of community was another vital nonmaterial force. This community spirit was not some mystical entity, but rather the collective value system of the urban center. Such systems, he argued, could be studied scientifically to determine their influence on people's lives.

quite recently. It wasn't until the late 1960's that we finally became alarmed about air, water, land, and noise pollution. Just how serious the environmental crisis has become is difficult to measure accurately. We know, for instance, that the rate of lung cancer is higher in urban than rural areas; that the rate of pulmonary emphysema has increased 500 percent in New York City in the past decade. But it is practically impossible to analyze how much of this is due to air pollution and how much might be related to other factors such as cigarette smoking.

Regardless of the precise dimensions of the problem, we have come to realize that something must be done. All levels of government have tried to devise codes to reduce the deadly smog that hangs over our cities. Industries and automobile manufacturers have begun to cooperate. Despite legislative efforts and the expenditure of funds in recent years,

progress has been slow. In some cities, there are now smog alerts, during which people with respiratory ailments are advised to remain indoors and children's playground activities are curtailed or carried on with the aid of face masks.

Progress in the battle against other forms of pollution has been equally slow. With few exceptions, streams and lakes are becoming more rather than less polluted. Sewage disposal systems have proved inadequate in nearly every major city. Metropolitan areas are finding it increasingly difficult to devise ways of collecting and getting rid of waste materials. As ecologists have pointed out, Americans produce nothing in greater abundance than garbage; it is estimated that each of us is responsible for 5.3 pounds of garbage every day. More than half the incinerator plants in the country are considered outmoded or inadequate, but no comprehensive means of correcting the situation has been started yet. In desperation, the cities of the San Francisco Bay Area devised a plan for loading garbage off a train (derisively called the "Twentieth Stenchery Limited") and transporting it 400 miles for dumping in a desolate region. Such measures, of course, merely add to the growing problem of land pollution. Alternative measures such as recycling waste materials to help conserve our valuable resources are still in an experimental stage.

Noise pollution works in more subtle ways; we can't see or feel the effects of urban noise which is increasing at the rate of 10 percent each decade. Recent studies have shown, however, that in addition to hearing loss, people subjected to high noise levels from any source—traffic, machinery, airplanes, loud music—are more likely to be tense and irritable and may be more susceptible to certain neuroses.

Urban Renewal

In the 1950's, when Americans were first beginning to notice that their cities were sick, the major rehabilitation effort was in the form of urban renewal projects. "Blighted" and decaying areas would be carved out and new buildings constructed. In this way, slums would be cleared and the downtown areas would gain a new life, hopefully luring suburbanites back into the central city, at least for shopping and business if not for living.

With tremendous sums of money from the federal and state governments (it has been estimated that redevelopment of a single acre in Manhattan costs the taxpayers $1 million), every major city in the country launched a renewal project. But like so many attempts to save the cities, the intentions were good, but the planning was insufficient. In dozens of cities slums were torn down and traditional neighborhoods destroyed, with worn out tenements and warehouses replaced by new

apartment buildings. But there was no place for the ghetto residents to relocate. These people couldn't afford the new apartments, and even if they could, they needed a place to live until the new buildings were constructed, a time lapse that often proved to be indefinite. The result: the ghetto area simply spread out in new directions, and the cleared area took on the appearance of a doughnut hole, ringed by a new "blighted" area.

There was considerable success, however, in renovating downtown areas. Most of the older cities received a much-needed face lift, and in many cases this led to a revitalization of the shopping and business districts. These beautification programs came under considerable criticism, though, from the poor, who felt the money should have been spent on education, parks, job training, and low-cost housing. The ghetto riots of the 1960's were at least partially an outgrowth of the frustrations felt over the failure of urban renewal to deal with these needs.

Programs such as Model Cities, job-training centers, and low-cost public housing have been launched to correct some of the uneven progress of earlier renewal efforts. In recent years, however, a new obstacle has arisen in the form of lack of funds to carry these projects through. Taxpayers and legislatures have proved equally reluctant to allocate still more billions to what seems to be an endless complex of urban problems. The problems, of course, get worse instead of better—in fact, time will only make solutions more difficult, particularly with the addition of some 100 million people to our urban society anticipated over the next quarter-century.

The Overlapping of Governments

A major difficulty in finding our way out of the urban wilderness is the structure of American government. Obviously problems of congestion, pollution, housing, traffic, and so on do not stop at the political boundaries of the city. The political divisions of our nation's federal, state, and local governments were designed for the rural society idealized by Jefferson; in modern urban society, these divisions cause almost hopeless confusion. The metropolitan region dominated by New York, for example, consists of 550 separate municipal governments, dozens of county governments, and three states. A problem such as air pollution or sewage disposal cannot possibly be solved without the cooperation of all these government structures. Occasionally such cooperation has been achieved. The Port Authority of New York, for instance, is a cooperative venture by city, county, and state governments which has virtual control over harbors, airports, bridges, and tunnels servicing 200 cities in two states (New York and New Jersey).

Another aspect of the problem of governmental control has to do with taxation. Most central cities have lost revenue as their wealthier inhabitants have fled to the suburbs, but the city cannot reduce its services which are used by commuting suburbanites as well. Moreover, the central city has the added burden of providing for higher concentrations of the aged and the poor. Some cities have sought to correct this imbalance by imposing a tax on all income earned within the city no matter where the wage earner lives. Such measures, of course, have often aroused heated opposition from suburbanites who have raised the old rallying cry of "no taxation without representation."

A more extreme solution to the overlapping of governmental control has been the experiments with some form of regional government which would service an entire metropolitan area. Following a plan developed in Toronto, Canada, such a government has been installed in Dade County, Florida, which includes the region around Miami. Called "Metro," this regional government controls such matters as housing codes, slum clearance, and air pollution. In addition, if local communities fail to meet Metro standards in such areas as public transportation, the Metropolitan government has the option of stepping in and operating the service itself. Other cities have adopted a wait-and-see attitude before deciding whether or not the Dade County experiment offers a model to be followed elsewhere.

The Future City

In general terms, the solutions to the urban dilemma are subject to 2 approaches: trying to alleviate immediate problems; or thinking in long-range terms, drawing plans for the city for 30 or 40 years from now. Both approaches are needed, and both are being followed to some extent, although major efforts have been in the direction of solving the most pressing problems.

To facilitate these efforts, the federal government has, of necessity, assumed a larger and larger role, particularly in the form of financing and the establishment of uniform standards. There are limits, however, to the effectiveness of placing these problems on the doorstep of the nation's capitol. In the first place, such a solution runs counter to the important American tradition of self-government and local control. Secondly, monolithic national bureaucracies cannot be sensitive to the needs and desires of each particular community.

In building for the future, countless schemes have already been proposed and some have been set in motion, at least experimentally. Architects and urban planners have devised a wide variety of concepts of what the future city should look like. Chicago's Hancock Tower represents one aspect of future design, high-rise cities. A different approach is offered by the "new cities" plans. In Reston, Virginia, and Columbia, Maryland, entirely new cities have been built, each designed to overcome or reduce the drawbacks of present cities. The cost of construction, of course, is staggering, but the planners felt the investment was well worthwhile if it offered an alternative to the haphazard growth of present urban areas. Unfortunately, both experiments have encountered financial difficulties and have not been as successful as hoped in luring residents away from established areas which, despite their drawbacks, seemed to offer greater economic security.

No matter what form our future cities take, perhaps the key to making them what we would like them to be lies in comprehensive planning. Such social planning so far has proved impossible. Attractive buildings, smooth traffic flow, modern educational facilities, clean air—all these are important considerations but not sufficient in themselves. In the last analysis, the ancient Greeks were right in saying, "the city is the people." If people are to survive in cities, they must build new cities and reconstruct old ones without disregarding the needs, desires, and goals of human beings. The skills of the social and behavioral scientists must be combined with those of engineers, architects, politicians, planners, and the people themselves.

SUMMARY

Cities have been part of human history for some 5000 years, but the development of urban societies has been a recent and revolutionary development. The impetus for the modern urban revolution has come from industrialization, increased agricultural output, and improved transportation and health facilities.

The rate of urban growth, combined with lack of planning, have shaped America's urban society and its current problems. Suburban sprawl and population growth have led to the development of highly congested metropolitan regions covering only a small fraction of the available land surface.

Urban society represents a sharp break with rural patterns of living, with 4 of the most noticeable characteristics being the *interdependence, heterogeneity, bureaucratic organization* and *impersonal relationships* of urban life.

Problems of crowding, environmental health, urban decay, and government overlapping make up the modern urban crisis. So far, satisfactory solutions have not been found. Whether or not man can survive in cities will depend, in large measure, on comprehensive and far-sighted social planning.

GLOSSARY

green ghetto   derisive term for a suburb.

invasion-succession pattern   a process in which one type of population moves into an area already occupied by another type (invasion). If the newcomers predominate over the older residents, the "invasion" becomes "succession." Often a factor in the creation of slums.

megalopolis   a term coined by Jean Gottman for such urban-dominated areas as the stretch along the eastern seaboard from Massachusetts to Virginia.

SMSA   a "Standard Metropolitan Statistical Area," as defined by the U.S. Census Bureau. A SMSA is an urban area with its suburbs; specifically, a county or counties with adjoining borders containing 1 or more cities of at least 50,000 people, with most of the people making their living in nonfarm occupations.

"strip" city   a narrow metropolitan area spread along either side of a highway.

urban revolution   the rapid development of urban societies within the last 25 years.

urban society   a society in which more than half the people live in urban areas.

urbanization   the 2 part process consisting of (1) a quantitative change involving growth of city populations, and (2) a qualitative change in which the society takes on general urban characteristics.

SUGGESTED READINGS

Banfield, Edward. *The Unheavenly City.* Boston: Little Brown & Co., 1970. An outspoken economist critizes liberal urban reforms in education, housing, jobs, and civil rights. Presents a view that is not very popular among modern sociologists.

Gottman, Jean. *Megalopolis: The Urbanized Northeastern Seaboard of the United States.* MIT Press, 1961, 1969. This is a long, complex study by a leading urbanologist. Gottman deals exclusively with the sprawling urban center that extends from New Hampshire to Virginia— "the main street of the nation." He is concerned with the problems of this unplanned congestion but also suggests that this "may be the cradle of a new order in the organization of inhabited space."

Hauser, P. M. and Schnore, Leo F. *The Study of Urbanization.* New York: Wiley, 1965. A wide ranging study of the urbanization process and its effects. Particularly good as an interdisciplinary approach, covering contributions of demographers, economists, sociologists, and anthropologists.

Jacobs, Jane. *The Death and Life of Great American Cities.* New York: Vintage Books, 1961. A very personalized view of the quality of city life. Jacobs, a journalist, criticizes the destruction of neighborhoods during urban renewal projects.

Starr, Roger. *Urban Choices: The City and its Critics.* Baltimore: Penguin Books, 1967, 1969. Starr spent a number of years as executive director of New York's Citizens' Housing and Planning Council. This experience probably accounts for his emphasis on realistic approaches to what he calls the "hard choices" city people must face.

Two Boston Boys Accused
In Fatal Stoning of Man

Stone Man to Death as He Fishes

21 SEIZED UPSTATE
ON NARCOTIC CHARGE

BABY KIDNAPPED
FROM A HOSPITAL

uspect in Slaying
Of 2 Officers Flees

THREE MORE SLAIN
IN VIRGIN ISLANDS

43 Indicted in Crackdown
On Heroin Dealers Here

CRIME IN 'VILLAGE'
PROTESTED BY 400

$10,000 Payoff to Mafia

cials Say Narcotics 'Hot Line' Is Wo...

They Saw Dad Die

Angry Thugs
Trail Victim
& Slay Him

BRONX MAN SEIZED
AFTER AUTO CHASE

School Destroyed
In Suspicious Fire
At Children's Home

6 Frustrating Hours in Harlem
On Trail of 11 Heroin Dealer

DRIVER CARRIES
NO MONEY...
TRUCK EQUIPPED WITH
SAFE NOT UNDER
DRIVERS CONTROL

17

CRIME

Crime and violence have existed in all societies, in all ages of history, but events of recent years have led Americans to wonder if our society may not be more susceptible to these ills than others. During the 1960's, the assassinations of John and Robert Kennedy and of Martin Luther King, combined with a series of well-publicized mass murders, raised serious questions about violence in America. Race riots, antiwar protests, and campus unrest added to our uneasiness and led to a series of nationwide surveys on the causes of violence and crime in our nation. And annual statistics seem to point to a steady and alarming increase in the rate of crime and juvenile delinquency, suggesting that we may be in the midst of a crime wave that threatens to go beyond our ability to control.

The result of these occurrences has been an increasing concern for the establishment of "law and order." Dozens of public opinion surveys have shown that the majority of Americans now consider crime and violence to be our major domestic problem; and few political office-seekers fail to make law and order one of the major pillars of their campaigns.

But the prevention and control of crime depend on much more than hiring more policemen, passing new laws, or "cracking down" in the courts. Effective remedies rely on a firm understanding of the nature and causes of the problem. We must know far more than we do now about the causes and extent of crime and juvenile delinquency; and we must carefully analyze those measures that show most promise in offering the control and prevention we desire. This chapter will give you some ideas about what has been learned about crime and violence and how much more is yet to be learned.

THE NATURE AND EXTENT OF CRIME

Current alarms over social issues often cloud our historical perspective; we tend to feel that things have never been so bad. In regard to crime, as with all our contemporary problems, it is important to view the present in terms of the past. Concern over crime is nothing new. It has been part of our national history since colonial days. Consider, for example, these comments about crime in America which appeared in newspapers nearly a century ago:

In San Francisco, "no decent man is safe to walk the streets after dark; while at all hours, both day and night, his property is jeopardized by arson and burglary."

"Gangs of 'hoodlums' roam the streets of New York, and in one central area, near Broadway, the police enter only in pairs, and never unarmed. . . ."

"Municipal law is a failure . . . we must soon fall back on the law of self-preservation."

"Crime, especially its more violent forms, and among the young, is increasing steadily and is threatening to bankrupt the nation."

One thing we must know about crime, then, is how it compares with the past; we have to analyze trends to determine if crime is increasing in relation to population, decreasing, or remaining about the same. Once a trend is recognized, we face the much more difficult task of trying to find out why change has occurred.

The Uniform Crime Reports

Our most accurate source of data on crime is provided by *The Uniform Crime Reports*, compiled by the Federal Bureau of Investigation. The complete report is published annually and provides information on all crimes known to state and local police from over 8000 agencies throughout the country.

Crime can be categorized in a number of ways, such as crime against property as distinct from crimes against individuals. American legal codes also make a distinction between *felonies* and misdemeanors. A misdemeanor is a less serious offense and is usually punishable by a fine or short-term imprisonment in a local jail. Felonies are more serious violations of law and involve confinement in a state or federal prison for a term of more than one year; some are considered *capital* crimes and are punishable by death. Although there are variations from state to state, the crimes of murder, arson, burglary, rape, robbery, and larceny are almost always considered felonies.

It is the index of more serious crimes that is usually regarded as a barometer of whether the crime rate is increasing or decreasing. Figure 17-1 shows the *Uniform Crime Report's* summary of the crime rate compared to population growth for the decade of the 1960's. The chart creates a clear and shocking picture of how much faster the crime rate seems to be growing than is population. Although the table shows *all* crimes, if only serious crimes are used, the rate is still growing more than 4 times as fast as population. On the basis of such evidence, we are clearly in a crime wave of alarming proportions.

Dispute Over Statistics

The FBI, realizing the possibility of error in reporting, exercises extreme caution in compiling its statistics, and refuses to publish any information that it considers invalid. Despite this care, the reports have been criticized on a number of counts. Some criminologists, for instance, suggest that much of the increase shown in the Reports merely reflects more accurate reporting methods. There seems to be some grounds for this stand. For years, for example, Chicago reported twice as many robberies as did New York, quite clearly a distortion since Chicago's population is about half that of "fun city." For a variety of reasons, apparently, New York police departments were reluctant to reveal the true robbery rate in their city. As a result, the FBI didn't include New York robbery reports in its figures for a number of years because they were so obviously inaccurate.

Other suggestions on distortions of the crime index were made in a report to the

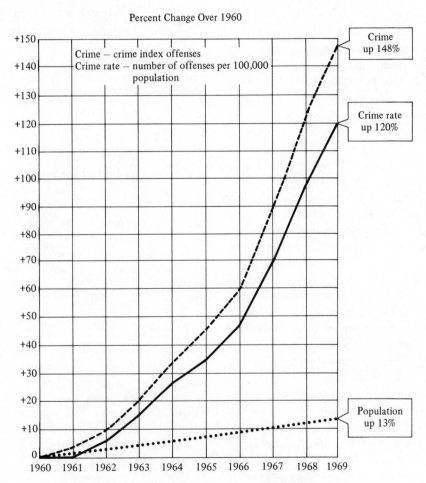

Percent Change Over 1960

FIGURE 17-1 Crime and Population, 1960-1969

Source: *Uniform Crime Reports, 1969*, Washington, D.C., Dept. of Justice, 1970.

President's Commission on Law Enforcement and Administration of Justice in 1967. "Because there is so much unreported crime," the report stated, "it is theoretically possible to have a 'crime wave' on the index charts, when in fact nothing but reporting habits have changed. Thus a crime scare could result from victim sophistication—a realization that only reported thefts can become valid income tax deductions or insurance claims, or a new willingness by nonwhites to report crimes to the police." The Commission itself, after an 18-month study, could not reach a firm conclusion on whether or not the crime rate is higher now than it has been in the past.

The FBI reports are also criticized on the grounds that they arouse fear by making things appear worse than they are. The so-called "crime clocks" are examples of what are considered sensationalist reports. The Bureau publishes statements such as: "An American woman is raped every 12 minutes. A house in the United States is burglarized every 27 seconds. Someone is robbed every 4 and a half minutes." Critics charge that such use of statistics create an unwarranted fear about a person's chances of being a victim of one of these crimes. A former U.S. Attorney General has pointed out that actually a person's chances of being a victim of a serious crime is about once in 400 years; he went on to say that these odds could be improved if one avoided family and associates because, according to statistics, most such crimes are committed between family members or friends.

Karl Menninger, a psychiatrist with a special interest in crime and punishment, summed up the doubts of many when he wrote: "No crime statistics are dependable: most crime is not reported. Most violent crime occurs in the home. Most nonviolent crime takes place in department stores. My own belief is that there is less violence today than there was 100 years ago, but that we have a much better press and communications to report it."

Despite these criticisms, many of them justified, the statistical evidence can't be discounted as meaningless. When all considerations are made for error and distortion, there still remains strong indication of a serious increase in crime. Two categories of crimes, for example, that are quite automatically reported and reported accurately are bank robberies and homicides. *The Uniform Crime Reports* show that bank robberies increased by 248 percent between 1960 and 1967; armed assault rose 84 percent in the 5 years between 1962 and 1967. Such figures as these have convinced even the skeptics that the increase in crime rate is serious, although disagreement continues over the precise amount of that increase.

Unreported crimes. One of the factors clouding the picture of the extent of crime in America is that countless numbers of crimes are never reported to the police. There are many explanations for this: some people are afraid that they will place themselves in danger if they report a crime; often crimes of robbery or theft seem too petty to be worth reporting; frequently people refrain because they "don't want to get involved"—there have been numerous cases of murders witnessed by dozens of people, none of whom called the police.

In 1966 a team of sociologists tried to determine how many serious crimes went unreported. Obviously the people interviewed were not likely to give information about such crimes in which they may have been implicated. Despite these limitations, the survey of 10,000 households revealed a rate of violent crime and serious property crimes twice as great as that reported to the FBI.

White collar crime. In 1940, sociologist William H. Sutherland challenged the belief that crime was associated with the "behavior of the poor." Police records, he pointed out, revealed only what are referred to as "conventional crimes"—those typically reported to the police such as murder, robbery, assault, and larceny. Prison records showed that 98 percent of those serving sentences for such crimes were members of the lower socioeconomic classes.

What these records failed to indicate, according to Sutherland, were certain offenses such as violations of the laws governing business and the professions, which are committed almost exclusively by members of the middle and upper classes. He coined the term "white-collar crime" to refer to such practices as price-fixing, income tax frauds, sale of de-

"It's nice to see some people still appreciate the value of a dollar."

PERSPECTIVE

THE PROVO EXPERIMENT: SELF-HELP FOR JUVENILE DELINQUENTS

When a 16-year-old boy—we'll call him Frank—appeared before a Juvenile Court Judge for the third time, he fully expected to be sent to a reformatory. He guessed that it would be the Utah State Industrial School and the main question on his mind was how long the sentence would be.

He was only mildly surprised when the judge told him that instead of a reformatory, Frank would become part of something called the Provo Program. Judge Paxman told Frank that it was a great opportunity for him—which sounded like the same old line he'd been hearing from adults for years.

Frank was taken to a place called Pinehills and then he had more questions. The building was an unpretentious frame house; no guards, no fences. What kind of place was this? What was the system and how did you beat it?

Inside, he was greeted by a man, obviously one of the "authorities," and Frank expected the usual orientation session. There wasn't any. He began to feel uncomfortable. What was going on? How long did he have to stay there? The man wouldn't answer any of his questions or tell him any of the rules. "Why don't you find out for yourself," the man told him.

The same confusing beginning greets all newcomers at Pinehills, and the confusion is intentional. Pinehills is part of what is called the Provo Experiment, a unique attempt to apply the findings of sociological studies to the rehabilitation of juvenile delinquents. Although it works closely with the Juvenile Court, the experiment is not a government program; instead it is the creation of a volunteer group of concerned citizens and professionals who call themselves the *Citizens' Advisory Council to the Juvenile Court*.

The Provo Program is built around the basic premise that the juvenile gang is largely responsible for a youth's delinquent behavior. As two sociologists connected with the program have written: "Although a 'bad' home may have been instrumental at some early phase in the genesis of a boy's delinquency, it must be recognized that it is now other delinquent boys, not his parents, who are current sources of support and identification." The way to change a boy's behavior, then, is through the group.

Putting this theory into practice, the 20 boys at Pinehills are divided into 2 groups. Although all of the boys are habitual delinquents who would otherwise be in reformatories, they continue to live at home and spend only part of each day at Pinehills. There is very little in the way of structure or rules, beyond attendance and hard work—instead each boy has to learn to rely on his own group. And part of each day is spent in group discussions where the boys try to "work through" their problems; instead of being told what is wrong with them and how they *ought* to behave, they explore their own behavior and its consequences, and begin the search for alternatives.

Frank was given no indoctrination so that from the beginning he would learn to rely on his group. At first he thought the whole idea was a gimmick, a system that you had to work your way around. So, after a couple of days, he simply didn't show up at Pinehills. No one said anything to him when he returned. Not a word. He was tempted to test the system further but already he was beginning to sense that his group was shunning him because of his behavior. He began to feel uneasy and insecure. He didn't know what was expected of him or even how long his "sentence" would be.

Over the next few weeks, Frank gradually began to see how the Provo Experiment operated. Everything depended on the group and how well you fit into it. The group had established its own norms, such as requiring that no one be released until all had succeeded in being completely honest about themselves in group discussions and until every boy had showed a willingness to help solve problems.

If a boy is slow to respond and continues to engage in delinquent behavior when away from Pinehills, the group will react. They know their own success depends on everyone. Consequently, they will either shun a persistent offender or chastise him. If this doesn't work, they will request that the individual be sent to jail on weekends until they think he is ready to become a working member of the group.

The Advisory Council—as well as the boys—believe firmly that "the crucial criterion for any treatment program is not what an individual does while in it, but what he does while he is *not* in it." For a new boy like Frank, this frequently sets up a tug-of-war between his old juvenile gang connections and his new peer group at Pinehills. In nearly all cases, the boy realizes that he has come to a critical crossroads and that if he turns to the Provo group for the support he needs, his chances of avoiding a long series of jail sentences are much better. Once the group feels a boy is ready to move on, he enters phase II of the Program, in which he is helped to find a job in the community, but still meets periodically with his group so that he doesn't lose their support.

The Provo Experiment is certainly not a final answer to the problem of juvenile delinquency. In fact, it has been criticized by some for its disregard of methods that have proved successful elsewhere, such as psychological counseling and vocational training. Perhaps the greatest advantage of the Program is to suggest that a number of the social sciences can make contributions to a coordinated program of rehabilitation.

Source: LaMar T. Empey and Jerome Rabow, "The Provo Experiment in Delinquency Rehabilitation," *American Sociological Review*, October, 1961, vol. 26, pp. 679-696, and LaMar T. Empey, *Alternatives to Incarceration*, Office of Juvenile Delinquency & Youth Development, HEW, 1967.

fective merchandise, fraudulent consumer "games," misleading advertising, and "kickbacks" for special favors.

Although they receive little publicity and are seldom brought into courts, Sutherland felt that these "respectable crooks" had a very harmful and widespread effect on society. One serious business violation can involve millions of dollars and affect the lives of thousands of people. Because the general public is aware that these illegal practices exist, they not only represent a betrayal of trust but lead to a lowering of social morale.

Of course, the fact that certain members of business and professional groups engage in illegal activity does not prove that crime is rampant among the upper classes. Neither does it completely discount the relationship between environmental factors and criminal activity. But it does seriously challenge those theories which have attempted to explain all types of criminality as the result of lower-class poverty, inadequate education, bad companions, poor housing, and lack of opportunity. Almost by definition, members of the middle and upper classes are those citizens who enjoy many of the advantages society has to offer. Yet these advantages do not prevent some of them breaking the law.

Organized Crime

Just as it is difficult to measure the extent of unreported and white-collar crimes, it is equally difficult to discover the precise dimensions of the activities of the organized crime "syndicates." Traditionally, the Mafia or syndicates have been known to engage in such activities as the manufacture and sale of bootleg liquor, in narcotics, peddling in labor racketeering, illegal gambling, prostitution, and the "fencing" of stolen merchandise. These activities have been going on for decades on an organized basis, but authorities can do no more than make educated guesses about the scope of the operations. Currently, the sale of narcotics seems to be the major income producer, with heroin alone producing a revenue of some 300 million dollars a year. Trade in marijuana and barbiturates is probably even higher. Some consider illegal gambling to be the primary activity of organized crime, with income estimated as high as $20 billion a year.

In recent years, there is increasing evidence that the syndicates have begun to "move underground" by infiltrating legitimate businesses—or what Al Capone called the "legitimate rackets." Such operations as vending machine businesses, food wholesaling, retail sales of beer and liquor, laundries, nightclubs, and record manufacture and distribution seem to be among the favorite targets. By pressure or monopolistic methods in these areas, organized crime can achieve much higher profit levels than would normally be the case in open competition. Combined with the continuing efforts to gain influence in various levels of government, particularly municipal governments, it becomes increasingly difficult for law enforcement authorities to gain much headway in cracking down on these nationwide operations.

Violent Protest as Crime

Campus unrest, antiwar demonstrations, race riots and draft protests are all seen by most Americans as further evidence of the breakdown of law and order in our country. Many social scientists, however, feel that such outbursts are temporary in nature and subside in time, much as the ghetto riots of the mid-1960's did. By way of evidence, they point out that violence in America, like crime, seems to run in cycles. There are at least 7 identifiable periods in our national history when violent protest was at least as rampant as it is today. For example, the draft riots during the Civil War resulted in over 2000 deaths in New York City alone in the space of just 5 days—a statistic that makes modern protests seem extremely peaceful by contrast. Similarly, the massive railroad strike of 1877 resulted in hundreds of deaths and the destruction of millions of dollars worth of buildings and railroad equipment.

A number of sociologists suggest that group violence today may be more frightening because of the publicity and the frequent advance indications that an explosive situation is likely to occur. A typical case developed during the Democratic National Convention in August, 1968, when millions of Americans watched the bloody confrontation between protesters and police on television. People saw the police engaged in often needless violence, not only against protesters but also against newsmen and innocent bystanders. It should be mentioned in this connection that police, although subject to discipline and tight organization, are also subject to the same characteristics of collective behavior you read about earlier. Under such circumstances, the maintenance of social control becomes increasingly difficult—there is, on the one hand, a tendency to overreact and give in to the forces of emotional contagion; or there may be a tendency to underreact and make the situation worse by doing little or nothing.

As with other aspects of crime and violence, our hope for the future lies in understanding the social factors that contribute to outbreaks of group violence. Understanding can lead to prediction, and this in turn creates a greater possibility of taking preventive action to forestall a "cycle" of violence or crime.

THEORIES ON THE CAUSES OF CRIME

If it is difficult to measure the extent of crime in America, it has proved even more difficult to sort out the various causes of criminal behavior. As we have seen, such behavior cannot be understood solely in terms of socio-economic class, educational level, or intelligence, although all of these have some bearing on the types of crime a person is likely to commit. Nor can we accept sweeping generalizations such as the idea that urbanization or poverty breeds crime. Our knowledge has to be much more precise—we have to discover what specific elements of the environment contribute to criminal behavior and why, and we cannot ignore white-collar crime in favor of concentrating on conventional crimes. While social science research is providing increasing amounts of information, we are nowhere near any final answers.

Some Tentative Findings

Most social scientists agree that there is a correlation between crime rate and urbanization. Studies of rural communities over a period of years have shown that as the community becomes more urbanized, the rate of crime goes up. Also, it has been noted that blacks who have moved from the rural South to northern cities show a crime rate far higher than the national average for blacks. The connection between density of population and crime rate is, of course, not a sufficient explanation of criminal behavior, but it does suggest that criminals are to a large extent shaped by their environment. In a word, criminals are made, not born.

On the other hand, psychologists and psychiatrists have suggested that personality development, particularly within the family, is the key element. Other psychological studies present persuasive indications that all criminals may be afflicted by some sort of mental disorder and that the so-called "normal" criminal simply does not exist.

A recent study by a husband-wife team of sociologists attempted to combine environmental factors with personality development. The study was a follow-up of an unsuccessful experiment in the control of juvenile delinquency which had taken place during the

1930's; the sociologists attempted to determine why, as adults, such a large percentage of the group had turned to a life of crime. Their research convinced the team that the influence of the family was the key factor. "Undeniably a slum neighborhood can mold a child's personality," they reported, "but apparently only if other factors in his background make him susceptible to the subculture that surrounds him. Cohesiveness in the family, consistent discipline, and affection from his parents seem to insulate a boy from 'criminal influence.'" The authors went even further in their conclusions by stating, "Of all the influences which play a part in the genesis of criminality, the *mother's personality* appeared to be most fundamental." Because of the many other variables involved, few criminologists would agree with such a strong statement.

Lack of a Single Theory

It should be clear from what has already been said that no single theory has been able to account for all types and instances of criminal behavior. Why, for example, should one person who has been exposed to a particular environment become a criminal while another person living under roughly the same conditions does not? Why is it that 2 persons with similar personality types may or may not commit a crime and may or may not commit the same kind of crime? Most criminologists agree that an act of crime results from a combination of many influences, among which environmental factors and psychological traits appear to be prominent. Most would also agree that much more research is needed in this field.

JUVENILE DELINQUENCY

As with crime, the legal definition of juvenile delinquency varies from state to state.

Usually an individual is considered a juvenile delinquent if he is between the ages of 7 and 17, and if his offense consists of some act that would be considered a crime if committed by an adult.

In addition, all states also define certain other types of behavior as juvenile offenses, such as habitual truancy or refusing to obey parents or guardians. All juvenile offenders are tried in special juvenile courts or in courts operating under special juvenile jurisdiction.

The extent of juvenile delinquency. As with adult crime, accurate statistics are hard to establish but all indicators suggest that juvenile delinquency is also increasing at a much faster rate than population. According to the *Uniform Crime Reports,* arrests for serious crimes by individuals under age 18 totaled well over one-half million in 1970; or to put it another way, nearly half of all people arrested for serious crimes were under age 18. What is more alarming than the figures themselves is the rate of increase of juvenile delinquency—between 1960 and 1968, arrests in this age group increased by 78.5 percent. This figure is somewhat distorted because the number of people in this age group is larger each year than it was the year before due to the "baby boom" of the late 1940's and 1950's. Even when this factor is taken into consideration, however, it is clear that the rate of juvenile delinquency is rising much faster than the population of this age category.

Another important development of the past decade has been the increased rate of arrests of girls under age 18. Throughout our history, males have been responsible for far more crimes in all age categories than were females—male criminals outnumber females by more than 7 to 1. Generally it is believed that this evidence does not prove that females are necessarily more virtuous than males, but rather that members of the 2 sexes were expected to fulfill different social roles. Strongly aggressive behavior is not only tolerated in males, but often encouraged. On the other hand, women have traditionally led a fairly protected existence, with closer ties to the home, and with the expectation of adhering rather strictly to established moral and legal codes. As the sexes have become more nearly "equal," not only have new opportunities been opened up for females, but they have also showed a marked increase in the incidence of crime. While arrests for all females has increased sharply in the past decade, the greatest jump has been in the juvenile category. Between 1960 and 1968, arrests of females under 18 increased by roughly 160 percent, or just about twice the rate of increase for juvenile males.

Delinquency and Urban Environment

In the search for the causes of delinquency and the reasons for its alarming increase in recent years, social scientists are dealing with much the same complex set of variables as they do in trying to explain all types of criminal behavior. As is the case with adult crime, the highest percentage of juvenile arrest occurs in the core areas of our cities. This fact has led many to search for the combination of causes in the ghetto areas of our cities. On the basis of studies in this field, the President's Commission on Law Enforcement and Administration of Justice attempted to draw a composite portrait of the "typical" juvenile delinquent and the forces that led to the early entrance into criminal behavior:

A sketch drawn from the limited information available shows that . . . the delinquent is a child of the slums, from a neighborhood that is low on the socioeconomic scale of the community and harsh in many ways for those who live there. He is 15 or 16 years old . . . one of numerous children . . . who live with their mother . . . His home may be broken . . . it may have a male head who is often drunk or in jail or in and out of the house. He may never have known a grown-up man well enough to identify with or imagine emulating. . . .

He may well have dropped out of school. He is probably unemployed, and has little to offer his employer. The offenses he and his friends commit are much more frequently thefts than crimes of personal violence, and they rarely commit them alone. Indeed, they rarely do anything alone, preferring to congregate and operate in a group . . . [1]

While this picture fairly well conforms to the general public's stereotyped impression of juvenile delinquency, it only describes some of the juvenile delinquents. In recent years, we have become more and more aware that delinquent behavior is also a problem in middle-class urban and suburban neighborhoods.

Middle-Class Delinquency

One reason that the Commission tended to associate delinquency with the inner-city environment is because that is the impression created by the records of police, detention centers, and prisons. The majority of arrests and convictions for serious juvenile offenses do involve a high percentage of the type of individual described above.

Delinquency in suburbs and middle-class neighborhoods is much like white-collar crime; it is there but it doesn't show up on the police blotters. Recent sociological studies have shown that delinquent behavior on the part of middle-class youth may be nearly as widespread as ghetto delinquency. One extensive survey in a Midwestern suburb revealed that the percentage of juveniles who admitted criminal behavior was nearly as high as that found in lower-class urban neighborhoods. The major difference was in detection, arrests, and convictions. The youths in the survey admitted that 90 percent of their law violations—usually shoplifting, buying alcohol,

[1]President's Commission on Law Enforcement and Administration of Justice, *The Challenge of Crime in a Free Society*, Washington, U.S. Gov't, Printing Office, 1968.

or destroying property—went undetected. More serious crimes led to more arrests, but 9 out of 10 of these arrests never resulted in court action. Although many in the sample admitted narcotics offenses, none of these had led to court action.

Criminologists have suggested that the primary reason that middle-class delinquency goes virtually unnoticed is that the police and courts tend to deal more leniently with middle-class offenders. There is considerable evidence to suggest that authorities deal much more harshly with the "tough kids"—the "hoods," particularly members of racial minorities. A polite, well-dressed youth from a "good" family usually escapes with nothing more than a lecture. A "child of the slums," picked up for the same offense, is much more likely to be arrested, especially if his behavior seems sullen or belligerent.

While much more study is needed, particularly in changes in family life, at least some of the upsurge of middle-class delinquency has been associated with basic changes in adolescent life. In the past, young people enjoyed much less freedom, and most teen-agers were more concerned with finding a job than with getting into college or having fun. Some social scientists have suggested that the "Protestant ethic"—which encouraged thrift, hard work, and good behavior—has been replaced by a "social ethic" which emphasizes the importance of getting along with people. If one's friends go in for thrill-seeking—through drugs, drinking, joy-riding, or criminal behavior—the youth feels the need to "go along with the crowd." Psychological studies have also indicated that a boy's desire to assert his masculinity may lead to deviant behavior in order to capture attention.

Delinquency and Gang Life

One of the key variables in the explanation of juvenile delinquency is the importance of the peer group, which appears to be much more significant for juvenile law breakers than adults. We have already seen that this is a factor in middle-class delinquency, and the Crime Commission mentioned in regard to ghetto delinquents that "they seldom do anything alone."

The delinquent pattern of behavior is learned from the gang and it is this group that provides the security, rewards, and sense of belonging that the youth needs. This would seem to be particularly true of young people who come from unhappy or broken homes; the delinquent subculture can provide some of the support the family fails to afford. When the gang finds itself in conflict with authority, this tends to solidify the group feeling—it is easy for them to feel that all representatives of authority are treating them unfairly and so they rely even more heavily on each other. As one team of sociologists concluded, "From the point of view of a gang member, the gang *is* the world."

PUNISHMENT

Throughout history, the rationale for the punishment of criminals has been two-fold: first, and most obviously, to make the offender suffer in some way for the crime that has been committed; second, to act as a deterrent—not only to prevent the prisoner from returning to criminal behavior, but to serve as an example to others who might be contemplating a crime. Gradually, we have also developed a more humane and practical theory that imprisonment should provide some means of rehabilitation enabling the offender upon release to become a functioning member of society. As a result, our attitudes toward punishment have remained in a state of transition for a long time— there is no consensus on what the nature and purpose of punishment ought to be.

The Effectiveness of Punishment

Particularly in times like the present, when the crime rate seems to be increasing at a frightening pace, the demand for "law and order" usually includes the demand that offenders be treated as harshly as the law allows. Criminologists, however, have long insisted that such treatment actually defeats its purpose—it does not deter others from crime and it tends to "harden" the criminal behavior of the prisoner.

Many criminologists and specialists in penology (punishment) argue that instead of "straightening out" the offender, our present prison system tends to reinforce criminal patterns of behavior. Perhaps the majority of prisoners would agree with the statement of one former convict that, "if you aren't a criminal when you go in, you are by the time you get out."

Prison life really amounts to a complete social system, with its own set of laws, norms, and values. Studies of the "prison subculture" have made it clear that adjustment to this life usually necessitates criminal or deviant behavior. Bribery of guards, petty theft, trade in drugs, willingness to fight for your "rights," and homosexuality all tend to make prison life a "training school for criminals."

In addition, many of our jails and prisons present a demoralizing, sterile environment which offers the prisoner little opportunity or incentive for learning job skills or developing other patterns of behavior that will be helpful in making a successful readjustment of life "on the outside." Considerable efforts have been made to improve conditions in state and federal prisons, but conditions remain deplorable in many areas, particularly in county and city jails where prisoners are usually confined for shorter periods. A report issued by the Justice Department in 1970 revealed that of 161,000 prisoners surveyed in county and city jails, more than half were awaiting trial or arraignment—many had been in prison for as long as 12 months without ever being brought to trial. The same report showed that 85 percent of county and city jails had no recreational or educational facilities, 50 percent had no medical staff, and 25 percent no visiting facilities. Considering such factors, it may not be surprising that economist Robert Heilbroner, in listing the 10 most important priorities for America in the 1970's, placed prison reform near the top of the list.

Capital Punishment

Recently the form of punishment that has aroused the most public controversy is capital punishment, or execution. The practice has been both opposed and defended on religious, moral, and humanitarian grounds. The major arguments, however, have revolved around whether or not it serves to deter criminals from committing those crimes that could lead to the death penalty—murder, treason, kidnapping, espionage, and bank robbery. Opponents of legal execution have argued that statistics show homicide rates are no lower in states that have kept the death penalty than they are in states that have abolished it. Defenders of capital punishment argue that the statistics are misleading and that even if a single life were saved, it would justify maintaining this type of punishment.

In response to these arguments, a number of states have abolished the death penalty, except for unusual crimes, and there is agitation in other states to abolish it. Although the debate is far from over, even states that maintain the death penalty have proved increasingly reluctant to use it. Between 1930 and 1960, there were 3742 executions in the United States, about 90 percent of them for murder. In the past decade, there have been fewer than 50.

Attempts to Reduce Recidivism

One of the major concerns of criminal justice has been to discover ways to reduce what is called *recidivism,* a term used to describe the repeating of criminal behavior after a prisoner is released. Two of the oldest methods to combat recidivism are *probation* and *parole.* A person who is placed on probation does not have to serve a prison sentence but reports periodically to a probation officer who attempts to guide the offender in making a more satisfactory social adjustment. Parole is different in that a prison term has already been served, but usually shortened by the parole period. The parolee is expected to observe certain rules of conduct and to report to a parole officer; after successful completion of a parole, the individual is restored to full freedom.

In addition, attempts are made to "rehabilitate" the criminal who is serving a prison term. These efforts include training for a trade, formal schooling, and individual counseling on why the convict turned to criminal behavior in the first place. So far, all of these methods have had little success in reducing the rate of recidivism. Figure 17-2 shows that recidivism remains alarmingly high, particularly with younger criminals. According to these nation-wide statistics, roughly two-thirds of those arrested for serious crimes will be arrested again within 6 years of their release from prison.

THE NEED FOR UNIFIED SOCIAL EFFORT

Even our brief survey of the problems of crime and punishment can lead one to despair over the magnitude and complexity of the problem. It is easy to agree with the harsh statement of former U.S. Attorney General Ramsey Clark in his book *Crime In America.*

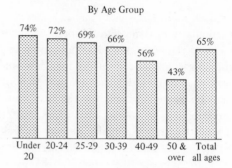

By Age Group

74% 72% 69% 66% 56% 43% 65%

Under 20 | 20-24 | 25-29 | 30-39 | 40-49 | 50 & over | Total all ages

Persons released in 1963 and rearrested within 6 years

FIGURE 17-2 Percent Repeaters

Source: *Uniform Crime Report, 1969,* Washington, D.C., Dept. of Justice, 1970.

"In its most direct contacts with crime," Clark wrote, "prevention, detection, apprehension, conviction, and correction—the American system of criminal justice fails miserably. Since most crime is never reported to the police, the agencies of criminal justice are ignorant of most of the conduct they are designed to control."

As Clark later makes clear, the problem must be combatted on all fronts simultaneously if our system of criminal justice is to lead to positive results. We need more efficient law enforcement, but we also need more adequate methods of rehabilitation, a swifter, modernized court system, prison reform, and a sound understanding of the causes of crime and delinquency as a means of seeking prevention.

In our desire for "law and order," for example, one often hears the demand for larger, more effective police forces. These are certainly needed—of the millions of serious crimes that are reported each year, only about 1 in 9 leads to conviction. As Clark points out, "At a time when our major domestic concern is crime and violence, the nation spends more on household pets than on police."

But adding more police is not enough. For one thing, we need more efficient means of gathering and presenting evidence and a revamped criminal court system. While 86 percent of murders lead to arrests, fewer than 25 percent result in conviction, often because of insufficient evidence or lack of coordination between prosecutors and police. And even if both police methods and the court system are improved, what purpose will this serve if two-thirds of those convicted return to crime when they have completed their sentences?

Some Steps in the Right Direction

So often with our major social problems, Americans have turned to the federal government for assistance. While the national government can help, nearly all observers agree that we must be careful not to move in the direction of massive national or state police forces. The local police force is the key to crime control in a democracy because it keeps law enforcement close to the people. The officer on the beat is a far better judge of the needs and problems of the neighborhood precinct than would be some national official functioning as part of a huge bureaucracy.

The federal government, therefore, has concentrated its efforts on assisting state and local law enforcement agencies and correctional institutions, rather than trying to assume control. One of the most promising steps has been established by the Crime Control Act of 1968. Under this law, the federal government has sponsored state coordinating councils designed to encourage closer cooperation among local police, prosecutors, courts, and corrections officers.

Other promising steps include innovative attempts at prison reform, especially at the state level. Despite a shortage of funds, there have been signs of considerable success in experiments with group therapy and temporary release programs which allow an inmate to leave prison during the day to work. More ambitious programs include "prisons without walls," which have attempted to create a more positive environment for inmates to reduce the feeling of a "deliberate, moral rejection of the criminal by a free society." Similar experiments, called "half-way houses" provide a transition between prison and society; the prisoners live in supervised dormitories but have considerable freedom of movement and are aided in the search for jobs. Much more, of course, needs to be done. Society, including the convict's family, tends to place a stigma on the released prisoner that creates difficulties in finding work and making a satisfactory social adjustment. An enlightened public is an important part of the rehabilitation process.

In regard to juvenile delinquency, attempts have been made to strengthen federal and state public assistance programs, local family and child guidance agencies, and the services of the juvenile court system. A much greater concentration of effort and expenditure of funds is needed in all 3 areas. And, as the report of the 1960 White House Conference on Children and Youth stated, "All programs . . . which really result in stronger, more stable and secure homes are, in reality, programs for the prevention of delinquency, even though that may not be their stated purpose." In addition, parents must be helped "to recognize and acknowledge the basic dignity and worth of their children as human beings . . . for a nearly total lack of self-esteem, or feeling of his own real worth, can be among the root causes of a child's delinquent behavior." At the same time, young people should be encouraged to understand that their increased freedom carries with it a responsibility to society and to each other.

THE VARIOUS PATHS TO SOCIOLOGICAL KNOWLEDGE
EDWIN H. SUTHERLAND

Edwin H. Sutherland's research into "white-collar crime" (first published in 1940) was not only an important addition to sociological knowledge, but also contributed to a nationwide reevaluation of crime. Americans had come to identify crime with lower-class individuals, with poverty and slums. Sutherland countered this view by aiming his research at "men of affairs, of experience, of refinement and culture, of excellent reputation and standing."

In the ordinary catalog of crime come the offenses of murder, assault, burglary, robbery, larceny, and public intoxication, among others. People who are accused of these crimes are dealt with by the police, juvenile or criminal courts, probational institutions or the correctional systems. But there is another kind of crime that is practiced by middle- and upper-class persons. ". . . persons of the upper socioeconomic class engage in much criminal behavior; . . . this criminal behavior differs from the criminal behavior of the lower socioeconomic class principally in the administrative procedures which are used in dealing with the offenders."

White-collar crimes are committed by persons, often of high respectability, in the course of their occupations. White-collar crimes include such business practices as violations in restraint of trade, misrepresentation in advertising, unfair labor practices. In the medical professions and in politics examples of such crime are: illegal sales of drugs, bribery, and fraudulent testimony in accident cases. The problem of white-collar crime is very serious. It is expensive and dangerous for the society in which it occurs.

Sutherland studied the records of 70 of the largest corporations in the United States. He found that the majority of them had been found guilty of some illegal act. Yet the majority were never brought to criminal courts. Most cases were settled out of court.

In addition, the perpetrators of white-collar crimes were not branded as criminals. The general public does not see these offenses in the same way as traditional crimes. Perhaps the reason for this public apathy is the diffusion of the effects of white-collar crime. It hurts the consumer through increased prices and taxes, but this does not seem the same as robbery. In addition, the higher status of the businessman protects him from the weight of public disapproval that the ordinary criminal suffers. Moreover, white-collar crime is sometimes committed by an organization like a corporation, so it is difficult to focus guilt on any one person. Yet the cheating of corporations can cost the public more than ordinary crimes.

While many felt—and continue to feel—that such crimes as sharp business practices were of quite a different nature than "traditional" crimes, Sutherland insisted that "White Collar crime is real crime . . . because it is in violation of the criminal law." Further, he argued, such crimes were perhaps more serious than others in eroding social trust and unity. The complex web of illegal and extralegal activities which emerged from the 1972 presidential election has made many Americans more aware of the thrust of Sutherland's arguments.

The Need for Further Study

It should be clear by now that one of the keys to the control and prevention of crime lies in acquiring more accurate knowledge of the factors that lead an individual into criminal behavior. Recent studies have provided important insights and suggested areas where more research is needed. But we are only on the threshold of finding out what we need to know. As criminologist Thorsten Sellin has stated, ". . . if it is to strike at the roots of crime, preventive social action must rest on an understanding of the causes of crime. To provide an explanation of crime is the still unfinished work of the social scientists, in particular sociologists, psychologists and psychiatrists."

SUMMARY

Finding the means for more effective control and prevention of crime depends first on acquiring a better understanding of the nature and causes of criminal behavior. Although there are definite signs that the rate of crime and delinquency is increasing much faster than population, there is no agreement on the exact proportion of this increase. Accurate measurement is made difficult by such factors as disagreement over statistics, and the "hidden" nature of such aspects of the problem as unreported crime, white-collar crime, organized crime, and the question of violent protest.

Social scientists have encountered even greater difficulty in trying to understand the web of factors causing criminal or delinquent behavior. Most criminologists agree that a combination of influences, including environment and psychological traits, is involved and that no single theory can adequately explain crime.

Like crime, juvenile delinquency is increasing at a faster rate than the population. In the last decade arrests of girls in particular have jumped. Many delinquents come from broken urban homes, but unreported middle-class delinquency may be as widespread as that of the ghetto. Pressures of adolescence and the influence of the peer group help cause delinquency.

A growing number of people have become convinced that imprisonment must include rehabilitation, as well as punishment, of the prisoner. Early measures to reduce recidivism, such as parole and probation, have met with little success. But newer programs, including group therapy, prisons without walls, and halfway houses, show signs of promise. Our changing attitudes toward the purpose of punishment are reflected in the continuing debate over the use of capital punishment. Most experts agree that prison reform, as well as better methods of law enforcement and court procedures, are badly needed. But these measures must be part of a unified effort on all fronts, including further research by social scientists.

GLOSSARY

capital punishment the death penalty.
crime any violation of a law that requires punishment of the offender; more loosely, harmful antisocial behavior.
criminology the scientific study of crime and criminals.
felony a serious crime, punishable by death, a term in a state or federal prison, or a large fine.
misdemeanor a lesser crime, usually punishable by a fine or confinement for less that a year in a local jail.
parole the process wherein a convicted criminal is released from prison, but is required to abide by certain restrictions and requirements for a specific period of time. If he successfully completes the parole, he is permitted to return to normal life.
penology the branch of criminology that studies the punishment and treatment of criminals.
probation the procedure whereby a person accused of a crime is permitted to remain at liberty under the supervision of a probation officer.
recidivism the habitual relapse into crime.
white-collar crime criminal acts, usually violations of the laws governing business and the professions, committed by middle- and upper-class citizens on the job.

SUGGESTED READINGS

Blumberg, Abraham S. (ed.). *Current Perspectives on Criminal Behavior: Original Essays on Criminology.* New York: Alfred A. Knopf, Inc., 1974. An impressive collection of articles on criminality, law enforcement, and corrections, all written by prominent sociologists.

Clark, Ramsey. *Crime in America.* New York: Pocket Books, 1970. Poignant observations on the nature, causes, prevention, and control of crime in America.

Cressey, Donald. *Other People's Money.* Belmont, California: Wadsworth Publishing Co., 1971. An investigation into embezzlement by a noted sociologist.

Gibbons, Donald C. *Changing the Law Breaker: The Treatment of Delinquents and Criminals.* Englewood Cliffs, N.J.: Prentice Hall, 1965. A novel approach to studying the causes of crime through analysis of social psychological factors related to the various types of criminal offenses.

Jackson, Bruce. *Outside the Law: A Thief's Primer.* New Brunswick, New Jersey: Transaction Books, 1972. A firsthand account of criminal lifestyles. Very interesting reading.

Maas, Peter. *Serpico.* New York: Bantam Books, 1973. A biography of a New York detective who must constantly fight against corruption in the N.Y.P.D. This work provides the details related to the Knapp Commission study of police corruption.

Quinney, Richard. (ed.). *Criminal Justice in America.* Boston: Little, Brown and Co., 1974. An interesting compilation of radically oriented essays on law, police, justice, and corrections in America.

Gresham M. *Crime and Society.* 2d ed. New York: Random House, 1967. A brief and easily read analysis of modern criminological theory and research.

———— *The Society of Captives: A Study of a Maximum Security Prison.* New York: Atheneum, 1965. A classic treatment of the organization of convict subcultures and the "pains of imprisonment."

18

WAR

One cannot travel far through the pages of human history without being led to the conclusion that warfare is the "normal" state of human affairs, and peace is little more than a lull between armed clashes. We tend to see these wars in isolation, each with its own set of causes, its own pattern of battles, maneuvers, triumphs and defeats, its own set of results. This pattern creates a feeling that wars are simply things that happen, events which are beyond human control.

In recent years, however, an increasing number of social scientists have begun to treat war as a separate field of study, trying to understand its nature and causes, and exploring the possible means for its prevention. They have wrestled with such questions as: What is the relationship between conflict, violence, and war? Are wars inevitable? Is there something inherent in human nature that leads to large-scale violence and war? Why does conflict sometimes lead to violence and other times to nonviolent resolution? These research efforts are just beginning to scratch the surface of this highly complex subject. Gradually, though, we are building up a body of knowledge to help answer these questions and to give us hope that war is a social phenomenon that can be controlled and perhaps eventually eliminated.

WAR AND THE WAR SYSTEM

In the modern world, we live with the constant threat of war. We have already been shocked by 2 global wars in this century, the last one responsible for the destruction of an estimated 50 million lives, and a staggering debt of human suffering and property damage. We all know that a third world war would make the previous 2 seem like minor skirmishes by comparison, and that a nuclear holocaust could lead to the end of civilization as we know it or even to the end of all life on this planet.

The "Balance of Terror"

In a desperate effort to avoid the catastrophe of another global war, the major nations of the world have followed the traditional path of seeking security through military strength. Over the past 25 years, the world has been divided into armed camps, each nation attempting to keep its military power at such a level that other nations will not dare to attack it.

Maintaining this "balance of terror" has become a self-perpetuating process. Neither side dares let the other develop a "first-strike capability." This has meant that, as weapons become increasingly sophisticated and destructive, old weapons must be discarded and a costly new arsenal built to keep pace with developments. In addition to the evergrowing stockpile of conventional and nuclear weapons, the major powers have felt it necessary to experiment with the lethal forces of chemical and biological warfare (CBW). These arsenals now include such items as botulism toxin, 1 ounce of which would be capable of killing 60 million people, and pneumonic plague, for which no one has yet developed an effective vaccine.

Perhaps the balance of terror will work; perhaps the fear of annihilation will succeed in preventing another total war. As Winston Churchill stated, "When the advance of destructive weapons enables everyone to kill everyone else, nobody will want to kill anybody at all." But as long as the weapons exist, the risk is there; either by accident or design, the arms buildup could plunge us over the brink.

The Cost of the Arms Race

Even though the "balance of terror" may so far have helped to prevent World War III, the cost of the spiraling arms race has placed a tremendous burden on the world's wealth and resources. Considering the agenda of problems humanity faces—the growing gap between population and food, saving our environment, creating decent standards of living, education, and health—this is a burden we can ill afford. According to a report of the U.S. Arms Control and Disarmament Agency: "Global military expenditures take more than seven percent of the world's gross product. In money terms they are equivalent to the total income produced by the one billion people living in Latin America, South Asia, and the Near East. They are greater by 40 percent than world expenditures on education at all levels of government and more than three times worldwide expenditures on public health."

"Brush-Fire Wars"

In the years since World War II ended, in 1945, the world has witnessed an unending series of limited wars, often referred to as "brush-fire wars" because they have been confined to small regions of the earth's surface. These small wars have been fought with con-

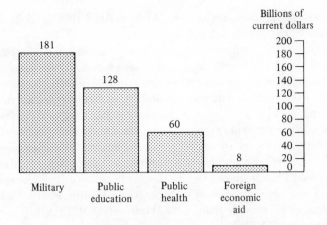

FIGURE 18-1 World military and other public expenditures, 1969

Source: U.S. Arms Control & Disarmament Agency, *World Military Expenditures, 1969*, Washington, 1970, p. 6.

ventional weapons, but some authorities say that we regard them as small only because they appear so in comparison with all-out nuclear war; in terms of destructive power, they have been a devastating continuation of World War II. In *The War Business*, George Thayer makes these conflicts seem anything but small: "Bombing tonnage in the Korean War," he writes, "exceeded all the tonnage dropped by the Allies in the Pacific Theatre of World War II. In the 'small' 6-day Sinai War of 1967, more tanks were committed to battle than by the Germans, Italians, and Allies together at the crucial 12-day battle of El Alamein in 1942. And from July 1965 to December 1967, more bomb tonnage was dropped on Vietnam than was dropped by the Allies on Europe during *all* of World War II."[1]

It has also been pointed out that these brush-fire wars are actually more divisive than large-scale war tends to be. They usually end

[1] Thayer, *The War Business,* Simon and Schuster, 1969. p. 18.

in some sort of a stalemate rather than a clear-cut victory for either side, leaving in their wake seething resentment that amounts to little more than an armed truce. In addition, these wars frequently are not supported by the total population of the nations involved and can lead to deep divisions within a country.

The Dangers of Militarism

In his final speech as President, Dwight Eisenhower gravely warned: "In the councils of government, we must guard against the acquisition of unwarranted influence, whether sought or unsought, by the military-industrial complex. The potential for this disastrous rise of misplaced power exists and will persist. . . ." These phrases have become the watchwords of those who sense some sort of conspiracy exists in America aimed at perpetuating and expanding the war system. Others argue that the very existence of a large war machine presents the constant danger that it will be used. General David Shoup, former Commandant of the Marine Corps, points out that military men are anxious to test their training in combat, to try new tactics, theories, and weapons in action, and, in so doing, to receive promotions. "Militarism in America," he concludes, "is in full bloom."

Those who defend our present security system are convinced that the dangers are exaggerated and, in any case, we have no choice but to accept those risks. They point out that there was more to President Eisenhower's "military-industrial-complex" speech than a warning. He went on to say: "A vital element in keeping the peace is our military establishment. Our arms must be mighty, ready for instant action, so that no potential aggressor may be tempted to risk his own destruction. . . . We have been compelled to create a permanent armaments industry of vast proportions."

ARE WARS INEVITABLE?

Many people are convinced that wars cannot be prevented; we have always had them and we always will. Some go a step further and argue that wars are not only inevitable but even necessary. Our nation was forged in war and the Union was preserved by war. Those who believe in radical change also frequently argue that large-scale violence is the only means to achieve such change. Algerian psychiatrist Frantz Fanon, whose book *The Wretched of the Earth* has become a handbook for revolutionary movements, presents the thesis that the peoples of the underdeveloped countries must resort to violence to throw off the yoke of European and American imperialism.

Others believe that large-scale violence not only can be prevented but, considering the risks involved, must be. In order to explore

TABLE 18-1 WORLD'S LARGEST REGULAR ARMED FORCES AND CHANGES FROM 1966-1968*

Country	1966 size	1968 size	Change
United States	3,094,000	3,500,000	+ 406,000
Soviet Union	3,165,000	3,220,000	+ 55,000
China	2,486,000	2,761,000	+ 275,000
India	879,000	1,033,000	+ 154,000
Turkey	450,000	514,000	+ 64,000
France	523,000	505,000	− 18,000
W. Germany	440,000	456,000	+ 16,000
Britain	438,000	427,000	− 11,000
Italy	376,000	365,000	− 11,000
Indonesia	352,000	340,000	− 12,000
Pakistan	278,000	324,000	+ 46,000

* Note: These figures do not include reserves (of which China may have more than 200 million) or guerilla forces.

Source: Institute for Strategic Studies, London, "The Military Balance, 1968-69."

more realistically the possible alternative to war, many social and behavioral scientists have searched for an understanding of the causes of what may be considered humanity's most urgent problem. No one has come up with anything approaching final answers, but it is worthwhile to examine some of the directions these explorations are taking.

Is Violence Inherent in Human Nature?

In recent years, a number of researchers have developed theories to explain violence and war in terms of the human nature. Ethnologist Konrad Lorenz, in *On Aggression*, has suggested that a fighting instinct against members of the same species has been bred into many animals in the course of evolution, an instinct which serves positive functions in preserving the strongest of the species. Yet once even the crudest weapons were developed, humans turned into natural killers of their own species.

Desmond Morris, author of *The Naked Ape*, believes that the distance between combatants was the crucial factor in turning humans into killers of each other. Both he and Lorenz had noted that many animals stop short of killing a member of their own species by what they called "appeasement gestures." A wolf, for example, who has lost a fight to another wolf, bares his throat in a signal of defeat, and this gesture alone is enough to satisfy the victor without resorting to killing his victim. Weapons that can be used at a distance render any such appeasement gestures meaningless. Morris concludes that "the moment the attacking is done from such a distance that the appeasement signals of the losers cannot be read by the winners, then violent aggression is going to go raging on." Both Lorenz and

Morris agree that this "aggressive instinct" explains why humans go to war, even if that war is carried out in the name of self-defense.

Robert Ardrey, a journalist with training as a social scientist, suggests that human beings are driven by the same natural desire exhibited by many animals to protect their territory from intruders of the same species. In *The Territorial Imperative*, he states: "If we defend the title to our land or the sovereignty of our country, we do it for reasons no different, no less innate, nor less ineradicable, than the lower animals. The dog barking at you from behind his master's fence acts from a motive indistinguishable from that of his master when the fence was built."

Is Violence Culturally Determined?

Many social and behavioral scientists vigorously disagree that war and violence represent instinctive behavior. Anthropologists are quick to point out that if a warlike instinct was inherent in human nature, it would be evident in all cultures. Many cultures, however, show distinctly nonviolent means of settling conflicts. Among Eskimos, for instance, rivals may settle their differences by "insult-contests" in which individuals publicly hurl epithets at each other until one is forced to retire because he has run out of words. The California Indians engaged in what has been called "token warfare"; the Indians of the Yurok, Maidu, and Miwok tribes met intruding hunting parties by hurling stones or spears at them from a fairly safe distance. The skirmish quickly ended when one faction chanced to wound or kill an opposing hunter. And some cultures, such as the Hopi, have been noted for the absence of warlike traits.

On the basis of such evidence, most social scientists would agree with the conclusion of

THE REPORT FROM IRON MOUNTAIN

In 1967, a controversial book, whose author or authors remain anonymous, argued that wars are so necessary that we cannot afford peace. Written in the language of social scientists, *The Report from Iron Mountain on the Possibility and Desirability of Peace* is actually a very clever satire, but so subtle in tone that many of its arguments have been taken seriously.

Here is a summary of some of the major arguments on the functions of war presented in the *Report:*

1. *Economic.* War-preparation is a "dependable system for stabilizing and controlling national economies." Employment levels can be maintained and different aspects of the economy strengthened whenever necessary; dangerous swings in the economy can be prevented by pumping money into or withdrawing it from war-related industries. War-preparation, therefore, is the great "stimulator of the national metabolism."

2. *Political.* "The permanent possibility of war is the foundation for stable government; it supplies the basis for general acceptance of political authority. It has enabled scientists to maintain necessary class distinctions, and it has ensured the subordination of the citizen to the state" by virtue of the tremendous power of nationalism. "No modern political ruling group has successfully controlled its constituency after failing to sustain the continuing credibility of an external threat of war."

3. *Social.* The military establishment "controls dangerous youth" through conscription. The military system is also the basis of loyalty to the state: "allegiance requires a cause; a cause requires an enemy."

4. *Cultural and Scientific.* In time of peace, the *Report* states, the art, music and literature of a society become "sterile" and "decadent." The truly great creative achievements are usually inspired by war. War has also provided a great stimulus for scientific and technological innovation: "Beginning with the development of iron and steel, and proceeding through . . . the age of atomic particles, the synthetic polymer, and the space capsule, all important scientific advances have been at least indirectly attributable to war."

5. *Ecological.* Wars have been useful in keeping populations ecologically in balance. Unfortunately, the author states, war is not "eugenically selective"— that is, the superior die as well as the inferior. But in nuclear war, with the killing of great masses, "the victims become more genetically representative of their societies."

In examining possible alternative systems, the *Report* concludes that no other program comes close to meeting "the functional requirements of a world without war."

Although recognizing that the *Report* was satirical in intent, the arguments presented seemed so close to the thinking of many people that a group of 8 prominent social scientists felt called upon to present counterarguments. In a book titled *Peace and the War Industry* (Aldine, Trans-action Books, 1970), the scholars present their answers to *The Report from Iron Mountain:*

1. *Economic.* War preparation is *not* necessary for "stabilizing and controlling national economies." In 1965, a blue-ribbon U.S. Committee on the Economic Impact of Defense and Disarmament concluded that "even general and complete disarmament would pose no insuperable problems; indeed it would mainly afford opportunities for a better life for our citizens." Other ways can be found of stabilizing the economy and, of course, the war industry uses up funds and resources that could better be used on important domestic programs.

2. *Political.* While wars have often been a time of heightened patriotism, they have also on occasion created deep divisions of opinion in the society. It is also pointed out that loyalty to one's country does not depend on the threat of an external enemy; Switzerland and other countries have remained free of such threats for long periods without any loss of national spirit. Far from being a factor that hardens class lines, war often serves as a great leveller of social classes and may even lead to social upheaval.

3. *Social.* Military service might "control dangerous youth" for short periods, but creates more serious problems in the individual's readjustment to civilian life. It may also encourage an "acceptance of violence" that carries over into domestic society.

4. *Cultural and Scientific.* Rather than causing a burst of creative activity, the authors argue that cultural achievement actually declines in time of war. The long period of wars during the French Revolution and the Age of Napoleon produced strikingly few important works of art or literature. And Nazi Germany, perhaps the prime example of a war-oriented society, was itself "sterile" and "decadent" in terms of artistic production. War has acted as a stimulus to scientific invention, but this does not mean that a nation is incapable of such innovations in times of peace. One can also raise the question of whether the quickened pace of scientific advancement is worth the price in human suffering.

5. *Ecological.* War has obviously not functioned as any sort of control on population growth. A survey of population-growth charts for this century shows that wars are just as likely to result in a sharp increase in population, such as the "baby boom" in this country. The idea that any war could be "eugenically selective" is clearly absurd—a nuclear war would destroy just as many of the "strong" as of the "weak."

Regarding alternatives to the war system, the authors argue that such alternatives do exist and all that is needed is the will to use them. We must find that will if we are to avoid the tremendous burdens of our defense systems and if we are to avoid a nuclear war that could destroy all life on this planet.

Kenneth Boulding: "We have not learned aggression," he states, "from our remote biological ancestors, nor have we learned territoriality from them. Insofar as aggression or territoriality play a part in human culture—and they do—each generation learns them from the previous generation and perhaps in a lesser degree from its own physical environment and random events."

Does Group Behavior Explain War?

Psychologist Gordon Allport has said that aggression in an individual cannot explain large-scale violence because "however pugnacious or frustrated an individual may be, he himself lacks the capacity to make organized warfare." As you learned in the chapter on Collective Behavior, people in groups often act in ways that they would not as separate individuals. Sociologists and social psychologists have studied a number of aspects of group behavior that help to explain, in part at least, why whole societies are able to become involved in the war-making process. Here are examples of some of the factors that have been examined:

Displacement. Displacement is a term used to describe the mechanism which allows a group to vent its feelings on an acceptable enemy—a scapegoat. During the 1920's and 1930's, for example, the Jews were convenient targets for the German people who had been humiliated by defeat in World War I and then encountered a series of frustrations in the chaotic years following that war. Encouraged by official Nazi propaganda, a large portion of the population vented their frustrations on the Jews by blaming them for all the hardships the country had experienced. Some national leaders have consciously tried to distract their country's population from domestic troubles by building up hatred for an external "enemy."

The image of the enemy. Related to a society's tendency toward ethnocentrism is the belief that other groups have intentions of causing harm to one's own nation or group. People build up an "image of the enemy" which allows them to act towards others in ways they wouldn't think of if they didn't have particular stereotypes in their minds. In time of war, the population of both sides will easily be persuaded that the enemy, and only the enemy, is guilty of horrible atrocities, and the feeling develops that the enemy is something other than human. An American soldier in Vietnam explained his "image of the enemy" to reporter Jonathan Schell by saying: "The trouble is, no one sees the Vietnamese as people. They're not people. Therefore it does not matter what you do to them."

Selective inattention. This term refers to the mechanism which allows us to screen out things that are threatening or dangerous. In time of war, people want to hear only of victories and tend to block from their minds signs that their nation may be losing. In a similar way, many people today simply ignore the destructive threat of nuclear weapons and even speak of "winning" a war between nuclear powers. We also select descriptive words that give a comfortable tone to unpleasant subjects. For example, we speak of *antipersonnel weapons* to describe shells that explode into tiny, lethal fragments covering a wide area, or a *nuclear umbrella* to convey a protective meaning concerning our stockpile of nuclear weapons.

Nationalism. Perhaps the most important element of group behavior in regard to warfare—and one of the most difficult to explain—is nationalism. Until fairly recent times, wars in Western societies were usually fought by small professional armies; it was not uncommon to hire "mercenaries" from another nation to help out, as was done by the British in the American Revolution. During the French Revolution, the nature of warfare changed dramatically when the hard-pressed revolutionary government turned to the *levee en masse*, a huge citizen army made up of zealous patriots. Since then, increasingly large proportions of the population have been involved in the waging of war. Since World War I, we refer to *total* war, because the entire populace contributes to the war effort in some way, and the civilian population is no longer immune from the suffering and death of war.

What is there in the spirit of nationalism that turns millions of normally peaceful human beings into willing cogs of a huge war machine? So far, no one has come up with any universally accepted explanation of the dynamics of nationalism. Most social scientists would agree, however, with the following quotation by John Good which offers a partial explanation by relating patriotism to religious fervor:

> As a citizen of a nation-state, the individual associates himself with other individuals in common loyalty and action, as he does in organized religion. Like religion, nationalism is developed through symbols. The national flag replaces the Christian cross, and the national anthem becomes the foremost hymn of the new religion. The hundreds of thousands of Americans who visit Washington, D.C. are, in a way, making a pilgrimage to a national shrine. The heroes of a nation's history become the saints of this new religion. Nationalism has also proved as intolerant of nonconformists as religion, and, like religion, the nation asks men to sacrifice their property and their lives.[1]

[2] John Good, *The Shaping of Western Society*, Holt, Rinehart & Winston, 1968.

The Role of Decision-Makers

But no matter how much hostility is built up between nations, war does not begin with the people of one nation suddenly picking up weapons and heading for the enemy. The decision to go to war is made by the governments of the nations involved. This fact often creates the tendency to excuse the populace for the existence of war and place all the blame on the decision-makers. One of the major defense arguments used at the Nuremberg War Crime Trials following World War II was that the Nazi officials on trial were not to blame for acts they committed because they were merely obeying orders.

There is no doubt that national leaders can play a determining role in the outbreak of war. This would be particularly true of such dictatorial regimes as Nazi Germany and Fascist Italy. But even the most powerful modern dictator cannot wage war without the support of a large portion of the population. Government leaders, then, may make the actual decision to go to war, but they do so only with the knowledge that they have the support of the people they govern.

In a democracy, the structure of government is designed to minimize the possibility of one man having the responsibility for making the ultimate decision. In the United States, technically, only Congress has the power to declare war, although numerous presidents have managed to involve the nation in combat without any such formal declaration. The long-lasting debate over U.S. involvement in Southeast Asia has raised unanswered questions about where the decision-making power should or actually does reside—with the President, the Congress, or the people.

In an age of instant communications and "push-button warfare," the burden of responsibility seems to rest with unusual weight on

THE VARIOUS PATHS TO
SOCIOLOGICAL KNOWLEDGE
C. WRIGHT MILLS

While many sociologists have striven for a detached objectivity in their work, others have used their research as a vehicle for outspoken social comment and criticism. No figure exemplifies this second attitude more than C. Wright Mills.

In a career cut short by a fatal heart condition, Mills often upset fellow sociologists with his harsh attacks on American culture, its various power structures, and what he foresaw as a relentless drift toward catastrophe (*The Causes of World War III,* 1958). In the 1970's, his concern with the uses and abuses of power seem strikingly relevant, although his writings spanned only the decades of the 1940's and 1950's. Studies of power in labor and business led him to a concern over how these power structures influenced those of government and the military. The idea that such power elites tended to be in close association was not new, but Mills raised alarm by arguing that the coalition was leading the nation toward ultimate destruction in "the name of crackpot realism."

Mills saw the danger as being in the institutional structure itself. For a person to exercise power, he had to use a source that was "something greater" than himself—that "something greater" being the institution. Changing the individuals in the elite would make little difference, except to the individuals involved; the abuses of power would simply be transferred to other hands. Mills felt it was necessary to stress this institutional basis of power to counteract the tendency of Americans to equate power positions with particular personalities.

In *The Power Elite,* published in 1956, Mills said the institution which most threatened the nation's existence was that of the military. This did not mean that a military *junta* was about to sieze control of the United States. Rather, he argued, that other elites found the military posture satisfying and expedient—the "crackpot realism" surrounding the need for national security was bound to work with the military to bring about holocaust. "Every man and every nation is either friend or foe," he wrote, "and the idea of enmity becomes mechanical, massive and without genuine passion. When virtually all negotiation aimed at peaceful agreement is likely to be seen as 'appeasement,' if not treason, the active role of the diplomat becomes meaningless; for diplomacy becomes merely a prelude to war or an interlude between wars. . . .''

Because the power elites were firmly in control, Mills felt that even if war were avoided for a time, we were heading toward a mass society where the fragmented populace would be increasingly manipulated and controlled. The United States, he said, had moved ''a considerable distance along the road to mass society. At the end of the road there is totalitarianism, as in Nazi Germany or in Communist Russia. We are not yet at that end. But surely we can see that many aspects of the public life of our times are more the features of a mass society than of a community of publics.''

The one hope Mills held out was that we might regain our ''moral sensibility'' before it was too late. But there was little in his writing to encourage optimism. Rather, he seemed to feel that the most he could offer was as bleak a prediction as possible, in the hope that some, at least, would listen.

the shoulders of the Chief Executive. Living in an international system marked by a high degree of suspicion and hostility, the President and his advisors operate under constant pressure and stress. A breakdown in communications, faulty intelligence reports, misperception of another power's intentions, an irrational act or an accident, or deliberate deception—any of these could place a national leader in the position of having to make an irrevocable decision.

THE ALTERNATIVES TO WAR

If the individual, whether common citizen or government leader, is innately aggressive, endowed with some killer instinct, then perhaps wars can be avoided only by some basic change in human nature. But, as we have seen, whatever the causes of aggressiveness, the social environment plays a determining role in the expression of that behavior. Therefore, we must decide what we can do with the environment—both national and international—to minimize the chance of total war, to reduce gradually the number of brushfire wars, and to find ways to reverse the arms buildup.

The approaches to improving the international environment are numerous and varied. Among the more extreme proposals are methods and procedures for gradually transferring a degree of sovereignty from the nation-state system to some supranational body, such as the United Nations, which would eventually attain a preponderance of military power in some form of international peace-keeping force. At least for the present, however, most people feel that such basic changes in the international system are utopian. Consequently, the majority of those concerned with war/peace issues advocate a variety of ways of building safeguards into the existing nation-state system. Most of these plans are based on trends or changes that are already in evidence. In general, these proposals are not mutually exclusive—that is, one can advocate maintaining a strong military force and yet work for limitations in armaments; this has been the approach of the U.S. government for a number of years. At the same time, advocacy of these limited goals does not rule out the possibility of working for the eventual goal of an international peace-keeping force, or even total global disarmament.

Here is a brief summary of some of the proposals for creating security within the framework of the present nation-state system.

1. *Deterrence.* The logic of maintaining security through military strength has already been mentioned in connection with the war system, and so have some of the limitations. In an age of increasingly sophisticated weapons, it becomes all but impossible to tell when a nation has achieved enough strength. One has to deal with such complicated questions as: how does the deterrent value of intermediate-range ballistic missiles compare with the value of intercontinental missiles? Or, how many more missiles does the U.S. need to offset the growing strength of the Soviet Union's nuclear submarine fleet? The constant debates in Congress over such issues attest to the complexity of the problem. There is also the question in the minds of many as to whether or not the traditional civilian control over the military can be maintained when the civilian element cannot understand the nature of the weaponry being used. Despite these drawbacks, deterrence remains the predominant method of trying to maintain security at the present time.

2. *Arms control.* For many years, the major powers have attempted to reach an understanding on some means of limiting or controlling the arms race. By and large, the success of these Strategic Arms Limitation Talks (SALT) has been meager. Two notable exceptions have been the Limited Test Ban Treaty, by which the leading members of the "nuclear club" agreed to stop indiscriminate testing of nuclear devices, and the Nuclear Non-Proliferation Treaty, signed by most of the nations of the world, which is designed to limit nuclear weapons to those nations which already possess them. Despite these achievements, arms control efforts have done little to slow down the stockpiling of destructive weapons or to limit the cost of the arms race.

3. *Increased international understanding.* The modern revolutions in technology, communications, and transportation are rapidly bringing the peoples of the world into closer contact with one another. Each year brings new additions to the growing list of international organizations; some are made up of private citizens or associations, some of government agencies, and they deal with a wide variety of functions. Cultural and student exchange programs continue to multiply, and such unilateral efforts as the Peace Corps and CARE enable some Americans to make a contribution in the worldwide struggle against poverty, disease, and hunger. Multinational business corporations have spread their activities over the globe with little regard for national boundaries. International Telephone and Telegraph, to cite just 1 example, has its main offices in New York, but 3 of its 4 research centers are in other countries, foreign production is equal to production in the United States, and its stockholders and employees represent dozens of countries. Already 25 percent of the world's production of goods and services is controlled by these global firms. Even Cold War tensions have yielded to the advantages of global business; the Italian auto firm Fiat is producing automobiles in the Soviet Union and an American manufacturer is considering building and selling trucks on Russian soil, using both American and Soviet personnel.

Increased contact between members of different cultures does not automatically lead to increased understanding. Such contacts may serve to reinforce ethnocentric stereotypes or may arouse feelings of nationalistic resistance. There are many who feel that firms such as I.T.T. may interfere in the politics of foreign nations by siding with the forces of stability even if this tends to foster dictatorial government. On the other hand, many observers are hopeful that a sense of world community is beginning to emerge—that more and more people are beginning to recognize that we are all members of the same species sharing common problems and aspirations on our fragile "spaceship earth."

4. *Improved decision-making.* Some experts feel that the international climate can be improved if the decision-making process is carried out with greater efficiency and far-sightedness. A well-informed and practically minded public can add a great deal toward achieving this goal. International affairs expert Roger Fisher, for example, claims that "critics of government" make intelligent decision-making difficult because they "regularly demand the wrong kind of performance from the official concerned with foreign affairs. They ask him to play to the grandstand, not to get results. They themselves judge performance not by international results but by the short-term affect on popularity."

5. *Functionalism.* In recent years, we have begun to see that the problems we face are global in nature. Such matters as environmental decay, poverty, the preservation of resources, the stresses of urbanization, and racial tensions do not stop at a nation's borders. They involve all cultures and all people. With this awareness has come the knowledge that cooperative action among all nations is needed to cope with these problems, and such cooperative effort is increasing each year. The United Nations has not proved as effective

a peace-keeping organization as many had hoped, but it has offered a useful means for international cooperation in a number of functions such as public health and economic development. Lincoln Bloomfield has said of these activities: "If the member states should find that the U.N. no longer serves their basic national interests in the political realm, they will still have to think long and hard before sacrificing this 'functional' realm, where cooperation has become not an option but a necessity."

Those who believe that what is called *functionalism* offers man's best hope for peace, stress the idea that we need more "functional arrangements" on an international level geared to dealing with the problems shared by all peoples. Such arrangements do not mean loss of loyalty to one's nation, but rather the recognition that for some purposes joint effort by many nations is necessary.

Whatever goals we pursue in the hope of creating a more stable international environment, we must recognize that the problem of war cannot be isolated from other elements of our "high-risk environment." The problems of population, poverty, hunger, scarcity of resources, and the growing gap between the "rich nations" and the "poor nations" create the sort of international tensions that make war not only possible but probable.

SUMMARY

The study of war and the means of preventing it is now recognized as a legitimate field of study in the social sciences, including sociology. The instability and excessive cost of our current security system make it essential that we find some alternative to war for settling human differences.

Gradually, research efforts are beginning to

yield results by increasing our understanding of the causes and nature of war and some of the ways wars might be prevented. While some social scientists argue that violence is inherent in man's nature, most believe that it is culturally determined. In either case, it is the social environment that makes possible the expression of aggressive feelings. Individual psychology, group behavior, and governmental decision-making all contribute to making war possible.

The search for alternatives to war have led some to advocate extreme proposals for changing the international system by transferring the war-making machinery to some international organization such as The United Nations. But, most people feel that limited goals are more realistic. Rather than changing the international system, they hope to build security into the current system by working for one or more possible alternatives. These include deterrence, arms control, increased international understanding, improved decision-making, and functionalism.

GLOSSARY

appeasement gesture   the gesture whereby one animal signals to another that he's given up a fight. Appeasement gestures allow animals to refrain from killing each other in struggle.

balance of terror   the status quo achieved when no nation dares to attack another because of its strong military power.

brush-fire war   term for any limited war since World War II.

displacement   the mechanism whereby group feelings are transferred from their original cause to an acceptable enemy or scapegoat.

first-strike capability   the ability to make the first military attack successfully because of sophisticated weaponry.

functionalism   an approach to human society that emphasizes the interrelated functions of all parts.

militarism   the spirit or policy which promotes military virtues and ideals; prevalence of a military way of thinking or predominance of a military class.

military-industrial complex   the association of private business and manufacturing interests with the development of arms and the growth of the national military establishment.

selective inattention   the mechanism which allows people to screen out from their minds matters that are threatening or dangerous.

SUGGESTED READINGS

Benoit, Emile. "Interdependence on a Small Planet." *Columbia Journal of World Business*, 1966. Available in reprints. A fascinating insight into the relationship between the problem of war and other elements of the high-risk environment.

Fisher, Roger. *International Conflict for Beginners.* New York: Harper & Row, 1969. A very readable analysis of the problems of decision-making and improving the international environment.

Frank, Jerome. *Sanity and Survival; Psychiatric Aspects of War and Peace.* New York: Random House, 1967. A psychiatrist's survey of some aspects of human behavior that make war possible and other aspects that offer hope for the peaceful resolution of conflict. Frank deals with such subjects as collective behavior, the role of decision-makers, the ability to see the "enemy" as something less than human, and the question of aggressive tendencies as part of human nature.

Fried, Morton, et al. (eds.). *War: The Anthropology of Armed Conflict and Aggression.* New York: Natural History Press, 1968. An examination of war and violent conflict from the perspective of anthropological studies.

Hardcastle, Gerald. (ed.). *Readings in World Order.* New York: World Law Fund, 1971. A series of readings explaining the causes and nature of war, including selections from Lorenz, Ardrey, Morris, and those who oppose their views.

McNeil, Elton B. (ed.). *The Nature of Human Conflict.* Englewood Cliffs, New Jersey: Prentice-Hall, 1965. A collection of essays dealing with some findings of social scientists on the nature of human conflict. The book is not easy reading, but represents a major attempt to apply the findings of the social sciences to such issues as aggression, violence, and war.

source references

1   Bierstedt, Robert, *The Social Order*, Fourth Edition, New York: McGraw-Hill Book Company, 1974.

Birenbaum, Arnold, and Edward Sagarin, *People in Places, The Sociology of the Familiar*, New York: Praeger Publishers, 1974.

Braude, Lee, *A Sense of Sociology*, New York: Praeger Publishers, 1974.

Hughes, Everett C., *The Sociological Eye, Selected Papers*, Chicago: Aldine Publishing Company, 1972.

Lenski, Gerhard E., *Human Societies, An Introduction to Macrosociology*, Second Edition, New York: McGraw-Hill Book Company, 1974.

Leslie, Gerald R., Richard Larson, and Benjamin Gorman, *Order and Change, Introductory Sociology*, New York: Oxford University Press, 1973.

Perry, John A., and Murray B. Seidler, *Patterns of Contemporary Society, An Introduction to Social Science*, San Francisco: Canfield Press, 1973.

Reynolds, Larry T., and James M. Henslin, *American Society: A Critical Analysis*, New York: David McKay Company, Inc., 1973.

Sanders, William, Editor, *The Sociologist as Detective, An Introduction to Research and Methods*, New York: Praeger Publishers, 1974.

Smelser, Neil J., Editor, *Karl Marx and Social Change*, Chicago: The University of Chicago Press, 1973.

2   Bell, Colin, and Howard Newby, *Community Study: An Introduction to Study of the Local Community*, New York: Praeger Publishers, 1973.

Brown, Robert, *Rules and Laws in Sociology*, Chicago: Aldine Publishers, 1973.

Coser, Lewis A., *Masters of Sociological Thought, Ideas in Historical and Social Context*, New York: Harcourt Brace Jovanovich, 1971.

Douglas, Jack D., *Understanding Everyday Life: Toward the Reconstruction of Sociological Knowledge*, Chicago: Aldine Publishing Company, 1970.

Greenberg, Martin H., Joseph Olander, Allan Turowetz, and Patricia Warrick, Editors, *Social Problems Through Science Fiction*, New York: St. Martin's Press, 1974.

Hage, Jerald, and Michael Aiken, *Social Change in Complex Organization*, New York: Random House, 1970.

Horowitz, David, *Radical Sociology: An Introduction*, New York: Canfield Press, 1971.

Labovitz, Sanford, and Richard Hagedorn, *Introduction to Social Research*, New York: McGraw-Hill, 1970.

Perry, John H., and Erna Perry, *The Social Web, An Introduction to Sociology*, New York: Canfield Press, 1974.

Reynolds, Larry T., and Janice Reynolds, *The Sociology of Sociology*, New York: David McKay Company, Inc., 1970.

3   Herskovits, Melville J., *Cultural Relativism: Perspectives In Cultural Pluralism*, New York: Random House, 1973.

Hoggart, Richard, *On Culture and Communication*, New York: Oxford University Press, 1972.

Howard, John R., Editor, *Awakening Minorities: American Indians, Mexican Americans, Puerto Ricans*, New Brunswick, N.J.: Trans-Action, 1972.

Le Vine, Robert A., and Donald T. Campbell, *Ethnocentrism: Theories of Conflict, Ethnic Attitudes, and Group Behavior*, New York: John Wiley and Sons, Inc., 1972.

Le Vine, Robert A., *Culture, Behavior, and Personality*, Chicago: Aldine Publishers, 1973.

McNickle, D'Arcy, *Native American Tribalism, Indian Survivals and Renewals*, New York: Oxford University Press, 1973.

Michael, Donald N., Editor, *The Future Society*, New Brunswick, N.J.: Trans-Action, 1970.

Rennison, G. A., *We Live Among Strangers*, Australia: Melbourne University Press, 1970.

Warwick, Donald P., and Samuel Andosherson, Editors, *Comparative Research Methods*, Englewood Cliffs, N.J.: Prentice-Hall, Inc., 1973.

4

Coser, Lewis A., *Greedy Institutions, Patterns of Undivided Commitment*, Riverside, N.J.: The Free Press, 1974.

Dunning, Eric, Editor, *Sports: Readings from a Sociological Perspective*, Buffalo, New York: University of Toronto Press, 1972.

Greeley, Andrew M., *The Denominational Society, A Sociological Approach to Religion in America*, Glenview, Illinois: Scott, Foresman and Company, 1972.

Greer, Colin, *The Great School Legend: A Revisionist Interpretation of American Public Education*, New York: Viking Press, 1973.

Heller, L. C., *The Death of the American University*, New Rochelle, New York: Arlington House, Publishers, 1973.

Herschfield, Robert S., Editor, *The Power of the Presidency*, Chicago: Aldine Publishers, 1973.

La Barre, Weston, *The Ghost Dance: The Origin of Religion*, New York: Delta Books, 1972.

McNamara, Patricia H., *Religion American Style*, New York: Harper and Row Publishers, 1974.

Segal, David R., *The Polity, Differentiation and Integration in Modern Democracy*, Glenview, Illinois: Scott, Foresman Company, 1974.

Turk, Herman, and Richard L. Simpson, Editors, *Institutions and Social Exchange, The Sociologies of Talcott Parsons and George C. Homans*, Indianapolis, Indiana: Bobbs-Merrill, 1971.

Turner, Jonathan H., *Social Institutions*, New York: McGraw-Hill, 1972.

5

Bernard, Jessie, *The Future of Marriage*, New York: World Publishing Company, 1972.

Bowman, Henry A., *Marriage for Moderns*, Seventh Edition, New York: McGraw-Hill Book Company, 1974.

Crosby, John N., *Illusion and Disillusion, The Self in Love and Marriage*, Belmont, California: Wadsworth Publishing Co., 1973.

Duberman, Lucile, *Marriage and Its Alternatives*, New York: Praeger Publishers, 1974.

Fuchs, Lawrence H., *Family Matters*, New York: Random House, 1972.

Goode, William J., Elizabeth Hopkins, and Helen A. McClure, *Social Systems and Family Patterns, A Propositional Inventory*, Indianapolis, Indiana: Bobbs-Merrill, 1971.

Jewell, Nancy M., Sarah Beserra, and Melody Matthews and Elizabeth Gatov, Editors, *Sex Codes of California and America*, Los Altos, California: William Kauffmann, Inc., 1973.

Kelley, Robert K., *Courtship, Marriage, and Family*, Second Edition, New York: Harcourt Brace Jovanovich, 1974.

Koller, Marvin R., *Families: A Multigenerational Approach*, New York: McGraw-Hill, 1974.

Leslie, Gerald R., *The Family in Social Context*, Second Edition, New York: Oxford University Press, 1973.

Morrison, Eleanor, and Vera Borosage, *Human Sexuality: Contemporary Perspective*, Palo Alto, California: The National Press, 1973.

Nye, F. Ivan, and Felix M. Berardo, *The Family: Its Structure and Interaction*, New York: The Macmillan Company, 1973.

Winch, Robert F., and Graham B. Spanier, Editors, *Selected Studies in Marriage and the Family*, Fourth Edition, New York: Holt, Rinehart and Winston, Inc., 1974.

6   Cole, Jonathan R., and Stephen Cole, *Social Stratification in Science*, Chicago: The University of Chicago Press, 1973.

Cole, Robert E., *Japanese Blue Collar: The Changing Tradition*, Berkeley, California: University of California Press, 1971.

Duncan, Otis Dudley, David Featherman, and Beverly Duncan, *Socioeconomic Background and Achievement*, New York: Seminar Press, 1972.

Eisenstadt, S. N., *Social Differentiation and Stratification*, Glenview, Illinois: Scott, Foresman and Company, 1971.

Hope, Keith, Editor, *The Analysis of Social Mobility: Methods and Approaches*, Oxford: Oxford University Press, 1972.

Laumann, Edward O., Editor, *Social Stratification, Research and Theory for the 1970's*, Indianapolis, Indiana: Bobbs-Merrill, 1970.

Levitan, Sar A., Editor, *Blue-Collar Workers: A Symposium on Middle America*, New York: McGraw-Hill, 1971.

Littlejohn, James, *Social Stratification: An Introduction*, New York: Humanities Press, 1972.

Lopreato, Joseph, and Lionel S. Lewis, Editors, *Social Stratification: A Reader*, New York: Harper and Row Publishers, 1974.

Reissman, Leonard, *Inequality in America, Social Stratification*, Glenview, Illinois: Scott, Foresman and Company, 1973.

7   Adams, Paul, and Associates, *Children's Rights: Toward the Liberation of the Child*, New York: Praeger Publishers, 1971.

Claussen, John A., Editor, *Socialization and Society*, Boston: Little, Brown and Company, 1968.

Crain, Robert L., and Carol Sachs Weisman, *Discrimination, Personality, and Achievement*, New York: Seminar Press, 1972.

Denzon, Norman K., Editor, *Children and Their Caretakers*, New York: E. P. Dutton, 1973.

Elkin, Frederick, and Gerald Handel, *The Child and Society, The Process of Socialization*, Second Edition, New York: Random House, 1972.

Hill, Reuben, and Rene Konig, *Families in East and West: Socialization Process and Kinship Ties*, Paris: Mouton and Company, 1970.

Malson, Lucien, *Wolf Children and the Problem of Human Nature*, New York: Monthly Review Press, 1972.

Roby, Pamela, *Child Care, Who Cares?, Foreign and Domestic Infant and Early Childhood Development Policies*, New York: Basic Books, 1973.

Silverstein, Harry, *The Sociology of Youth, Evolution and Revolution*, New York: The Macmillan Company, 1973.

Theobald, Robert, *Futures Conditional*, Indianapolis, Indiana: Bobbs-Merrill, 1972.

8   Back, Kurt, *Beyond Words: The Story of Sensitivity Training and the Encounter Movement*, Baltimore, Maryland: Penguin Books, 1973.

Chambliss, Bill, *Box Man: A Professional Thief's Journey*, New York: Harper and Row Torch Books, 1972.

Heine, Patricke Johns, *Personality in Social Theory*, Chicago: Aldine Publishing, 1971.

Huber, Joan, Editor, *Changing Women in a Changing Society*, Chicago: The University of Chicago Press, 1973.

Levine, Sol, and Norman A. Scotch, Editors, *Social Stress*, Chicago: Aldine Publishing, 1970.

Lundberg, Margaret, *The Incomplete Adult: Social Class Restraints in Personality Development*, Westport, Connecticut: Greenwood Press, 1974.

Mischel, Harriet N., and Walter Mischel, *Readings on Personality*, New York: Holt, Rinehart and Winston, 1973.

Sebald, Hans, *Adolescence, A Sociological Analysis*, New York: Meredith Corporation, 1968.

Smelser, Neil J., and William T. Smelser, Editors, Second Edition, *Personality and Social Systems*, New York: John Wiley and Sons, 1970.

Teague, Bob, *Letters to a Black Boy*, New York: Walker and Company, 1968.

9 Bahr, Howard M., *Skid Row, An Introduction to Disaffiliation*, New York: Oxford University Press, 1973.

Blum, Jeffrey D., and Judith E. Smith, *Nothing Left to Lose, Studies of Street People*, Boston: The Beacon Press, 1972.

Collins, Alice H., *The Lonely and Afraid, Counseling the Hard to Reach*, Indianapolis, Indiana: Odyssey Press, 1969.

Finch, Stuart M., and Elva O. Poznanski, *Adolescent Suicide*, Springfield, Illinois: Charles C. Thomas Publishing, 1971.

Mead, Margaret, *Culture and Commitment, A Study of the Generation Gap*, Garden City, New York: Doubleday, Anchor Press, 1970.

Ollman, Bertell, *Alienation: Marx's Conception of Man in Capitalist Society*, New York: Cambridge University Press, 1971.

Polsky, Ned, *Hustlers, Beats, and Others*, Garden City, New York: Doubleday, Anchor Press, 1967.

Raab, Earl, *Major Social Problems*, New York: Harper and Row Publishers, 1973.

Schacht, Richard, *Alienation*, Garden City, New York: Doubleday, Anchor Press, 1970.

Yablonsky, Lewis, *Robopaths*, Indianapolis, Indiana: Bobbs-Merrill, 1972.

10 Altbach, Philip G., *Student Politics in America*, New York: McGraw-Hill Book Company, 1974.

Becker, Howard S., Editor, *Campus Power Struggle*, New York: E. P. Dutton, 1973.

Clinard, Marshall B., *Sociology of Deviant Behavior*, New York: Holt, Rinehart and Winston, 1973.

Denisoff, R. Serge, *The Sociology of Dissent*, New York: Harcourt Brace Jovanovich, 1974.

Edge, D. O., and J. W. Wolfe, Editors, *Meaning and Control*, New York: Barnes and Noble Books, 1973.

May, John D., *What Should Be Done?, Debates Before the Advocates*, Palo Alto, California: The National Press, 1973.

Merton, Robert K., and Robert Nisbet, *Contemporary Social Problems*, Third Edition, New York: Harcourt Brace Jovanovich, 1971.

McClelland, David C., William N. Davis, Rudolf Kahn, and Eric Wannem, *The Drinking Man*, New York: The Free Press, 1972.

Rains, Prudence M., *Becoming an Unwed Mother, A Sociological Account*, Chicago: Aldine Publishing Company, 1974.

Roach, Jack L., Janet K. Roach, Editors, *Poverty*, Baltimore: Penguin Books, 1972.

Rubington, Earl, *Alcohol Problems and Social Control*, Columbus, Ohio: Charles E. Merrill Publishing Company, 1973.

11   Coser, Lewis A., *The Functions of Social Conflict*, Glencoe, Illinois: The Free Press, 1956.

Glazer, Nathan, and Patrick D. Moynihan, *Beyond the Melting Pot*, Cambridge, Mass.: Massachusetts Institute of Technology Press, 1970.

Hodges, Harold M., Jr., *Conflict and Consensus: An Introduction to Sociology*, Second Edition, New York: Harper and Row, 1974.

Hunt, Chester L., and Lewis Walker, *Ethnic Dynamics*, Homewood, Illinois: Dorsey Press, 1974.

Jacobs, Alfred, and Wilford Spradlin, Editors, *The Group as an Agent of Change*, New York: Behavioral Publications, 1974.

Marx, Gary T., Editor, *Muckraking Sociology: Research as Social Criticism*, New Brunswick, New Jersey: Trans-Action, 1972.

Report of the National Advisory Commission on Civil Disorders, New York: Bantam Books, 1968.

Rist, Ray C., *The Pornography Controversy: Changing Moral Standards*, New Brunswick, New Jersey: Trans-Action, 1974.

Tedeschi, James T., Editor, *The Social Influence Process*, Chicago: Aldine-Atherton, Inc., 1972.

Van Den Berghe, Pierre, Editor, *Intergroup Relations: Sociological Perspectives*, New York: Basic Books, 1972.

12   Argyle, Michael, *Social Interaction*, Chicago: Aldine Publishing Company, 1970.

Chaney, David, *Process of Mass Communication*, New York: Herder and Herder, 1972.

Kirschner, Allen and Linda, Editors, *Readings in the Mass Media*, Indianapolis, Indiana: Odyssey Press, 1971.

Krupar, Karen P., *Communication Games*, New York: Free Press, 1973.

Makay, John J., Editor, *Exploration in Speech Communication*, Columbus, Ohio: Charles E. Merrill Publishing Co., 1973.

Mehrabian, Albert, *Nonverbal Communication*, Chicago: Aldine Publishing Company, 1972.

Miller, George A., Editor, *Communication, Language and Meaning*, New York: Basic Books, 1973.

McLuhan, Marshall, *Understanding Media, The Extensions of Man*, New York: McGraw-Hill, 1965.

Sandman, Peter M., David Ruben, and David Sachsman, *Media: An Introductory Analysis of American Mass Communication*, Englewood Cliffs, New Jersey: Prentice-Hall, Inc., 1972.

Scheflen, Albert E., *How Behavior Means*, Garden City, New York: Doubleday, Anchor Press, 1974.

Wells, Alan, *Picture Tube Imperialism? The Impact of U.S. Television on Latin America*, New York: Orbis Books, 1972.

13   Barton, Allen H., *Communities In Disaster: A Sociological Analysis of Collective Stress Situations*, Garden City, New York: Doubleday, Anchor Press, 1969.

Chen, Lincoln, Editor, *Disaster in Bangladesh*, New York: Oxford University Press, 1973.

Elsner, Henry Jr., Editor, *Robert E. Park: The Crowd and the Public, and Other Essays*, Chicago: The University of Chicago Press, 1972.

Gerlach, Luther P., and Virginia H. Hine, *People, Power, and Change, Movements of Social Transformation*, Indianapolis, Indiana: Bobbs-Merrill, 1970.

Gunn, John, *Violence*, New York: Praeger Publishers, 1973.

Hughes, Helen Macgill, Editor, *Crowd and Mass Behavior*, Boston: Holbrooke Press, Inc., 1972.

Oberschall, Anthony, *Social Conflict and Social Movements*, Englewood Cliffs, New Jersey: Prentice-Hall, Inc., 1972.

Orum, Anthony M., *Black Students Protest, A Study of the Origins of the Black Student Movement*, Washington, D.C.: American Sociological Association, 1972.

Short, James E., and Marvin E. Wolfgang, Editors, *Collective Violence*, Chicago: Aldine Publishing Company, 1972.

Shibutani, Tamotsu, *Improvised News, A Sociological Study of Rumor*, Indianapolis, Indiana: Bobbs-Merrill, 1966.

Turner, Ralph H., and Lewis M. Killian, *Collective Behavior*, Englewood Cliffs, New Jersey: Prentice-Hall, Inc., 1972.

14 Forman, Robert E., *Black Ghettos, White Ghettos and Slums*, Englewood Cliffs, New Jersey: Prentice-Hall, Inc., 1971.

Georgakas, Dan, *Red Shadows: The History of Native Americans from 1600-1900, from the Desert to the Pacific Coast*, Garden City, New York: Doubleday and Company, 1973.

Gist, Noel P., and Anthony Dworkin, Editors, *The Blending of Races, Marginality and Identity in World Perspective*, New York: John Wiley and Sons, 1972.

Kinloch, Graham C., *The Dynamics of Race Relations*, New York: McGraw-Hill Book Company, 1974.

Liebman, Charles S., *The Ambivalent American Jew*, Philadelphia: The Jewish Publication Society of America, 1973.

Newman, William W., *American Pluralism, A Study of Minority Groups and Social Theory*, New York: Harper and Row, 1973.

Rossi, Peter H., Editor, *Ghetto Revolts*, New York: E. P. Dutton, 1973.

Simpson, George E., and J. Milton Yinger, *Racial and Cultural Minorities, An Analysis of Prejudice and Discrimination*, Fourth Edition, New York: Harper and Row, 1972.

Snyder, Clifford L., and Ernest Hildebrand, Editors, *Red and Yellow, Black and Brown*, New York: Rinehart Press, 1972.

Stroud, Drew McCord, Editor, *The Majority Minority Viewpoints*, New York: Rinehart Press, 1973.

Thompson, Daniel C., *Sociology of the Black Experience*, Westport, Connecticut: Greenwood Press, 1974.

Yin, Robert K., Editor, *Race, Creed, Color, or National Origin*, Itaska, Illinois: F. E. Peacock Publishers, Inc., 1973.

15 Atchley, Robert C., *The Social Forces in Later Life, Introduction to Social Gerontology*, Belmont, California: Wadsworth Publishing, 1972.

Berelson, Bernard, Editor, *Population Policy in Developed Countries*, New York: McGraw-Hill, 1974.

Hartley, Shirley Foster, *Population, Quantity Versus Quality*, Englewood Cliffs, New Jersey: Prentice-Hall, Inc., 1972.

Penchef, Esther, *Four Horsemen: Pollution, Poverty, Famine, Violence*, New York: Canfield Press, 1971.

Pierson, George W., *The Moving American*, New York: Alfred A. Knopf, 1973.

Quick, Horace F., *Population Ecology*, Indianapolis, Indiana: Pegasus, 1974.

Reid, Sue Titus, and David L. Lyon, *Population Crises, An Introductory Perspective*, Glenview, Illinois: Scott, Foresman and Company, 1972.

Singer, S. Fred, *Is There an Optimum Level of Population?*, New York: McGraw-Hill, 1971.

Symonds, Richard, and Michael Carder, *The United States and the Population Question*, New York: McGraw-Hill, 1973.

Westoff, Charles F., Editor, *Toward the End of Growth, Population In America*, Englewood Cliffs, New Jersey: Prentice-Hall, 1973.

16   Crane, Jacob L., *Urban Planning—Illusion and Reality*, New York: Vantage Press, 1973.

Davis, Kingsley, *World Urbanization, 1950-1970*, Vol. II, *Analysis of Trends, Relationships, and Development*, Berkeley, California: Institute of International Studies, University of California, 1972.

George, Carl J., *Urban Ecology: In Search of an Asphalt Rose*, New York: McGraw-Hill, 1974.

Gordon, Daniel H., Editor, *Social Change and Urban Politics: Readings*, Englewood Cliffs, New Jersey: Prentice-Hall, 1972.

Greer, Scott, *Urban Renewal and American Cities*, Indianapolis, Indiana: Bobbs-Merrill, 1965.

Harr, Charles M., *The End of Innocence, A Suburban Reader*, Glenview, Illinois: Scott, Foresman and Company, 1972.

McKelvey, Blake, *American Urbanization, A Comparative History*, Glenview, Illinois: Scott, Foresman and Company, 1973.

Mumford, Lewis, *The City In History, Its Origins, Its Transformation, and Its Prospects*, New York: Harcourt Brace Jovanovich, 1968.

Suttles, Gerald P., *The Social Construction of Community*, Chicago: The University of Chicago Press, 1973.

Wright, W. D. G., and D. H. Stewart, Editor, *The Exploding City*, Chicago: Aldine Publishing Company, 1972.

17   Gazell, James A., and G. Thomas Gitchoff, *Youth, Crime, and Society*, Boston: Holbrooke Press, Inc., 1973.

Grupp, Stanley E., Editor, *Theories of Punishment*, Bloomington: Indiana University Press, 1971.

Hartjen, Clayton, *Crime and Criminalization*, New York: Praeger Publishers, 1974.

Hills, Stuart L., *Crime, Power, and Morality, The Criminal Law Process in the United States*, Scranton: Chandler Publishing Company, 1971.

Johnson, Elmer H., *Crime, Correction, and Society*, Homewood, Illinois: The Dorsey Press, Inc., 1973.

Nettler, Gynn, *Explaining Crime*, New York: McGraw-Hill, 1974.

Phillipson, Michael, *Understanding Crime and Delinquency, A Sociological Introduction*, Chicago: Aldine Publishing, 1974.

Reckless, Walter C., and Simon Dinitz, *The Prevention of Juvenile Delinquency*, Columbus, Ohio: Ohio State University Press, 1972.

Smith, Alexander B., and Harriet Pollack, *Crime and Justice in Mass Society*, Corte Madera, California: Rinehart Press, 1972.

Zimring, Franklin E., and Gordon J. Hawkins, *Deterrence*, Chicago: The University of Chicago Press, 1973.

18   Beitz, Charles R., and Theodore Herman, *Peace and War*, San Francisco: W. H. Freeman and Company, 1973.

Clark, Grenville, and Louis Sohn, *Introduction to World Peace Through World Law*, Chicago: World Without War Publications, 1973.

Dougherty, James E., *How To Think About Arms Control and Disarmament*, New York: Crane, Russak and Company, 1973.

Elliot, R. S. P., and John Hickie, *Ulster: A Case Study on Conflict Theory*, New York: St. Martin's Press, 1972.

Knapp, Daniel L., and Kenneth Polk, *Scouting the War on Poverty*, Lexington, Massachusetts: D. C. Heath and Company, 1971.

Levitan, Sar A., and Karen Cleary, *Old Wars Remain Unfinished: The Veterans' Benefits System*, Baltimore, Maryland: The Johns Hopkins University Press, 1973.

Levey, Charles J., *Spoils of War*, Boston: Houghton Mifflin Company, 1974.

Pilisuk, Marc, *International Conflict and Social Policy*, Englewood Cliffs, New Jersey: Prentice-Hall, Inc., 1972.

Sampson, R. V., *The Discovery of Peace*, New York: Pantheon Books, 1973.

Tolley, Howard J., *Children and War: Political Socialization to International Conflict*, New York: Teacher's College Press, 1973.

index